Heath's College Handbook of Composition

9th edition

Heath's College Handbook of Composition

Langdon Elsbree ■
Claremont Men's College

Frederick Bracher ■
Pomona College

Nell Altizer ■
University of Hawaii

D. C. Heath and Company
Lexington, Massachusetts   Toronto

Cover design by Leonard Preston,
inspired by the *Book of Kells.*

Published simultaneously in Canada.

Printed in the United States of America.

Paperbound International Standard Book Number: 0–669–00562–2

Clothbound International Standard Book Number: 0–669–99960–1

Library of Congress Catalog Card Number: 76–9332

Authors' Preface

In preparing the ninth edition of this *Handbook*, we have made basic revisions throughout, especially in the rhetoric chapters. Students, teachers, and other helpful critics have asked for reorganizing of these opening sections. The rhetoric now begins with the word, continues with a discussion of paragraphs, and concludes with a discussion of the paper as a whole. Several chapters from the eighth edition have been condensed and unified, and all of the rhetoric chapters have been rewritten in part or wholly. We hope this progression from diction to paragraphing to the complete argument will offer a more coherent structure.

Other important changes include a new research paper and discussion of its planning and form, keyed to *The MLA Style Sheet;* an updating of various examples and a scrutiny of our prose to eliminate possible sexual stereotyping; and revisions throughout to increase clarity and brevity. At the same time, we have tried to keep the features our friends and critics have liked, not least the use of student sentences and student papers. Such examples occasionally show traces of their original awkwardness even after correction, but they are the kinds of sentences students struggle with and they seem to us better than the contrived illustrations which no one can believe in.

Once again we are indebted to colleagues, students, and reviewers for critiques and suggestions. A number of people have assisted, including those formally acknowledged in the seventh and eighth editions, but no one has had a more important part in the ninth edition than our editor, Holt Johnson. His tactfulness, thoroughness with detail, and good-humored assistance at all stages have been invaluable.

On behalf of the authors,

L. E.

Acknowledgments

WILLIAM COLLINS + WORLD PUBLISHING COMPANY, from *Websters New World Dictionary of the American Language*, Second College Edition. Copyright © 1976 by William Collins + World Publishing Co., Inc.

THOMAS Y. CROWELL COMPANY, from *Funk & Wagnalls Standard College Dictionary*. Copyright © 1963, 1966, 1968, 1973 by Funk & Wagnalls Publishing Company, Inc. Used by permission of the publisher.

MARY ELLMAN, from *Thinking About Women*. Reprinted by permission of Harcourt Brace Jovanovich, Inc., and Macmillan, London and Basingstoke.

ROBERT L. HEILBRONER, from *The Great Ascent*, pp. 33–34. Copyright © 1963 by Robert L. Heilbroner. By permission of Harper & Row, Publishers, and William Morris Agency, Inc.

HOUGHTON MIFFLIN COMPANY, from *The American Heritage Dictionary of the English Language*. Copyright © 1969, 1970, 1971, 1973, 1975, 1976, Houghton Mifflin Company. Reprinted by permission.

LANGSTON HUGHES, from "The Negro Artist and the Racial Mountain." Copyright 1926 by Langston Hughes. Renewed. Reprinted by permission of Harold Ober Associates Incorporated.

G. & C. MERRIAM COMPANY, from *Webster's New Collegiate Dictionary*. Copyright © 1976 by G. & C. Merriam Co., Publishers of the Merriam-Webster Dictionaries. By permission.

OGDEN NASH, from *Verses From 1929 On* by Ogden Nash. Copyright 1930 by Ogden Nash. By permission of Little, Brown and Co. "Reflections on Ice-Breaking" originally appeared in *The New Yorker*. By permission of the Estate of Ogden Nash and J. M. Dent Ltd. from *The Face Is Familiar*.

DAVID C. STEWART, from "The Movies Students Make" copyright © 1965 by Harper's Magazine Inc. Reprinted from the October, 1965 issue of *Harper's Magazine* by permission of the author.

Contents

5

Forceful Sentences 83

6

Coherent Sentences 105

7

8

9

10

11

12

13

15

16

Spelling

17

Mechanics

18

Definitions of Grammatical Terms

Index

Heath's College Handbook of Composition

9th edition

The Development of English 1

Much of the uproar over the "bad English" written by students today (and the "good English" their parents were taught to write) is the result of misunderstandings of the way English has developed (its history) and the way it works today (its grammar). This section attempts to clear up some of the apparent contradictions that disturb people when they try to think about the English language. It may not improve your ability to write, but it should throw some light on the paradox that everybody speaks English and most people write it, but only a few are thought to write "good grammatical English."

Any living language, like a biological organism, is undergoing constant, gradual change. The English we know and use today is only one stage in a long, and presumably endless, process of gradual development. Everyone who has read Chaucer knows that his English was different from ours, and if we go back another five centuries, we find a still different stage of English—so different from that used today as to be unintelligible to all but the scholar.

Here is a sentence written by King Alfred about the year 880. It concerns the *hors-hwael*, "horse-whale," or as we say today, "the whale-horse," or *walrus:*

> Hīe habbath swīthe aethele bān on hiora tōthum, ond hiora hȳd bith swīthe gōd tō sciprāpum.

All but two of these words are in common use today, but they have changed so much over the centuries as to be unrecognizable to most of us.

We might guess at the archaic verb-ending -*eth* and translate two words as "haveth" and "be-eth"—that is, *have* and *be*. A linguist who knew the facts of grammatical and phonetic change in English could interpret *bān* as "bone," *tōthum* as an old plural form of *tooth*, *hӯd* as "hide" (skin), *gōd* as "good," and *scipræpum* as "shipropes." He would recognize *aethele* as akin to German *edel*, meaning "noble," and *swīthe* as an intensive, like *very*. If we know that *hīe* and *hiora* correspond to *they* and *their*, and that some prepositions have changed their meanings if not their written forms, we can translate:

> They have a very noble bone in their teeth (i.e., tusks), and their hide (rawhide) is very good for shipropes.

Historical linguistics is concerned with the principles of change from one stage of a language to another. Linguistic evolution is gradual: phonetic change proceeds by the accumulation of slight variations in sound which may hardly be noticed by the people who make them. Today many people pronounce "going to" as "goin to" or "gawn ta" or even "gonna"* without being aware of these differences. Similarly, in the past the sound of English words varied slightly from speaker to speaker, or from place to place, and an increment of small changes has brought about the difference between King Alfred's English and Chaucer's, and between Chaucer's and our own. There were other kinds of change as well: new words were borrowed, old words disappeared, spellings varied, meanings shifted. But phonetic change—that is, change in the sound of the language—is basic for a linguist.

Phonetic changes are often regular enough to be generalized into principles. Old English *rāp* (pronounced to rhyme with Modern American English *top*) became something like "rawp" in Chaucer's day and has become *rope* in our own time. If you say these three words in front of a mirror, you will notice that the vowel in *top* is made with the mouth spread wide toward the sides. To pronounce "rawp" you will move your lips so that your open mouth is in the shape of an approximate square. To pronounce *rope* you round your

---

*The spellings used here to indicate different pronunciations of "going to" illustrate some shortcomings of the English alphabet. There are no letters to indicate unmistakably the vowel sounds we have tried to suggest by "gawn ta." Linguists have provided such symbols [gɔn tə], and enough others to indicate fairly accurately all the sounds used in English. For any serious study of linguistics, learning a phonetic alphabet is indispensable.

lips into a still smaller opening, even protruding your lips a little. This account is oversimplified, but it suggests a kind of principle: the change from old English *rāp* to Modern English *rope* involves progressive rounding of the mouth. The principle can be checked by looking at similar words; Old English *bān, rād, hām,* and *stān,* have become Modern English *bone, road, home,* and *stone* by the same principle of progressive rounding.

Some of the consonants have also changed, and the changes can often be described by phonetic principles. A number of English consonant sounds can be arranged in pairs according to the way they are formed. The tongue is held in approximately the same position for pronouncing *s* and *z;* the difference in sound depends on whether our vocal cords vibrate to produce the voiced *z* or we whisper the voiceless *s.* Here are some other examples:

voiced	*voiceless*
b	p
d	t
g	k
v	f

A change from a voiced consonant to its voiceless counterpart is fairly common, and we can find many instances in the history of English of the opposite change, from voiceless to voiced. (Notice the difference, which is not indicated by the spelling but can be heard, between the *s* in *house* and the *s* in *houses.*) But there is no simple explanation for a change from a voiceless *s* to a *g,* nor from a *d* to an *f,* and in fact such changes have seldom if ever occurred in the history of English. Phonetic change seems to occur only along what a geologist would call "natural lines of cleavage." These natural lines in language can often be explained by a careful study of the mechanisms of speech.

Historical linguists in the nineteenth century noticed that there are marked similarities between some English words and words with the same meaning in other European languages. Consider, for example, English *mother,* Old English *modor,* Dutch *moeder,* German *mutter,* Celtic *mathair,* Latin *mater,* Greek *meter,* and Lithuanian *moter.* Such similarity can hardly have been accidental, and it raised some questions. Were these words all variants of a common original? If so, what was the original?

By comparing thousands of related words in different languages, historical linguists could note some relationships: Latin is more like

Greek than like Dutch; Dutch is more like English than like Russian. Romance languages (French, Spanish, Italian, etc.) have many close similarities, and since it can be shown historically that the Romance languages have evolved from dialects of Medieval Latin, it seems likely that other European languages have evolved as descendants of a single very ancient language. This hypothesis is now supported by so much circumstantial evidence that it is almost universally accepted by linguists. The original parent language is called Indo-European, since some of its branches are spoken in Iran and northern India as well as in Europe. No record of Indo-European remains, since the people who spoke it had not invented a writing system. But comparative linguists have worked out a good many of the principles of phonetic change operating in the Indo-European languages and have reconstructed many words of the parent language.

Data from other sciences have contributed to our knowledge of the location and way of life of this hypothetical Indo-European people, and linguistic research has helped the historian. For example, since a good many widely separated languages in the family have similar words for *salmon, turtle, honey,* and *beech* tree, it is a fair assumption that the parent language had these words and that the speakers were acquainted with these things. The geographic limits of these animals and plants can be determined: the turtle did not live north of Germany; the beech tree did not grow naturally much to the east of the Vistula river in Poland; the line marking the occurrence of the honey bee can be drawn on a map.

Somewhere within these boundaries, in the fourth millenium B.C., the Indo-European tribesmen lived as small farmers, who kept cows for milk, knew and used the wheel, and were organized into patriarchal families. Paul Thieme locates the original homeland of the Indo-Europeans on the Baltic coast, between the Vistula and the Elbe, in what is now East Germany and Poland. Other linguists have placed it farther east and south, in what is now the Ukraine. But there is general agreement that the original homeland was in central Europe rather than in Asia.

During the third millennium the tribes began migrations which took them east to Persia (present-day Iran) and India, south to Italy and Greece, north to Scandinavia, and west to Spain and the British Isles. As they separated, they developed their own dialects, which eventually became the separate languages of the Indo-European family.

The changes which, over the centuries, produced the branch of the Indo-European family to which English belongs are often regular enough to be described in general "laws." For example, it can be shown that the Germanic languages (English, Dutch, German, Scandinavian, and some others) all went through a regular change of consonants in the first millennium B.C., whereas other Indo-European languages, like Greek, Latin, or Sanskrit, preserved for the most part the original consonants. In the Germanic languages, an original Indo-European voiced *b* became the voiceless *p*. Latin *labia* preserves the original *b*, but English *lip* shows the change to *p*. Similarly, Latin *turba* (crowd, group) keeps the original Indo-European consonants, but English *thorp* (village) shows, among other things, the shift of *b* to *p*.

Turba and *thorp* are thus related by being descended from a common Indo-European root, and they are called *cognates*. Words that are borrowed by one language from another usually do not show the phonetic changes that distinguish the Germanic languages from their Indo-European brothers and sisters. For example, we have borrowed the Latin stem of *turba* directly into English in such words as *turbid, turbulent,* and *disturb.* Borrowings are relatively recent; cognates go back to the early stages of each language. The words for *mother* listed on page 3 are presumably all cognates, descendants of a common Indo-European ancestor which probably sounded something like "mah-tár." Within historical times we have borrowed *maternal* and *matron* from Latin and Old French.

The following lists show other changes which make up the Germanic Consonant Shift, often called "Grimm's Law." The Indo-European consonants are represented here by roots of Latin and Greek words, instead of less familiar words from Sanskrit or Lithuanian. After each root, some English words borrowed from Latin or Greek are added in parentheses to indicate the meaning. Since they are borrowings, they preserve the original Indo-European consonants.

Indo-European *d*	becomes	Germanic *t*
ed- (*edible*)		eat
dic- (*dictate, diction*)		teach
Indo-European *g*	becomes	Germanic *k*
gen- (*generate, genus*)		kin
ager ("field," as in *agriculture*)		acre

Indo-European *p*	becomes	Germanic *f*
pyr (*pyre, pyrotechnics*)		fire
pullus (*pullet, poultry*)		fowl
Indo-European *t*	becomes	Germanic *th*
tu (*second person pronoun*)		thou
frater (*fraternal*)		brother
Indo-European *k*	becomes	Germanic *h*
cornu (*cornet, cornucopia*)		horn
canis (*canine*)		hound

With a little knowledge of Greek and Latin roots, some ingenuity, and a good dictionary, a student will be able to find other examples of the Germanic Consonant Shift and of borrowed words which preserve the original Indo-European consonants.

Exercise 1

Look up the etymologies of the following pairs of words, keeping in mind the Germanic Consonant Shift.

1. canine, hound
2. domestic, tame
3. gusto, choose
4. intrude, threaten
5. octopus, eight, foot
6. peril, fear
7. pedal, foot
8. piscatorial, fish
9. subjugate, yoke
10. tension, thin

The Indo-European family includes almost all the languages of Europe, from Scandinavia to Greece, from Russia to Ireland, and some of the languages spoken in Armenia, Iran, and northern India. Among the latter, Sanskrit is specially important to the linguist since it is the oldest recorded Indo-European language, appearing first in the *Vedas*, ancient religious books of India written down in the second millennium B.C.

There are many other language families in the world, but the only important non-Indo-European languages in Europe are Finnish and Hungarian, which belong to the Finno-Ugric family. Basque, spoken in the Pyrenees along the border between France and Spain, is a linguistic mystery; it has no known relatives and may be a lone survivor of the lost Iberian languages spoken in the Late Stone Age throughout Southern Europe.

The Germanic tribes who invaded Great Britain in the fifth century came from the low country around the base of the Danish peninsula.

They conquered all of the island except Scotland and Wales and imposed their Germanic dialects on the Celts who survived the invasion. (Celtic languages still persist in Scotland, Wales, Ireland, and the Breton peninsula in France.) Old English, as the Anglo-Saxon dialects of the invaders are now called, was not written down until after the arrival of Christian missionaries from Rome in the year 597. Like their modern counterparts the world over, these missionaries wrote down the language of the natives in the Roman alphabet, and they taught English monks to write and make translations. In so doing, they rendered a great service to historical linguistics, for they provided us with the earliest specimens of the English language.

To this Old English language stock, a great many words borrowed from other languages have been added. Some Latin words used for place names in the first century, when the Roman legions established army posts throughout the island, have remained on the map. Most conspicuous is the Latin word for "camp," *castra*, which frequently appears in place names like Lancaster, Winchester, Worcester, and the like. More Latin words were borrowed when Christianity was introduced into England, and since the Renaissance, a great many Latin and Greek words, especially those dealing with education, law, and science, have been borrowed, sometimes by way of French. In the following sentence, all italicized words are of Latin origin.

> Today the *curriculum* of our *educational institutions—elementary, secondary,* and *collegiate—* is *administered* by *deans, superintendents, coordinators,* and *principals* as well as *professors* and other *faculty members.*

The traditional fields of study often have Greek names: *geography, theology, economics, physics, psychology, mathematics, philosophy, botany.* Modern physics has taken Greek roots to form such words as *thermodynamics, atomic, cyclotron, electronics, gamma-ray,* and *proton.*

French words were borrowed in increasing numbers after the Norman Conquest, especially in the thirteenth and fourteenth centuries. A famous passage in Scott's *Ivanhoe* reminds us that language can reflect differences in social class. The Saxon serfs in *Ivanhoe* used English words for the animals they tended: *ox, cow, sheep, swine.* Their Norman overlords had little need for the names of the animals but were interested in the end product; they used French words for the different kinds of meat that appeared on their tables: *beef, veal, mutton,* and *pork.*

French words make up the largest part of the borrowed words in our everyday vocabulary, but the English-speaking peoples have borrowed words from almost every language they have come in contact with. *Sky* and *happy* and *window* come from Scandinavian; *flannel* and *whiskey* from Celtic; *tub, yacht,* and *pump* from Dutch; *pretzel, kindergarten,* and *hamburger* from German. From Italian come words like *balcony, piazza,* and *umbrella,* as well as many terms used in music and art. Spanish has contributed *cigar, alligator, mosquito,* and many words used in the American Southwest, like *canyon, rodeo, lariat,* and *mesa.* From Hebrew have come *camel* and *sabbath;* from Arabic, *algebra* and *sugar* and *alcohol.* Many words for fruits and flowers come ultimately from Persia: *peach* and *orange, tulip* and *lilac;* and we have borrowed *tea* and *mandarin* from China, *kimono* and *tycoon* from Japan, *pajama* and *bungalow* from India, and *gong* and *gingham* from Malaysia. Modern English has borrowed words of other languages very freely.

Exercise 2

In a good dictionary, look up the ultimate origin of the following borrowed words:

1. alkali	8. lute
2. alligator	9. Negro
3. amethyst	10. potato
4. bamboo	11. skipper
5. calico	12. skunk
6. cherub	13. stirrup
7. isolate	14. syrup

Since Old English times, the language with its borrowed additional vocabulary has changed steadily. Englishmen have apparently always had a tendency to telescope and shorten words—a tendency which today sometimes reduces *extraordinary* from six syllables to three: "extráwdnry." Old English *hlāf-weard* (literally, "loaf-guard") meant the leader of a tribe; *hlāf-dige* (literally, "loaf-kneader") meant a woman. Both words were shortened in Middle English to *loverd* and *lavedi,* and they have been further shortened in Modern English to *lord* and *lady.*

Many changes in the form of words fall into regular patterns like that already mentioned in the change from Old English *rāp* to *rope.* A pattern of vowel changes, very common in German where it is called *umlaut*, also appears in Old English and has produced such pairs of words as *man* and *men*, *strong* and *strength*, *blood* and *bleed*, *goose* and *geese*, *full* and *fill*, *mouse* and *mice*. Voiceless consonants tend to become voiced when they occur between vowels: contrast *house* and *houses*, *bath* and *bather*, *wife* and *wives*. Especially in the vicinity of vowels like *i* or *e*, a *k*-sound may become palatalized to *ch*, as in *chill* (compare *cool*), Green*wich* (compare Ber*wick*), and Win*chester* (compare Lan*caster*). Palatalization also distinguishes verb from noun in *bake* and *batch*, *speak* and *speech*, *stick* and *stitch*. Other forms of palatalization account for pairs like *skirt* and *shirt*, *gard(en)*, and *yard*, *drag* and *draw*.

Initial *k* disappeared before an *n*, and *w* before an *r*, though we still preserve a record of the earlier pronunciation in modern spelling: *knee*, *know*, *knight*; *wrap*, *wreck*, *wrong*. Inflectional endings, once as common in English as in Latin, have mainly eroded away. In King Alfred's time there were still three different declensions of the noun, and one of them had six different forms, illustrated in *stan, stanes, stane, stanas, stana, stanum*. Today *stone* has only two phonetic forms, *stone* and *stones*, though in spelling we distinguish two more, *stone's* and *stones'*. The inflection of verbs has been similarly simplified, and we have given up entirely the old inflection of adjectives. The final *e*'s which trouble students trying to read Chaucer aloud are vestigial remnants of earlier inflectional endings. Today their only function is to indicate the pronunciation of the preceding vowel, as in *hate* compared with *hat*, or *site* with *sit*.

The constant erosion of word endings has increased the importance of word order in modern English. In a highly inflected language, like Latin, the function of a word in the sentence (subject, object, etc.) is indicated mainly by case endings. One can write "puer puellam amat" or "puellam amat puer" without changing the meaning of the sentence. So long as a reader knows that *puer* (boy) is in the nominative case and that adding an *m* to *puella* (girl) makes the case of the noun objective, he will translate the sentence correctly as "boy loves girl."

In English, lacking case endings for nouns, we indicate the function by the position of the noun. If it precedes the verb, it is the subject; if it follows the verb, it is usually the object. There is a great difference in meaning between the sentence "Boy loves girl" and the inverted sentence "Girl loves boy." Pronouns still show a case distinction between *I* (subject) and *me* (object), between *he* and *him* or *she* and *her*. But even so, we usually put *I* before the verb and *me* after it.

In modern English word order is functional in more subtle ways than simply indicating case; precise degrees of emphasis or tone can be conveyed by the position of a word or phrase, as the sections on sentence coherence (Chapter 6) in this book demonstrate.

Exercise 3

The second word in each of the following pairs shows a change in form. What phonetic principles explain the various changes? Look for changes in *sound,* not in spelling.

1. calf, calves
2. dike, ditch
3. food, feed
4. kirk, church
5. long, length

6. louse, lousy
7. proud, pride
8. stink, stench
9. tug, tow
10. use (noun), usable

Exercise 4

Look up in a good dictionary the Old English forms of the following words, and note the consonant sounds that have been dropped in Modern English:

1. eye
2. leap
3. loud
4. lee

5. nil
6. rack (and ruin)
7. retch
8. ring

Just as the spoken forms of words change by slow degrees over a long period of time, so do the meanings of words. Old English *hlāf-weard* must once have meant something like "loaf-keeper" (compare modern *breadwinner*), but along with the change in form to *lord* there has been a considerable change in meaning. Such semantic changes do not follow regular principles, but one can often trace the psychological connections between the different meanings of a word. *Head* means, basically, a part of the body. But it is easy to see how this meaning was extended, as a kind of metaphor, in such phrases as "head of lettuce," "head of a pin," "come to a head," "headmaster," "newspaper headline," "head on a glass of beer," "headwaters," and "headland." Latin *candidatus* originally meant "dressed in white"—i.e., in one's best toga. Since aspirants for public office dressed in white, *candidate* has come to mean a person seeking office, but the original idea of whiteness has disappeared entirely. English *hearse* came, through Old French, from Latin *hirpex*, a rake or harrow. When it first appeared in English it meant a frame with candles on which a coffin was placed. The frame with candles sticking up around the edge looked like a primitive harrow. Later the meaning changed to a device for carrying a coffin and eventually to the leading Cadillac in a funeral procession.

Some meanings are expanded, or generalized. *Gossip* originally had the fairly specific meaning of "god-parent," but it became generalized to any talkative person, and eventually to what he or she said. *Barn* at first meant a place for storing barley. *Manuscript* originally meant "written by hand," but since the invention of the typewriter, the word has been expanded to mean an author's typed or written copy, as distinguished from a printed version. By the same kind of change, some airplanes can now "land" at sea.

Other words become more specialized in meaning. In Shakespeare's time, *deer* still meant any kind of wild animal ("Rats and mice and such small deer"), but today it means only one kind. *Starve* meant "to die" in Chaucer's time: the little boy in the Prioress's Tale "sterved" of a cut throat. Today the word means to die from lack of food, or even just to be very hungry.

A few words which once had a derogatory meaning have become complimentary terms. *Shrewd* used to mean harmful or malicious, from the supposedly poisonous small animal called a shrew. Today a good many people would be pleased to be described as "shrewd." Similarly, *knight* once meant a servant boy, and only under the feudal system did the word acquire its present honorific sense.

A great many words have undergone the opposite change. *Hussy* is a contraction of Old English *huswif*, "house wife," and originally had none of its present depreciatory sense. *Wanton* and *lewd* once meant simply undisciplined or untaught. A *knave* was once merely a boy, a *boor* was simply a farmer, and a *villain* a farm laborer at a villa, or village.

Folk etymology—a bad guess as to the meaning or origin of a word—may cause a change in the form of a word. *Crayfish* (American and Irish *crawfish*) comes from a misunderstanding, and hence misspelling, of Middle English *crevis*. A *penthouse* represents an English misunderstanding of Old French *apentis*, from Latin *appendix*, "an addition to." An *umpire* was originally *a nompere* (Old French *nonper*, not one of a pair of contestants), but the *n* of the original word was taken by the English to be the last letter of the article *an*.

Exercise 5

Look up the etymologies of the following words, and try to account for the changes in meaning:

1.	adder (snake)	8.	cretin
2.	auger	9.	marshal
3.	belfry	10.	newt
4.	bishop	11.	pretty
5.	bridegroom	12.	shrive
6.	can (as in *ashcan*)	13.	volume
7.	churl	14.	wiseacre

Even a brief look at the history of English shows that changes in the form and meaning of words have been taking place at every stage of the language, and they are still going on today, in spite of the efforts of teachers and textbooks. Historical linguistics gives little encouragement to those who would guard the purity of English by fixing it in a permanent form. Changes are slow, however, and any one generation finds the language fairly stable. Dictionaries attempt to record the current state of the language, though they often include archaic or obsolete forms and meanings.

At any given stage, a language constitutes a system: certain ways of putting words together are acceptable while others are not. The system of a language at a given stage is its *grammar,* but the word *grammar* is used in other senses, too. W. Nelson Francis, in his often reprinted article, "Revolution in Grammar" (*Quarterly Journal of Speech,* October 1954), makes some useful distinctions. The meaning just described, which Francis calls Grammar 1, is the actual structure of a language—the way in which English words *must* go together if sentences are to be acceptable to other people who speak the language. Certain patterns of verbal sounds are used by all people who speak English; other patterns are never used. When a child learns to speak English—to use these acceptable patterns—he has at least made a start at learning the grammar of English in this first basic sense. A schoolboy may not know that he knows Grammar 1, but he would find a statement like "This my is book" unacceptable and "This is my book" a perfectly normal English sentence. Even though he cannot explain *why* the first sentence is wrong, he knows that it just isn't English.

Consider the following sentences:

1. Send me your new address.
2. Send your new address to me.

3. Send to me your new address.
4. Send your new address me.

No one would object to the first two sentences, though the pattern of the second sentence is probably a little less common. The third sentence, though intelligible, sounds stilted, slightly foreign. We would not be apt to use it ourselves, though we would understand it readily if a foreigner spoke it. The fourth sentence, however, is just not English, and everyone who recognizes this knows at least a part of Grammar 1.

The second meaning of *grammar* is suggested by a phrase like "a grammar of the English language," or by the word *grammarian*. If we want to know *why* "This my is book" is wrong, we need some systematic description of the acceptable forms and patterns of words in English sentences. Such generalized, explanatory descriptions may be called Grammar 2. The plural form "descriptions" is purposely used to indicate that there is no single correct way of describing and explaining English. Grammar 2 is any theoretical account of Grammar 1.

Language, like walking, is initially learned by trial and error. All normal children eventually learn to walk, though they may never learn exactly what happens to nerves and muscles when they are walking. Similarly, every normal child learns to speak the language of the adults around him, and he thus acquires the Grammar 1 of his particular dialect without conscious effort. If he wants to know, or is required to learn, the "theory" of the language he uses every day, he will have to study Grammar 2.

Is there any practical advantage to studying Grammar 2? There may be, though probably not so much as you think. Knowing something about the process of walking may improve our efficiency when we walk; it may help us distribute our weight properly and thus avoid weakened or flattened arches. Similarly, a knowledge of Grammar 2 may lead to greater efficiency in our use of the language; it may increase our knowledge of the possibilities of Grammar 1. It will not help much with simple sentences like "Send me your new address," but it may help us to communicate precisely more subtle or more complex meanings, or to redistribute the weight in a sentence so as to emphasize one part and play down another.

In the mind of the public, however, the chief reason for studying grammar at all is to enable us to speak and write "correct" English and to avoid "bad grammar." This is the third sense of the word in common use. Grammar 3 usually consists of prescriptive rules for "correct" English usage. Don't say "between you and I"; the preposition *between* requires a complement in the objective case. Don't say "Everyone brought their own lunch"; *everyone* is singular in number and must be followed by a singular pronoun. And so on.

Many people uncritically assume that studying Grammar 2, an analytic description of the language, is a necessary first step in correcting "errors" like those in the preceding paragraph, which are the main concern of Grammar 3. It may be that some grammatical analysis is useful in explaining why certain constructions are "wrong," but common sense suggests that a complete theoretical account of the structure of English is hardly necessary for correcting errors in, say, agreement of subject and verb. Furthermore, an underlying assumption has not been proved: that if a student understands the theory of a language consciously, this knowledge will become usable on the subconscious level, where languages are really learned. Finally, linguists have raised serious doubts about the adequacy of the traditional Grammar 2 that has been taught since the Renaissance. Intelligent students are disturbed by the many exceptions to the grammatical principles they are taught, and linguists would add to the charge of inconsistency that of incompleteness.

Traditional Grammar 2 is concerned primarily with written, rather than spoken, English, and it thus simply ignores some very important ways of signaling meaning, like accent and pitch. A classic example from C. C. Fries is this headline:

PROFESSOR RAKES LEAVES AFTER CHAPEL

If we stress the word *rakes* and pronounce it with a relatively high pitch, we produce "Professor Rakes leaves after chapel." But if we stress the second syllable of *professor* and the word *leaves*, pronouncing both with a higher pitch than we give to *rakes*, we are saying "Professor rakes leaves after chapel." The point is that traditional Grammar 2 ignores completely the intonation of a sentence, an important element of spoken English.

Furthermore, traditional Grammar 2 attempts to fit written English into a theoretical framework derived from classical languages. The categories of our traditional grammar were borrowed from Latin and Greek. These are both highly inflected languages, in which the relationship between words is indicated by adding an ending to the root word. English has lost most of its inflectional endings; it depends on word order, rather than word endings, to indicate the difference between "Dog bites man" and "Man bites dog." The so-called parts of speech—eight categories into which all words are supposed to fit —had some meaning in Latin. One can tell from its form that *quies* is a noun, *quiesco* is a verb, and *quietus* is an adjective. But in English the word *quiet* may be, without change of form, a noun (*peace and quiet*), a verb (*to quiet down*), or an adjective (*a quiet hour*). To apply the Latin concept of parts of speech to English words is bound to produce some confusion. Since many English words fit into several categories, how can we say what part of speech a given word is?

One way out of the difficulty is to use terms like *noun, verb,* or *adjective* to refer to function in a sentence. That is, let function determine the part of speech, instead of vice versa. If *brick* is used to name an object, it is a noun. If it is used to describe an object (*a brick wall*), it is an adjective. This functional approach to grammatical analysis, using traditional Latin names to indicate function in a sentence, works fairly well for a rough analysis of sentence structure. But linguists have argued that new categories, derived from English as it is spoken rather than borrowed from Latin, might be more accurate and more useful.

In an effort to arrive at a Grammar 2 derived inductively from English, C. C. Fries studied fifty hours of transcribed telephone conversations among educated middle-class citizens of Michigan, analyzing their actual speech patterns. His book *The Structure of English* proposed new categories for English grammar, and they have since been modified and used by many structural linguists. Structural linguistics applies to English the objective approach used by anthropologists studying a native language in the field. Making no advance assumptions, the structural linguist tries to limit himself to statements about the forms of words and their structure in sentences, regardless of their meaning. Structural linguists pride themselves on being scientific: their statements are tentative (subject to change or qualification in the light of further data), verifiable by anyone who knows Grammar 1, and objective (they describe what is, instead of what should be). Though linguists do not yet agree on all details of structural analysis, nor on the terminology to be used in describing it, the method has uncovered some very important features of English which were obscured by traditional grammar.

More recently, however, a new school of linguists has been pointing out some shortcomings of structural linguistics. Perhaps the most serious, in the eyes of theorists, is that structural linguistics accounts for only part of a language: that is, it is limited to the "corpus" of words and sentences that it analyzes, and a manageable corpus must always be smaller than the entire language. If we were to analyze the structure of that part of the English language represented by fifty hours of telephone conversations among typical Americans (as Fries did), we could work out inductively some plausible principles for the formation of the past tense of verbs and the plural form of nouns. But suppose, as is not unlikely, that in the chosen fifty hours no one happened to use the words *weave* and *ox*. The grammar derived from this corpus would be incomplete since it would fail to note that the past tense of *weave* is usually *wove*, rather than *weaved*, and that the plural of *ox* is *oxen*. Since any corpus is only a sample of a language, a grammar derived from the corpus is likely to be incomplete.

What some linguistic theorists wanted was an abstract method that could be used to "generate"—i.e., account for—all the possible constructions in the language that native speakers would agree were acceptable, and none of the constructions that native speakers would reject. Such a system not only would be a significant addition to knowledge, but might provide a basis for ultimate computer translation from one language to another. Using concepts and symbols drawn from mathematics and symbolic logic, Noam Chomsky has devised the outlines of a system of this kind—a generative grammar that theoretically would account for all possible English sentences. Because of its use of "grammatical transformations" (rules for transforming one constituent structure into another), Chomsky's system is commonly called "Transformational Grammar," though the more general term "Generative Grammar" is sometimes employed.

Most linguists agree that transformational grammar gives the completest and most accurate description of the structure of English, and some have tried to make this particular Grammar 2 the basis of teaching English in the schools. Such an effort would be reasonable if it were generally agreed that the goal of English courses is a full understanding of the structure of English. But few schools or colleges aim so high. The student already knows (in the sense of being able to use) the basic Grammar 1 of his language, and English courses usually offer only the rough analysis considered necessary in the teaching of Grammar 3. For this, the terminology of the traditional Grammar 2 seems adequate, and it has the additional advantage of being at least in part familiar to most college students. This handbook attempts to utilize some of the insights of modern structural analysis without discarding entirely the older terminology.

Whatever system of grammatical analysis is used, we must meet squarely a basic question raised increasingly by modern linguists:

are the "errors" catalogued by Grammar 3 really errors? Is there a standard by which we can call certain usages correct and others wrong?

In some areas, like vocabulary, the answer is a qualified yes. All language is based on a social agreement to attach certain meanings to verbal symbols, and we all agree that in English *bread* is something we eat, not something we build walls with. There may be slight disagreement about the exact limits of a word's meaning: whether a certain bakery product is to be called *bread* or *cake*, for example. But it is our general agreement about the meanings of English words that makes communication possible, and we can say unequivocally that Mrs. Malaprop was wrong when she referred to "an allegory on the banks of the Nile."

Since the eighteenth century, a good many people have tried to give equally certain answers to questions about correct usage—about ending sentences with prepositions, or using contractions like *ain't*. Communication is not involved here: one construction conveys the meaning as well as the other. Is one usage right and another wrong? Among the rich varieties of expression possible in English, is there such a thing as *the* correct way of speaking or writing?

It is easy to ridicule this question as naive. To show its supposed triviality, Bergen Evans cites a hypothetical case: a student takes a mouse to a biologist with the question "Is this a correct mouse?" Such a question would seem nonsensical to a scientist. A biologist can tell about the species, age, sex, and physical condition of a mouse, but he has no standard for determining the "correctness" of mice. Evans is implying, of course, that linguistics, like other sciences, should be descriptive rather than evaluative, and he bolsters this point by citing another hypothetical example. Suppose you want to make a grammar of the Eskimo language. The first thing you must do is to find some Eskimos. Then you must listen to what they say, record it, and by trial and error figure out how the language works. If while you are doing this, someone says, "Yes, but is this correct Eskimo?" all you can answer is, "Well, this is what they say in Baffinland." You might add that in Greenland they say it a little differently, but the implication is clear that the question is as nonsensical as the question about the correct mouse. What the Eskimos say is a fact, and all a linguist can do is record, analyze, and describe the facts. If English is what English-speaking people say and write, a linguist must base his analysis on what people are speaking and writing, without worrying about its "correctness."

Is one man's English, then, as good as that of the next? Are there no errors to be corrected by Grammar 3? It depends on the meaning one attaches to the term *error*. Certainly there are differences in the way different people speak English. When these differences are conspicuous, fairly regular, and confined to a particular area, we accept them as regional dialects, like Southern or Down East, or as racial, like the Black English dialect, widely spoken by Americans of African ancestry. But to a linguist, dialects are not necessarily limited to particular regions or races. People of different social classes in the same region may speak differently (on one side of the tracks "He don't" is common; on the other, nearly everyone says "He doesn't"), and any family is apt to have its own peculiarities of pronunciation, vocabulary, and syntax. It is probably true, in the last analysis, that no two people speak the language in precisely the same way—that is, each person has his own dialect (or idiolect, as the linguist would call it) of English. Why should any one dialect be called correct and others wrong?

The answer comes, in part, from history. In the past, the dialect of a metropolis has often gained prestige among the rural or provincial citizenry and has eventually been accepted as the standard. Modern English is a direct descendant of the dialect spoken in and around London in the fourteenth century. Furthermore, the written language of metropolitan areas has an advantage in its wider range of sentence patterns and its very much larger vocabulary, as compared with the dialects spoken in the provinces or backwoods.

But there is a sociological answer, too. In any given period there are apt to be differences between the language used by the educated classes and that used by uneducated people, rural or urban; and these differences almost always reflect different degrees of social prestige. In some countries, where society is more rigorously stratified than in the United States, one's speech determines one's social level, as Eliza Doolittle demonstrated in *My Fair Lady*. Language is not so important as a determinant of social prestige in the United States, but there is still a wide difference between the more prestigious "edited English" of the professional and executive classes and the dialects spoken, and sometimes written, by the less educated. It is unscientific for a linguist to ignore this difference, either by denouncing and banishing one level as "bad English," or by pretending that one level is "as good as" the other, since so many people speak it. Scientific objectivity calls for an accurate description of each dialect, and such a description should include some indication of the contexts in which either level gains or loses prestige for the speaker.

The kind of English prescribed by Grammar 3 might thus be redefined as a particular dialect of English which has special prestige because of the people who use it. A student ought to be able to write this dialect even though he usually speaks on a much more colloquial level. Why should we study the endless idiosyncracies of English spelling? *Beleive* is just as intelligible in written contexts as *believe*, but a person who misspells the word may lose caste in the eyes of others. Why should students be taught to write "I felt bad" instead of "I felt badly"? Because most people need to be concerned about the effect of their language on others. A person who confuses adjectives and adverbs may still communicate his meaning clearly enough, but he will reveal an ignorance of Grammar 3 which many people still regard as deplorable.

The motives behind studying Grammar 3 may thus be ultimately snobbish. The rules are often arbitrary conventions, without historical or rational justification, but they represent a level of usage found in practically all books, magazines, and newspapers; and this level of English cannot be ignored by teachers in a fluid society in which people are constantly trying to move upward in the social scale. Since this level of speech is not necessarily part of the Grammar 1 that children acquire unconsciously by imitating their elders, edited English, like table manners and polite behavior, must be studied and learned if one is to share whatever prestige attaches to speaking and writing "correctly."

Dictionaries and handbooks of composition usually try to distinguish different levels of English usage. When descriptive labels like *provincial, slang*, or *substandard* are used, they are meant as approximate guides to the social acceptability of different kinds of English. Almost everyone recognizes examples drawn from vocabulary. *Tired* is the normal English word, appropriate in both speech and writing, to indicate the feeling which follows overexertion. *Exhausted* is a little more literary; it is more apt to appear in writing than in speech. *Fatigued* is almost purely literary; though you know the word, you have probably never actually spoken it in conversation, and if you use it in informal writing, the chances are that your style is pompous. *Tuckered out* sounds provincial, as though the speaker came from the backwoods or were deliberately affecting folksy language. *Pooped* and *beat* are slang; you would not be likely to use either term when talking to the president of your college or in a letter applying for a job. A handbook is simply shirking part of its job if it does not point out that, things being what they are, the use of *like* as a conjunction may cast doubt on the social and educational background of the writer, even though one can find many examples of the usage on television and in the advertising columns of magazines.

In this handbook, the rules and the descriptive labels attached to examples of usage, are not meant to be final judgments on what is, and what is not, correct by some mythical standard of "pure" English. Our purpose is more modest and more utilitarian; we are trying, among other things, to provide a guide for the perplexed. We are saying that, in our opinion, the level of usage implied by these rules and prescriptions is that of the people who determine the prestige-values of the language: editors, writers, and educators. If you choose to violate the rules they follow, you should do so deliberately, not unwittingly.

The Dictionary and Levels of Usage

2

2a Use of the Dictionary

Like all languages, English is continually changing. New words are added as names are required for new inventions, discoveries, and ideas: *laser, meson, transistor, cybernetics, apartheid.* Old words acquire new meanings as they are used in new ways: *half-life* (physics), *snow* (television), *software* (computers), *cartridge* (high-fidelity recording). Some old words disappear as the need for them vanishes; a whole vocabulary dealing with horse-drawn vehicles is on its way out. Words gain or lose prestige: *strenuous* and *mob* are now standard words, although they were once considered slang. *Negro,* once considered a neutral word, has taken on bad connotations and is now widely replaced by *Black.*

A dictionary is an attempt to record the current uses and meanings of words. Though many people believe that a dictionary tells them what a word *ought to* mean, or how it *should be* used, a modern dictionary tries to be an accurate and objective record of what is actually being said and written. It discriminates among the current meanings of a word and tries to indicate the ways in which each is used. Since words and constructions differ in prestige value, a conscientious lexicographer will also try to record the current status of words, usually by labels such as Dialectal or Regional, Obsolete or Archaic, Informal, Colloquial, Nonstandard, or Slang.

Large, unabridged dictionaries include a history of the past meanings of words, biographical and geographical data, guides for pronunciation, spelling, and punctuation, and a variety of other useful information. The large dictionaries in established widespread use in most college libraries include:

The Oxford English Dictionary, 12 volumes and Supplement, Clarendon Press, Oxford, 1933. Supplement A–G, 1972. (This is the standard historical dictionary of the language; it traces and illustrates the development of each word from its earliest appearance to the present.)

Webster's New International Dictionary of the English Language, Second Edition, G. & C. Merriam Co., Springfield, Mass., 1954.

Webster's Third New International Dictionary of the English Language, G. & C. Merriam Co., 1961. (This dictionary gives few usage labels.)

The Random House Dictionary of the English Language, New York, 1966.

Webster's New Twentieth Century Dictionary of the English Language, Second Edition, New York, 1958.

Unabridged dictionaries are invaluable for occasional reference, but more practical for the student are the following abridged desk dictionaries. All are reliable, but some instructors may have preferences, which they will indicate.

The American Heritage Dictionary of the English Language, Houghton Mifflin Company, Boston

Funk and Wagnalls Standard College Dictionary, Harcourt, Brace & World, Inc., New York.

The Random House College Dictionary, New York.

Webster's New Collegiate Dictionary, G. & C. Merriam Co., Springfield, Mass.

Webster's New World Dictionary, Collins, William & World Publishing Co., Inc., Cleveland, Ohio.

(1) Abbreviations and Symbols

To use a dictionary effectively, you must understand the abbreviations and symbols it uses. These are explained in its introductory section. Here are entries from four collegiate dictionaries.

spelling & syllabication
↓

etymology
↓

2a

¹**im•ply** (im plī′) *vt.* **-plied′, -ply′ing** [ME. *implien* < OFr. *emplier* < L. *implicare,* to involve, entangle < *in-,* in + *plicare,* to fold < IE. base °*plek-,* to plait, wrap together, whence Gr. *plekein,* to braid: cf. FLAX] **1.** to have as a necessary part, condition, or effect; contain, include, or involve naturally or necessarily [drama *implies* conflict] **2.** to indicate indirectly or by allusion; hint; suggest; intimate [an attitude *implying* boredom] **3.** [Obs.] to enfold; entangle —*SYN.* see SUGGEST

↑
usage label

¹With permission. From *Websters New World Dictionary of the American Language,* Second College Edition. Copyright © 1976 by William Collins + World Publishing Co., Inc.

pronunciation   *part of speech*
↓   ↓

meanings

²**im•ply** (im•plī′) *v.t.* **•plied, •ply•ing 1.** To involve necessarily as a circumstance, condition, effect, etc.: An action *implies* an agent. **2.** To indicate or suggest without stating; hint at; intimate. **3.** To have the meaning of; signify. **4.** *Obs.* To entangle; infold. —Syn. See INFER. [< OF *emplier* < L *implicare* to involve < *in-* in + *plicare* to fold. Doublet of *EMPLOY.*]

—**Syn. 1.** *Imply* and *involve* mean to have some necessary connection. *Imply* states that the connection is causal or inherent, while *involve* is vaguer, and does not define the connection. **2.** *Imply, hint, intimate, insinuate* mean to convey a meaning indirectly or covertly. *Imply* is the general term for signifying something beyond what the words obviously say; his advice *implied* confidence in the stock market. *Hint* suggests indirection in speech or action: our host's repeated glances at his watch *hinted* that it was time to go. *Intimate* suggests a process more elaborate and veiled than hint: she *intimated* that his attentions were unwelcome. *Insinuate* suggests slyness and a derogatory import: in his remarks, he *insinuated* that the Senator was a fool.

full discussion of synonyms

²From *Funk & Wagnalls Standard College Dictionary.* Copyright © 1963, 1966, 1968, 1973 by Funk & Wagnalls Publishing Company, Inc. Used by permission of the publisher.

inflected forms

³**im•ply** ĭm-plī′) *tr.v.* **-plied, -plying, -plies. 1.** To involve or suggest by logical necessity; entail: *His aims imply a good deal of energy.* **2.** To say or express indirectly; to hint; suggest: *His tone implied a malicious purpose.* **3.** *Obsolete.* To entangle. —See Synonyms at **suggest.** —See Usage note at **infer.** [Middle English *implien, emplien,* from Old French *emplier,* from Latin *implicāre,* infold, involve, IMPLICATE.]

³Reprinted by permission from *The American Heritage Dictionary of the English Language.* © 1969, 1970, 1971, 1973, 1975, 1976, Houghton Mifflin Company.

⁴**im•ply** im-′plī *vt* **im•plied; im•ply•ing** [ME *emplien,* fr. **MF** *emplier,* fr. L *implicare*] **1** *obs* : ENFOLD, ENTWINE **2** : to involve or indicate by inference, association, or necessary consequence rather than by direct statement <rights ~ obligations> **3** : to contain potentially **4** : to express indirectly <his silence *implied* consent> **syn** see SUGGEST *ant* express

↑   ↑   ↑
illustration of use   *synonyms*   *antonyms*

⁴By permission. From *Webster's New Collegiate Dictionary* © 1976 by G. & C. Merriam Co., Publishers of the Merriam-Webster Dictionaries.

(2) Information Found in a Dictionary

Spelling and Syllabication   When more than one spelling is given, the one printed first is usually to be preferred. Division of the word into syllables follows the conventions accepted by printers.

Pronunciation   A key to the symbols used to indicate pronunciation of words is usually printed on the front or back inside cover of the dictionary. Some dictionaries also run an abbreviated key to pronunciation at the bottom of each page or every other page. Word accent is shown by the symbol (′) after the stressed syllable or by (′) before it.

Parts of Speech   Abbreviations (explained in the introductory section of the dictionary) are used to indicate the various grammatical uses of a word: e.g., *imply, v.t.* means that *imply* is a transitive verb. Note that some words can be used as several different parts of speech. *Forfeit,* for example, is listed first as a noun, and its various meanings in this use are defined. Then its meaning when used as an adjective is given, and finally its meaning as a transitive verb.

Inflected Forms   Forms of the past tense and past and present participles of verbs, the comparative or superlative degree of adjectives, and the plurals of nouns are given whenever there might be doubt as to the correct form or spelling.

Etymology   The history of each word is indicated by the forms in use in Middle or Old English, or in the language from which the word was borrowed. Earlier meanings are often given.

Meanings   Different meanings of a word are numbered and defined, sometimes with illustrative examples. Some dictionaries give the oldest meanings first; others list the common meanings of the word first.

Usage Labels   Descriptive labels, often abbreviated, indicate the level of usage: Archaic, Obsolete, Colloquial, Slang, Dialectal, Regional, Substandard, Nonstandard, etc. Look up the meanings of these words in the dictionary you use. Sometimes usage labels indicate a special field, rather than a level of usage: e.g., *Poetic, Irish, Chemistry.* If a word has no usage label, it may be assumed that, in the opinion of the editors, the word is in common use on all levels; that is, it is *standard* English. Usage labels are often defined and illustrated in the explanatory notes in the front of a dictionary. Check yours; it is important to understand how the labels are used.

Synonyms   Words that have nearly identical or closely related meanings often need careful discrimination to indicate the precise connotation of each. A full account of the distinctions in meaning between synonyms (for example, *suggest, imply, hint, intimate,* and *insinuate*) may be given at the end of the entry for the basic word, or cross references to its synonyms may be provided.

Exercise 1

In looking up the meanings of words, try to discover within what limits of meaning the word may be used. Read the definition as a whole; do not pick out a single synonym and suppose that this and the word defined are interchangeable. After looking up the following words in your dictionary, write sentences which will unmistakably illustrate the meaning of each word.

anachronism	innocuous	precocious
eminent	materiel	sinecure
fetish	misanthropy	sophistication
hedonist	nepotism	taboo
imminent	philanthropy	travesty

Exercise 2

Look up each of the following words both in an unabridged dictionary and in an abridged one, and write a report showing how the larger volume explains the use of each word more discriminatingly and clearly than the smaller one does. State the exact title, the publisher, and the date of both dictionaries.

Bible	Christian	court	idealism
catholic	color	evolution	liberal

Exercise 3

How may the etymologies given by the dictionary help one to remember the meaning or the spelling of the following words? (Note that when a series of words has the same etymology, the etymology is usually given only with the basic word of the series.)

alibi	insidious	privilege
capitol	isosceles	sacrilegious
cohort	magnanimous	sarcasm
concave	malapropism	subterfuge
denouement	peer (noun)	thrifty

Exercise 4

Most dictionaries put abbreviations in the main alphabetical arrangement. Look up the following abbreviations and be ready to state in class what they mean:

at. wt.	colloq.	E.T.A.	K.C.B.	LL.D.	PBX
CAB	e.g.	ff.	l.c.	OAS	QKtP

Exercise 5

Consult the dictionary for the distinction in meaning between the members of each of the following pairs of words:

neglect—negligence   instinct—intuition
ingenuous—ingenious   nauseous—nauseated
fewer—less   eminent—famous
admit—confess   criticize—censure
infer—imply   increment—addition

Exercise 6

In each sentence, choose the more precise of the two italicized words. Be able to justify your choice.

1. Many in the class were *disinterested, uninterested* and went to sleep.
2. His charming innocence is *childlike, childish.*
3. The problem is to assure the farm workers *continuous, continual* employment.
4. She is *continuously, continually* in trouble with the police.
5. I am quite *jealous, envious* of your opportunity to study in Europe.
6. She is so *decided, decisive* in her manner that people always give in to her.
7. If we give your class all of these privileges, we may establish *precedents, precedence* which are unwise.
8. She always makes her health her *alibi, excuse* for her failures.

Exercise 7

Find the precise meaning of each word in the following groups, and write sentences to illustrate that meaning.

1. abandon, desert, forsake
2. ludicrous, droll, comic
3. silent, reserved, taciturn
4. meager, scanty, sparse
5. knack, talent, genius
6. anxious, eager, avid

2b Levels of Usage

(1) Standard English

STANDARD ENGLISH includes the great majority of words and constructions that native speakers would recognize as acceptable in any situation or context. All words in a dictionary that are not specifically labeled are, in the judgment of the editors, Standard English and acceptable for general use. However, a good many words and constructions have, for various reasons, a more limited use and these are commonly labeled in dictionaries. For example, words used in some sections of the country but not in all, like *carry* in the sense of "escort to a dance or party," will be labeled REGIONAL or DIALECTAL. If the usage is more localized, like *arroyo* (a dry gully), the word will be labeled *Southwestern U.S.*, or *New England*, or whatever. Other labels explain words still found in books but no longer in common use, like OBSOLETE (for example, *deer* used in the sense of "any animal," as in Shakespeare's "Rats and mice and such small deer") or ARCHAIC (very old but preserved for historical or poetic reasons, like *olden*).

In addition to such geographic or temporal limitations on word use, most people feel that certain kinds of language, or certain dialects, have more or less prestige because of the people who use them. In the past, the language of the educated upper class was thought of as Good English, and all other dialects or levels were ignored or condemned as incorrect, ungrammatical, or illiterate. To the modern linguist, all the dialects spoken by different groups in American society are equally valid varieties of English, but they are not always appropriate in serious public writing.

In a country where many people are trying to improve their position in an open society, differences in prestige among dialects need to be pointed out. The usual way to do this in a handbook is to attach Usage Labels to words which are limited in some way. This handbook, in addition to regional and temporal labels, tries to indicate levels of acceptability by using the following labels: STANDARD (acceptable in formal and informal use), FORMAL, INFORMAL, (or general), COLLO-

QUIAL, SLANG, and NONSTANDARD. The overlapping of various levels and labels (in capital letters) can be seen in the following diagram.

Levels of Usage

Edited English {	FORMAL INFORMAL (General)	Not Labeled
Spoken English {	COLLOQUIAL SLANG NONSTANDARD	Labeled

Notice that Edited English, the main concern of this handbook, is not labeled in most dictionaries. Accordingly, any word that *is* labeled in your dictionary should be used sparingly, if at all, in public writing.

Sharp lines cannot always be drawn between the levels indicated by these labels, but relative differences are clear. *Fatigued* and *exhausted* are more formal than *tired,* which in turn is more formal than *bushed* (Colloquial) or *pooped* (Slang). *Fatigued* seldom occurs in speech and is usually found only in technical or poetic writing. *Tired* is acceptable in any spoken or written context. *Bushed* would be used mainly in familiar conversation or in writing among friends. The slang term *pooped* would seldom appear in serious writing, and then only for its shock value or its slightly comic effect.

As we have seen, levels of usage, like the language itself, undergo changes from generation to generation. Such changes have been especially rapid in recent decades. During the past fifty years, the center of Edited usage has moved away from the Formal level toward the Informal. Especially in magazines and newspapers, good writers are more apt to use colloquialisms and even slang rather than risk the stilted pomposity of Formal English in a commonplace context. Many once-forbidden words are coming up in the world, too. *Ain't* used to be universally regarded as Nonstandard; today, though it is generally disapproved even in informal writing, some dictionaries label it Nonstandard only when it is used to mean "has not" or "have not," as in "I ain't got any." As a result of a campaign by the advertising industry, *like* is now widely used as a conjunction ("like a cigarette should"; "tell it like it is"), though recent dictionaries continue to label this usage Nonstandard or Colloquial. It seems likely that, eventually, this use of *like* will be generally acceptable, despite the distaste of purists. Meanwhile, if your dictionary indicates by a usage label that a word is limited in its use, you will do well to keep that word out of your serious writing—that is, an article for a college magazine (unless you are trying for some special effect), a term paper, or a letter of application.

The basic principle of good usage is to fit the level of your language to the situation and to the expected reader. Formal English is for formal occasions, like Commencement or a funeral, or for official personages, like college presidents in their public speech and writings. You would not be apt to use the noun *gripe* in a Commencement address, an obituary or a letter to the President. Conversely, language suitable for a letter of application might be inappropriate in the locker room or a poker game. In making such discriminations, your own sense of the language (your Grammar 1), aided in doubtful cases by the dictionary, will have to serve you. But before your dictionary can help you with such problems, you must study the meaning of the labels it uses. The labels used in this handbook are explained below.

(2) Formal English

FORMAL ENGLISH appears in scholarly or scientific articles, formal speeches, official documents, and any context calling for scrupulous propriety. It makes use of words and phrases like "scrupulous propriety," which nobody would use in speech and which would seldom appear in ordinary writing. As another example, consider the word *scrutinize*. This is a perfectly good word that everyone knows, but its use is almost entirely limited to formal written English, and even there it is not common. It is apt to give a bookish flavor to ordinary writing, and it is almost never used in speech. (Try to imagine yourself handing a friend a piece of writing with the request "Scrutinize this.") Formal English also includes technical language—the specialized vocabularies used in such professions as law, medicine, and the sciences. Technical language can be very precise and economical, but it is Greek to the ordinary reader and out of place in most Edited English. A good general rule is to use formal or technical language, like best clothes, only on special occasions.

(3) Edited English

EDITED ENGLISH is the written language of books from reputable publishers, good magazines, and many newspapers. It is defined, not merely by choice of words, but by generally accepted conventions of spelling, punctuation, grammatical patterns, and sentence structure. In this section, we are considering Edited English primarily as it is reflected in choice of words. But the general purpose of all the rules laid down in this handbook is to enable you to write Edited English, the normal means of official communication in the professions and in the upper levels of business and industry.

Authorities, it must be admitted, often differ among themselves. Many handbooks, including this one, deplore the use of *contact* as a verb meaning "to get in touch with." Theodore Bernstein of the *New York Times*, though he dislikes the usage, admits in *The Careful Writer* that it is a useful verb and "will undoubtedly push its way into standard usage sometime." The most recent editions of three leading dictionaries differ widely: one accepts the usage, with no label, as standard English; one gently reproves it as an "Americanism"; the third labels it *Informal* and disapproves its use in Edited English.

Faced with such disagreement, what practical conclusion can we draw? If you use *contact* as a verb and someone challenges it, you can of course defend yourself by citing *Webster's New Collegiate Dictionary*, which makes no objection to it. But being challenged is a nuisance, and your defensive explanations are seldom convincing. If the main purpose of your writing is to get something said, don't use words that are likely to be challenged or that need lengthy defense.

(4) Colloquial English

COLLOQUIAL ENGLISH means, literally, conversational English. Everyone's language is more casual and relaxed among friends than in public speech or writing. Colloquial expressions are part of Standard English, since everyone uses them, but they may be jarringly out of place in formal contexts or in serious writing. Examples are words like *rock hound*, to *get away with* something, *sure* in the sense of "certainly" (I sure would like . . .), or a *square deal*. When words and constructions are labeled *Colloquial* (some dictionaries use *Informal* for the same purpose), you should consider their possible effects on a reader before writing them. If in doubt, look for an accepted synonym.

(5) Nonstandard English

The label NONSTANDARD indicates the wide variety of usages not generally accepted in writing: misspellings, unconventional punctuation, illiterate grammatical constructions, and certain widely heard expressions that educated people have qualms about writing. Examples are words like *nowheres, hain't,* especially in double negative constructions like "I hain't got none," and constructions like *he don't,* or *of* for *have* in sentences like "I would of gone. . . ." Expressions labeled *Nonstandard* have no place in serious Edited English, except in direct quotation.

(6) Dialect

A DIALECT is a form of the native language spoken in a particular region of the country or in a large geographical area by a particular group of persons. Its vocabulary and grammatical structures often differ from Standard English, which is the dialect of prestige and power in the United States. Within the region or among the group, however, the dialect may be more prestigious than Standard English. Dialect words are often colorful and vigorous: *varmint, poke, blood, polecat, da kine, foxy, streak-o-lean, talk story, branch water.* Some dialects, such as that in the Southeast, retain words from the early settlers—*reckon, yonder*—and echo grammar that was in use before Latin rules were imposed on English syntax. There's no question about what the dialect phrase "it don't bother me none" means, even though double negatives were banished from Standard English in the eighteenth century. Black dialect retains the "be" verb in its aspectual sense, as a state of being, a form now lost to Standard English. "I be working when he be bothering me" is not the same sentence as "I am working when he bothers me," its standard English approximation. An important distinction is lost in translation.

Often people create dialects in order to speak to one another. Black Dialect began as a means of communicating among slave traders (who were not always English), English slave owners, and persons sold into slavery who spoke a number of African languages. The pidgin dialect of Hawaii came about when persons from radically differing language families—the Tagalogs of the Philippines, Portuguese, Hawaiians, Japanese, Chinese—needed to communicate as they worked under English overseers side by side in the cane fields. The dialect is characterized by the absence of features which give English speakers difficulty: prepositions, tenses of verbs, articles. Because the dialects are spoken, the many inflections of English are not needed. Neither Black Dialect nor Hawaiian Pidgin consistently obeys the agreement rule. Students who are bi-dialectal, that is, fluent in Standard English and a dialect, are wise to be aware of those areas where their spoken and written voices conflict; they should proofread scrupulously to make sure they have followed the conventions of Edited English.

(7) Regional English

The label REGIONAL refers to a usage which is considered reputable in certain areas of the country, but which has not gained nationwide acceptance. These words are not necessarily nonstandard in the regions where they are found, and sometimes they are useful additions to the local vocabulary. But for general college writing, they should not be used when equivalent words in national currency are available. Some examples of regional words are *crack grass* for *crab grass*, *monkeychop* for *chipmunk, you all* to refer to one person, *eastworm* or *angle dog* for *angleworm*.

(8) Slang

SLANG is the label given to words with a forced, exaggerated, or humorous meaning used in extremely informal contexts, particularly by persons who wish to set themselves off from the average, respectable citizen.

To call a man whose ideas and behavior are unpredictable and unconventional "a kook" and to describe his ideas as "for the birds" or "way out" apparently satisfies some obscure human urge toward irreverent, novel, and vehement expression. Some slang terms remain in fairly wide use because they are vivid ways of expressing an idea which has no exact standard equivalent: *stooge, lame duck, shot* of whiskey, a card *shark*. Such words have a good chance of becoming accepted as Standard English. *Mob, banter, sham,* and *lynch* were all once slang terms. It is quite likely that, eventually, useful slang words, like *honkytonk* or *snitch* will be accepted as standard colloquial English.

A good deal of slang, however, reflects nothing more than the user's desire to be different, and such slang has little chance of being accepted into the language. Newspaper columnists and sports writers often use a flamboyant jargon intended to show off their ingenuity or cleverness. For centuries criminals have used a special, semisecret language, and many modern slang terms originated in the argot of the underworld: *gat, scram, squeal,* or *sing* (confess), *push* (peddle). Hippies and rock musicians have developed a constantly changing slang which seems intended to distinguish the user as a member of a select group or inner circle.

Whatever the motive behind it, slang should be used with discretion. Its incongruity in a sober, practical context makes it an effective way of achieving force and emphasis.

ACCEPTABLE SLANG   His book is so intelligently constructed, so beautifully written, so really acute at moments—and so *phony*.

But most slang terms are too violent to fit comfortably into everyday writing. Furthermore, slang goes out of fashion very quickly through overuse, and dated slang sounds more quaint and old-fashioned than Formal English. *Tight* has worn well, but *boiled, crocked, fried,* and *plastered* may soon be museum pieces.

The chief objection to the use of slang is that it so quickly loses any precise meaning. Calling a person a *fink*, a *square*, or a *creep* conveys little more than your feeling of dislike. *Cool* and *crummy* are the vaguest kind of terms, lumping all experience into two crude divisions, pleasing and unpleasing. Try to get several people to agree on the precise meaning of *square* and you will realize how vague and inexact a term it is. The remedy is to analyze your meaning and specify it. What exactly are the qualities which lead you to classify a person as a *square*, or as a *weirdo?*

If, despite these warnings, you must use slang in serious writing, do it deliberately and accept the responsibility for it. Do not attempt to excuse yourself by putting the slang term in quotation marks. If you are ashamed of a slang term, do not use it.

Exercise 8

With the aid of a dictionary and your own linguistic judgment (i.e., your ear for appropriateness), classify the following Standard English words as Formal, Informal, or Colloquial.

1. crank, eccentric, [a] character
2. hide, sequester, ditch
3. irascible, cranky, grouchy
4. increase, boost, jack [up the price]
5. decline, avoid, pass [up]
6. pass [out], faint, swoon
7. necessity, [a] must, requirement
8. inexpensive, [a] steal, cheap
9. snooty, pretentious, affected
10. room, domicile, pad

Exercise 9

For each of the following Standard English words supply one or more slang terms and, to the best of your ability, judge which are so widespread that they have already begun to creep into highly informal writing (e.g., letters to friends; college newspaper columns) or seem likely to do so in the near future.

Example: to become excited [to be turned on by, *slang*]

1. money
2. to relax
3. a skilled performer
4. to be going steady or in love
5. failure
6. to tell off
7. pleasant or enjoyable
8. to play a part
9. liquor
10. to ignore or disregard
11. complaint
12. a dull person
13. unconventional person
14. to be unfairly treated
15. puzzling

Exercise 10

Pick five or six slang terms widely used around campus and ask at least five people to define the meaning of each term in Standard English. Write the results and your conclusions.

Effective Diction 3

Diction, or choice of words, is the foundation of good style. The word *diction* is derived from the Latin *dicere*, to say, and ultimately from the Indo-European root *deik*, to show, or to point out, as its kinship with the Latin word for finger, *digitus*, and the English *digit* reveals. When we don't know the name for something we point to it. Written words are ways of pointing out things we do not always see to persons who are not there.

No word, of course, can ever duplicate what we touch and see or the turmoil that we feel. Recognizing this limitation of language, writers who are attentive to diction achieve precision by selecting words which most nearly approximate their thoughts. That even the most scrupulous stylists are occasionally misunderstood is evidence that no system of communication is perfect. But too often apprentice writers have the suspicion or hope that under, over, or behind what appears on the page lies a meaning that can be discovered, not by going through the words, but by brushing them aside. For the unskilled writer words seem barricades which obstruct understanding. "You *know* what I'm saying," such a writer insists, but no one knows what goes on in our heads until we choose the words that say precisely what we mean.

To do this we need a large, active vocabulary that we can use confidently in writing as well as passively in reading. Good writers own and use dictionaries. Look up both the meaning and pronunciation of the unfamiliar words you come across in reading and those which seem familiar but which you cannot define. Keep a vocabulary notebook and use these words frequently in conversation and writing. You may blunder in getting acquainted with a new word, for context often determines diction. But the awareness you will gain of a word's appropriateness is worth the risk of having a word circled on the returned manuscript.

3a Denotation and Connotation

Words resonate, and connotations are the echoes, the overtones. They have little to do with the denotations or literal meanings, but they often dictate what is suitable diction. *House, home,* and *domicile* all have the same denotation—a place of residence. But their connotations are quite different: *house* emphasizes the physical structure; *home* suggests family life, warmth, comfort, affection; *domicile* has strictly legal overtones.

The connotation of each word must be appropriate to the context. It would not be possible to write a sentimental song entitled "House, Sweet House," nor would it seem fitting to call the guest residence of the President of the United States "Blair Home." Similarly, the word *skull* is appropriate in a medical book or ghost story, but its connotations make it unsuitable in an advertisement for men's clothing: not "a hat to suit each type of *skull*" but "a hat to suit each type of *head*."

Colors connote a variety of associations beyond their literal definition as qualities which differ on the basis of absorbed or reflected light. A translator of the Spanish poet, García Lorca, for example, can count on English readers bringing the associations of youth, vigor, freshness, spring to the translation of "Verde que te quiero verde" as "Green, how much I want you green," even though the music of the Spanish line is lost. When Andrew Marvell three centuries ago praised "a green thought in a green shade," he knew very well that readers of English after his lifetime would bring to the phrase associations of grass, trees, growth, life, tranquility. Blue thoughts would be moody and troubled, yellow thoughts sprightly, brown thoughts pensive and melancholy, black thoughts foreboding.

Since English, along with some other languages, uses color words to designate racial groups, we should be alert to connotations which might result from unconscious or primitive reactions to the physical world. Our fears of the night, the absence of the sun's light and warmth, contribute to the negative overtones some speakers still associate with the word *black,* and which have produced the words *blackhearted, blackmail, blacklist.* The campaign of American Blacks to offset the negative connotations of the word with the positive ones of power and beauty and to strip the word *white* of its exclusive associations with purity, holiness and innocence represents a conscious effort by users of the language to alter the ways in which our minds respond to words.

Poets and children know that a similarity of sounds often prompts an association of words. "Sticks and stones may break my bones, but names will never hurt me," a taunted child chants with the grim bravado of the wounded. The magical power of the incantation, invoked in the midst of evidence which proves the contrary, is created by the alliteration of the words or the repetition of initial consonants —*st* and *st, b* and *b, n* and *n*—as well as by the true rhyme of *stones* and *bones.* The harmony of sound and syllable gives the authority of truth to what is a strategic falsehood. Besides sounding alike, *bones* and *stones* associate on the basis of shared qualities: they are gray-white in color, hard, dry. They can be used as weapons, lead to death, lie together in tombs, which is itself a slant rhyme for the words. The poet, Phyllis Thompson, concludes a poem: "When I die, I will turn to bone/like these. And dust of bone. And then, like God,/to stone," relying on the assonance or vowel repetition to give the lines the finality of a well fabricated design. *Rocks* and *bones* do not associate in the same way, neither do *stones* and *skin* even though they begin with the same letter.

Such word communities are not described in dictionaries or in a thesaurus, but we can recognize them by paying close attention to the sounds of words.

3b Abstract and Concrete

Words which name specific, tangible things are concrete; words which designate general qualities, categories, or relationships are abstract. A general term like *food* is a name for a whole group of specific things—from vegetable soup to T-bone steak to strawberry shortcake. If you want to make a statement about all foods, the general term is appropriate: "Food is becoming more and more expensive." But do not use the general term when concrete details and specific words are called for.

VAGUE AND GENERAL   For dinner we had some really good food.

SPECIFIC   For dinner we had barbecued steaks and sweet corn.

VAGUE AND GENERAL   She liked to argue about controversial subjects.

SPECIFIC   She liked to argue about politics and religion.

Note that specific *and* general *are relative, not absolute terms. In the following list, which runs from specific to more general, any of the four terms might be used to refer to a famous tree growing on campus:*

SPECIFIC   Charter Oak (one particular tree)

LESS SPECIFIC   oak (includes thousands of trees)

MORE GENERAL   tree (includes oaks, pines, palms, etc.)

MORE GENERAL   plant (includes trees, flowers, bushes, etc.)

Tree is more specific than *plant*, but more general than *oak*.

Many common nouns and adjectives were once the names of places and persons: *maudlin* (Mary Magdalen), *tawdry* (St. Audrey), *laconic* (Laconia), *romance* (Rome). Language begins in the concrete. We can trace most English words back to Indo-European roots which plunge into the firm soil of the tangible world. Indeed, the word *concrete* derives from the Latin prefix *com* (together) and the word *crescere* (to grow), which itself grows out of the name for the Roman earth goddess, *Ceres,* a curious beginning for a word which today denotes pavements and connotes the covering of growing things.

When we are learning a language we ask for the names of what we see, hear, smell, touch, taste: red, thunder, burning, smooth, salty. Later we begin to classify the particulars of our experience into categories which are abstract: color, sound, odor, texture, flavor. The word *abstract*, a combination of the prefix *ab* (away from) and *trahere* (to pull) means literally "to take away from." The process of abstraction takes the particularities away from things and arranges them in groups according to their sameness. It deals in generalities rather than in specifics.

Teachers of writing with good reason urge their students to be specific, to be concrete. Too often students write in vague generalities which seem to have no reference to the world of particular experience. We cannot, of course, avoid the abstract altogether. Nor should we, for we must organize the evidence gathered by our senses into summaries and concepts. The best writing moves gracefully from abstract to concrete and back from particular to general. Writing of the poet, William Wordsworth, Margaret Drabble ballasts abstract statement with vivid, concrete images:

> **To people who do not know or do not like his poetry, he presents an image made up of all kinds of forbidding and unpleasant characteristics:** he is a pious, grey-haired, elderly Victorian grandfather; a puritanical, humorless water-drinker; a lover of Nature, friend to butterflies, bees and little daisies; in fact, a sentimental, tedious old bore, with a moral reflection ready for any subject that should come up, from Alpine scenery to railways or his neighbour's spade.

The less skillful writer might have ended the sentence with the colorless abstraction, *characteristics*, but Drabble uses her keen eye for detail to fill out a portrait of the poet as he exists in the minds of his detractors.

3c   Weak and Vigorous Verbs

Anemic writing often results when, rather than using a vigorous verb, we connect subject and complement with a form of the verb *to be*. Such forms, known as *linking* (or *copulative*) verbs, also include *become, seem, appear, remain,* etc. We cannot, of course, write without linking verbs, especially when indicating logical equivalents:

> "Yoruk doctors, with extremely rare exceptions, were women—all their great doctors were women." (Theodora Kroeber)

The linking verb were *functions as an equal sign in mathematics and is appropriate to Kroeber's sentence.*

Acceptable in speech, the phrase "the reason is because" weakens written assertions. Don't waste words: "The reason I like the play is because Nora walks out the door." Be assertive: "I like the play because Nora walks out the door."

Make your verbs work. Good writers enliven their observations by selecting sharp verbs and by using verbals as modifiers. Consider these sentences from an essay by the Black poet, Langston Hughes:

> Let the blare of Negro jazz bands and the bellowing voice of Bessie Smith singing Blues penetrate the closed ears of the colored near-intellectuals until they listen and perhaps understand. Let Paul Robeson singing Water Boy, and Rudolph Fisher writing about the streets of Harlem, and Jean Toomer holding the heart of

Georgia in his hands, and Aaron Douglas drawing strange black fantasies cause the smug Negro middle class to turn from their white, respectable, ordinary books and papers to catch a glimmer of their own beauty.

The verbs which make the assertion of the statement, *let, penetrate, listen, understand, cause, to turn, to catch,* are reinforced by the continuous action of the participles, *bellowing, singing, writing, holding,* and *drawing.* Even the nouns *blare* and *glimmer* contribute energy, since they can function in other contexts as verbs.

Occur, took place, prevail, exist, happen, and other verbs expressing a state of affairs have legitimate uses, but they are often colorless, tossed in merely to complete a sentence.

WEAK   In the afternoon a sharp drop in the temperature occurred.
STRONGER   The temperature dropped sharply in the afternoon.

WEAK   Throughout the meeting an atmosphere of increasing tension existed.
STRONGER   As the meeting progressed, the tension increased.

Linking verbs completed by an adjective or participle are usually weaker than concrete verbs.

WEAK   He was occasionally inclined to talk too much.
STRONGER   Occasionally he talked too much.

WEAK   In some high schools there is a very definite lack of emphasis on the development of a program in remedial English.
STRONGER   Some high schools have failed to develop programs in remedial English.

Unnecessary use of the passive voice also produces weak sentences (see Chapter 5, page 97).

3d   Jargon

There are two kinds of jargon: the technical language used by certain professionals and the empty generalities that are the bluff of the incompetent, unthinking writer. We should take pains to excise from our writing the jargon which obscures the obvious. Ponderous, wordy, vague, inflated writing is characteristic of those bureaucrats, publicists, government employees, college professors, and students who hope that the dense air of their prose will give depth and authority to commonplace ideas.

Our minds are numbed everyday by foggy phrases like *capability factors, career potential, culturally disadvantaged, socio-personal development, substantive social interaction, protective reaction strike, inoperative fiscal procedures.* It is not easy to escape from this widely publicized network of confused language, but if we learn to recognize the stylistic flavor of jargon, we may avoid it in our own writing. Jargon words are, by and large, abstract rather than concrete, and contain more than one syllable (as if the jargon writer assumed that the addition of a syllable would add weight to the word). Jargon words are often nouns masquerading as verbs: *concretize, minimize, finalize, interiorize.* Sometimes nouns are turned into adverbs or adjectives by the addition of the suffix *wise: languagewise, subjectwise, moneywise, weatherwise.* Jargon is best deflated by a translation into clear English:

> A corollary of reinforcement is that the consequences of respond-ing may be represented exhaustively along a continuum ranging from those that substantially raise response likelihood, through those that have little or no effect on response likelihood, to those that substantially reduce response likelihood. An event is a posi-tive reinforcer if its occurrence or presentation after a response strengthens the response. Sometimes good grades, words of praise, or salary checks act as positive reinforcers. An object or event is a negative reinforcer if its withdrawal or termination after a response strengthens the response. Often bad grades, shame, or worthless payments act as negative reinforcers. The above notion sounds complex and difficult to apply but is indeed ex-tremely simple.

The relatively plain English of the third and fifth sentences con-trasts vividly with the puffy syllables, the awkward constructions, the straining adverbs and unclear substantives which clutter the rest of the paragraph. What the writer wants to say is, as he notes, fairly simple, though abstract:

> The psychological principle of reinforcement means that the likelihood of a learned response is increased if a person is re-warded for responding correctly. Good grades, words of praise, or salary checks act as positive reinforcers. Bad grades, shame, or worthless payments are negative reinforcers in that a response is strengthened only if such consequences are eliminated.

In addition to being obscure and tiresome, jargon, when it conceals or distorts the reality it describes, can be dangerous, even deadly. The phrase *anti-personnel detonating devices* obscures the bitter reality of

bombs which kill men, women, and children. Similarly, the devious-
ness of official statements like "The U.S. cannot foreclose any option
for retaliation" distracts us from the protest we might register had
the writer said what he meant: "The U.S. will use nuclear weapons if
necessary."

3e   Idiom

In English we rely on prepositions to indicate subtle but
essential relationships between words. To take a stand *on* an issue,
to be *in* a quandary, *out of* luck, *off* your rocker—these idiomatic
expressions make a kind of spatial sense. But some verbs require
prepositions which are arbitrary and cannot always be explained.
How can persons who are learning English and know the words *take,
in, up, down,* and *over,* deduce the meaning of *take in* (comprehend),
taken in (fooled), *take up* (begin to do something), *take down* (humil-
iate), *take over* and *overtake?* They can't; they must learn each idiom
separately. Here are some idiomatic uses of prepositions:

Abide *by* a decision
agree *with* a person; *to* a proposal; *on* a procedure
argue *with* a person; *for* or *against* or *about* a measure
angry *at* or *about* something; *with* a person
compatible *with*
correspond *to* or *with* a thing; *with* a person
differ *from* one another in appearance; differ *with* a person in opinion
independent *of*
interfere *with* a performance; *in* someone else's affairs
listen *to* a person, argument, or sound; listen *at* the door
with regard *to* or *as* regards
stand *by* a friend; *for* a cause; *on* an issue
superior *to;* better *than*
wait *on* a customer; *for* a person; *at* a place; *in* the rain; *by* the hour

Idiom demands that certain words be followed by infinitives, others
by gerunds. For instance:

infinitive	*gerund*
able to go	capable of going
like to go	enjoy going
eager to go	cannot help going
hesitate to go	privilege of going

If two idioms are used in a compound construction, each idiom must be complete.

INCOMPLETE   He had no love or confidence in his employer.
COMPLETE BUT AWKWARD   He had no *love for,* or *confidence in,* his employer.
IMPROVED   He had no love for his employer and no confidence in him.
INCOMPLETE   I shall always remember the town because of the good times and the friends I made there.
COMPLETE   I shall always remember the town because of the *good times I had* and the *friends I made* there.

3f   Pretentious Diction

Pretentious diction, like the pretentious person, is stiff, attitudinizing, phony—in short, a bore. Our diction becomes pretentious if we always choose the polysyllabic word over the word of one syllable, a Latinate word when an Anglo-Saxon one will do, flowery phrases in place of common nouns and verbs. Writing should be as honest and forthright as plain speech. And since we have the opportunity to revise and edit what we write, it should be even more economical, direct, and to the point.

Sometimes ordinary words seem inadequate to carry the weight we wish thoughts to have, so we encumber statements with ornate language:

A perusal of the tomes penned by the ancient bards can influence our future life patterns.

The sentence is saying little more than "the study of ancient books can teach us how to live," but the pompous and wordy language is out of proportion to the statement it makes.

Occasionally we lapse into pretentious diction in an attempt to give our prose a lofty or poetic tone. To protect yourself against this, read your writing aloud to a classmate. If he or she looks uncomfortable or laughs at the wrong places or seems annoyed by the tone, examine the diction of your paper for phony phrases, for words that don't sound like you.

Be wary of words which swell hard facts into tepid air: *impecunious* for *poor, inebriated* for *drunk, interred* for *buried, expired* for *died, pulchritude* for *beauty, perambulate* for *walk, lacerate* for *cut, alleviate* for *relieve, utilize* for *use, attired* for *clothed, abandoned* for *left, verdant* for *green.* As you consult dictionaries and a thesaurus in order to develop your vocabulary, note the fine distinctions among synonyms and listen to the sounds of the words to judge whether they will strike your reader as false or genuine.

3g   Wordiness and Euphemism

Writing which is needlessly repetitious has a strained, awkward tone. If handled carefully, repetition can be effective:

> A *people* that grows accustomed to sloppy writing is *a people* in process of losing grip *on its* empire and *on its*elf.
>
> Ezra Pound

Pound emphasizes his declaration by restating the subject and repeating the preposition on *and the pronoun* its *as a reflexive.*

Often, however, repetition is cumbersome:

AWKWARD Probably the next problem that confronts parents is the problem of adequate schooling for their children.

There is no reason for emphasizing problem *and no excuse for clumsily echoing its sound in the cautious* probably.

IMPROVED The parents' next problem is finding adequate schooling for their children.

Read your writing aloud to catch offenses to the ear which are elusive to the eye. Alliteration and other repetition of sounds, functional in poetry, are rarely suited to expository prose.

UNSUITABLE Henderson set some kind of record by sliding farther on the slippery slope than anyone else had slid.

Intensives such as *really, very, so, much*, which may give emphasis to conversation, weaken written language. They are usually attempts to relieve the writer of finding a word that is emphatic in itself. Why settle for *really angry* when there are *enraged* and *furious*, with *so sad* when there are *desolate, doleful, crushed*, with *very bad* when there are *wicked, detestable, rotten, vile*?

Often when we want to avoid harsh facts we resort to a particular kind of circumlocution, the *euphemism*. The Greek word means "good speech," but euphemisms seldom are good for writers. Too often they are cosmetics to cover up painful realities. To avoid facing the cold finality of death people have always used euphemisms: *passed on* or *passed, gone west, met his Maker, gone to her reward*.

The *dear departed* rests in his casket in the *slumber room,* often having been *prepared* by the *funeral director* who today is likely to preside at a *memorial service* instead of a funeral. Ultimately, the *loved one* is not buried but *laid to rest,* not in a graveyard but in the *Valley of Memories.* Such sentimental wordiness is intended to comfort the bereaved by pretending that death is sleep, but its effect is one of stilted insincerity. There is no need, however, to go to the opposite extreme and speak ill of the subject. *Croak* and *kick the bucket,* while brisk and salty, are no closer to the fact of dying than *wrestled with the Angel of Death and was vanquished.*

3h   Figurative Language

A statement which advises you to prune deadwood from your writing uses a metaphor which implicitly compares language to a growing tree and revising to the gardener's art of cutting out decayed and useless limbs. We speak in pictures all the time, calling them figures of speech. Words often contain images of the world around us. I *see* what you mean, we say; it is *as clear as day.* These are dead metaphors, the clichés of everyday speech which we rely on for quick communication, but which make for dull writing. The more we are aware of the pictures words make, the better we will be able to use them.

The word *metaphor,* the comparison of two different things on the basis of a shared quality, is itself a buried metaphor, since it means to transfer or carry across. When we compare, we are carrying a trait from one thing to another as if over a bridge or a road. Metaphor says one thing *is* another:

"the prairie is an anvil's edge . . . the houses are sentinels" (Scott Momaday).

A *simile* uses the words *like* or *as* to state a comparison:

"I sensed a wrongness around me, like an alarm clock that had gone off without being set." (Maya Angelou)

A comparison can be extended into an *analogy* which not only illustrates a point, but suggests an argument or point of view, as Mary Ellman does in her startling analogy between astronauts and pregnant women:

The astronaut's body is as awkward and encumbered in the space suit as the body of a pregnant woman. It moves about with even more graceless difficulty. And being shot up into the air suggests submission too, rather than enterprise. Like a woman being carted to a delivery room, the astronaut must sit (or lie) still, and go where he is sent. Even the nerve, the genuine courage it takes simply not to run away, is much the same in both situations—to say nothing of the shared sense of having gone too far to be able to change one's mind.

In an *allusion* the comparison made is between some present event, situation, or person and an event or person from history or literature. Usually it is a brief reference to something which the reader is assumed to be familiar with, as when Adrienne Rich says of a woman who reads about women in books written by men:

"She finds a terror and a dream, she finds a beautiful face, she finds La Belle Dame Sans Merci, she finds Juliet or Tess or Salome, but precisely what she does not find is that absorbed, drudging, puzzled, sometime inspired creature, herself, who sits at a desk trying to put words together."

A sense of audience should determine what allusions, if any, are appropriate. While you should expect intelligence in persons who read what you write, there is no point in throwing away allusions or in alienating your readers by appearing to be more knowledgeable than they.

Trite Metaphors

Figures of speech which may have been fresh when they were first coined become trite and stale in time. We call such worn out figures of speech dead metaphors or clichés. Writing filled with clichés is dull, banal, hackneyed. By and large, we are wise to the politician who claims that he is all for *mom and apple pie,* for *God's country* and *man's best friend,* for the *man on the street* and *the little woman,* whose *place is in the home,* which is a *man's castle* where the *apple of his eye* and *the chip off the old block* are lucky to live in the *land of opportunity* where *every boy can grow up to be president.* But you should also watch out for similar tired expressions in your own writing. Here is a modest list of clichés you would do well to *avoid like the plague:*

abreast of the times	last but not least
acid test	live from hand to mouth
agony of suspense	other side of the coin
as luck would have it	poor but honest
beat a hasty retreat	proud possessor of
bitter end	quick as a flash
bolt from the blue	reigns supreme
breathless silence	rotten to the core
checkered career	slow but sure
cool as a cucumber	straight from the shoulder
deep, dark secret	tempest in a teapot
depths of despair	undercurrent of excitement
doomed to disappointment	walking on air
few and far between	water under the bridge
green with envy	wave of optimism
heave a sigh of relief	wended their way
hit the nail on the head	worth its weight in gold

Mixed Metaphors

Create metaphors out of your own observations and with your own eyes, but be careful that your metaphors make logical and visual sense. Often the metaphors impressed like fossils into everyday words become so faint we have difficulty seeing them. Unless we pay close attention to what words mean, we can make some bizarre assertions:

> He was saddled with a sea of grass-roots opinion that his campaign workers had ferreted out for him.

Such a surrealistic image is a badly mixed metaphor. Combinations as confused as this one can often be caught by picturing what the words are saying.

> The administration jettisoned the groundwork laid by the student government.

> He penetrated the impervious gaze of his challenger.

Can we *jettison groundwork, penetrate* the *impervious?* Ask of your nouns and verbs: can it sensibly be done, even in the liberal world of metaphor?

A cheerful curiosity about words and their earthy origins, a respect for their resonances, and a pleasure in your own power to create new and striking images will instruct you in diction better than any language handbook. "Words must be shouted into, like wells, rather than joined in a series like pipelengths," the translator Ben Belitt writes in a compound simile which rings with associations of echos and water. Call down into words, squint at them against the light to see their changing colors, bite them like dimes to test their mintage and their savor. "Words," says the poet Yeats, "alone are certain good."

Exercise 1

With the help of a dictionary (and perhaps a dictionary of Roman and Greek mythology) discover the concrete particular in which each of these abstract words originated. Write a brief explanation of why and how you think some of these words came to mean what they mean today.

cereal	cupidity	hackneyed	panic
chapter	erotic	infant	paradise
comma	genius	language	surgery

Exercise 2

Analyze the following paragraph from a memo distributed by a Communications Department. Is it jargon and why? What clichés or submerged figures of speech can you find? Do they conflict with one another? Translate the paragraph into Standard English if you can, and if not, be prepared to say why.

All courses (process or outcome) in the University system that are judged to contain written or oral communication goal statements should constitute a set of courses from which a student must select some number. This client-oriented marketplace approach to core requirements is a solution. Enrollment determines which courses will survive and which will not. However, academic tradition is rife with distrust of student judgment; and it can result in a self-fulfilling prophecy where faculty compete in playing to the "house" because they are convinced that ultimately only those who do will survive. This solution is usually condemned without trial.

Exercise 3

Analyze the diction of the following sentences for exactness, connotation, figures of speech. Be prepared to discuss what words would more effectively express what the writer was trying to say.

1. Thus the young athletes are the workhorses that made the ends of the budget meet to form a vicious circle.
2. Our balloons of egotism filled with the air of freshman knowledge were soon to be pricked by the pin-points of self-awakening.
3. As the town grew, the theatre obtained a foothold in the hearts of the citizens.
4. This is the Achilles' heel of their position. For once a set of ideas are ruled fair game for witch-hunters, Pandora's box has been opened, and there is no ending.
5. Drinking seems to have its claw in the economy of San Francisco.
6. Our tariff wall will continue to be an unsurmountable obstacle until we throw a span across the ebb to link the rest of the world to our industrial growth.
7. Poring through *Paradise Lost* was like wading in deep water.
8. A good education is the trunk for a good life for it is the origin of all the branches which are your later accomplishments.
9. His immaturity may improve with age.
10. The basic objective of the indoctrination program is to build strong class spirit and to weed out those who are leaders in the class.
11. Darwin's *Origin of Species* began an epic of materialism.
12. Margaret Mead's book had a great success because Americans are grossly interested in sex.
13. I flitted away my first three years in college.
14. Jefferson and Madison were two of the most prolific characters our nation produced at that time in history.
15. The reason I like Christina Rossetti's *Goblin Market* is because it shows how love between sisters triumphs over the prowess of darkness.

Exercise 4

On the basis of sound association and of your knowledge of words, make an educated guess as to the lexical meaning of the following archaic words. Then look up the words in Charles MacKay's *Lost*

Beauties of the English Language. If you arrived at a meaning different from that listed in MacKay, explain the reasons for your definition.

crambles (n)	roaky (adj)
flathers (n)	sculsh (n)
glunch (v)	skime (v)
jugbitten (adj)	slive (v)
mazle (v)	slodder (n)
mirkshade (n)	sloom (v)
overword (n)	snurl (v)
pleach (v)	suckets (n)
prog (v)	tartle (v)
quillet (n)	ugsome (adj)

Exercise 5

Write a short essay or prepare a class discussion using examples from your own experience in which you defend or deny the truth of this Confucian maxim: "If language is incorrect, then what is said is not meant. If what is said is not meant, then what ought to be done remains undone."

3

Glossary of Usage

This Glossary discusses only the more commonly misused words which crop up frequently in student prose. In recommending that you observe rules of usage, no one is suggesting that you abandon your natural speech for what may to your taste seem stilted. But remember that written language is selective. It is the cultivation of that which grows wild and natural in our speech. Teachers of language, like practiced gardeners, tend to be conservationists. Before becoming annoyed with what may seem to you petty complaints, consider that your teacher and the editors of handbooks and dictionaries are attempting to preserve distinctions which you may not know exist. Roger Sales devotes a number of pages in his book *On Writing* to a concept that will be lost should the distinction between *disinterested* and *uninterested* not be preserved. Rather than decide that the difference in prefixes is inconsequential, read the entry in this chapter and then read his argument. The choice of whether or not to observe standards of usage is yours, but the choice should be an informed and prudent one.

a, an   Indefinite articles. *A* is used before words beginning with a consonant sound, *an* before words beginning with a vowel sound. Before words beginning with *h*, use *an* when the *h* is silent, as in *hour*, but *a* when the *h* is pronounced, as in *history*.

above   Colloquially used as an adjective: "The above remarks." In writing, this usage should be confined to legal documents.

accept, except   Different verbs which sound alike. *Accept* means "to receive," *except* "to leave out."

> I *accepted* the diploma.

> When assigning jobs, the dean *excepted* students who had already worked on a project.

adapt, adopt   To *adapt* is to change or modify to suit some new need, purpose, or condition.

> Man can *adapt* to many environments. The movie was *adapted* from a novel.

> To *adopt* something is to make it one's own, to choose it.

> The couple *adopted* a child. Our club *adopted* "Opportunity knocks" as its motto.

adverse, averse   Often confused, but important to distinguish. *Adverse* means "antagonistic" or "unfavorable."

>   *Adverse* weather forced postponement of the regatta.

>   *Averse* means "opposed to"; only sentient beings can be *averse*.

>   She *was averse* to sailing under such conditions.

affect, effect   Words close in sound and therefore often confused. *Affect* as a verb means "to influence." *Effect* as a verb means "to bring about."

>   Smoking *affects* the heart.

>   How can we *effect* a change in the law?

>   As a noun *effect* means "result."

>   One *effect* of her treatment was a bad case of hives.

>   The noun *affect* is a technical term used in psychology.

aggravate   Means "to intensify" or "to make worse."

>   The shock *aggravated* his misery.

>   Colloquially it means "to annoy," "irritate," "arouse the anger of."

ain't   A nonstandard contraction of *am not, is not,* or *are not.* Not to be used in formal writing.

all ready, already   Not synonyms. *All ready* refers to a state of readiness.

>   The twirlers were *all ready* for the half-time show.

>   *Already* means "by or before the present time."

>   Has the game *already* started?

all right   Unlike the pairs of words in the preceding and following entries, *all right* stands alone. There is no word *alright,* although many people, misled by the existence of *altogether* and *already,* assume that there is.

all together, altogether   *All together* refers to a group with no missing elements.

>   If we can get our members *all together,* we can begin the meeting.

>   *Altogether* means "completely."

>   You are *altogether* mistaken about that.

allude, refer   To *allude* is to make an indirect reference.

>   Did her letter *allude* to Sam's difficulties?

>   To *refer* is to call attention specifically to something.

>   The instructor *referred* us to Baudelaire's translations of Poe.

3

allusion, illusion, delusion   An *allusion* is a brief, indirect reference.

> Anyone who speaks of "cabbages and kings" is making an *allusion* to *Alice in Wonderland.*

An *illusion* is a deceptive impression.

> He enjoyed the *illusion* of luxury created by his imitation Oriental rugs.

A *delusion* is a mistaken belief, implying self-deception and often a disordered state of mind.

> She fell prey to the *delusion* that she was surrounded by enemy agents.

among, between   *Among* always refers to more than two.

> He lived *among* a tribe of cannibals.

Between is used to refer to two objects or to more than two objects considered individually.

> The scenery is spectacular *between* Portland and Seattle.

> The governors signed the agreement *between* all three states.

amoral, immoral   Anything *amoral* is outside morality, not to be judged by moral standards.

> The behavior of animals and the orbits of the planets are equally *amoral.*

Anything *immoral* is in direct violation of some moral standard.

> Snatching an old lady's purse is generally considered to be an *immoral* act.

amount, number   *Amount* is used as a general indicator of quantity; *number* refers only to what can be counted.

> An immense *amount* of food was prepared for the picnic, but only a small *number* of people came.

but   Often used colloquially in such idioms as *I can't help but think.* In writing *I can't help thinking* is preferred. If the nonstandard expression *I don't know but what he wants to do it* leads to confusion (does he or doesn't he?), it should be avoided in speech, too.

can, may   In formal speech and in writing, *can* is used to indicate ability, *may* to indicate permission.

> If you *can* open that box, you *may* have whatever is in it.

In informal questions, *can* is often used even though permission is meant.

> *Can* I try it next? Why *can't* I?

censor, censure To *censor* something (such as a book, letter, or film) is to evaluate it on the basis of certain arbitrary standards to determine whether it may be made public.

> All announcements for the bulletin board are *censored* by the department secretary.

Censor is often used as the equivalent of "delete."

> References in the report to secret activities have been *censored*.

Censure means "to find fault with," "to criticize as blameworthy."

> Several officers were *censured* for their participation in the affair.

compare to, compare with, contrast with *Compare to* is used to show similarities between different kinds of things.

> Sir James Jeans *compared* the universe *to* a corrugated soap bubble.

Compare with means to examine in order to note either similarities or differences.

> *Compare* this example *with* the preceding one.

Contrast with is used to show differences only.

> *Contrast* the life of a student today *with* that of a student in the middle ages.

concur in, concur with *Concur in* refers to agreement with a principle or policy.

> She *concurred in* their judgment that the manager should be given a raise.

Concur with refers to agreement with a person.

> She *concurred with* him in his decision to give the manager a raise.

contact The use of *contact* as a verb meaning "to get in touch with" has gained wide acceptance, but a more exact term such as *ask, consult, inform, meet, see, telephone,* or *write* is generally preferable.

continual, continuous The first is widely used to indicate an action which is repeated frequently, the second to indicate uninterrupted action.

> We heard the *continual* howling of the dog.

> The dog kept a *continuous* vigil beside the body of his dead master.

data, phenomena, criteria Latin plural, not singular forms, and so used in formal writing. But the use of *data* (rather than *datum*) with a singular form is widespread.

> These *data* have been taken from the last Census Report.

Criteria and *phenomena* are always plural. The singular forms are *criterion* and *phenomenon.*

Scientists encountered a *phenomenon* that could not be evaluated under existing *criteria.*

different from, different than   *Different from* is always acceptable usage.

College is *different from* what I had expected.

Different than, when used to avoid wordiness or awkwardness, is also acceptable.

College is *different* now *than* it was twenty years ago.

disinterested, uninterested   *Disinterested* means "unbiased," "impartial." *Uninterested* means "without any interest in," or "lacking in interest."

Though we were *uninterested* in her general topic, we had to admire her *disinterested* treatment of its controversial aspects.

due to   In writing *due to* should not be used adverbially to mean *because of.*

COLLOQUIAL   He made many mistakes, *due to* carelessness.
PREFERRED   He made many mistakes *because of* carelessness.
IN WRITING

Due to is an adjective and usually follows the verb *to be: His illness was due to exhaustion.*

either, neither   As subjects, both words are singular. When referring to more than two, use *none* rather than *neither.*

Either red or pink is appropriate.

I asked Leahy, Mahoney, and another Irishman, but *none* of them was willing.

enthused   Either as a verb (he *enthused*) or adjective (he was *enthused*), the word is strictly colloquial. In writing use "showed enthusiasm" or "was enthusiastic."

equally as good   A confusion of two phrases: *equally good* and *just as good.* Use either of the two phrases in place of *equally as good.*

Their TV set cost much more than ours, but ours is *equally good.*

Our TV set is *just as good* as theirs.

-ess   Feminine ending acceptable in such traditional words as *waitress, actress, hostess.* But many persons object to *poetess, authoress, sculptress* as patronizing and demeaning. Unless an *-ess* word has a long history and you are sure there are no objections to its use, it is best to avoid it.

etc.   Avoid the vague use of *etc.;* use it only to prevent useless repetition or informally to represent terms entirely obvious from the context.

VAGUE	The judge was honorable, upright, dependable, *etc."*
PREFERRED	The judge was honorable, upright, and dependable.
STANDARD	Use even numbers like four, eight, ten, *etc.*

Avoid *and etc.,* which is redundant.

expect   Colloquial when used to mean "suppose," "presume": I *expect* it's time for us to go.

> PREFERRED   I *suppose* it's time for us to go.

factor   Means "something which contributes to a result."

> Industry and perseverance were *factors* in her success.

Avoid using *factor* to mean vaguely any thing, item, or event.

> VAGUE   Ambition was a *factor* which contributed to the downfall of Macbeth.

Since factor includes the notion of "contributing to," such usage is redundant as well as vague and wordy.

> PREFERRED   Ambition contributed to the downfall of Macbeth.

farther, further   In careful usage *farther* indicates distance; *further* indicates degree and may also mean "additional." Both are used as adjectives and as adverbs: *a mile farther, further disintegration, further details.*

faze, phase   *Faze* is a colloquial verb meaning "to perturb," "to disconcert." *Phase* as a noun means "stage of development" (a passing *phase*); as a verb it means "to carry out in stages." Be wary of *phase in* and *phase out,* which have the ring of jargon.

fewer, less   *Fewer* refers to number, *less* to amount. Use *fewer* in speaking of things which can be counted and *less* for amounts which are measured.

> *Fewer* persons enrolled in medical schools this year than last.

> *Less* studying was required to pass Chemistry than we had anticipated.

flaunt, flout   Commonly misspelled, mispronounced and, therefore, confused. *Flaunt* means "to exhibit arrogantly," "show off."

> He *flaunted* his photographic memory in class.

Flout means "to reject with contempt."

> They *flouted* the tradition of wearing gowns at graduation by showing up in bluejeans.

flunk   Colloquial for *fail*. In formal writing, I *failed* (not *flunked*) the test.

former, latter   Preferably used to designate one of two persons or things. For designating one of three or more, write *first* or *last*.

get, got, gotten   *Get to* (*go*), *get away with*, *get back at*, *get with* (something), and *got to* (for *must*) are widely used in speech but should be avoided in writing. Either *got* or *gotten* is acceptable as the past participle of *get*.

good   An adjective. Should not be used in formal writing as an adverb meaning "well."

COLLOQUIAL	She plays tennis *good*.
STANDARD	She plays tennis *well*. She plays a *good* game of tennis.

had have, had of   Nonstandard when used for *had*.

NONSTANDARD	If he *had have* (or *had of*) tried, he would have succeeded.
STANDARD	If he *had* tried, he would have succeeded.

had ought   Nonstandard as a past tense of *ought*. The tense of this verb is indicated by the infinitive which follows.

He *ought to go;* she *ought to have gone*.

hanged, hung   When *hang* means "to suspend," *hung* is its past tense.

The guards *hung* a black flag from the prison to signal the execution.

When *hang* means "to execute," *hanged* is the correct past tense.

After the flag was *hung*, the prisoner was *hanged*.

hardly, barely, scarcely   Since these words convey the idea of negation, they should not be used with another negative.

NONSTANDARD	We *couldn't hardly* see in the darkness.
	We *hadn't barely* finished.
STANDARD	We *could hardly* see. We *had barely* finished.

hopefully   Though widely used in speech to mean "it is to be hoped," or "I hope" (*Hopefully*, a check will arrive tomorrow), the adverb *hopefully* is used in writing to mean "in a hopeful manner":

They spoke *hopefully* of world peace.

imply, infer   *Imply* means "to suggest" or "hint"; *infer* means "to reach a conclusion from facts or premises."

His tone *implied* contempt; I *inferred* from his voice that he did not like me.

insupportable, unsupportable   Often confused, but not synonymous. *Insupportable* means "unable to be endured."

> The noise of the bulldozers during the lecture was *insupportable*.

Unsupportable means "not capable of support."

> The building program, though imaginative, is financially *unsupportable*.

inter, intra   As a prefix *inter* means "between" or "among": *international, intermarry; intra* means "within" or "inside of": *intramuscular, intramural.*

irregardless   A nonstandard combination of *irrespective* and *regardless.*

> *Regardless* (or *irrespective*) of the minority opinion, we included the platform in the campaign.

its, it's   Often confused. *Its* is the possessive form of *it.*

> My suitcase has lost one of *its* handles.

It's is the contracted form of *it is* or *it has.*

> *It's* a good day for sailing.

> *It's* been a month since I mailed the check.

kind, sort   Colloquial when used with a plural modifier and verb: *These kind* (or *sort*) of books *are* trash.

> STANDARD   *This sort* of book *is* trash.
> *These kinds* of books *are* classics.

In questions, the number of the verb depends on the noun which follows *kind* (or *sort*).

> What kind of *book is* this?
> What kind of *books are* these?

kind of, sort of   Colloquial when used to mean "rather."

> COLLOQUIAL   I thought the lecture was *kind of* dull.
> STANDARD   I thought the lecture was *rather* dull.

Also colloquial when followed by *a* or *an:*

> What *kind of a* house is it? It is *sort of a* castle.

> PREFERRED   What *kind of* house is it?
> IN WRITING   It is *a sort of* castle.

latest, last   *Latest* means "most recent"; *last* means "final."

I doubt that their *latest* contract proposal represents their *last* offer.

lay, lie   Often confused. *Lay* is a transitive verb meaning "to put" or "place" something. It always takes an object. Its principal parts are *lay*, *laid*, *laid*. *Lie* is intransitive; that is, it does not take an object, and means "to recline" or "to remain." Its principal parts are *lie*, *lay*, *lain*. When in doubt, try substituting the verb *place*. If it fits the context, use some form of *lay*.

PRESENT TENSE	I *lie* down every afternoon.
	Every morning I *lay* the paper by his plate.
PAST TENSE	I *lay* down yesterday after dinner.
	I *laid* the paper by his plate two hours ago.
PERFECT TENSE	I *have lain* here for several hours.
	I *have laid* the paper by his plate many times.

let's   Contraction of *let us*. In writing, it should be used only where *let us* can be used.

COLLOQUIAL	*Let's don't* leave yet. *Let's us* go.
STANDARD	*Let's not* leave yet. *Let's* go.

liable, likely, apt   In careful writing, the words are not interchangeable. *Likely* is used to indicate a mere probability.

They are *likely* to be chosen.

Liable is used when the probability is unpleasant.

We are *liable* to get a parking ticket.

Apt implies a natural tendency or ability.

She is *apt* to win the musical competition.

like   The use of *like* to introduce a clause is widespread in informal English, especially that used by advertising agencies. In edited writing, *as*, *as if*, and *as though* are preferred.

COLLOQUIAL	This rose smells sweet, *like* a flower should.
STANDARD	This rose smells sweet, *as* a flower should.
	This perfume smells *like* roses.

However, don't always avoid *like* in favor of *as*, or you may end up in ambiguities.

As Lady Macbeth, she was disturbed by the sight of blood.
Does the writer mean "in the role of Lady Macbeth" or "similar to Lady Macbeth?"

literally Means "precisely," "without any figurative sense," "strictly." It is often inaccurately used as an intensive, to emphasize a figure of speech: "I was *literally* floating on air." This makes sense only if one is capable of levitation. Use the word *literally* with caution in writing.

loan, lend, Traditionally, *lend* is a verb, *loan* a noun, but *loan* is also used as a verb, especially in business contexts.

The company *loaned* us money for the down payment.

most As a noun or adjective, *most* means "more than half."

Most of us plan to go to the dance.

Most people admire her paintings.

As an adverb, *most* means "very."

His playing was *most* impressive.

Most is colloquial when used to mean "almost," "nearly."

COLLOQUIAL   *Most* everyone was invited.
PREFERRED   *Almost* everyone was invited.
IN WRITING

myself Correctly used as a reflexive: I cut *myself*, sang to *myself*, give *myself* credit. Colloquial when used as an evasive substitute for *I* or *me*.

COLLOQUIAL   My brother and *myself* prefer coffee.
                      She spoke to my brother and *myself*.
PREFERRED   My brother and *I* prefer coffee.
IN WRITING   She spoke to my brother and *me*.

of *Could of, may of, might of, must of, should of,* and *would of* are slurred pronunciations for *could have, may have, might have, must have, should have,* and *would have;* they are nonstandard in writing.

off of A colloquial usage in which *of* is superfluous.

COLLOQUIAL   Keep *off of* the grass.
PREFERRED   Keep *off* the grass.
IN WRITING

outside of Correct as a noun: He painted the *outside of* the house. Colloquial as a preposition: He was waiting *outside of* the house. Omit the *of* in writing. Nonstandard as a substitute for *except for, aside from*.

part, portion A *part* is any piece of a whole; a *portion* is that part specifically allotted to some person, cause or use.

We planted beans in one *part* of our garden.

She left a *portion* of her estate to charity.

party   Colloquial when used to mean "person," as in "The *party* who telephoned left no message." Write *person.*

percent   In formal writing use *percent*, or *per cent*, only after a numeral— either the spelled-out word (six) or the numerical symbol (6). The sign (%) is used only in strictly commercial writing. The word *percentage*, meaning "a part or proportion of a whole," is used when the exact amount is not indicated.

> A large *percentage* were Chinese.

> Thirty-one *percent* were Chinese.

real   Colloquial when used for "very." Write *very* hot, not *real* hot.

regarding, in regard to, with regard to, in relation to, in terms of   These windy phrases are usually dispensable. Replace them with concrete terms.

> WORDY   *With regard to* grades, she was very good.
> CONCRETE   She *got* very good grades.

Reverend   In formal writing should be preceded by *the* and followed by a title or full name, or both.

> *The Reverend Mr.* (or *Dr.*) *Carter* preached.

> *The Reverend Amos Carter* led the march.

The widely-used form *Reverend Amos Carter* is deplored by usage panels but accepted by the clergy. The use of *the reverend* as a noun, to mean "a clergyman," is strictly colloquial.

sarcasm   Not interchangeable with *irony. Sarcastic* remarks, like *ironic* remarks, convey a message obliquely, but sarcasm contains the notion of ridicule, of an intention on the part of the writer to wound. Only persons can be *sarcastic*, while both persons and events can be *ironic.*

> The sergeant inquired *sarcastically* whether any of us could tell time; it was *ironic* that his watch turned out to be ten minutes fast.

sensual, sensuous   Both words refer to impressions made upon the senses. Their connotations, however, are widely different. *Sensual* most often carries unfavorable connotations. It is applied primarily to the gratification of appetite and lust.

> *Sensual* delights are often considered inferior to spiritual pleasures.

Sensuous, on the other hand, is used literally or approvingly of an appeal to the senses (the *sensuous* delight of a swim on a hot day), and can even refer to such abstract appeals as those found in poetry.

> Milton's *sensuous* imagery calls upon sight, touch, and even smell to form the reader's impression of Eden.

set　　A transitive verb meaning "to put" or "place" something. It should be distinguished from *sit*, an intransitive verb.

PRESENT TENSE	I *sit* in the chair.
	I *set* the book on the table.
PAST TENSE	I *sat* on the chair.
	I *set* the book on the table.
PERFECT TENSE	I *have sat* in the chair.
	I *have set* the book on the table.

shall, will　　The distinction is rapidly fading, although many grammarians still conjugate the verb as *I shall, you will, he will, we shall, you will, they will*. Most writers, however, now use *will* throughout. *Shall* may still be used for emphasis (He *shall* be heard); since it is less common than *will*, it has a formal tone. See page 327.

should, would　　Generally interchangeable in modern American usage, though they formerly followed the pattern of *shall* and *will*. Each word does, however, have some special uses. *Should* substitutes for "ought to" (He *should* go on a diet); *would* for "wanted to" (He could do it if he *would*). *Should* indicates probability (I *should* be finished in an hour); *would* indicates custom (He *would* always call when he got home).

so, such　　Avoid using *so* and *such* as vague intensifiers: I am *so* glad; I had *such* a good time. The full forms, which should always be used, are *so . . . that, such . . . as*.

I was *so* glad to find that print *that* I bought copies for all my friends.

Such a good time *as* that is worth repeating.

some　　Colloquial when used as an adverb meaning "somewhat" (I am *some* better today) or when used as an intensifying adjective (That was *some* dinner).

PREFERRED	I am *a little* (or *somewhat*) better today.
IN WRITING	That was *an excellent* dinner.

sure　　Colloquial when used for "certainly, "surely," as in "He *sure* can play poker."

that, which　　*That* is largely confined to introduce restrictive clauses, which limit or define the antecedent's meaning and are not set off by commas.

The law *that* gave women the right to vote was passed in 1920. *Which* is used to introduce non-restrictive clauses, which are not essential to the meaning of the sentence and are set off by commas.

The 19th Amendment, *which* gave women the right to vote, was passed in 1920.

toward, towards Interchangeable. *Toward* is more common in America, *towards* in Britain.

transpire In formal writing, where the word properly belongs, it means "to become known." It is colloquial in the sense of "happen," or "come to pass."

try and Often used for "try to," but should be avoided in writing. I must *try to* (not *try and*) find a job.

unique Adverbs such as *rather, more, most, very* are colloquial when used to modify *unique*. Since the word means "being the only one of its kind," no thing can be more (or less) unique than another.

This copy of the book is *unique*.

This copy of the book is *very rare*.

up Do not add a superfluous *up* to verbs: We opened *up* the box and divided the money *up*. Write: We opened the box and divided the money.

***very** and *much* with past participles** A past participle that is felt to be a part of a verb form, rather than an adjective, should not be immediately preceded by *very* but by *much, greatly,* or some other intensive. A past participle that can be used as an adjective may be preceded by *very*.

COLLOQUIAL	He was *very* disliked by other students.
	He was *very* influenced by the teacher.
PREFERRED	He was *very much* disliked by other students.
IN WRITING	He was *greatly* influenced by the teacher.
	He was a *very* tired boy.

wait on Colloquial for *wait for*.

ways Colloquial in such expressions as *a little ways*. In writing, the singular is preferred: *a little way*.

where . . . to, where . . . at Colloquialisms whose prepositions are redundant or dialectal.

COLLOQUIAL	*Where* are you going *to? Where* is he *at?*
PREFERRED	*Where* are you going? *Where* is he?
IN WRITING	

who, whom (For the choice between these forms see the section on Case, page 318.)

-wise   Commercial jargon when attached to nouns in such combinations as *taxwise, languagewise, timewise, moneywise.* To be avoided in serious writing.

would have   Colloquial when used in *if* clauses instead of *had.*

COLLOQUIAL	If he *would have stood* by us, we might have won.
PREFERRED IN WRITING	If he *had stood* by us, we might have won.

write-up   Colloquial for a description, an account, as in "a *write-up* in the newspaper."

Sentences 4

4a   Elements of a Sentence

This section is a highly simplified summary of the Grammar 2 of English. That is, it attempts to analyze the language you use every day (your Grammar 1) and make a generalized description of the way it operates. For any kind of grammatical analysis, it is necessary to *classify* the words and groups of words that make up a sentence. To classify means simply to group together words that are alike in some respects and to give names to the classes thus formed.

Let's start with a kind of classification you may never have thought of, though structural linguists use it all the time. *Pen, telephone, tax,* and *fluid,* for example, are alike in that they often appear after words like *the, a,* or *this: a pen, the telephone, this tax.* Words of this class also take inflectional endings to indicate the plural, usually a suffix including the letter *s: telephones, fluids, taxes.* Another class is made up of words to which inflectional suffixes like *-ed* can be added: *ask, asked; cry, cried; walk, walked.* A third class consists of words to which *-er* and *-est* can be added: *happy, happier, happiest; swift, swifter, swiftest.*

As names for these classes, let's adopt the ones used by traditional grammar: we'll call the first class NOUNS (words that name something), the second class VERBS (words that assert something), and the third class ADJECTIVES (words that describe or limit the meaning of a noun). However, as we go on to classify more and more words, it will become apparent that these classes must be broadened. Traditional grammar will suggest that a word like *man* should be put in the first class, even though the plural is *men*, not *mans*. Similarly, in the second class we will want to put such a word as *weave*, even though, instead of taking an *-ed* ending, it is inflected *wove*. The third class will be widened to include some words which do not add *-er* and *-est*, like *beautiful*, which is inflected *more beautiful, most beautiful*.

In widening the classes, traditional grammar makes use of another set of similarities: it puts words into classes not merely by their position in a sentence or by their forms (the way they can be inflected), but by their *functions* in a sentence. That is, traditional grammar says that *man, pen,* and *tax* belong together in a class because they name something; whereas *rich* and *beautiful* and *cold* belong together in another class because they modify (that is, describe or limit) something.

Modern linguists have proposed alternative classifications which may well provide a more accurate and complete analysis of grammatical structures and relationships than the categories of traditional grammar do. But for the limited sort of analysis needed in a handbook, which tries merely to explain why certain constructions are "grammatical" without offering a complete system of grammar, the traditional classifications and the old names have the advantage of simplicity and familiarity. And they can be made consistent enough to be relevant and usable.

Many of the supposed inconsistencies of traditional grammar are caused by the fact that most English words can function in more than one way, and hence fit into more than one class. The word *poor* belongs in the class with *happy* and *swift* because it can take the suffixes *-er* and *-est* to make *poorer* and *poorest*. But the sentence "The poor usually eat poor food" shows that *poor* can also be used like words of the first class described above. *The poor* belongs with *the telephone, the pen,* etc., even though it does not take an *-s* suffix like *telephones*.

Into what class, then, do we put the word *poor?* The answer is no class, until we see the word used in a sentence. In a sentence, the form and position will indicate the word's meaning and grammatical function. *The poor* names an economic class; in this construction, the word belongs with other names like *telephone* or *fluid*. In the construction *poor food, poor* describes the quality of food; it belongs in the class with *rich, hot,* and *good*.

Once it is clear that grammatical analysis deals not with isolated words but with words used in sentences, various systems of classification are possible. For the present purpose, classifying words by their *functions* in a sentence provides a simple and usable tool, adequate for the needs of a composition course.

There are four functions of words in sentences: to name things, to assert things, to modify (describe, identify, or limit) other words, and to connect other parts of a sentence. Groups of words (what linguists call *constructions*) may have the same functions as single words: such groups are called PHRASES or CLAUSES—see 4a(5) and 4a(6).

class	*function*	*types*
substantive	to name	nouns, pronouns, gerunds
predicative	to assert	verbs
modifier	to describe or limit	adjectives, adverbs, participles
connective	to join elements	conjunctions, prepositions

Note that a GERUND (a verb form used as a noun, like *swimming* in "Swimming is good exercise") is classified along with nouns and pronouns, and that a PARTICIPLE (a verb form used as an adjective as in "*floating* beer can" or "*torn* paper") is put with the modifiers.

The basic unit of discourse, and the starting point of grammatical analysis, is the sentence. Sentences do a number of things: ask questions (INTERROGATIVE SENTENCE) or answer them, issue commands or requests (IMPERATIVE SENTENCE), or, most often, make statements. In speech they are not always explicitly complete. The single word "Going?" may serve in place of the full question "Are you leaving the party already?" and the answer may be the single word "Yes," just as the answer to the question "Where do you live?" may be no more than "On Elm Street." These answers are abbreviated sentences—a short way of saying "I am leaving the party," or "I live on Elm Street." Questions and answers, commands or requests are special types of the sentence, with their own grammatical characteristics. (Commands usually omit the subject; questions are indicated by a peculiar word order.) But the typical sentence in written English is a statement.

(1) Subject and Predicate

A statement says something about something, and to make a statement you need to *name* what you are talking about and *assert* something about it. The grammatical term for the word or words that name what you are talking about is the SUBJECT. The PREDICATE is the assertion you make about the subject.

subject	*predicate*
Edison	invented the light bulb.
The storm	cut off our lights.
A coyote	howled all night.
I	like spices.
My younger brother	does not like spices.

The subject is usually a noun or PRONOUN (a word used in place of a noun), though it may be a phrase or clause, as will be explained later. The predicate may contain a number of different words used in different ways, but the essential part is a VERB, a word that asserts something.

(2) Modifiers

It is possible to make a complete sentence of two words, a subject and a verb:

Rain fell.

Few sentences, however, are as simple as this. We usually add other words whose function is to describe the subject or the verb:

A gentle rain fell steadily.

Here *gentle* describes rain and *steadily* describes how it fell. Such words are called MODIFIERS, and they may be attached to almost any part of a sentence. Although modifiers usually describe, they may also indicate how many (*three* books, *few* books), which one (*this* pencil, *the* pen, *my* pencil), or how much (*very* gently, *half* sick, *almost too* late).

Modifiers are divided into two main classes: ADJECTIVES and AD-VERBS. Any word which modifies a noun, pronoun, or gerund is an adjective in function; an adverb is any word which modifies a verb, an adjective, or another adverb.

Very hungry men seldom display good table manners.

In this sentence, *hungry, good,* and *table* are adjectives, describing or indicating what kind of men and manners. *Very* is an adverb since it modifies the adjective *hungry; seldom* is an adverb modifying the verb *display.*

Adjectives and adverbs have different forms to indicate relative DEGREE. In addition to the regular, or "positive," form (*slow, comfortable, slowly*), there is the COMPARATIVE degree (*slower, more comfortable, more slowly*), and the SUPERLATIVE degree (*slowest, most comfortable, most slowly*). The examples illustrate the rule: adjectives with more than two syllables form the comparative and superlative degrees by the words *more* and *most,* instead of the suffixes *-er* and *est.* All adverbs ending in *ly* use *more* and *most* to indicate degrees of comparison.

(3) Identifying Subject and Verb

The analysis of any sentence begins with the identification of the simple subject and the verb. Look first for the verb: a word or group of words that often states an action or happening. Some forms or tenses of a verb are really phrases, including one or more AUXILIARY VERBS—I *was hit,* I *have been hit;* I *had taken,* I *shall have taken.* Verbs which do not add *-ed* to form the past tense are called IR-REGULAR VERBS—*swim, swam; eat, ate,* etc. A person learning English remembers these verb forms by memorizing their PRINCIPAL PARTS—*swim, swam, swum; eat, ate, eaten,* etc.

> I *sprained* my wrist.
> Joe Miller *wrote* me a letter.
> The fire *burned* out.
> He *has* never *painted* landscapes before.
> (*In this sentence the two parts of the verb are separated by the adverb* never.)

Some verbs merely assert, with varying degrees of certainty, that something is—or looks or sounds or seems or appears to be—something. These are called LINKING VERBS, or COPULAS.

> He *is* a fine mechanic.
> She *seems* intelligent and dependable.
> There *were* two reasons for believing his story.
> The troops *looked* weary.

When you have found the verb, ask yourself the question, "Who or what ....?" putting the verb in the blank space. The answer to the question is the subject, and if you strip away the modifiers you have the SIMPLE SUBJECT.

> A long, dull speech followed the dinner.

What followed the dinner? A *long, dull speech.* But *long* and *dull* are adjectives describing *speech;* the simple subject is *speech.*

This method is especially helpful when the normal order of the sentence is inverted (that is, when the subject comes *after* the verb) or when the sentence begins with an introductory word like "there." In the sentence "Across the Alps lies Italy," the verb is *lies.* What lies across the Alps? The answer is the subject, *Italy.*

Consider the sentence "There was a serious error in the first paragraph." The verb is *was,* and the predicate asserts that something "was in the first paragraph." What? The word *there* does not name anything and hence cannot be the subject. The answer to the question is "a serious error," and *error* is the simple subject.

Note that in a sentence which asks a question the subject often follows some form of the verb *have* or *be,* or a form of an auxiliary verb.

verb	*subject*	
Have	**you**	a match?
Is	**he**	dependable?

auxiliary	*subject*	*verb*	
Have	**you**	**returned**	the books?
Did	**she**	**buy**	a lock?
May	**they**	**come**	in?
Has	**the purse**	**been found?**	

	auxiliary	*subject*	*verb*
What kind of lock	**did**	**you**	**buy?**

In an imperative sentence the subject is not expressed. Since a command or request is addressed directly to someone, that person need not be named.

subject	*verb*	
( )	**Come**	in.
( )	**Shut**	the door.

	subject	*verb*	
Please	( )	**take**	this to the post office.

A sentence may have several nouns as its subject, since it is possible to make one assertion about several things. Such a construction is called a COMPOUND SUBJECT.

compound subject
The **trees and plants** were dying.
Richmond, Wills, and Hyatt have been elected.

Similarly, it is possible to use a COMPOUND PREDICATE—that is, to make several assertions about one subject.

compound predicate

The car *swerved, skidded,* and *ran* into the ditch.
Marilyn *washed* her face and *dressed* for dinner.

Exercise 1

Pick out the simple subjects and the verbs in the following sentences. Note that either the subject or the verb may be compound.

1. After locking the door, the flight attendant sat down at the rear of the plane.
2. Invisible to us, the pilot and copilot were checking the instruments.
3. Signs warning passengers not to smoke and to fasten their seat belts flashed on.
4. Directly beneath the signs was a door leading to the pilot's compartment.
5. Altogether there were about sixty passengers on the plane.
6. In a few moments the plane moved, slowly at first, and then roared into life.
7. After taxiing out to the airstrip, the pilot hesitated a moment to check the runway.
8. Then with a sudden rush of speed the plane roared down the runway and gradually began to climb.
9. Below us, at the edge of the airport, were markers and signal lights.
10. The football field and the quarter mile track enabled me to identify the high school.

(4) Complements

Some verbs, called INTRANSITIVE verbs, require nothing to complete them; that is, in themselves they make a full assertion about the subject.

After meeting all the relatives, my cousin *left.*
In a heavy rain, cabbage *may explode.*

TRANSITIVE verbs, however, are incomplete by themselves. If one says only "I bought," the reader is left hanging in mid-air and is apt to ask "What did you buy?" Words which answer such a question, and thus complete the assertion, are called *complements* of the verb.

subject	verb	complement
I	bought	a scarf.

The commonest type of complement is the DIRECT OBJECT of a transitive verb, illustrated in the sentence above. The direct object is usually a noun or pronoun, though it may be a phrase or a clause, and it usually names the thing acted upon by the subject.

subject	verb	direct object
My niece	built	a water clock.
They	chased	the soccer ball.

The easiest way to identify a direct object is to say the simple subject and verb and then ask the question "What?" My niece built what? The answer *clock*, is the direct object of the verb *built*. Note that the direct object may be compound.

subject	verb	direct object
I	borrowed	a tent, a sleeping bag, and a gas stove.

In addition to a direct object, certain verbs (usually involving an act of giving or telling), may take an INDIRECT OBJECT, a complement that receives whatever is named by the direct object. Consider the sentence "The Constitution grants us certain rights." What does the Constitution grant? *Rights* is the direct object. Who receives them? *Us* is the indirect object—the receiver of what is named by the direct object. Note that the same meaning could be expressed by a phrase beginning with *to* or *for:*

The Constitution grants certain rights *to us.*
I told *her* a lie = I told a lie *to her.*
I wrote *him* a check = I wrote a check *for him.*

Linking verbs, or copulative verbs, sometimes require a SUBJECTIVE COMPLEMENT, a word which completes the predicate by giving another name for the subject, or by describing the subject. In the sentence "Floyd is the clerk," *clerk* cannot be called the direct object since it is merely another name for Floyd, and it can be made the subject of the sentence without changing the meaning: "The clerk is Floyd." (Contrast "Floyd fired the clerk," in which the direct object, *clerk*, names another person, who is acted upon by Floyd. Making *clerk* the subject of this sentence changes the meaning entirely.) A noun which serves as a subjective complement of a linking verb is usually called a PREDICATE NOUN.

Linking verbs may also be completed by an adjective which describes the subject. Such a subjective complement is called a PREDICATE ADJECTIVE.

The concert was *routine* and **unimaginative**.

Routine and *unimaginative* describe concert, but instead of being directly attached to the noun ("a routine, unimaginative concert"), they are joined to it by the linking verb *was* and become predicate adjectives.

Exercise 2

Pick out the subjects and verbs in the following sentences. Identify direct objects, indirect objects, predicate nouns, and predicate adjectives.

1. As a wedding present, my uncle gave us a picture.
2. It was an original sketch by Dufy.
3. The technique was interesting, since Dufy had used only a few simple lines.
4. It seemed an early work, according to a friend to whom I showed it.
5. We hung it in the living room and it looked good.
6. I wrote my uncle a note and thanked him for the picture.
7. We enjoyed it for several months, until my friend told us its value.
8. Then we worried about burglars, and we wrote my uncle again asking if he would give us a less valuable picture.

(5) Phrases

A group of words may have the same function in a sentence as a single word. For example, in the sentence "The train to Boston leaves in ten minutes," the group of words *in ten minutes* modifies the verb *leaves* in exactly the same way as an adverb like *soon*. Similarly, *to Boston* functions like an adjective: it describes and identifies *train*. Such groups of words, which do not make a complete statement but which function like a single word, are called PHRASES. Phrases may be named for the kind of word around which they are constructed—prepositional, participial, gerund, or infinitive. Or they may be named by the way they function in a sentence—as adjective, adverb, or noun phrases. *To Boston* in the sentence above is a prepositional phrase used as an adjective.

Prepositional Phrases

A PREPOSITION is a word which, by connecting a noun or pronoun (its object) to the rest of the sentence, forms a modifying phrase. Prepositions are good examples of what linguists call "structure words": that is, their primary function is to hold structures together, rather than to convey lexical meaning. More specifically, they produce PREPOSITIONAL PHRASES, which function as modifiers. The following are prepositions in phrases:

> an agreement *between us,* a motel *in New Orleans,* a piece *of paper,* slid *under the table,* walked *for an hour,* try *with all my strength.*

Some of the most common prepositions are *of, by, with, at, in, on, to, for, between, through, from.* Prepositional phrases usually modify nouns or verbs, and they are accordingly described as adjective or adverb phrases.

        adjective   *adverb*
The lyrics *in the musical* were written *by Stephen Smith.*

Verbals and Verbal Phrases

A VERBAL is a verb form used as some other part of speech. *Fishing* may be used as part of a verb in a construction like "We were fishing for perch," but it may also be used as an adjective, to modify a noun: "a fishing rod." A verbal which modifies a noun is called a PARTICIPLE. Note that a participle may be in the past tense, as well as in the present—"a *used* car with *cracking, worn* upholstery." When a verb form ending in *ing* is used as a noun, it is called a GERUND: "Hunting is his hobby." In this sentence, *hunting* is the subject of the sentence. Gerunds may also be used as the objects of verbs or of prepositions.

     obj. of verb   *obj. of prep.*
He loves *hunting* and supports himself by *training* dogs.

One other type of verbal is common: the INFINITIVE. This is the ordinary form of the verb preceded by the preposition *to* (to run, to see). Infinitives are frequently used as nouns—as subject or object of a verb.

 subject   *object*
To win is his chief concern, and he hates *to lose.*

Since they are verb forms, participles, gerunds, and infinitives may take objects and they may be modified by adverbs or by prepositional phrases. A verbal with its modifier and its object, or subject, makes up a verbal phrase and functions as a single part of speech, but it does not make a full statement.

PARTICIPIAL PHRASE   *Flying some strange foreign flag,* a ship was entering the harbor.

Here the participle "flying," with its object and the modifiers of the object, describes "ship."

GERUND PHRASE   *Scaling a long slippery barracuda* takes strong hands.

Here the phrase—gerund, object, and the modifiers of the object—is the subject of the sentence.

INFINITIVE PHRASE   The rules required us *to arrive at 7:30.*

The infinitive has a subject, "us," and a modifying prepositional phrase, "at 7:30."

Absolute Phrases

An ABSOLUTE PHRASE consists of a participle with a subject (and sometimes a complement) grammatically unconnected with the rest of the sentence but usually telling when, why, or how something happened.

The floodwater having receded, people began returning to their homes.
I hated to leave home, *circumstances being as they were.*

Appositive Phrases

An APPOSITIVE is another name for something already indicated—a noun added to explain another noun: "Helen Fitzgerald, *the novelist,* was guest speaker." Appositives with their modifiers make up phrases, since they function as a unit to give further information about a noun.

APPOSITIVE PHRASE   Her subject was "Male Chauvinism," *a surprising choice for that audience.*

Note that appositives are ordinarily set off by commas. For exceptions, see page 338.

Exercise 3

Pick out the phrases in the following sentences. Identify them as prepositional, participial, gerund, infinitive, or appositive, and be ready to describe their function in the sentence.

1. On Tuesday I came home expecting to drive my car, a shiny new convertible, into the garage.
2. To my surprise, I found a ditch between the street and the driveway.
3. A crew of men had begun to lay a new water main along the curb.
4. Hoping that I would not get a ticket for overnight parking, I left the car in the street in front of the house.
5. For three days a yawning trench separated me from my garage.
6. Finding a place to park was difficult, since all the neighbors on my side of the street were in the same predicament.
7. By Friday the workmen had filled up the ditch, but my car, stained with dust and dew, looked ten years older.
8. I had to spend the weekend washing and polishing it.
9. My wife, a strong advocate of justice, suggested sending the city a bill for the job.
10. My refusal convinced her that men are illogical, improvident, and easily imposed upon.

(6) Clauses

Any group of words which makes a statement—that is, which contains a subject and a predicate—is called a CLAUSE. Except for elliptical questions and answers, every sentence must contain at least one clause.

Independent and Dependent Clauses

Though all sentences must contain a clause, not all clauses are sentences. Some clauses, instead of making an independent statement, serve only as a subordinate part of the main sentence. Such clauses, called DEPENDENT or SUBORDINATE, perform a function like that of adjectives, adverbs, or nouns. INDEPENDENT CLAUSES, on the other hand, are capable of standing alone as complete sentences. They provide the framework to which modifiers, phrases, and dependent clauses are attached in each sentence. Any piece of connected discourse is made up of a series of independent clauses.

"While I was sitting on the steps" is a clause, since it contains a subject, *I*, and a verb, *was sitting*. But it is a dependent clause; in meaning it is incomplete (what happened?) and it would normally be used as a modifier. Its purpose is to tell *when* something happened, and the complete sentence should state what did happen.

dependent clause   *independent clause*
While I was sitting on the steps,   I heard a siren.

A dependent clause is usually connected to the rest of the sentence by a relative pronoun (*who, which,* or *that*) or by conjunctions like *while, although, as, because, if, since, when,* or *where.* These are called SUBORDINATING CONJUNCTIONS because they introduce clauses which are elements of a sentence rather than independent statements. Notice how the addition of a subordinating conjunction to an independent clause makes the clause dependent. Here are two independent clauses, each a complete sentence:

independent clause   *independent clause*
We stayed home.   It was beginning to snow.

Adding the subordinating conjunction *because* makes the second clause dependent; written as a separate sentence, "because it was beginning to snow" would be a fragment. If joined to the preceding clause, however, it modifies the verb *stayed,* giving the reason for our staying.

independent clause   *conj. & dependent clause*
We stayed home   **because** it was beginning to snow.

In sentences dependent clauses are used like nouns (as subjects or objects) or as modifiers, like adverbs and adjectives.

Noun Clauses

A NOUN CLAUSE functions as a noun in a sentence. It may be a subject or a complement in the main clause, the object of a preposition or of a gerund.

NOUN CLAUSE   **That he couldn't jump twenty-two feet** was obvious.
The noun clause is used as the subject of the sentence.

NOUN CLAUSE   He said **that he could jump only twenty feet.**
The noun clause is used as the direct object of the verb "said."

NOUN CLAUSE   Sell it to **whoever will buy it.**
The noun clause is used as the object of the preposition "to."

NOUN CLAUSE   Keep out of trouble by doing **what comes naturally.**
The noun clause is used as the object of the gerund "doing."

Adverb Clauses

An ADVERB CLAUSE is a dependent clause used to modify a verb or an adjective or an adverb in the main clause.

ADVERB CLAUSE   We ate *whenever we felt like it.*
 "Whenever we felt like it" modifies the verb "ate."

ADVERB CLAUSE   The trip was as pleasant *as we had hoped.*
 The clause "as we had hoped" modifies the adjective "pleasant."

ADVERB CLAUSE   The train arrived sooner *than we had expected.*
 The clause "than we had expected" modifies the adverb "sooner."

Adjective Clauses and Relative Pronouns

A dependent clause used to modify a noun or pronoun is called an ADJECTIVE CLAUSE.

ADJECTIVE CLAUSE   The salesman *we met yesterday* showed us his library, *which includes all the first editions of Dorothy Sayers.*
 The adjective clause "we met yesterday" modifies the noun "salesman"; the adjective clause "which includes all the first editions of Dorothy Sayers" modifies the noun "library."

Adjective clauses are usually introduced by a RELATIVE PRONOUN, which serves both as a pronoun and as a subordinating conjunction. Its function can be seen by some examples.

 Ken was a leader; Ken never failed us.

This sentence consists of two independent clauses, but it would be more idiomatic to substitute a pronoun for the second "Ken."

 Ken was a leader; *he* never failed us.

If, instead of using the personal pronoun *he,* we substitute the relative pronoun *who,* the second clause becomes dependent.

 Ken was a leader *who* never failed us.

"Who never failed us" no longer will stand as an independent sentence; but when it is joined to the first clause, it functions as an adjective, modifying *leader.*

 The relative pronouns *who* (and *whom*), *which,* and *that* always have two functions: they serve as subordinating conjunctions, connecting dependent clauses to independent ones, but they also function like nouns, as subject or complement in the dependent clause. Often the relative pronouns can be omitted: "I received the book [*which, that*] I ordered."

Exercise 4

Find the simple subject and verb of each clause in the following sentences. Point out the main clauses and the dependent clauses, and be prepared to state the function in each sentence of each dependent clause.

1. The movie director who did much to perfect the one-reel Western as a distinct genre was D. W. Griffith.
2. Shortly after he had entered movies in New York, Griffith achieved immediate success with his first film, which he directed in 1908.
3. Between 1908 and 1913, while he was directing Westerns, Griffith continually worked with techniques which, though they had been introduced by others, were developed and refined by him.
4. Griffith was delighted by the Western because it offered opportunities for spectacle and scope.
5. He found that the Western was an ideal genre in which to experiment with close-ups and with cross-cutting, the techniques he employed to build narrative suspense.
6. Some critics have pointed out that Griffith was more interested in dramatic situations which lent themselves to lively visual treatment than he was in the details of plot or conventional justice.
7. He would willingly let the villains go free whenever he felt the dramatic situation warranted it.
8. The close-up of the outnumbered settlers grimly hanging on and the panoramic view of the battle seen from afar were characteristic Griffith shots.
9. In 1915, Griffith produced *The Birth of a Nation,* the first great spectacle movie.
10. It made use of many of the techniques he had developed while he was making one-reel Westerns.

4b　Types of Sentences

Sentences are traditionally classified, according to their structure, as simple, complex, compound, and compound-complex.

4b

(1) Simple Sentences

A SIMPLE SENTENCE consists of one independent clause, with *no* dependent clauses attached, although it may have modifying phrases.

subject   *verb*
SIMPLE   The   children hurriedly   left   for school.

mod. phrase   *subj.*   *verb*
SIMPLE   Slumped in the bottom of a skiff,   I   floated
peacefully along.

Simple sentences are not necessarily short and jerky, but their overuse is apt to make one's writing seem both choppy and childish. So-called "primer" style is caused by a succession of short simple sentences. The remedy is to combine some of them into complex sentences (see page 86).

(2) Complex Sentences

The COMPLEX SENTENCE contains one independent clause and one or more dependent clauses, which express subordinate ideas.

independent clause   *dependent clause*
COMPLEX   We lost touch with the Carters   after they moved.

ind. clause   *dependent clause*
COMPLEX   He was a man   who had many close friends.

dependent clause
COMPLEX   Although the spray contained endrin,

dependent clause   *independent clause*
which may harm people, she used the poison
on tomato plants.

The complex sentence has the advantage of flexibility; it can be arranged to produce a variety of sentence patterns. It also provides selective emphasis, since the subordination of dependent clauses throws the weight of the sentence on the main clause.

(3) Compound Sentences

The COMPOUND SENTENCE consists of two or more independent clauses.

	ind. clause		*ind. clause*
COMPOUND	He notified the office,	and	the manager corrected the error.

	ind. clause		*ind. clause*
COMPOUND	This sentence is compound	;	it has two main clauses.

(4) Compound-complex Sentences

When a compound sentence contains dependent clauses, the whole is sometimes described as a COMPOUND-COMPLEX SENTENCE.

dependent clause

COMPOUND-COMPLEX   Although the critics gave it good reviews,

independent clause
the play never attracted the public, and

independent clause
the producers closed it reluctantly after two weeks

dependent clause
because they could not afford the losses.

Exercise 5

Classify the following sentences as simple, compound, complex, or compound-complex. Identify the subject, verb, and complement, if any, of each clause. Describe the function of each dependent clause.

1. When Renaissance physicians began to study human anatomy by means of actual dissection, they concluded that the human body had changed since the days of antiquity.
2. Galen, an ancient Greek physician, was generally accepted as the authority on anatomy and physiology.
3. His theory of the four humors, blood, phlegm, bile, and black bile, was neat and logical, and authorities had accepted it for centuries.
4. Similarly, his account of the structure of the human body, revised by generations of scholars and appearing in many printed editions, was generally accepted.
5. If dissection showed a difference from Galen's account, the obvious explanation was that human structure had changed since Galen's time.

6. One man who refused to accept this explanation was Andreas Vesalius, a young Belgian physician who was studying in Italy.
7. Asked to edit the anatomical section of Galen's works, Vesalius found many errors in it.
8. Galen's statement that the lower jaw consisted of two parts seemed wrong to Vesalius, who had never found such a structure in his own dissections.
9. He finally concluded that Galen was describing the anatomy of lower animals—pigs, monkeys, and goats—and that he had never dissected a human body.
10. When he realized that Galen could be wrong, Vesalius began a study which came to be recognized as his major work: a fully illustrated treatise on the human body based on actual observation.

Forceful Sentences 5

A good sentence should have impact. If you merely spray your reader with a cloud of words, he may not even notice what you are trying to say. Your sentence should be as coordinated, well-timed, and accurate as a good fencer's thrust. It should be tightly organized rather than sprawling, and its choice of words should be both precise and concise.

5a   Sentence Unity

A unified sentence should make a single main point, or have some good reason for making more than one. In any case, it should produce a single effect. It can contain many details if the subordinate relationship of most of them is made clear by the grammatical structure.

DETAILS IN SEPARATE SENTENCES   The barber pole originally represented an arm or leg wrapped in bandages. Barbers were also the surgeons in those days. The jars of colored water in a chemist's shop represented the medicines and elixirs offered for sale. Three gold balls are the traditional sign of a pawnbroker. They originally indicated the shop of a banker or moneylender. Most villagers in those days could not read. The signs indicated where these essential services could be found.

ONE UNIFIED SENTENCE   The barber's pole (originally intended as a limb swathed in bandages), the chemist's coloured jars, the banker's three gilt balls, were marks of identification for those (and they were most of the village) who could not read.

—LOUIS KRONENBERGER

If the writer thinks of a sentence as a container into which all available information is to be indiscriminately dumped, he will wind up with a mess, like the following:

OVERCROWDED   The earliest known examples of sculpture date from the Old Stone Age, which was more than 20,000 years before the time of Christ and is sometimes called the Paleolithic Period, making sculpture one of the oldest arts known to man, many pieces of ancient sculpture having been found in caves or old burial grounds in various parts of the world.

Perhaps the main point of all this is meant to be the great antiquity of the art of sculpture. If so, that idea should be stressed and all the other details subordinated or omitted.

IMPROVED   Sculpture is one of the oldest arts known to man: the earliest examples, found in caves or burial grounds, go back to the Old Stone Age, more than 20,000 years ago.

If a writer temporarily loses sight of the main point, unrelated ideas may creep into a sentence. They may be important in some sense, but unless they contribute to making the main point, they should be eliminated in revision.

UNRELATED IDEAS   The pilot of an airplane, whether he flies a Piper Cub or one of the giant jetliners which have two decks, carry over 300 passengers, and are now in use throughout the world on most runs of 3,000 miles or more, must depend on his instruments.

IMPROVED   The pilot of an airplane, whether he flies a Piper Cub or a giant jetliner, must depend on his instruments.

UNRELATED DETAILS   When I set out to gather material for my feature story, the town library, which has an unusually good reference collection thanks to the generosity of one of the early settlers who established an endowed fund for reference works, was my first stop.

The generosity of the early settler, though certainly commendable, is not relevant to the point the writer seems to be trying to make.

IMPROVED   When I set out to gather material for my feature story, my first stop was the town library, which has an excellent reference collection.

The relationship between two ideas may be perfectly clear to the writer (after all, he thought them up) but may baffle the reader if the unifying principle is only implied.

OBSCURE RELATIONSHIP   Road maps, I discovered, cost a quarter, but I was used to the old days and took only one.

IMPROVED   Road maps, which in the old days were free, now cost a quarter, and so I took only one.

OBSCURE RELATIONSHIP   Being from San Diego, I wear only half my pajamas.

The sentence suggests the interesting if unintended generalization that all people living in San Diego wear only "half" their pajamas. The student has omitted a logical step in the cause-and-effect relationship.

IMPROVED   Since I came from San Diego, which is warm most of the year, I wear only my pajama bottoms.

OBSCURE RELATIONSHIP   Maturing faster because of parents' divorcing does not hold true in all cases. The child may become timid and insecure.

The writer is assuming a connection between the child's shock at the divorce and his growth. This connection should be made explicit.

IMPROVED   When parents divorce, the shock may hasten the maturing of the child. But divorce may, in some cases, retard maturity by making the child timid and insecure.

Two ideas which belong together in the sense that one ought to follow the other do not necessarily belong in the same sentence. Putting them together in one sentence may suggest a closer relationship than actually exists.

FALSE UNITY   After locking the house, I left the key with the real estate agent, and I hope you will soon find another tenant.

IMPROVED   After locking the house, I left the key with the real estate agent. I hope you will soon find another tenant.

No one deliberately writes disorganized sentences, lacking in unity or crammed with excessive detail. Such faults, as well as the primer sentences discussed in the next section, are usually due to oversight: the writer is so intent on what he thinks he is saying that he fails to notice how his sentences will sound to a reader. The best way to find out how a sentence sounds is to read it *out loud*. If you hesitate, stumble, or have to start over, if your voice rhythms cannot encompass all the material, you had better start revising the sentence or the paragraph. Reading aloud is also an excellent way of detecting the wordiness and repetition discussed in Section 5b.

(1) Excessive Detail

Length alone does not make a sentence good or bad. By using parallel structure, proper subordination, and carefully selected connectives as guide posts, an experienced writer can compose sentences which are well unified even though long. There is a natural psychological limit, however. If a sentence contains too many ideas or details, none of them will stand out and the sentence will seem overcrowded and pointless.

OVERCROWDED   On the forward end of the boat I built a little deck of plywood, which extended about one third of the way aft and into which I cut a hole for the mast, made of two pieces of plywood glued together, and I made the boom in the same way.

IMPROVED   On the forward end of the boat, I built a little deck of plywood and cut a hole in it for the mast. I made both the mast and the boom by glueing two pieces of plywood together.

OVERCROWDED   When the cry for woman's suffrage was first heard there was immediate opposition to it, which continued for a long time until men finally began to realize that women were entitled to the same rights as themselves, and in 1920 the Nineteenth Amendment was ratified.

This sentence includes too many ideas: the beginning of the women's suffrage movement, opposition to it, continued opposition, gradual change of public opinion, and the ratification of the Nineteenth Amendment. It should be broken down into at least two sentences.

IMPROVED   When the cry for woman's suffrage was first heard there was immediate opposition to it, and this opposition continued for a long time. Gradually, however, men realized that women were entitled to the same rights as themselves, and in 1920 the Nineteenth Amendment was ratified.

(2) Primer Sentences

Short, jerky sentences like those found in a second-grade reader are an offense to the ear and a sure sign that the writer has not troubled to define his meaning. Since every detail is put as a main clause, none seems more important than another; the reader has to guess what the main point is. Less important elements should be put into subordinate constructions like dependent clauses, participial phrases, or appositives. Reading out loud what you have written is the best way of detecting the awkward abruptness of primer sentences.

PRIMER SENTENCES The train was three hours late. There had been a freight wreck ahead somewhere. We finally reached Riverbank. The station was dark and deserted.

SUBORDINATED The train was three hours late because of a freight wreck up ahead, and when we finally reached Riverbank, the station was dark and deserted.

Experienced writers of fiction—Hemingway is a notable example—sometimes use a string of short, simple sentences for special effects. In expository writing, however, longer unified sentences with the less important ideas subordinated are usual.

PRIMER SENTENCES Peter Ratcliff is a free-lance writer and printer. He has lived in this city for five years. He is a member of the Citizens' Charter Review Committee. Now he is running for the City Council. His main concern is to make the Council receptive to the needs and ideas of the people.

SUBORDINATED Peter Ratcliff, a free-lance writer and printer who has lived in this city for five years and is a member of the Citizens' Charter Review Committee, is running for the City Council on a platform of making the Council receptive to the needs and wishes of the people.

(3) False Coordination

Just as the reader expects ideas of lesser importance to be put in subordinate clauses and phrases, so when he finds statements in coordinate constructions, he expects them to be of equal weight and importance. If sentence elements are not really equal in importance, do not confuse the reader by connecting them with coordinating conjunctions: *and, or* and *nor, but.* Subordinate one of the elements.

FALSE COORDINATION In English courses we had to learn many rules of grammar, and very few of these rules are taken seriously today.

IMPROVED Few of the rules we had to learn in English courses are taken seriously today.

FALSE COORDINATION The topographic map showed the trail going all the way to Jackhammer Springs, and I could usually trust these maps and so I decided to go ahead, but it was beginning to get dark.

IMPROVED   The topographic map, which I could usually trust, showed the trail going all the way to Jackhammer Springs, and so I decided to go ahead even though it was beginning to get dark.

(4) Faulty Subordination

Do not put the main idea of a sentence into a subordinate construction, like a dependent clause or a modifying phrase.

FAULTY SUBORDINATION   The night watchman walked past the building at 9:20, noticing that the door was unlocked.

Which is more important, the unlocked door or the watchman walking past?

IMPROVED   When the night watchman walked past the building at 9:20, he noticed that the door was unlocked.

FAULTY SUBORDINATION   Ruth Benedict is the author of **Patterns of Culture,** in which she praises the Zuñi Indians for their ceremonial life and its cooperative attitude toward the natural world.

IMPROVED   In her **Patterns of Culture,** Ruth Benedict praises the Zuñi Indians for their ceremonial life and its cooperative attitude toward the natural world.

In some cases, of course, the context alone determines which ideas are relatively more or less important. If you were stressing your own experience in a narrative, the following sentence would be satisfactory:

I used to work for the Arco Electronics Company, which went bankrupt yesterday.

If you were writing mainly about the Arco Electronics Company, you would probably subordinate the first clause:

The Arco Electronics Company, where I used to work, went bankrupt yesterday.

(5) Excessive Subordination

The House-that-Jack-built sentence, which trails off into a series of "that . . . that . . ." or "which . . . which . . ." clauses should be rewritten. Such sentences may be confusing and are always tiresome.

EXCESSIVE SUBORDINATION   The prize was finally awarded to a girl who was the niece of the man who was president of the company which sponsored the contest which caused all the dispute.

REVISED   The prize winner was the daughter of the president of the company which had sponsored the disputed contest.

Notice that in the revised sentence, the logical subject is also the grammatical subject. The sentence is not really about the prize, but about the winner of it.

EXCESSIVE SUBORDINATION   The examples are not very clear in the books which are used in the courses which are required for freshmen who didn't pass the placement tests. They don't receive much help in the review sections, which is why many freshmen who buy these books won't use them.

REVISED   Freshmen who are required to take makeup courses because they failed placement tests get little help from the textbooks assigned. They complain that the examples are not very clear and that the review sections are inadequate, Many freshmen won't use the texts at all.

Exercise 1

Revise the following sentences by putting the main ideas in main clauses and less important ideas in subordinate clauses. Be prepared to explain why you have chosen certain ideas as the main ones and to explain the form of subordination you have used.

1.   An especially big wave rolled in, when I finally managed to get my line unsnagged.
2.   Many of his home run records still unbroken and his life-time batting average one of the highest ever achieved, Babe Ruth batted for the Yankees.
3.   The ocean was choppy, causing the fishermen to have little luck and to return to the pier disappointed.
4.   The population of Latin America, ranging from Indians who live as their ancestors did hundreds of years ago to highly educated men and women in modern cities like Buenos Aires and Rio de Janeiro, is varied.
5.   He was trying to kill a bee inside the car, driving off the road as a result.
6.   Contact lenses are worn next to the eyeballs and have advantages over ordinary glasses, since contact lenses are invisible, are kept unfrosted by the eyelids, and correct faulty corneas.

7. The horse came up to the first jump, when he stumbled and threw Janet off.

Exercise 2

Revise the following sentences by subordinating the less important ideas. Be prepared to explain the choices you make and the form of subordination you have used.

1. The potter must roll the clay out on a flat surface, and a surface that the clay will not stick to.
2. Five hundred citizens were too many to meet at one time, and so instead the Council was divided into ten smaller groups.
3. The job was interesting, and the pay was good, but finally I decided not to accept it and I regretted my decision later.
4. Gertrude Stein and Hemingway were contemporaries, and Stein was one of the first to recognize Hemingway's genius as a writer.
5. Scientists are continually developing new photographic equipment, and now they have devised ways of photographing planets as far away as Mars by rockets which relay the pictures back to Earth.
6. I got the note from my parents, and I gave it to my teacher, but he just scowled at me, but finally he said I could take the afternoon off.

Exercise 3

Revise the following student sentences by eliminating the excessive subordination.

1. In 1666 when he sent a beam of white light through a glass prism which broke the beam up into bands of colored lights which resembled a rainbow, Isaac Newton showed that what we normally think of as white light is actually made up of light which consists of different colors, a discovery which revolutionized the science of optics, which was in its infancy before Newton.
2. When I bought my parrot from the pet store on the Mall, where I had visited several times and spent hours gazing at the cages because I so badly wanted a bird of my own, I was so excited that

I could hardly contain myself as I rushed home to begin training him from the booklet which I had also bought at the store.

3.   At the beginning of the story, which takes place in Sicily at some unknown time in the past, Verga makes us realize that the main character is called "La Lupa," which means the wolf, because the villagers are superstitious people who believe in the devil and other evil forces that can take human form.

Exercise 4

Revise the following sentences to improve their unity. Be prepared to explain the changes you have made.

1.   I usually enjoyed an appointment with my dentist, and he would make me feel good because he complimented me on my teeth.
2.   The swimming pool was intended for college students only, but is now open to townspeople as well.
3.   The train was late, causing me to miss my appointment and lose the client.
4.   The picture which won first prize was in water color. It was an abstract painting. Most people criticized it, but the judges liked it.
5.   The first book I consulted lacked an index, and next I tried an almanac.
6.   The Greek word *papyros* originally meant thin sheets of paper made from a certain Egyptian reed, from which we have borrowed our modern word *paper* and which now means any kind of writing material.
7.   The United Nations, which was founded in San Francisco more than twenty-five years ago when many of the major diplomats of the world were there, has increased greatly in size, many of the new members being the small nations which have recently gained their independence.
8.   Freud grew up in Vienna, doing some of his most creative psychoanalytic research in that city.
9.   There were about ten women out for field hockey, and we only had four weeks before our first match, so we worked very hard to get in condition, but three of our best players caught the flu and so we didn't do well against our opponents.
10.   The match burned his fingers. He tried to light his pipe in the wind, and he dropped it on the ground when he burned himself.

5b Concise Sentences

The impact of a sentence can be weakened by dilution—that is, too many words per unit of sense. A wordy sentence tastes flat and watery, like a weak cup of coffee. Although your main concern in a first draft is to get your ideas down on paper before they slip your mind, in revision you should be ruthless in cutting out unnecessary words and phrases.

Note that there is a difference between brevity and conciseness. Brevity is not always a virtue; conciseness almost always is. Any statement can be made brief by omitting detail. But details are often essential and must be included. Conciseness means stating the necessary details without wasting words.

BRIEF STATEMENT   I failed the job.

CONCISE STATEMENT   Last month I sold only 60 percent of the quota set by the company.

WORDY   The pill had the desired effect of tranquilizing the dog and served the purpose of keeping him asleep until we arrived at our ultimate destination at a time approaching midnight.

CONCISE   The pill kept the dog asleep until we reached camp late that night.

Note in the preceding sentence that vagueness ("our ultimate destination") often goes hand in hand with wordiness.

WORDY   Under present circumstances I have come to the conclusion that my answer must be in the negative.

CONCISE   My answer is no.

(1) Wordy Constructions

Answering a young man's question about how to become a good writer, Sydney Smith once said, "You should cross out every other word. You have no idea what vigor it will give to your style." Though exaggerated, the advice makes a good point. In revision, cross out every word that is not essential. To find out what is essential and what is mere padding, read your sentences aloud.

WORDY   It should be observed whether your dog is eating weeds, rubbish, or other things not part of his usual diet, for if he is participating in such behavior, you may know that this is a symptom of his having worms.

CONCISE   Notice whether your dog eats weeds, rubbish, or other things not part of his usual diet, for if he does, he may have worms.

WORDY   It is requested by the management that the audience refrain from using flash attachments for the purpose of picture taking during the performance.

CONCISE   The management requests that the audience not take pictures during the performance.

The term *deadwood* is applied to constructions which have become, through overuse, as meaningless and as unconscious as clearing one's throat. Expressions like "proceeded to . . . ," "it is my opinion that . . . ," "because of the fact that . . . ," seldom add anything to the sentence and usually weaken it by dilution.

DEADWOOD   It is the opinion of the present writer that tax cuts are not well calculated to bring about an increase in spending on the part of the consumer.

CONCISE   I think that tax cuts are unlikely to increase consumer spending.

(2) Redundant Phrases and Clauses

A phrase which carelessly repeats what has already been said is redundant. It usually causes no misunderstanding, but it is a sign of sloppy writing.

REDUNDANT   In this country of ours, everything has become so large in size that the individual feels isolated and unable to cooperate together with others.

IMPROVED   In our country, everything has become so large that the individual feels isolated and unable to cooperate with others.

REDUNDANT   When the poet writes in his poem that the character was never "odd in his views," he means to imply that the man was a conformist, accepting the standards of his society in all aspects.

IMPROVED   When the poet writes that the character was never "odd in his views," he implies that the man was a conformist.

REDUNDANT   Over the years, Smathers becomes suspicious that he is being exploited *by people who want to take advantage of him and use him.*
The student has ignored the meaning of "exploited."

REDUNDANT The criticisms I will make are major ones *which ought to be given careful consideration because of their importance.*

If anything is "major" (or "basic" or "fundamental"), then of course it "ought to be given careful consideration."

REDUNDANT We like to be appreciated and admired for our talents *which we possess* and we hope to be praised for our achievements *that we have attained as individuals.*

The student forgot the meaning of the word "our."

Some other redundant phrases include:

attractive *in appearance*   red *in color*
connected *up* with   refer *back* to
expert in *the field of*   repeat *again*
the reason *why*   several *in number*
our modern society *of today*   square *in shape*

(3) Unnecessary Repetition

Careless or unnecessary repetition of words or phrases is apt to distract the reader from what you are saying and underline the awkward way in which you are saying it.

AWKWARD REPETITION The question of who is to be considered needy is a hard question to answer.

IMPROVED The question who is to be considered needy is hard to answer.

FOCUS LOST If *one* examines the *story* carefully, *one* will find that the hidden symbolism in the *story* makes the *story* stand for something more than *one* first found in the *story.*

The repetition of "story" and "one" obscures a simple idea—that if one reads the story carefully, he discovers a symbolism which deepens it.

INEFFECTIVE After having opened your *presents, you* find that *you* have received just about every conceivable *present* in the world, except the *present you* have been hinting you would like to receive.

IMPROVED After opening your presents, you find that you have received just about everything conceivable except the present you have been hinting for.

5c   Standard Sentence Patterns

The basic pattern of the typical English sentence is Subject—Verb—Complement. Probably most of your sentences will follow this pattern, but within it a great deal of variation is possible. The order of subject and complement can be reversed; modifying phrases and clauses can be moved about from place to place. Familiarity with a wide variety of sentence patterns will enable you to vary the rhythm and movement of your prose. It will also help you to achieve more precise emphasis on certain points.

A LOOSE SENTENCE puts the main idea first and then adds qualifications or supplemental information.

LOOSE SENTENCE   I will pick up the car later, probably when I get off work this afternoon.

LOOSE SENTENCE   I can feel the loneliness that haunted him as I read between the lines of his letters.

In both sentences, the main idea is in the independent clause; the dependent clause is added at the end.

A PERIODIC SENTENCE, on the other hand, suspends its main point until all the subordinate details have been spelled out. Hence, the ending of a periodic sentence is usually emphatic.

PERIODIC   As I read between the lines of his letters, I can feel the loneliness that haunted him.

PERIODIC   Frost's seriousness and honesty; the bare sorrow with which, sometimes, things are accepted as they are, neither exaggerated nor explained away; the many, many poems in which there are real people with their real speech and real thoughts and real emotions—all this, in conjunction with so much subtlety and exactness, such classical understatement and restraint, makes the reader feel that he is not in a book but in a world, and a world that has in common with his own some of the things that are most important in both.

—RANDALL JARRELL

This sentence includes a great many details explaining (at the very end of the sentence) why the reader feels himself "not in a book but in a world," and an important world as well.

There is no question here of correctness; both loose and periodic sentences are correct in structure. But since they have different effects, each has its proper uses. A long periodic sentence, like the one just quoted, has the force of compression and is a product of careful craftsmanship. In formal or rhetorical writing such a sentence can be very effective, but too many periodic sentences may make your everyday writing sound stilted, formal, or contrived.

What is usually desirable is variety in sentence patterns, and to achieve variety a writer must become aware of the different effects produced by changes in structure and order.

(1) Weak Sentence Patterns

A loose sentence can have so long a tail of appended afterthoughts that it may seem to just trail away into thin air. The end of a sentence is usually a key spot and should contain an important idea. Continuing to add trivial details at the end has the same effect as letting your voice trail away into a mumble.

TRAILING   It is in this scene that Lear finally realizes that he has been deceived by the promises that his older daughters have made to him earlier in the play when he thought they were being sincere and didn't see them for what they really were.

Read this aloud and note the fatigue the sentence causes. Wordiness often produces trailing sentences.

EMPHATIC   In this scene Lear finally realizes that he has been deceived by the promises of his older daughters.

Pruned of such redundant phrases as "earlier in the play" and such clauses as "when he thought they were being sincere," the sentence is clear and emphatic.

TRAILING   I quit regretfully when the strain in the office became too great because of inadequate staff and inefficient equipment.

EMPHATIC   When the strain of working with inadequate staff and inefficient equipment became too great, I regretfully quit the office.

(2) Anticlimax

Build a climax by arranging a series of items in increasing order of importance and by placing the most important idea last. Otherwise an unintentional anticlimax may occur.

ANTICLIMAX   Einstein was a deeply philosophical man, a great mathematician, and a fair amateur violinist.

PASSIVE CONSTRUCTIONS

CLIMACTIC ORDER   Einstein was a fair amateur violinist, a great mathematician, and a deeply philosophical man.

ANTICLIMAX   She has won all the delegates in Ohio, California, and South Dakota.

CLIMACTIC ORDER   She has won all the delegates in South Dakota, Ohio, and California.

Don't build the reader up to a letdown unless you are being deliberately ironic or humorous.

DELIBERATE ANTICLIMAX   He owes his success to hard work, perseverance, and his father-in-law.

DELIBERATE ANTICLIMAX   The long climb to the summit rewarded us with a spectacular view, invigorating air, and sore feet.

(3) Passive Constructions

When the grammatical subject of a sentence names the doer of the action asserted by the predicate, the verb is in the active voice.

ACTIVE VOICE   When you pay your bill, we *will reinstate* your charge account.

When the subject names the person or thing that is acted upon, the verb is in the passive voice.

PASSIVE VOICE   When your bill is paid, your charge account *will be reinstated.*

The passive voice is appropriate when the doer of an action is unknown or is irrelevant to the statement being made. Scientists, for example, often use the passive voice to emphasize that what is important is the experiment, not the person who performs it. "Two cc. of water were added, and the test tube was heated" . . . , etc.

APPROPRIATE PASSIVE   Lost parcels *may be claimed* at the office.

APPROPRIATE PASSIVE   The painting *was stolen* in 1925.

Usually, however, the person who performs an action is important, and the subject of the verb should name him or her. Overuse of passive constructions leads to weak sentences, like the following:

WEAK PASSIVE   Every night Mr. Richardson's lawn *had to be watered* by me.

IMPROVED   Every night I *had to water* Mr. Richardson's lawn.

WEAK PASSIVE   The picnic *was enjoyed* by everyone who went on it.

The passive construction here has led the writer to add an unnecessary identifying clause, "who went on it."

IMPROVED   Everybody *enjoyed* the picnic.

One way to avoid weak and wordy sentences is to use the passive voice only when you have some good reason for doing so. Many dangling modifiers are the result of unnecessary passive constructions:

PASSIVE CONSTRUCTION AND DANGLING MODIFIER   Having baked the potatoes, the steak *was put* on the grill.

Changing the verb to the active voice requires a subject, like "we" or "I" or "the chef," which also anchors the dangling modifier.

IMPROVED   Having baked the potatoes, we *put* the steak on the grill.

WEAK AND WORDY PASSIVE   Disapproval *was felt* by even the enemies of the accused woman as well as her friends because of the illegal methods indulged in by the sheriff when evidence *was being collected.*

IMPROVED   Even the enemies of the accused woman disapproved of the sheriff's illegal methods of collecting evidence.

(4) False Subject

Do not bury your real subject (what you are mainly talking about) in some subordinate part of the sentence. Make the real subject the grammatical subject, and notice how much stronger the sentence becomes.

FALSE SUBJECT   We can readily see how fame was achieved by a man named Patrick Henry, who said "Give me liberty or give me death."

This sentence is really about Patrick Henry. Make him the subject.

IMPROVED   Patrick Henry achieved fame for saying "Give me liberty or give me death."

Overuse of the passive voice often leads to a false subject, which can make the sentence confusing as well as wordy.

PASSIVE VOICE AND FALSE SUBJECT   The changes which *had been made* in the conservation bill by the Committee *were accepted* by the Senate, which voted to pass the bill.

As it stands, one can hardly tell what happened here. Who did what? The real subject is "the Senate" and what it did was to pass a bill. Say it that way.

IMPROVED   The Senate passed the Conservation bill as amended in committee.

Beginning a sentence with "There is . . ." or "It is . . ." is an accepted idiomatic construction in English.

CORRECT   There is no reason to doubt his honesty.
"There" is an introductory word; the grammatical subject is "reason."

CORRECT   It is true that he had been drinking at the time.
In this idiomatic construction, "it" anticipates the actual grammatical subject, the clause "that he had been drinking." The writer uses this construction to imply that a concession is being made.

Used unnecessarily or unthinkingly, however, this idiom can be awkward, weak, or repetitious.

AWKWARD AND WEAK   It was to see Paul Revere's house that I walked to the North End.

IMPROVED   I walked to the North End to see Paul Revere's house.

WEAK AND REPETITIOUS   It was about that time that I came along.

IMPROVED   About that time I came along.

Exercise 5

Analyze the techniques employed in the following student sentences: the use of periodic and balanced sentences, the placement of words in key positions, the use of climactic order, and effective repetition. If you think some of the sentences are weak, revise them and be prepared to explain your changes. If you think some of the sentences are too labored and self-consciously emphatic, tame them, and be prepared to explain your changes.

1. Ada's large, dark eyes, usually so clear and full of laughter, were lack-lustre and were sunk in deep circles of worn brown skin, and her naturally dark skin looked sallow and overlaid with a fine mask of lines. Against her mother's countenance, Ada's was a pale, young, and confused face.

2.　We are all foreigners. Although we live in the United States and claim the title "American," foreign blood runs through our veins. The first generation of our family came to America for opportunities and independence. But America did not greet them with the fruitfulness they had expected. Instead, they found that the hard road to success was one they had to travel by themselves, despite the barrier of their foreign language and foreign ways. Naturally, they wanted their children to become more successful than they themselves had been. I am one such child.

3.　G. K. Chesterton has said, "Only those will permit their patriotism to falsify history whose patriotism depends on history." Such men, according to Chesterton, do not love their country; they love a theory about their country. To judge from the history books I used in school, the American patriot's theory depends on a West that was conquered only by white cowboys, the rugged sort who spent most of their time fighting other cowboys or Mexicans and Indians. Yet from a recently published book, *The Negro Cowboys*, written by Philip Durham and Everett L. Jones, I learned that there were more than 5,000 Negro cowboys, and that they lived together with the white cowboys and shared the same hardships. I learned that is was a unit of Negro cavalry who captured Geronimo and that it was a Negro cowboy who helped bring in Billy the Kid. Though the Negro cowboys broke horses, herded cattle, and occasionally turned renegade, it has taken until 1965 for a history of their deeds to be published. Until now, I have been given a falsified history, a patriot's theory of our country's history.

Exercise 6

Revise the following sentences to eliminate the trailing construction by placing the more important words at the beginning or end of the sentence.

1.　The Industrial Revolution has progressed during the last two centuries, changing the life of everyone in Europe and now having its effect on the people in Africa and Asia.

2.　I like to watch television, although I don't get much of a chance because I don't get home from practice until after six and then have to eat my supper before I start my homework, which isn't finished before 10:30.

3.　A scientific fact is one in which the conditions by which the fact

was discovered can be duplicated by someone else, achieving the same result.
4. The remote setting of the village answers the questions of why there is so much ignorance among the people who live in it, it would seem.
5. He strongly opposed the motion for several reasons which he had.

Exercise 7

Revise the following sentences as necessary to gain greater effectiveness.

1. To cool off that evening, she drank a coke, a pitcherful of iced tea, and a glass of water.
2. She was valedictorian in her senior year after doing average work in her freshman and sophomore years and beginning to show her real abilities in her junior year.
3. There are two holidays which I especially enjoy, these being Christmas and spring vacation.
4. The worst driver of all is the driver who is positive he couldn't cause an accident and who doesn't care if other people are careless, speeding, or not quite sober, because he is sure that nothing can happen to him while he is driving.
5. The turtle nipped the boy on the finger when he put a finger into its box.
6. The two roommates finally saw each other again, many years later at a professional convention in New York, in a hotel lobby.
7. The pickets began their dramatic sit-in when the manager of the building scoffed at their requests.
8. The silent films produced America's greatest comedians, including Harry Langdon, Buster Keaton, Charlie Chaplin, and many others who could be mentioned.

Exercise 8

One way to alert yourself to wordy sentences is to write them deliberately. For each sentence in the following exercises, give yourself 5 points if you succeed in making it wordier without adding anything to the meaning. Perfect score 100.

(1) Pad out each of the following sentences by using the passive.
    1. The football team won all of its home games last season.

2. Lock all doors and leave the keys at the desk.
3. The Valley String Quartet decided to hold extra rehearsals during the week and agreed to postpone other activities.
4. He cut the wood with his ax.
5. Some college students choose medicine as a career as early as the beginning of their sophomore year.

(2) Pad out each of the following sentences by adding dead phrases or clauses.
    1. Many writers dislike personal publicity because the lionizing keeps them from their work.
    2. The apartment rooms were small, boxlike, and painted in a hideous green.
    3. The City Council agreed to work with the Board of Education to determine the principles for zoning schools and homes.
    4. In 1960, Kennedy won by a very small majority.
    5. Sometimes I study from 8 P.M. to 2 A.M.

(3) Pad out each of the following sentences by using the verb *to be* and a clumsy complement to replace the precise verb.
    1. I like musical comedies and I collect record albums of them.
    2. David Riesman, author of *The Lonely Crowd,* thinks many Americans lack a firm sense of individuality.
    3. Mrs. Spaulder lives in Cincinnati but teaches school in the suburbs.
    4. Distance bicycling requires stamina and ten gears.
    5. He has given up cigarettes and now he feels better.

(4) Pad out each of the following sentences by expanding the modifiers into phrases and clauses.
    1. A *mano* is a hand stone for grinding corn in a large hollowed stone *metate.*
    2. A biographer lacks the artistic freedom of a novelist because the biographer cannot invent his characters or move them about as he pleases.
    3. Since Paul was tired when he took the Civil Service examination, he missed several easy questions and did poorly on familiar topics.
    4. A number of educational theories and practices still regarded as dangerously "modern" and "progressive" date back to Rousseau.
    5. If my mother, born in the Kentucky backwoods, had stayed there and spoken only with her childhood friends, she would never have had to change her speech habits; only when she

moved north and began associating with teachers and business people did she realize how much people scorned her grammar and pronunciation.

Exercise 9

Reduce the wordiness in the following student sentences. Be prepared to explain your changes.

1. It is my intention to be affiliated with some large automobile manufacturer in connection with sales of cars and accessories.
2. There are all too many instances of condemnation of a person by his fellow men before "sufficient knowledge" has been found.
3. I was especially interested in going to the University of Southern California because of the fact that it was near home.
4. Respect is the individual's personal ability to be aware of another person's unique individuality.
5. Owing to the fact that quick action was taken by this employer, a major crisis was averted.
6. He is often thought to have a lack of responsibility; hence, he is not trusted to any great extent by those who know him.
7. I am now very sorry that I didn't find reading a meaningful and worthwhile experience when I was younger.
8. The reason that Lincoln kept in close contact with his generals by writing them letters was that he felt that he was responsible as commander-in-chief for the running of the war.

Exercise 10

This is a brief review exercise: Make the following sentences more forceful by proper subordination and the elimination of trailing construction, anticlimactic constructions, and unnecessary words.

1. The common cold is a communicable disease which can be passed on by one person to another.
2. Political scientists attempt to regard political events with an unbiased attitude, attempting also to find and apply scientific principles which are valid.
3. Our whole civilization is becoming very lax—lax about raising our children, lax about crime rates, lax about credit buying.

4. In assessing the local political situation, one cannot leave out of account the fact that Roberts won over Mrs. Ackwell by a majority of the voters who went to the polls.

5. She is certainly not worried about her financial resources, for she puts on an act at the Flamingo Club, bringing her in over $500 a week.

6. Parts of Asia and Europe have already become communistic, but the people in the countries which have turned communist do not know what communism is in its pure form, I think.

Coherent Sentences 6

A sentence is coherent when its various parts are properly connected and when the relationships between the parts are clear to a reader. To the writer, who knows what is being said, the parts of a sentence always seem to be connected. To the reader, however, implied connections may not always be clear. Lacking the writer's advantage of knowing the meaning in advance, the reader may be baffled by ambiguous reference of pronouns, by misplaced or dangling modifiers, by needless shifts in tense, and by faulty parallel construction. At the very least, he will be irritated by incoherent sentences; at worst, he will misunderstand them.

The time to check sentences for coherence is in revision. Ask yourself, "Could this sentence be misread or misunderstood?" instead of just hoping that someone will understand it. If there is any doubt, revise the sentence.

6a Parallel Structure

When the parts of a sentence are properly connected, any native speaker of the language will recognize the pattern as acceptable. We are used to having nouns connected by *and*: "bacon and eggs" or "bacon, eggs, and a waffle," where the *and* is implied between the first two elements of the series. Likewise, three prepositional phrases in a series is a normal pattern: "of the people, by the people, and for the people."

Elements in this kind of series pattern or any two elements properly connected by *and* have the same grammatical function and are said to be in parallel construction. A noun phrase can be parallel with another noun phrase; a subordinate clause can parallel another subordinate clause, but not a participle. John Ruskin lists the qualities required of great art in four subordinate clauses:

For as

(1) the choice of the high subject involves all conditions of right moral choice, and as
(2) the love of beauty involves all conditions of right admiration, and as
(3) the grasp of truth involves all strength of sense, evenness of judgment, and honesty of purpose, and as
(4) the poetical power involves all swiftness of invention, and accuracy of the historical memory,

the sum of all these powers is the sum of the human soul.

We use parallel structure constantly in our speech, joining two or more compound (that is, parallel) verbs or adjectives or phrases or clauses by one of the coordinating conjunctions, most often *and*. A single sentence can contain many kinds of parallel structure; note the parallel noun phrases within clauses (3) and (4) of Ruskin's statement.

(1) Coordinating Conjunctions

Sentence elements jointed by the coordinating conjunctions *and, or, nor, but* should be in parallel grammatical structure.

FAULTY He likes to swim in the summer and skiing in the winter.
Here an infinitive is incorrectly paralleled with a gerund.

PARALLEL He likes *to swim* in the summer and *to ski* in the winter. *Or* He likes *swimming* in the summer and *skiing* in the winter.

FAULTY Every player is taught to work with the team and that good sportsmanship must be shown.
Here and *joins an infinitive phrase and a subordinate clause beginning with* that.

PARALLEL Every player is taught *to work* with the team and *to show* good sportsmanship.

(2) Elements in a Series

Faulty parallelism of elements in a series is one of the commonest faults in coherence.

FAULTY I concluded that she was intelligent, witty, and liked to make people uncomfortable.

The first two elements are adjectives: the second is a predicate—a verb with an infinitive phrase as a complement.

The faulty parallelism can be corrected by making all three elements adjectives:

PARALLEL I concluded that she was intelligent, witty, and malicious.

Or the sentence can be corrected by inserting another "and" to make clear which elements parallel which.

PARALLEL I concluded that she was intelligent *and* witty and liked to make people uncomfortable.

FAULTY Harrison signed up as the camp counselor in charge of evening programs, swimming, sailing, and to lead occasional overnight hikes.

PARALLEL Harrison signed up as the camp counselor in charge of evening programs, swimming, sailing, and occasional overnight hikes.

(3) Repetition of Words

To make a parallel construction clear, you may need to repeat a conjunction, preposition, or other preceding word.

FAULTY The advisor told the girl that she spent far too much time in useless fretting and she needed confidence in herself.

The omission of "that" to introduce the second subordinate clause causes misreading.

PARALLEL The advisor told the girl *that* she spent far too much time in useless fretting *and that* she needed confidence in herself.

FAULTY Frank needed Elaine because she was his reminder of his past glory and she would also help get him into the right circles through her family.

PARALLEL Frank needed Elaine *because* she was his reminder of his past glory *and because* she would also help him get into the right circles through her family.

FAULTY The vineyard is often visited by tourists who sample the grapes and connoisseurs of wine.

PARALLEL   The vineyard is often visited *by* tourists who sample the grapes *and by* connoisseurs of wine.

(4) Correlatives

Some conjunctions, called correlatives, occur in pairs: *either . . . or, neither . . . nor, not only . . . but also, both . . . and.* Be sure to place the first correlative so that the construction which follows will parallel the construction following the second correlative. That is, if you write "James is not only ....*a*.... but also ...*b*......," be sure that *a* and *b* are in parallel structure.

FAULTY   Blake is not only famous for his poetry but also for his illustrations.
"Not only" is followed by the adjective "famous" with a prepositional phrase modifying it. "But also" is followed by a prepositional phrase. Correct this by moving "not only."

PARALLEL   Blake is famous *not only* for his poetry *but also* for his illustrations.

FAULTY   He either is a liar or a remarkably naive person.

PARALLEL   He is either a liar or a remarkably naive person.

FAULTY   The Legislature hoped both to raise taxes and stimulate business.
Placing "both" after "to" would make the two verbs parallel but it would produce an awkward split construction: "to both raise . . ." A smoother sentence would result from adding another "to."

IMPROVED   The Legislature hoped both to raise taxes and to stimulate business.

(5) Subordinate Clauses

A subordinate clause should not be connected to its main clause by *and* or *but.*

FAULTY   She is a woman of strong convictions and who always says what she thinks.
This error can be corrected either by omitting the coordinating conjunction:

CORRECT   She is a woman of strong convictions, who always says what she thinks.

or by writing two subordinate clauses:

PARALLEL   She is a woman who has strong convictions and who always says what she thinks.

FAULTY   In the middle of the sleepy village is a statue dating from 1870 *and which* shows General Lee on horseback.

PARALLEL   In the middle of the sleepy village is a statue *which* dates from 1870 *and which* shows General Lee on horseback.

FAULTY   *He* appeared before the committee with a long written statement, *but which* he was not allowed to read.

CORRECT   *He* appeared before the committee with a long written statement, *but he* was not allowed to read it.

Fault corrected by changing relative clause to a main clause.

(6) Sequence of Ideas

To be effective, elements in parallel structure should be parallel in sense. Used carelessly, parallel structure can lead to an illogical series or an awkward sequence of ideas.

INCOHERENT   His slumping business, his friends, and even his wife Mary could in no way offer him a chance to find the happiness he had known while in college.

The three items are not parallel in meaning. A man might reasonably be expected to find a chance for happiness in those closest to him, his friends and his wife. But he would hardly be expected to find happiness in a "slumping business."

REVISED   His friends and even his wife Mary could in no way offer him a chance to find the happiness he had known while in college.

MISLEADING   During her last year in law school, she rose to the top of her class, worked on the legal review, and married the day after graduation.

REVISED   During her last year in law school, she rose to the top of her class and worked on the legal review. She married the day after graduation.

Exercise 1

Revise the following sentences by giving parallel structure to coordinate ideas.

1. The bandleader told us to wear our uniforms next time and that we should expect a long rehearsal.
2. Among the primitive uses of fire were protection from wild animals and for preparing food.

3. When I was in grade school, my parents spent a lot of time on my homework with me, and then when I got to high school letting me do it myself.
4. The columnist argued that sports stars should be well paid because of their relatively short period of greatness and that they must achieve security for later on.
5. The congressman said we need comprehensive federal pollution laws to make enforcement easier and also for standardizing the regulations passed by individual states.

Exercise 2

Identify the cause of faulty parallelism in each of the following sentences and make the needed correction.

1. Applicants for the position must be United States citizens, willing to work abroad, and qualify under security regulations.
2. In the remedial reading clinic he learned how to coordinate his eye movements, how to scan for information, and how frequent reviewing for key ideas helps.
3. The opera's opening performance was spirited, colorful, and with many people attending.
4. During the summer, they planned to hitchhike along Route 40, to stop at interesting places, and take sidetrips whenever they felt like it.
5. John Brown was either regarded as a patriotic martyr or a crazed fanatic.
6. The flasks were difficult to fill, not only because their necks were narrow but also they were slippery and hard to hold.
7. The bumper crop of rice neither helped the farmer nor were the customers helped.
8. At the campground we met a Mr. Osborn from somewhere near San Francisco and who had his whole family with him.
9. And on these hunting trips, Sam teaches the boy when to kill and when not to, ability, patience, and endurance.
10. If you get ambitious, you might even shoot nine holes of golf from your new four-cylinder golf cart, or with your neighbor go bowling at that new air-conditioned alley, or you might even go and play miniature golf.

6b   Faulty Reference of Pronouns

The antecedent of every pronoun—the person or thing to which the pronoun refers—should be immediately clear to the reader. Try to put yourself in the position of the person reading your sentences. If the pronoun is too far away from its antecedent, or if there are two possible antecedents, a reader may be uncertain of your meaning. Reading the first draft of a paper aloud may help you to catch pronouns with doubtful antecedents.

(1) Ambiguous Reference

Do not use a pronoun in such a way that it might refer to either of two antecedents. If there is any possibility of doubt, revise the sentence to remove the ambiguity.

AMBIGUOUS   Virginia told her sister that she was unforgiving.

Who was unforgiving—Virginia or her sister?

CLEAR   Virginia confessed to her sister, "I am unforgiving."

CLEAR   Virginia said to her sister, "You are unforgiving."

AMBIGUOUS   In *Nostromo* Conrad's style is ironic and his setting is highly symbolic, so that it sometimes confuses the reader.

Does "it" refer loosely to Nostromo, *Conrad's style, his setting, or a combination of these?*

CLEAR   Conrad's ironic style and highly symbolic setting in *Nostromo* sometimes confuse the reader.

CLEAR   In *Nostromo,* Conrad's style is ironic, and his highly symbolic setting sometimes confuses the reader.

(2) Remote Reference

A pronoun too far away from its antecedent may cause misreading. Either repeat the antecedent or revise the sentence.

REMOTE   Two major highways converge at the sign, each lined with huge, ugly billboards rising above the corn stalks and obscuring the gently rolling hills. It is a convenient location for hitching rides.

The pronoun "it" is too far removed from its antecedent, "sign."

CLEAR   Two major highways converge at the sign, each lined with huge . . . . The *sign* is a convenient location for hitching rides.
Antecedent repeated.

CLEAR   Two major highways converge at the sign, a convenient location for hitching rides. Each highway is lined . . . .
The sentences have been recast.

REMOTE   The waitress locked the door, slapped at the flies, and then sat down wearily to rest for a minute before cleaning up the litter. But they gave her no peace.
The antecedent, "flies," is too remote.

CLEAR   The waitress locked the door, slapped at the flies . . . . *But* the *flies* gave her no peace.

CONFUSING   The Tzotzil Indians are only nominal Catholics, using its symbols and adapting them to the traditional Mayan religion.
Antecedent of "its" has to be inferred from the noun "Catholics."

CLEAR   The Tzotzil Indians are only nominal Catholics, using the symbols and names *of the Church* and adapting them . . . .

MISLEADING   The botanist told us the plants' names which were all around us.

CLEAR   The botanist told us the names of the *plants which* were all around us.

(3) Awkward Use of *his or her*

A problem arises from the fact that English has no singular pronoun to refer generically to both male and female persons. Strictly speaking, one would logically follow a noun like "student" with "his or her" or even "his/her," to indicate that the term "student" includes members of both sexes. But to write "Each student is responsible for his/her books," is awkward, and many people feel that even "his or her books" is repetitious.

In the past it has been accepted that the masculine pronoun can stand for both sexes: "Each student is responsible for his books," just as *man* has been understood to mean the human race, including both men and women. Recently, however, writers and publishers have begun to eliminate discriminatory language practices—words or constructions that may reflect the dominance of the male in western society. Women argue, with justice, that they are being ignored when a writer uses *his* to refer to both men and women, and many feel that terms like *congressman* or *policeman* help to perpetuate the false assumption that these positions are occupied only by men.

To avoid this, substitute alternative terms with no indication of gender, like *member of congress, representative* or *senator, police officer.* The plural pronouns *they, their, them* and neutral terms like *one, person, people* may also be used.

ACCEPTABLE Students are responsible for their books.

People in England like unchilled beer. (Instead of "The Englishman likes his beer unchilled.")

In England one usually drinks unchilled beer.

However, in order to avoid strained circumlocutions or awkward plurals, it may at times be preferable to use *his* to mean both his and hers, as it has done for centuries.

(4) Loose Use of *this, that,* or *which*

In informal usage, the relative pronouns *this, that,* and *which* are frequently used to refer to the whole idea of a preceding clause or sentence. In formal usage, these pronouns are usually expected to have a particular word as their antecedent. No hard and fast rules can be given here. Sometimes the broad reference is clear and a change would be awkward.

ACCEPTABLE BROAD REFERENCE The game ended a little before ten, which gave us plenty of time to catch our train home.

ACCEPTABLE BROAD REFERENCE At first glance, the desert seems completely barren of animal life, but this is an illusion.

Frequently, however, broad reference makes a sentence sound awkward. It may also be ambiguous if the preceding clause contains a noun which might be mistaken for the antecedent. If you are in doubt, recast the sentence to eliminate the pronoun or give the pronoun a definite antecedent.

LOOSE The beginning of the book is more interesting than the conclusion, which is very unfortunate.

On the first reading, the pronoun "which" seems to refer to "conclusion," although it is intended to refer to the whole main clause.

CLEAR Unfortunately, the beginning of the book is more interesting than the conclusion.

The misleading pronoun has been eliminated.

LOOSE   In the eighteenth century, more and more land was converted into pasture, which had been going on to some extent for several centuries.

CLEAR   In the eighteenth century, more and more land was converted into pasture, *a process which* had been going on to some extent for several centuries.

The vague reference has been corrected by the inclusion of the summarizing noun "process" to give the pronoun "which" an antecedent.

(5) Indefinite Use of *it, they,* and *you*

English contains a number of idiomatic expressions in which the impersonal use of the pronoun *it* is correct: "It is hot," "it rained all day," "it is late." The pronoun *it* is also used correctly in sentences like "It seems best to go home at once," in which *it* anticipates the real subject, *to go home at once.* Avoid, however, the unexplained *it,* the *it* that needs a clear antecedent and has none.

VAGUE   Our neighbor was a semiprofessional golfer who took every spare moment he could get to practice *it.*

CLEAR   Our neighbor was a semiprofessional golfer who took every spare moment he could get to practice *his game.*

The indefinite use of *they* is always vague and usually sounds childish.

VAGUE   If intercollegiate sports were banned, they would have to develop an elaborate intramural program.

CLEAR   If intercollegiate sports were banned, *each college* would have to develop an elaborate intramural program.

VAGUE   They are finally beginning to pave the street outside our house.

CLEAR   The street outside our house is finally being paved.

CLEAR   The city is finally beginning to pave the street outside our house.

The indefinite use of the pronoun *you* to refer to people in general is widespread: "In Sparta you had to be strong to survive." Formal usage, however, still prefers the impersonal pronoun *one* or a passive verb unless the context clearly implies a definite audience or person addressed.

INFORMAL   You shouldn't take sulfa drugs without a doctor's prescription.

FORMAL   One should not take sulfa drugs without a doctor's prescription.

STANDARD   Sulfa drugs should not be taken without a doctor's prescription.

Exercise 3

Revise the following sentences to correct the ambiguous reference of pronouns.

1. The runner lunged towards the tape, threw out his chest, and snapped it.
2. In the course of the argument, Jack told his father that he needed a new car.
3. It wouldn't hurt people to read about criminals because they live in a different kind of world and they don't have to follow their example.
4. Both parents were there when the twin brothers graduated together, and we couldn't help noticing how happy they were.
5. Under Roosevelt's leadership, the Democratic party, which had not really been united under one president for some years, came together effectively for a time. Historians tend to agree that this was a case of the right man at the right moment.
6. The hives buzzed with activity, and the beekeeper covered himself with netting before going after the honey and then motioned for us to follow at a distance. It was about fifty feet away.
7. In Joyce's novel, he delights in complex puns and in playing with words.
8. The spider gently shook the strands of his web as he scurried towards the fly and the moth. Although they were barely visible, they were obviously strong.
9. Engineering is the profession that applies scientific knowlege to the building of such things as bridges, harbors, and communication systems. This is my ambition.
10. Ethics must not be understood to be the same thing as honor because this is not the case.
11. When there is no harmony in the home, the child is the first to feel it.
12. Most of the students at the work camp were inexperienced, and many of them had never seen raw poverty before, but on the whole they were up to it.
13. It says in the brochure that in England they drink tea instead of coffee.

14. Fielding's *Shamela* successfully used farcical incident and character development as tools for his satire in the novel.

15. Since the white settlers held the Indians to be of no significant value, they regarded their rights as equally nonexistent. This is exemplified by several incidents in Kroeber's account.

6c Dangling Modifiers

A modifier is "dangling" when there is no word in the sentence for it to modify.

In the sentence "Swimming out into the lake, the water felt cold," the writer took it for granted that the reader would assume someone was swimming. But the only noun in the main clause is *water,* and the participial phrase cannot logically modify *water*—the *water* was not *swimming out into the lake.*

Note the position of the dangling modifier: almost all dangling modifiers occur at the beginning of a sentence. They can be corrected in either of two ways:

(1) By supplying the noun or the pronoun which the phrase logically modifies:

    modifier   *word modified*
    Swimming out into the lake,   **I** felt the water grow colder.

(2) Or by changing the dangling construction into a complete clause:

    As I swam out into the lake, the water felt colder.

(1) Dangling Participial Phrases

           modifier   *word modified*

DANGLING   **Walking** along the trestle,   a **train** suddenly appeared.
    The sentence is grammatically illogical: do trains walk?

IMPROVED   **Walking** along the trestle, **I** suddenly saw a train.

IMPROVED   **As I** walked along the trestle, a train suddenly appeared.
    In this sentence the introductory clause modifies the verb appeared.

DANGLING The mountains were snow-covered and cloudless, *flying* over the Rockies.

Dangling modifiers at the end of a sentence are less frequent than those at the beginning, but they are often confusing and always awkward.

IMPROVED When *I* flew over the Rockies, the mountains were snow-covered and cloudless.

IMPROVED *Flying* over the Rockies, we saw snow-covered, cloudless mountains.

DANGLING Having followed directions carefully, my *cake* was a great success.

IMPROVED Since *I* had followed directions carefully, my cake was a great success.

(2) Dangling Gerunds

DANGLING After *explaining* my errand to the guard, an automatic *gate* swung open to let me in.

The gate can't explain; one must infer the subject of "explaining."

IMPROVED After *I* had explained my errand to the guard, an automatic gate swung open to let me in.

DANGLING Before *climbing* the mountain, our *lunches* were packed in bags.

Note that a change from the active to the passive voice will often correct the dangling modifier.

IMPROVED Before *climbing* the mountain, *we* packed our lunches in bags.

(3) Dangling Infinitives

DANGLING *To be considered* for college, the aptitude *test* must be taken.

IMPROVED To be considered for college, a *student* must take the aptitude test.

DANGLING In order to become a top entertainer, all types of audiences must be pleased.

"All types of audiences" are not going to become "a top entertainer."

IMPROVED In order to become a top entertainer, an *actor* must please all types of audiences.

The agent capable of the act is specified.

(4) Dangling Elliptical Clauses

Subject and main verb are sometimes omitted from a dependent clause (*while going* instead of *while I was going*, or *when a child* instead of *when he was a child*). If the subject of such an elliptical clause is not stated in the rest of the sentence, the construction may dangle.

DANGLING   When six years old, my grandmother died.

DANGLING   At the age of six, my grandmother died.

In both examples, the implied subject of the elliptical clause, "I," is omitted. Correct the dangling modifier by including subject and verb.

IMPROVED   When *I was* six, my grandmother died.

DANGLING   While sleeping, the covers were kicked off her bed.

The implied subject of the elliptical clause is "she." Make it the subject of the main clause.

IMPROVED   While sleeping, *she kicked* the covers off her bed.

An alternative method is to make the implied subject of the elliptical clause the subject of a dependent clause:

IMPROVED   While *she* was asleep, *she kicked* the covers off her bed.

DANGLING   Do not apply the paint until thoroughly stirred.

IMPROVED   Do not apply the paint until *it* has been thoroughly stirred.

(5) Permissible Introductory Expressions

Some verbal phrases, like *in the first place, judging from past experience, considering the situation, granted the results,* or *to sum up,* have become well-established as introductory phrases and need not be attached to any particular noun.

ACCEPTABLE   Judging from past experience, he is not to be trusted.

ACCEPTABLE   Granted the results, what do they prove?

ACCEPTABLE   To sum up, all evidence suggests the decision was a fair one.

An absolute phrase consists of a participle with a subject (and sometimes a complement) grammatically unconnected with the rest of the sentence and usually telling when, why, or how something happened. It is not a dangling modifier.

CORRECT   The floodwater having receded, people began returning to their homes.

CORRECT   The weather being warm, we took light sleeping bags with us.

Exercise 4

Revise the following sentences to eliminate the dangling modifiers.

1. When waiting for the dentist, every sound from the office is nerve-wracking.
2. After correcting my original calculations, the problem was finally solved.
3. Having seen Beckett's *Waiting for Godot,* my attitude toward modern drama has changed completely.
4. The directions were clear, and my trouble could have been prevented, if followed correctly.
5. After hurrying to answer the phone, the operator told the woman the other party had hung up.
6. In order to see the comet in detail, a small telescope was set up in the backyard.
7. The zoning petition was widely supported, after having canvassed many people in the neighborhood and stirred up concern about the proposed high-rise apartment building.
8. Being covered with plastic, I did not expect the car seats would be cool, having sat in the hot parking lot for several hours.
9. At last able to earn my car insurance, my parents allowed me to buy my own car.
10. Although tired and out of practice, the last set of the tennis match was too much of a personal challenge for me to resist.

6d   Misplaced Modifiers

Since word order is often crucial to meaning in English, try to place modifiers as close as possible to the words they are intended to modify. Consider, for example, what happens in the following sentence when the adverb *only* is moved about in it:

The notice said *only* [said *merely*] that clients were invited to see the exhibit on the third floor.

The notice said that *only* clients [clients *alone*] were invited to see the exhibit on the third floor.

The notice said that clients were invited *only* [invited for the one purpose] to see the exhibit on the third floor.

The notice said that clients were invited to see the exhibit on the third floor *only* [third floor *alone*].

Most modifying phrases and clauses can be moved around to various positions in the sentence. An introductory clause, for example, can be shifted from the beginning of a sentence to the middle or the end.

Whatever the public may think, I am sure that Picasso will be remembered as one of the greatest artists of our times.

I am sure, *whatever the public may think,* that Picasso will be remembered as one of the greatest artists of our times.

I am sure that Picasso will be remembered as one of the greatest artists of our times, *whatever the public may think.*

This freedom, however, has its dangers. Movable modifiers may be placed so as to produce misreadings or real ambiguities. Unlike the dangling modifier, which cannot logically modify any word in the sentence, the misplaced modifier may seem to modify the wrong word or phrase in the sentence:

AMBIGUOUS   He sent us the full story of his rescue from the Ozarks.

The phrase "from the Ozarks" should be placed closer to the word it is meant to modify, "sent."

CLEAR   He sent us from the Ozarks the full story of his rescue.

AMBIGUOUS   Peacefully nibbling on the lawn, Jim finally found his pet rabbit.

To prevent an image of Jim grazing on the lawn, put the modifying phrase as close as possible to "rabbit."

CLEAR   Jim finally found his pet rabbit peacefully nibbling on the lawn.

(1) Misplaced Adverbs

AMBIGUOUS   I have followed the advice *faithfully* given by the manual.

REVISED   I have *faithfully* followed the advice given by the manual.

The adverb has been placed nearer the word it is intended to modify.

AMBIGUOUS   The woman scolded the boy for playing with matches *severely.*

REVISED   The woman *severely* scolded the boy for playing with matches.

(2) Misplaced Phrases and Clauses

MISPLACED PHRASE   He lost the chance to make large profits *through the work of imitators and plagiarists.*

CLEAR   *Through the work of imitators and plagiarists,* he lost a chance to make large profits.

MISPLACED PHRASE   Hamlet stabs Laertes with a poisoned sword *in the last act.*

CLEAR   *In the last act* Hamlet stabs Laertes with a poisoned sword.

MISPLACED CLAUSE   He searched around and found an old bus schedule in the drawer *that was out of date.*

CLEAR   He searched around and found in the drawer an old bus schedule *that was out of date.*

(3) Squinting Modifiers

Avoid placing a modifier in such a position that it may refer to either a preceding word or a following word.

SQUINTING   The child who lies *in nine cases out of ten* is frightened.

CLEAR   *In nine cases out of ten,* the child who lies is frightened.

SQUINTING   The tailback who injured his knee *recently* returned to regular practice.

CLEAR   The tailback who *recently* injured his knee returned to regular practice.

CLEAR   The tailback who injured his knee returned *recently* to regular practice.

(4) Split Constructions and Infinitives

Avoid separating the parts of tight grammatical constructions. Separating the parts of a verb phrase or an infinitive by an inserted modifier can give the reader an awkward jolt.

AWKWARD   The operator told him that he *should, if he expected to get his call through, place* it soon.
The verb phrase is needlessly broken up by the modifier.

IMPROVED   The operator told him that he *should place* his call soon *if he expected to get it through.*

AWKWARD   *I, more than the rest of my family, **have been losing** sleep* since we got a color television set.

Try reading this sentence aloud to see why a single pronoun subject should not be separated from its verb and complement.

IMPROVED   *More than the rest of my family, **I have been losing** sleep* since we got a color television set.

Split infinitives—that is, infinitives with a modifier between the *to* and the verb (*to personally supervise*)—may be awkward, especially if the modifier is long.

AWKWARD   I should like *to, if I ever get the chance, **take*** a trip to Mexico.

IMPROVED   I should like **to take** a trip to Mexico *if I ever get the chance.*

Frequently, however, an adverb fits naturally between the two parts of an infinitive:

ACCEPTABLE   Some young couples regard children as a nuisance, but as they grow older they begin **to actually look** forward to having a family.

If the modifier is moved, the emphasis is slightly changed: ". . . but as they grow older they actually begin to look forward. . . ."

ACCEPTABLE   We expect in the coming year **to more than double** our assets.

Exercise 5

Revise the following sentences to correct misplaced words, phrases, and clauses.

1. She wore a ribbon in her hair which was a light pink.
2. The film about the life of the sea otter which I saw downtown was very interesting.
3. He wrote his book on gambling in Iowa.
4. We camped in a small shelter near the edge of the cliff which had not been used for months.
5. Bread which rises rapidly too often will have a coarse texture.
6. The dean told me I could return to school in a high rage.
7. He was hit by a rotten egg walking back to his apartment one night.
8. Wild and primitive, with hidden snags and rapids on one side, jungle and savage natives on the other, danger is ever present.
9. I promised during the evening to call her.
10. Often she would spend hours on the edge of the beach watching her small son build a sand castle with half-closed eyes.

Exercise 6

Revise the following sentences to correct the split constructions.

1. At the end of the period we were told to promptly hand in our bluebooks.
2. The pharmacist told her she should, since she needed the medicine in such a hurry, have the doctor phone in the prescription.
3. The term *reactionary* can be applied to political, social, or economic (or a combination of the three) beliefs.
4. After nicking a submerged rock, the canoe began to slowly but steadily leak and to gradually settle deeper in the water.
5. She told him to for Heaven's sake shut up.

 Confusing Shifts

Consistency of structure makes sentences easier to read. If the first clause of a sentence is in the active voice, do not shift to the passive voice in the second clause unless there is good reason for the change. Similarly, avoid shifts in tense, mood, or person within a sentence unless they reflect an intentional shift in focus.

(1) Confusing Shifts of Voice or Subject

Shifting from the active to the passive voice almost always involves a change in subject; thus a shift in voice may make a sentence doubly awkward.

SHIFT IN SUBJECT AND VOICE   After *I* finally *discovered* an unsoldered wire, the *dismantling* of the motor *was begun.*

The subject shifts from "I" to "dismantling." The voice shifts from the active "discovered" to the passive "was begun."

CONSISTENT   After I finally discovered an unsoldered wire, *I dismantled* the motor.

The sentence would be logically consistent if both verbs were in the passive voice: "After an unsoldered wire was found, the motor was dismantled." But the passive voice is unnecessary here.

SHIFT IN VOICE   *He left* the examination after his answer *had been proofread.*

Who proofread the answer?

CONSISTENT   He left the examination after *he had proofread* his answer.

CONFUSING SHIFT IN SUBJECT   As the guests entered the church, appropriate seats were assigned by the ushers conducting them.

IMPROVED   As the guests entered the church, they were conducted to appropriate seats by the ushers.

(2) Confusing Shifts of Person or Number

A common shift in student writing is from the third person (*he, she, they, one*) to the second person (*you*); another is from a singular number (*a person, one, he*) to a plural (*they*). These errors usually occur when the writer has no particular individual in mind but is thinking of anybody or everybody and is stating some vague general truth applicable to all.

CONFUSING SHIFT IN PERSON   When *you* try hard enough, *one* can do almost anything.
Confusing shift from the second to the third person.

CONSISTENT   When *you* try hard enough, *you* can do almost anything.

CONSISTENT   When *one* tries hard enough, *one* [or *he*] can do almost anything.

CONFUSING SHIFT IN PERSON   *I* could find only one fault with my new gun. When *you* fired it, gas would leak through the action.
Confusing shift from first to second person.

CONSISTENT   *I* could find only one fault with my new gun. When *I* fired it, gas leaked through the action.

CONFUSING SHIFT IN NUMBER   When *a person* gets an early start, *they* can work more efficiently.
Confusing shift from singular to plural number.

CONSISTENT   When *a person* gets an early start, *he* can work more efficiently.

(3) Confusing Shifts of Mood or Tense

If you begin a sentence with an order or command (*imperative* mood), do not shift without reason to a statement (*indicative* mood).

CONFUSING SHIFT IN MOOD   First stir in the flour; then you should add the butter and salt.

The first clause is an order, the imperative mood; the second clause is a statement giving advice, the indicative mood.

CONSISTENT   First stir in the flour; then add the butter and salt.
Both clauses in the imperative mood.

ACCEPTABLE   After you have stirred in the flour, add the butter and salt.
First clause modifies the imperative verb "add."

If you begin a sentence in the past tense, do not switch to the present unless you have good reason to do so.

CONFUSING SHIFT IN TENSE   I *stood* on the starting block and *looked* tensely at the water below; for the first time in my life I *am* about to swim the 50-yard freestyle in competition.
Confusing shift from past to present.

CONSISTENT   I *stood* on the starting block and *looked* . . . I *was* about to swim . . . .

CONSISTENT   I *stand* on the starting block and *look* . . . I *am* about to swim . . . .

CONFUSING SHIFT IN TENSE   At the beginning of the *Divine Comedy*, Dante *finds* that he has strayed from the True Way into the Dark Wood of Error. As soon as he *realized* this, Dante *lifted* his eyes in hope to the rising sun.
When you use the historical present, the tense normally used for summarizing plots of narratives, take special care not to lapse into the past tense.

CONSISTENT   At the beginning of the *Divine Comedy*, Dante *finds* that he has strayed from the True Way into the Dark Wood of Error. As soon as he *has realized* this, Dante *lifts* his eyes in hope to the rising sun.

Exercise 7

Correct shifts in voice, person, number, mood, or tense in the following sentences.

1. After I finished planting my garden, the seeds were watered daily.
2. The matinee was enjoyed by all the children because they saw two monster films.
3. A person can always find something to criticize if they look hard enough.
4. In the school I attended, you had just five minutes between

classes, and that was not enough time for most of us.

5. Don't ride the clutch; you should keep your left foot off the pedal.

6. Because he was so naive, Candide listens to almost anybody he meets.

7. Parson Adams went to London to try to sell his sermons and finds out that people are neither kind nor generous; he does not worry about taking money with him because he thought that people would be hospitable to him.

8. Thus, in *The Way of All Flesh,* Butler is telling his readers to look ahead; he tells them not to be caught without knowing what is going on around you.

9. Of course, knowing how to use one's leisure is also important, but I do not think that it is up to the college to more or less arrange your social life, as many colleges do.

10. Fifty years ago, your house was the center of your everyday life; today, we Americans practically live in our cars.

6f   Mixed Constructions

Do not begin a sentence with one construction and conclude it with another. English is full of alternative constructions, and it is easy to confuse them in a first draft and to produce a monster with the head of one sentence and the tail of another.

MIXED   By requiring citizens to install pollution controls in their cars is one way to protect the air we breathe.

As it stands, the sentence begins with a modifying phrase which is then used as the subject of the verb is.

CORRECT   By requiring citizens to install pollution controls in their cars, we can protect the air we breathe.

CORRECT   Requiring citizens to install pollution controls in their cars is one way to protect the air we breathe.

(1) Dependent Clauses Used as Subjects or Complements

Using a dependent clause as subject or complement of a verb can produce a badly mixed construction.

MIXED   Because he ran out of gas made him late for work.

CORRECT   Because he ran out of gas, he was late for work.

CORRECT   Running out of gas made him late for work.

(2) Adverbial Clauses Used as Nouns

A frequent cause of mixed construction is the illogical use of "when" or "where" as part of the complement of "is"—the "is when" or "is where" habit:

MIXED   One thing which keeps me from enlisting *is when* I think of kitchen police.

The clause "when I think of kitchen police" is a modifier, not a thing. What is needed to complete the sentence is some kind of substantive.

CORRECT   One thing which keeps me from enlisting **is the thought** of kitchen police.

MIXED   A fanfare *is where* trumpets are sounded.

An adverb clause is misused as a noun; the verb "is" needs a substantive here.

CORRECT   A fanfare **is a flourish** of trumpets.

Though widely used, "the reason . . . is because . . ." construction is both redundant and wordy. Instead of writing *"The reason* American teams perform well at the Olympics *is because* they have been well trained," drop either "the reason" or "is because."

CORRECT   American teams perform well at the Olympics because they have been well trained.

CORRECT   The reason American teams perform well at the Olympics is that they have been well trained.

(3) Idiomatic Comparisons

English has idiomatic ways of making comparisons, and these do not contain interchangeable parts. In making comparisons, use the same idiom throughout the sentence.

MIXED   The amateur mechanic will find plastic easier to work with than with metal.

What is easier than working with metal? Working with plastic. Write it that way.

CORRECT   The amateur mechanic will find plastic easier to work with than metal.

CORRECT   The amateur mechanic will find it easier to work with plastic than [to work] with metal.

Exercise 8

In the following student sentences, analyze the constructions that have been mixed and revise the sentences.

1. Since cheating in schools instigates distrust on so a large scale that I think all people caught cheating should be punished as a lesson to all.
2. Because Joyce's stories are written with the greatest skill makes each and every character come alive before the reader's eyes.
3. In the container is where the experiment takes place.
4. For college students, I feel that teaching assistants who read papers for the professors are really a disadvantage to the student.
5. It would be hard for me to say what the outlook on life a person with this disease would have.
6. In choosing the class play, we found small reading groups much easier to work with than with the whole committee together.
7. In my high school, which is rated as one of the best in the state, it is my opinion that it was much too easy.
8. As the volume of sound increases in the earphones, the nearer the submarine is approaching.
9. In my study of campus slang, to get an A on a test or in a course is where you "ace" it.
10. Of course, if I decide to become an engineering major doesn't mean that it is too late to change later on.
11. By defining the term "socialism" accurately will save us argument.
12. When waiting for the mail on the day a check from home is expected is very frustrating.

6g   Incomplete Constructions

Do not omit words and expressions necessary for grammatical completeness.

INCOMPLETE   Worse still, he had a seven-day journey∧the fort.
   "To" is needed to complete the meaning of the predicate.

INCOMPLETE   The very sound of the poem gives the feeling∧fleeting light and life.

"Of" completes and clarifies the predicate's meaning.

(1) Incomplete Verb Forms

When the two parts of a compound construction are in *different tenses,* the auxiliary verbs should usually be fully written in so that their meanings will be clear.

INCOMPLETE   Fishing **has** and always **will be** a profitable industry in Alaska.

"Be" is the proper auxiliary for "will" but not for "has." One cannot say "Fishing has be and always will be . . . ."

COMPLETE   Fishing **has been** and always **will be** a profitable industry in Alaska.

When there is *no change* in tense, part of a compound verb can be omitted:

ACCEPTABLE   Tickets will be sent to all students who have signed up for the trip and [who have] paid the fee.

In sentences whose predicate is the linking verb *to be,* make certain that the verb agrees with its subject in number.

INCOMPLETE   He *was lecturing* and the students *taking* notes.

The singular "was" cannot be used with the plural "students."

COMPLETE   He *was lecturing* and the students *were taking* notes.

(2) Idiomatic Prepositions

English idiom requires that certain prepositions be used with certain adjectives and verbs: we say, for example, "interested *in,*" "aware *of,*" "devoted *to.*" We expect others "to agree *with,*" or "to object *to,*" or even "to protest *against,*" our plans. Be sure to use the proper idiomatic preposition with each part of a compound construction. Your dictionary will often help here.

INCOMPLETE   He was **oblivious** and **undisturbed by** the noise around him.

COMPLETE   He was **oblivious to** and **undisturbed by** the noise around him.

INCOMPLETE   No one could have been more **interested** or **devoted to** his students than Mr. Beattes.

COMPLETE No one could have been more *interested in* or *devoted to* his students than Mr. Beattes.

(3) Incomplete and Inexact Comparisons

In comparisons do not omit words necessary to make a complete idiomatic statement.

INCOMPLETE He is as tall, if not taller, than his brother.
As it stands, the sentence says that he is "as tall . . . than his brother."

COMPLETE He is *as* tall *as* his brother, if not taller.

INCOMPLETE Leonardo had one of the greatest, if not the greatest, minds of all times.
Two idioms: "one of the greatest minds" and "the greatest mind."

COMPLETE Leonardo had one of the greatest *minds,* if not the greatest *mind,* of all time.

Comparisons should be complete, logical, and unambiguous.

INCOMPLETE Her salary was lower than a typist.
Is a typist low?

COMPLETE Her salary was lower than *that of* a typist.

COMPLETE Her salary was lower than a *typist's* [salary].

INCOMPLETE The food here costs no more than any other restaurant.
Can one buy the food and a restaurant at the same low price?

COMPLETE The food here costs no more than [it does] *at* any other restaurant.

Avoid the illogical use of *than* and *any.*

ILLOGICAL For many years the Empire State Building was taller than any building in New York.
"Any building in New York" includes the Empire State Building. Can it be taller than itself?

REVISED For many years the Empire State Building was taller than *any other* building in New York.

Make sure that the reader can tell what is being compared with what.

INEXACT Claremont is farther from Los Angeles than Pomona.

CLEAR   Claremont is farther from Los Angeles than Pomona *is.*

CLEAR   Claremont is farther from Los Angeles than *it is* from Pomona.
In the two revisions, both terms of the comparison are completely filled in.

INEXACT   Philsoc Gas gives more and better mileage for the dollar.
More than what? Mule teams? Many commercials and advertisements only pretend to give information: by conveniently omitting any standard of comparison, they do not commit themselves to any real claims.

If clearly indicated by the context, the standard of comparison need not be specified:

CLEAR   Boulder Dam is big, but the Grand Coulee Dam is bigger.

Note that the words *so, such,* and *too* when used as comparatives are completed by a phrase or clause indicating the standard of comparison.

CLEAR   I'm *so* tired *that I could drop.* I had *such* a small breakfast *that I was starving by noon,* and when we stopped for lunch, I was *too* tired *to eat.*

Exercise 9

Revise the following sentences by filling out the incomplete or illogical constructions.

1.   The Japanese are at least as inventive as the United States or Germany.
2.   Disneyland is as large, if not larger, than any other amusement park in the country.
3.   The Hondas and Yamahas weigh less and are cheaper.
4.   My father complained that his income tax was higher than last year.
5.   The distributor was cleaned and the points adjusted.
6.   Vale did some of her best work and learned a great deal from her high school history teacher.
7.   Because of their climate and soil, Florida and Texas raise more citrus than all the states put together.
8.   According to our map of Arkansas, Fort Smith is farther from Little Rock than Pine Bluff.
9.   As your Class Secretary, I have and will continue to send you all the news that I receive about the class of '71.

10. Trying to analyze my good points and weaknesses made me a happier and secure person.

Exercise 10

The following student sentences contain faults discussed in the preceding chapter on coherence—faulty parallelism, faulty reference of pronouns, dangling and misplaced modifiers, confusing shifts, and mixed and incomplete constructions. Identify the cause or causes of faulty coherence in each sentence, and then revise the sentence.

1. Entering the door, after walking up several steps made of concrete, there is a policeman sitting behind his desk, who will gladly give you any needed information.
2. The politician has dinners given, circulars printed, and attends rallies.
3. If someone knows that a certain person is a "cheat," they wouldn't want to be around them and they wouldn't trust him.
4. By the way she tells the story is indication enough of how Mansfield feels.
5. I found Charlie Macklin to be the closest thing to perfection, but at the same time still being human, than any other I have either read about or known in real life.
6. Pulled through a broken window with pieces of glass scattered about, a passing motorist rescued a woman in her home early this morning, which was blazing.
7. One advertisement shows a washing machine "growing" before our eyes to be ten feet tall, and in a different commercial for soap portrays a giant in your washer who labors to clean your clothes.
8. Some occupations in which following directions might not be important are where a person is an artist, a potter, a novelist, or some other creative artist.
9. Although surprising to students, this writer feels that in most questionable cases, the uncertainty of science should be presented for what it is.
10. While personally finding nothing to recommend Marx's system, it is fitting to examine him in order to see how and why so many people have believed in it.
11. He certainly didn't look like a man of my father's age and he certainly didn't have a particle of dignity that I so commonly associated with my father of having.

12. Paul has different ideas about schooling than the school principal.
13. Just because our campus radio station plays so much popular music is no reason for the college to cut its funds.
14. The Lilliputians are much more like the human race than the giants.
15. After being locked in the cabin about two hours, our first roll call of the evening took place.

The Paragraph as a Unit 7

Let us begin with a few simple questions about paragraphs, and let us agree that because these are simple questions, they may be hard ones. Exact definitions and pat examples would be neat, but they are unlikely to reflect the varied possibilities and uses which writers have discovered in paragraphs. So let us try to answer the following questions: What are paragraphs? What can they do? How can they be made more effective?

What are paragraphs? The standard answer is that a paragraph is both a unit in itself and part of a larger whole; that paragraphs help to indicate the structure of a composition; and that paragraph division is a conventional sign that one point is completed, the next point about to begin. So far as it goes, the answer is true enough. What a word is to a sentence, or a sentence to a paragraph, the paragraph may be to an essay, a story, or a chapter—a part which is integral to the whole and which gains its full meaning from the whole. Or, like certain words ("Ouch!") and sentences ("Trespassers will be prosecuted"), a paragraph can stand alone, more or less contented and self-contained—a gem of an answer, a smug point of view, another way of looking at things. What, then, is insufficient about the standard answer? Nothing, except that it suggests paragraphing is like drawing static squares:

We still want to know about the different ways the boxes can be made to hold a variety of things:

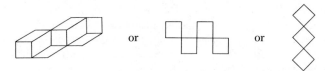

We will take up these considerations in the second and third questions and, later, in Chapter 8 on "Effective Paragraphs."

What can paragraphs do? Well, we know they break up a page of type and make it more readable: they provide both focus and rest stops for the reader. They isolate individual features of a landscape the writer wishes to look at, and thus they allow both writer and reader to linger over—or hurry by—this feature. Too many paragraphs, like too many commands to "See this!" "Note that!" and "Look here!," fragment our attention and make us glance at a page superficially. Too few paragraphs in a work, like the guide who wants us to take in the whole landscape at once, lead us to see nothing clearly. Most beginners probably want to look at too many things too quickly, or else skip from one sight to another because they don't know how to focus. In either case, the consequences are brief, fuzzy paragraphs. We need not only to look more steadily and fully at the individual parts but also to study the way each part contributes to the total impression.

Paragraphs single out, connect, and control tempo. But they obviously do other things. They help tell stories, describe processes, distinguish differences, report findings, and push conclusions. They help clarify feelings, understand motives, and excite emotions. Paragraphs *make something happen*. When we are writing well, we find that we are getting into our subject and discovering new connections and examples as we go along. On such lucky occasions, we usually paragraph by the dynamic feel that one section is complete and that we're eager to get on with the next one, which is already teasing our consciousness. Later, during the rewriting and revision ("re-seeing"), we combine, break up, thin out, or rework our paragraphs more systematically. We now have an overall view, a clear structure, to work with and to improve.

Finally, how can paragraphs be made more effective? As far as any short discussion can answer this, the next chapter will suggest some techniques for improving paragraphs, and it will point to some models used (often unconsciously) by experienced writers to accomplish particular ends. One trait of any effective paragraph is that it is *unified,* and we can ask certain questions (after the writing) that help ensure unity: Does the paragraph read smoothly? Does it hang together? Unified paragraphs are not magically created by indented openings or by other graphic devices, but they do have certain elements we can look for.

7a Paragraph Division

As a unit in itself, each paragraph should deal with a single topic or aspect of a topic. It should have a central idea or purpose, and each sentence in the paragraph should aid in developing this central idea and making it clear. But before you test for unity in any single paragraph, you should consider the relationship of that paragraph to the work as a whole. *The essential principle in dividing material into paragraphs is making sure that each paragraph will show a significant turn in your thought.* (If you have been working from an outline, check back and be sure that your paragraphs come at important points in it).

One way to achieve unity in paragraphs is by a careful analysis of the material and the coverage of the thesis statement. This technique works especially well when you can discriminate distinct stages or steps in a process, distinct requirements for a particular position or job, distinct aspects of a person's character, etc. Notice in the following student theme how the writer's unified paragraphs (in nonindented style, with spacing) reflect his unified, carefully stated thesis and his clear topic sentences.

A Beet Gatherer

```
A mechanical sugar-beet gatherer, like
many other agricultural machines, is far
from perfect. Its main imperfection is
that it leaves beets behind, either by
```

breaking them off or missing them
altogether. Thus, someone is needed to
walk behind the machine, pick up all the
beets missed, and toss them into the truck.
This is not a complex task, admittedly,
but it is one which requires a good deal of
stamina for walking, a sharp eye, and the
mastery of some special techniques.
[THESIS]

A most important qualification for the job
is knowing how to walk rapidly and steadily
over ground which has many large clods on
it. The machine moves about four miles per
hour and leaves behind it a line of
plowed-up dirt about four feet in width.
The beet gatherer has to walk upon this
plowed dirt (which has large clods every
few feet) about as fast as the average
person can walk, and for periods up to
seven hours without any appreciable time
for rest, except the lunch break. On certain types of ground, like dry adobe, the
machine may leave as many as one hundred
beets in a quarter mile of travel. When
this occurs, it is impossible for the
gatherer to keep up with the machine, and
he must either leave some beets behind or
stay behind himself, pile the beets in the
field, and pick them up later.

The beet gatherer also needs a keen eye.
The beets are about the same color as the
dirt around them--this is especially true
of the light-colored, sandy soils--and it
is difficult to see the beets while walking
at a rapid rate. To offset this difficulty,
he has to familiarize himself with the
shapes of beets, their sizes, and roughly
where they will be found in the row. He
acquires this familiarity by experience,
but even so, sometimes he is fooled.

The beet gatherer soon learns certain
techniques which help him do his job more

```
efficiently. For instance, his walking
step becomes different from the average
person's. He picks up his feet more, in
much the same manner as a person tramping
through deep snow. This step enables him
to avoid large clods while he maintains a
rapid rate of motion. He also learns how to
carry beets (up to fifteen or twenty) in
the crook of his arm in a manner similar to
that of a football player who is carrying
the ball. Even in work like this, pride in a
job efficiently done in some measure com-
pensates for the physical discomfort
involved.
```

Here, the writer has specified in his thesis the minimum qualifications of a beet gatherer. He has established an *orderly sequence* of significant ideas and therefore has made the job of paragraphing much easier. Each paragraph discusses only *one* of the different qualifications and fills it out with relevant specific detail. Each paragraph, in short, is unified in itself and is a logical subdivision of the whole composition.

7b The Topic Sentence

You may have noticed that a writer often begins a paragraph with a sentence that summarizes the paragraph's content, as in the preceding piece, "A Beet Gatherer": "A most important qualification for the job is knowing how to walk rapidly and steadily over ground which has many clods on it," or "The beet gatherer also needs a keen eye." These are topic sentences. Topic sentences perform the same function for the individual paragraph that the thesis does for the whole paper. *A topic sentence summarizes the central idea of a paragraph.* It is a valuable aid in securing paragraph unity: the writer can use it in the rough draft as a guide to the paragraph's content, and in revision as a means of ensuring that everything in a paragraph is connected. It helps a writer to control the paragraph's focus and to cut out details which are irrelevant.

Topic sentences are usually found at or near the beginning of a paragraph. Here, they are a kind of promise writers make themselves of what is going to be talked about. Topic sentences also prepare the reader for what is to come. They are the declaration of the paragraph's independence. A topic sentence, however, may be placed anywhere in the paragraph—in the middle, after some transitional sentences, or at the end, as a conclusion. There is nothing sacred about starting with a topic sentence; the beginning of the paragraph just happens to be the place most writers naturally pause, reflect, and center their thoughts. Notice in the following student paragraphs how the topic sentences at the beginning help unify the material that comes after.

Opening with Topic Sentence

> Rachel Carson has used simple illustra-
> tions to get important information over to
> the reader without using complex technical
> terms. Rather than tell her readers that
> scarps mark the upper part of a great
> fault, along which the crustal block under
> Valley X moved in relation to the range,
> she simply mentions that the crust of the
> earth fell into folds and wrinkles and
> that valleys were formed. Miss Carson's
> statement is clearer to the average reader
> than the technical one, and yet it gets the
> same point across. Similarly, because
> most people already know what sponges,
> jelly-fish, worms, and starfish look like,
> Miss Carson has chosen these to represent
> her specific examples of early animal
> life. They give the reader a general idea
> of all primitive animal life, since each
> one is representative of a specific
> phylum.

In this example, the writer uses the topic sentence at the beginning as a broad generalization which she then illustrates. The key phrases "simple illustrations" and "without using complex technical terms" give the writer a framework into which to fit her observations.

In the example which follows, the student has used the topic sentence to summarize the main point he wishes to make about Hardy's novel.

Opening Topic Sentence

In Jude the Obscure, Hardy shows the <u>disappearance of the traditional, isolated rural community and its ways, and the failure of those born into this dying order to find meaning in it.</u> Very early in the novel, we are told by the eleven-year-old Jude that the village of Marygreen is a "small, sleepy place." There is nothing here to hold a young man's interest or allegiance. The thatched cottages are disappearing and the quaint old church has been torn down and replaced by an ugly modern Gothic building. The very bones of Jude's ancestors are unmarked since the iron crosses set up with the new church have rusted away in the rain. Nature herself, the essence of the rural community, has nearly left the pages of this novel. Here there is a mention of sunshine, there of rain or fog. But the earth is no longer a vital force in men's lives. There are no seasonal celebrations—so often found in Hardy's earlier novels— to recall the eternal cycles of birth, courtship, and death. Jude becomes a lonely exile who walks on paved streets and lives in city apartments where the seasons pass largely unnoticed.

When a topic sentence comes in the *middle* of a paragraph, it usually ties the sentences which precede it to the material which follows it. When it *concludes* the paragraph, the topic sentence usually pulls together a long series of details which have been designed to lead up to it, often serving as a climax. Notice how the topic sentence functions in each of the following examples.

Topic Sentence in the Middle

Then something unforeseen happened. The waters of the River, shut out from much land, rose higher upon the lands that were left, and so broke over many dikes and again flooded the farms. The white men cursed, thinking that the rains must have been heavier than before; they decided to build levees a little higher and be safe for ever. ***In those years that followed, a confusion as of a nightmare fell upon, the Valley.*** More and more levees were built, and each one made the water rise so that men had to build up the old ones higher still. The white men would not withdraw from the lands, and neither in their peculiar madness would they all work together against the River. Instead, in the dark rainy nights a man might break his neighbor's levee to lower the water-level against his own; so, not with shovels, but with loaded guns, men patrolled the levees, like savages brandishing spears against the river-god.

Topic Sentence at the End

At last, although the white men hated the very sound of the words, they began to talk more and more of "the government" and "regulation." Then finally came engineers who looked shrewdly not at one part of the River, but at the whole. They measured snow and rain, and the depth of streams. They surveyed; they calculated with many figures how high the levees must be and how wide the channels between. Gradually even the fiercest fighters among the white men came to see that the River (which was always the whole River) was too great for any man or company of men. Only the Whole People could hope to match the Whole River. ***So, after many years of disaster the white men began to live in a truce with the river.***

—GEORGE R. STEWART

Not *every* paragraph you will write will have a topic sentence, though the practice of including a focusing sentence in each paragraph is a good one. In some cases, the topic sentences may be omitted entirely without violating unity. *But it should always be possible to summarize a paragraph's central idea or thought in a single sentence.* For instance, in the following student paragraph, though it has no topic sentence, the central idea might be summarized thus: "The long school day at the medieval University of Paris demanded much from the students."

Topic Sentence Left Implied

```
Classes at the medieval University of
Paris began at 5 a.m. First on the agenda
were the ordinary lectures, which were the
```

> regular and more important lectures. After
> several ordinary lectures and a short,
> begrudged lunch hour, students attended
> extraordinary lectures given in the after-
> noon. These were supplementary to the
> ordinary lectures and usually given by a
> less important teacher, who may not have
> been more than fourteen or fifteen years
> old. A student would spend ten or twelve
> hours a day with his teachers, and then
> following classes in the late afternoon,
> he had sports events. But after sports, the
> day was not over. There was homework, which
> consisted of copying, recopying, and
> memorizing notes while the light per-
> mitted. Nor was there much of a break.
> Christmas vacation was about three weeks,
> and summer vacation was only a month.

If your papers are criticized for disunified paragraphs, you should certainly make a conscientious effort to write a clear topic sentence for each of your paragraphs. Similarly, you can often clarify an assigned reading by locating and underlining the topic sentences for the paragraphs that confuse you. The great value of the topic sentence for the reader and writer alike is its function in focusing on the main idea and in giving the paragraph direction.

7c Length of Paragraph

The principle which governs paragraph length is the *reader's convenience.* If each sentence is a separate paragraph, the reader will be unable to see the groupings the writer has in mind. Pages consistently cluttered by short, underdeveloped paragraphs scatter the reader's attention. If, on the other hand, there are too many sentences in the paragraph, the reader will be unable to see the subdivisions of the material clearly. Paragraphs which run consistently to more than a page are little better than no paragraphing at all, since the reader is forced to make the subdivisions of material for himself.

Ordinarily, then, a paragraph should consist of more than one sentence but less than a page. But note that paragraphs vary considerably in length in different kinds of writing. In formal, scientific, or scholarly writing they are sometimes as long as 250 words. In ordinary magazine articles the average length is about 150 words. In newspapers the average is 50 words or less. Good questions to ask yourself are "Should any of my paragraphs be written as two, for clarity?" and "Are there any noticeably short paragraphs so closely related that they should be combined?" If the writer of the first theme which follows had questioned himself about the paragraphing on his opening page, he would have revised it for greater unity. Here is a major part of the first page, followed by the student's revision.

Disunified: Groupings Unclear

(1.) In Barchester Towers Anthony Trollope's most fully developed character is Mr. Slope. Slope is the nearest Trollope comes to a villain.

(2.) He commits the mortal sin of the age-- the disrupting of social order. Barchester is a quiet, easygoing Victorian province and Mr. Slope is a pusher who upsets the harmony of this clerical paradise.

(3.) But Slope is not wholly despicable. Although he is an opportunist, he is not a hypocrite.

(4.) Slope believes wholeheartedly in the religion he teaches and dedicates himself realistically and entirely to its furtherance.

(5.) He craves no materialistic benefits but only the power to convey his beliefs. However, Slope violates the "natural laws" of society by disturbing the social order and he must suffer. . . .

Paragraphs Combined for Unity

In Barchester Towers Anthony Trollope's most fully developed character is Mr. Slope. Slope is the nearest Trollope

comes to a villain; he commits the mortal
sin of the age--the disrupting of social
order. Barchester is a quiet, easygoing
Victorian province and Mr. Slope is a
pusher who upsets the harmony of this
clerical paradise.

Paragraphs #1 and #2 combined (nonindented spaced style).

But Slope is not wholly despicable.
Although he is an opportunist, he is not a
hypocrite. He believes wholeheartedly in
the religion he teaches and dedicates
himself realistically and entirely to its
furtherance. He craves no materialistic
benefits but only the power to convey
his beliefs.

Paragraphs #3, #4, and #5 (first sentence) combined.

Nevertheless, Slope violates the "natural
laws" of society by disturbing the social
order and he must suffer. . . .

By joining the first two paragraphs together and the second two
together, the student achieved greater unity. The reader can now
more easily follow the student's argument that (a) Slope commits the
mortal sin of disrupting social order, and (b) Slope sincerely wants
power only to further his religious beliefs. The student might even
have joined the first four paragraphs into one unified whole. But as it
stands, his revision eliminates the needlessly short paragraphs and
groups the ideas more conveniently.

The student who wrote the following composition did not build it
up painfully by adding one paragraph to another; rather, he con-
ceived of the experience as a unified and coherent one, with movement and continuity. Nevertheless, the subject was obviously far too
long to appear as a single paragraph, so he located the phases he
wished to emphasize and made these his paragraphs. His paper illustrates how unity helps continuity.

I Surrendered

Social order, it is said, can only be
maintained through the restriction and
prohibition of our often whimsical
impulses (taking off from school or work,

swimming nude, open sex), and we find
ourselves inhibited by a civilization that
was supposed to ensure our well-being.
Parents, the law, and public opinion
condition us to keep the lid tightly
clamped on our drives for free and outward
expression of inner needs: we are made to
stop and evaluate our actions and thoughts
and to feel guilty when they are not
acceptable. And because this guilt often
makes us tense and ill-at-ease, we give up
and submit. This is what I understand
Freud to be saying in Civilization and Its
Discontents, and this is what I learned to
be the melancholy fact when I went
hitchhiking up the West Coast with my
sleeping bag and thoughts of "doing my
own thing."

My hitchhiking trip with a white friend
from Long Beach to Canada was plagued by
social pressure even before it began. Two
weeks before we started, reports over the
news about hitchhikers being axed in their
sleeping bags, as well as drivers being
robbed, beaten, or killed, did not make
our trip sound like a good idea to my
family. My family was also concerned that
reports like these make drivers hesitant
of stopping for anyone unless they have a
gun under the seat. That was just the
beginning, though. I could have handled
the fears others had for me, but the guilt
I was made to feel was harder to cope with.

My brother-in-law and I had a long
discussion about the dangers of
hitchhiking. The list was a frightening
one that included the possibility I might
be hassled and jailed by the police or be
robbed and stranded. I felt quite guilty
about running off and frolicking around
while everyone worried about me, and this
guilt took some of the pleasure--the
thrill, day-to-day suspense, and
excitement--out of the trip and made me
wary.

My brother-in-law and I also discussed
the fact that very few blacks hitchhike
in the live-on-the-road manner I was about
to, which means sleeping in forests, com-
munes, or in freeway shrubbery, or going
into strange towns and meeting all kinds
of people. He suggested that if tension in
any given situation forced a serious
racial confrontation, my friend would
surely turn to the safe side and against
me. This kept me wondering all through the
trip, and to my dismay, kept me looking for
hints of racism in him, which took some of
the pleasure out of the trip. It also made
me feel guilty for suspecting him. My
brother-in-law and I also talked about the
fact that, instead of hitchhiking, I
should be working to pay for college.
Feeling all this guilt, and sensing the
concern of my parents, I still set out with
my friend.

We carefully heeded (out of fear)
California's policy on hitchhiking.
Hitchhiking is illegal, but the law is not
usually enforced if the hikers stay on the
curb. We had no problems at all until just
south of San Luis Obispo, where we were
searched for weapons. There we were
insulted by a pair of California Highway
Patrol officers while they went over us.
Among the many insults was the one directed
at me, asking me who I was going to rape
next. But, knowing how public opinion
would side with the police if we
retaliated, we kept our mouths closed. We
knew that if the police reported subduing
a couple of wandering, violent hippies,
then the stereotype of the hippie
(shiftless young bums begging for food and
for money to buy drugs with) would justify
the police in the public's view and set
people's minds at ease. So we checked our
natural impulse to fight back, but we were
angry with ourselves for having to do so.

We felt guilty for not standing up for our rights.

Even with that episode behind us, the rest of the trip didn't bring me the pleasure I'd hoped for. The possible presence of dope in the cars of the young people who picked us up made me uneasy. But not my friend. He indulged heavily in marijuana all the way up the coast whenever he could get some. I knew that if we were arrested for dope it would go on my record, damage my chances in the future, and hurt my family badly. I would be ashamed and guilt-ridden. I was very worried about the presence of dope around me, even back in the deepest woods near Eureka, California. There, at one in the morning, my friend and another hiker who joined up with us smoked as much marijuana as they could hold. I was fearful that a band of night-roaming vigilantes would swarm on us and take us away. In Canada itself, I felt guilty the very first time I got in line for a feed-in. I was overly self-conscious because the food was paid for by Canadian taxpayers and was meant for needy people. We had enough money to buy food.

It now seems that everything we did, beginning with the very thought of hitchhiking, was meant to prove we weren't as trapped as the people we left behind. But when it came to the wild, free expression of inner drives, I couldn't throw off the wet blanket of society. I couldn't even go skinny dipping in the Russian River because there were people around and I was afraid of what they might think if I stripped. We loved Canada and its forests, but we came back. Even though the air and water were like nectar in comparison to that of Los Angeles, we came back to the smog and noise and people. We discarded the forests, rivers, and meadows for the benefits and security of our social surroundings. I surrendered.

Samuel Reece

7d   **Short Paragraphs**

To call attention to an important shift in the line of thought, or to emphasize a crucial point, you may occasionally want a very short paragraph. Sometimes, a short paragraph will serve both these purposes. In any case, such paragraphs should be used *sparingly*. Notice in the following example that the student might have joined his short paragraph of rhetorical emphasis to either of the other paragraphs. He chose instead to make the two sentences into a separate paragraph and thus to stress the importance of his early training and the shock he was to receive.

Turning Point Stressed

> . . . I know from personal experience the truth of Erich Fromm's criticism that the American male is forced to repress his feelings. Our society does tend to suspect emotional outbursts in a man as signs of "abnormality." From childhood onward, I was taught to "control" my emotions. I was told constantly that good little boys don't cry; they act like big strong men. The little boy who fell off his tricycle and got up with a smile was admired and recommended as a model to be emulated by the rest of the tricycle set. Nor were feelings of pain the only emotion I was encouraged to suppress. Anger, hostility, envy, and melancholy were all taboo, and this training was almost impossible to resist.
>
> By the age of thirteen, I was a true believer in this Spartan code. It was at this age that I was first startled into doubting it.
>
> My uncle had been ill but had kept this fact secret from. . . .

Short paragraphs are also used for dialogue. *In a narrative, any direct quotation, together with the rest of a sentence of which it is a part, is paragraphed separately.* The reason for this convention is to make immediately clear to the reader the change of speaker.

Identified Speakers Paragraphed Separately

"But 'glory' doesn't mean 'a nice knock-down argument,'" Alice objected.

"When *I* use a word," Humpty Dumpty said, in a rather scornful tone, "it means what I choose it to mean—neither more nor less."

"The question is," said Alice, "whether you *can* make words mean so many different things."

"The question is," said Humpty Dumpty, "which is to be master—that's all."

—LEWIS CARROLL

This same convention is usually observed in cases where the speaker is not named each time.

Unidentified Speakers Paragraphed Separately

"Hello," she said. "Are you awake?"

"Where have you been?"

"I just went out to get a breath of air."

"You did, like hell."

"What do you want me to say, darling?"

—ERNEST HEMINGWAY

However, a short quoted speech which is closely united with the context is sometimes included in a paragraph of narration:

Short Dialogue Included

Now and then Mr. Bixby called my attention to certain things. Said he, "This is Six-Mile Point." I assented. It was pleasant enough information but I could not see the bearing of it. I was not conscious that it was a matter of any interest to me. Another time he said, "This is Nine-Mile Point." Later he said, "This is Twelve-Mile Point." They were all about level with the water's edge; they all looked alike to me; they were monotonously unpicturesque. . . .

—MARK TWAIN

7

Exercise 1

Select any two of the following statements. Use each as the topic sentence for a unified paragraph.

1. Students often learn more from each other than they do from their classes.
2. Unless they rebel, adolescents can't grow up.
3. Slogans like "Progress is our most important product" are misleading because progress is an attitude toward achievement, not the achievement itself.
4. Most of us are more prejudiced than we realize.
5. Beginnings are more exciting than endings.

Exercise 2

Choose one of the following exercises and write a unified paragraph based on it.

1. Try to capture the mood and feel of a specific place that meant a great deal to you in your childhood—a room, a park, a field, whatever.
2. Try to catch the mood and feel of a specific and repeated experience that meant a great deal to you in your childhood—a holiday, an occasion with the family, a private ritual of your own, whatever.
3. Try to catch the mood and feel of a specific place or experience which you frequently seek out now.

Exercise 3

In the following selections find and mark the topic sentence. Be prepared to explain why your choice is the most complete summary or statement of the paragraph's idea.

If we would discover the little backstairs door that for any age serves as the secret entranceway to knowledge, we will do well to look for certain unobtrusive words with uncertain meanings that are permitted to slip off the tongue or the pen without fear and without research, words which, having from constant repetition lost their metaphorical significance, are unconsciously taken for objective realities. In the thirteenth century the key words would no doubt be God, sin, grace, salvation, heaven, and the like; in the nineteenth century, matter, fact, matter-of-fact, evolution, progress; in the twentieth century, relativity, process, adjustment, function, complex. In the eighteenth century the words without which no enlightened person could reach a restful conclusion were nature, natural law, first cause, reason, sentiment, humanity, perfectibility (these last three being necessary only for the more tender-minded, perhaps).

—CARL L. BECKER

Disease from contaminated food or beverages was very common a few generations ago, and nutritional deficiencies were almost the rule. Now laboratories check on the safety of what we eat and drink. Furthermore, the nutritional requirements of man are now well known, and in the Western World, at least, we have the means to satisfy them. But all this theoretical and practical knowledge does not guarantee that nutrition will not present problems in the immediate future, even assuming that economic prosperity continues. On the one hand, modern agriculture and food technology have come to depend more and more on the use of chemicals to control pests and to improve the yields of animal and plant products. The cost of food production would enormously increase without these chemicals, and for this reason their use is justified. Unfortunately, however, and despite all care, several of them eventually reach the human consumer in objectionable concentrations. As more and more substances are introduced in agriculture and food technology every year, it will become practically impossible to test them all with regard to long-range effects on human health, and the possibility of toxic reactions must be accepted as one of the inevitable risks of progress.

—RENÉ DUBOS

In many ways, we break down children's convictions that things make sense, or their hope that things may prove to make sense. We do it, first of all, by breaking up life into arbitrary and disconnected hunks of subject matter, which we then try to "integrate" by such artificial and irrelevant devices as having children sing Swiss folk songs while they are studying the geography of Switzerland, or do arithmetic problems about rail-splitting while they are studying the boyhood of Lincoln. Furthermore, we continually confront them with what is senseless, ambiguous, and contradictory; worse, we do it without knowing that we are doing it, so that, hearing nonsense shoved at them as if it were sense, they come to feel that the source of their confusion lies not in the material but in their own stupidity. Still further, we cut children off from their own common sense and the world of reality by requiring them to play with and shove around words and symbols that have little or no meaning to them. Thus we turn the vast majority of our students into the kind of people for whom all symbols are•meaningless; who cannot use symbols as a way of learning about and dealing with reality; who cannot understand written instructions; who, even if they read books, come out knowing no more than when the went in; who may have a few new words rattling around in their heads, but whose mental models of the world remain unchanged and, indeed, impervious to change. The minority, the able and successful students, we are very likely to turn into something different but just as dangerous: the kind of people who can manipulate words and symbols fluently while keeping themselves largely divorced from the reality for which they stand; the kind of people who like to speak in large generalities but grow silent or indignant if someone asks for an example of what they are talking about; the kind of people who, in their discussions of world affairs, coin and use such words as megadeaths and megacorpses, with scarcely a thought to the blood and suffering these words imply.

—JOHN HOLT

Exercise 4

In the following paragraphs, several sentences have been italicized as possible topic sentences. For each paragraph, choose the sentence which you think is the most complete summary or statement of the paragraph's main idea. Be prepared to justify your choice by showing in detail how it more adequately summarizes the paragraph's contents than the other possible topic sentences do. If none of the alternatives seems acceptable, write your own topic sentence.

Let us define a plot. We have defined a story as a narrative of events arranged in their time-sequence. **A plot is also a narrative of events, the emphasis falling on causality.** "The king died and then the queen died" is a story. "The king died, and then the queen died of grief" is a plot. The time sequence is preserved, but the sense of causality overshadows it. Or again: "The queen died, no one knew why, until it was discovered that it was through grief at the death of the king." This is a plot with a mystery in it, a form capable of high development. **It suspends the time-sequence, it moves as far away from the story as its limitations will allow.** Consider the death of the queen. If it is in a story we say "and then?" If it is in a plot we ask "why?" **That is the fundamental difference between these two aspects of the novel.** A plot cannot be told to a gaping audience of cave-men or to a tyrannical sultan or to their modern descendant, the movie-public. They can only be kept awake by "and then—and then—" They can only supply curiosity. *But a plot demands intelligence and memory also.*

—E. M. FORSTER

Inside the play-ground an absolute and peculiar order reigns. *Here we come across another, a very positive feature of play: it creates order, is order.* Into a very imperfect world and into the confusion of life it brings a temporary, a limited perfection. *Play demands order absolute and supreme.* The least deviation from it "spoils the game," robs it of its character and makes it worthless. *The profound affinity between play and order is perhaps the reason why play, as we have noted in passing, seems to lie to such a large extent in the field of aesthetics.* Play has a tendency to be beautiful. *It may be that this aesthetic factor is identical with the impulse to create orderly form, which animates play in all its aspects.* The words we use to denote the elements of play belong for the most part to aesthetics, terms with which we try to describe the effects of beauty: tension, poise, balance, contrast, variation, solution, resolution, etc. Play casts a spell over us; it is "enchanting," "captivating." *It is invested with the noblest qualities we are capable of perceiving in things: rhythm and harmony.*

—JOHAN HUIZINGA

Exercise 5

The following selection was originally written as six paragraphs. Try outlining it, first. Then indicate where, in your opinion, the five divisions should be made and be able to give reasons for your choice. In dividing the selection, try to find topic sentences for your paragraphs.

To begin to understand economic development we must have a picture of the problem with which it contends. We must conjure up in our mind's eye what underdevelopment means for the two billion human beings for whom it is not a statistic but a living experience of daily life. Unless we can see the Great Ascent from the vantage point of those who must make the climb, we cannot hope to understand the difficulties of the march. It is not easy to make this mental jump. But let us attempt it by imagining how a typical American family, living in a small suburban house on an income of six or seven thousand dollars [in 1963], could be transformed into an equally typical family of the underdeveloped world. We begin by invading the house of our imaginary American family to strip it of its furniture. Everything goes: beds, chairs, tables, television set, lamps. We will leave the family with a few old blankets, a kitchen table, a wooden chair. Along with the bureaus go the clothes. Each member of the family may keep in his "wardrobe" his oldest suit or dress, a shirt or blouse. We will permit a pair of shoes to the head of the family, but none for the wife or children. We move into the kitchen. The appliances have already been taken out, so we turn to the cupboards and larder. The box of matches may stay, a small bag of flour, some sugar and salt. A few moldy potatoes, already in the garbage can, must hastily be rescued, for they will provide much of tonight's meal. We will leave a handful of onions, and a dish of dried beans. All the rest we take away: the meat, the fresh vegetables, the canned goods, the crackers, the candy. Now we have stripped the house: the bathroom has been dismantled, the running water shut off, the electric wires taken out. Next we take away the house. The family can move to the toolshed. It is crowded, but much better than the situation in Hong Kong, where (a United Nations report tells us) "it is not uncommon for a family of four or more to live in a bedspace, that is, on a bunk bed and the space it occupies— sometimes in two or three tiers—their only privacy provided by curtains." But we have only begun. All the other houses in the neighborhood have also been removed; our suburb has become a shantytown. Still, our family is fortunate to have a shelter; 250,000 people in Calcutta have none at all and simply live in the streets. Our family is now about on a par with the city of Cali in Colombia, where, an official of the World Bank writes, "on one hillside alone, the slum population is estimated at 40,000— without water, sanitation, or electric light. And not all the poor of Cali are as fortunate as that. Others have built their shacks near the city on land which lies beneath the flood mark. To these people the immediate environment is the open sewer of the city, a sewer which flows through their huts when the river rises."

—ROBERT L. HEILBRONER

Effective Paragraphs 8

How can paragraphs be made effective? Though we can't enumerate all the possibilities, we do have a couple of standards for testing paragraph effectiveness—*development* and *coherence*. And we also have some useful techniques and models to help us write more effective paragraphs and to help us rewrite weak ones. A word of explanation about these techniques and models is needed.

We often use these methods quite unconsciously because we understand the material we're working with. To put it another way, what happens in the paragraph—the shape and form it assumes—is often determined by the subject itself. If we are analyzing the kinds of tapes and records students buy, we quite naturally classify; if we are discussing the choice between two jobs or professions, we will probably compare and contrast them. In short, in the words of the American architect Louis Sullivan, "Form follows function." These methods can help us revise and reorganize ineffective paragraphs, or suggest ways of handling materials when we are not sure how to proceed. Readers expect (usually unconsciously) to see the methods observed, and may be confused if the pattern is violated without apparent reason—for example if the paragraph jumps confusingly back and forth in time or from one location to another. These methods are often most valuable when we are revising a rough draft, a defective section, or an unsatisfactory paper. For most of us, who are not born writers, it is during revision that we have our best chance to improve a paper.

8a Paragraph Development

Although its central idea may be clear, an undeveloped paragraph may be brief, general, thin, or dull. Developing a paragraph requires that the writer take time to see clearly and say accurately what his or her generalities signify. It means filling out the bare statement with specific detail. It certainly does not mean padding out a simple statement or repeating the same idea in different words. Unless the writer shows how his generalities apply in detail to particular cases, how his conclusions differ from someone else's or what specifically has led him to his view, the reader remains uninformed and unpersuaded. Undeveloped paragraphs are one of the commonest and most irritating weaknesses in student writing. Consider the following scrawny, lazy paragraphs:

Undeveloped

> I arrived here at Millberry College on Saturday, September 20. One of the first things I learned of was the dinner the following evening which each freshman was supposed to attend with his faculty advisor. I found my advisor was Mr. Ward.
>
> We met in his room in West Hall. We obviously couldn't all eat there, so Mr. Ward had arranged that we eat at Dr. Miller's house.
>
> As we walked to Dr. Miller's I began to talk with the others of our group of about ten.
>
> Mr. Ward was not what I had expected of a faculty member. He was not over fifty years old. He was not wearing thick glasses. He was, in contrast, about twenty-six, rather athletic looking, and a very interesting conversationalist, not only in his own field, but in every subject we discussed.
>
> My classmates, most of whom I had not met before, were also a surprise. There were no socially backward introverts, interested only in the physical sciences,

as I had feared. I found instead some very interesting people with whom I immediately wanted to become friends. Some were interested in sports, some in hobbies, some in card games, and all in sex. Each individual had something to offer me.

The Millers did a marvelous job of preparing the dinner. We did a marvelous job of eating it. However, the real purpose of the dinner was to become acquainted with at least two of our faculty members and about ten of our fellow students. In this endeavor we were also quite successful, for the discussions begun during the meal lasted for a long time after and, as a matter of fact, some of them were continued the next day.

This year's advisor dinner was very rewarding and I believe it should remain a tradition. The students really get to know each other, and a few of the faculty are pleasantly surprised.

A reader might well wonder why the dinner should be continued as a tradition. Nothing the writer says carries real conviction because nothing is developed concretely. These paragraphs raise more questions than they answer: (1) Why should the writer have expected the faculty to resemble his caricature of them as ancient, near-sighted bores? (2) What was Mr. Ward's "field" and what did he talk about as a "very interesting conversationalist"? (3) What "sports," "hobbies," and "card games" was the writer so pleased to discover he shared in common with his classmates? (4) If the meal was so memorable, what was it and how many servings did he have? If it wasn't important, why give two vague sentences to it? (5) What was talked about so enthusiastically and "for a long time after" the meal?

The writer has substituted jargon (the pretentious phrasing "very interesting conversationalist," "socially backward introverts"), vague generalities ("some were interested in sports, some in hobbies, some in card games"), and unexplained events (the dinner discussion) for specific detail. The paragraphs are not developed; they merely repeat the same idea unconvincingly—that the advisor's dinner was a good chance to discover that faculty and students were in some vague way "interesting" and "rewarding," not what the writer "had expected."

Concrete diction cuts out fuzziness and gives a paper sharpness and depth. Consider these sentences: "The Millers did a marvelous job of preparing the meal. We did a marvelous job of eating it." Do they mean the Millers barbecued two dozen hamburgers and tossed a spicy bean salad for a delicious buffet meal on paper plates? Or do they mean the Millers gave a sit-down dinner, complete with white linen, silver setting and candlelight, and served roast turkey, hot rolls, and two vegetables? Either of these alternatives is better than the empty generality of the original. A buffet dinner for thirteen people implies a relaxed host and hostess, students going back for several helpings, and comfortable informality. A sit-down dinner for thirteen people implies a busy host and hostess, reserved freshmen, hushed requests for the gravy, and long, earnest discussion as the coffee lingers in cups and the candles melt. Whatever the case was, specific wording would help the reader *see* the event and prepare him for the writer's conclusion about it.

To get specific detail by specific wording, writers think in concrete images to recall and *re*-create the taste, touch, sound and sight as clearly as possible. In doing so, writers are trying to give the reader as much relevant information as they can. For example, in the following two versions of the same paragraph the student has improved the second by more complete information. Her revision is not much longer than the original but it tells far more. It is the choice of words, not the number of words, which creates an image. The underlined passages indicate the places where she has made her major changes.

Vague Original

> Though the air was uncomfortable, the sand was soothing and warm, and I dug a hole into it and piled it up until it half-covered me from the air. I sat there, shivering in the air, until the sand began falling away from me. I tried to bury my legs again, but the sand was dry and it would not stay in place. I tried to find damp sand near me, but in a short time it also dried out and wouldn't stay in place. So I rested for a while and watched the sea rise and fall and the various objects it threw onto the beach. Seaweed and other things were washed up, then carried back in a regular rhythm.

Revision for Concreteness

> Though the air was <u>cold</u>, the sand <u>felt soft</u>
> <u>and warm</u>, and I dug <u>a damp trough</u> in it and
> piled it up around my <u>legs until I had a</u>
> <u>body only from the waist up.</u> I sat there,
> <u>shivering in the cool mist,</u> until the sand
> began <u>to crumble</u> down around me. I tried to
> <u>gather it back up</u> on my legs, but it had
> <u>dried and kept slithering down again in</u>
> <u>little shifting rivers.</u> I dug with my
> <u>hands beside me</u> until I came to damp sand
> which I piled on my legs, but in a short
> time it too <u>dried and slipped away.</u> So I
> rested <u>my head on my knees</u> and watched the
> sea rise <u>and fall and rise and fall,</u>
> <u>bringing with it,</u> to the beach, something
> new each time: <u>a loop of rust-colored</u>
> <u>seaweed, a shell,</u> a rock, <u>a small jelly-</u>
> <u>fish. And falling away,</u> it would <u>often take</u>
> <u>with it</u> what it had <u>just brought.</u>

Notice that the writer has done more than make the diction specific.
She has developed her paragraph by adding extra detail and slowed
down the tempo of the narrative. She has tried to make the reader
see and feel what happened.

Developing a paragraph requires that a writer give content to
generalities by using *relevant* details and illustrations. These details
may be found in particular actions, sensory impressions, objects,
processes. But they must be *selected*, not merely inventoried. Details
become boring—mere padding—when the writer confuses quantity
with quality. If, for example, an American student has been asked
by his Polish correspondent what a "drugstore" is, the American
should not try to explain it by listing every type of cold tablet, sleeping pill, foot powder, lipstick, face cream, hair remover, shaving
lotion, cigarette, stale candy, and garish paperback it sells. But
neither should he content himself by saying a drugstore fills prescriptions and sells medical supplies and cosmetics. The correspondent
can get this broad definition from a dictionary. The American might
begin with such a definition, and then suggest through selected details
that "medical supplies" *range* from cough syrups through pink
bandages and that cosmetics *range* from green fingernail polish
through perfumed hair rinses. Without trying to be exhaustive, he
would try to suggest the odd variety and specialization of items covered by the general terms "medical supplies" and "cosmetics."

(1) Development by Detail

If your instructor comments that your paragraphs are inadequately developed, you can do several things. First, examine the paragraph or paragraphs carefully for all vague generalities, needlessly abstract words, and clichés, and underline them. For instance:

> When they are young, children are free and
> can be themselves. They are protected
> from nature's hardships by our modern-day
> society and by our complex technology.
> They only have to keep out of trouble.
> Mostly, they are free to do whatever they
> want. But as they get older, they have more
> and more duties and responsibilities
> put upon them. They begin to lose their
> freedom and become conformists.

Such phrases as "When they are young" may be changed to "Before they start elementary school"; "free and can be themselves" to "playful, spontaneous, and imaginative"; "protected from nature's hardships" to "protected from hunger, disease, and the weather." Underlining may also reveal that certain generalities, if they mean anything at all, are untrue or need extensive qualification: Do children who bike to school, who roam where they wish afterwards, and who spend time in the evenings with their friends really "lose their freedom and become conformists"? Or, to take a very different view, is it true that our "modern-day-society" or our "complex technology" "protect" a ghetto child from rats, crime, poverty, sickness, and dilapidated firetraps?

Many undeveloped paragraphs result from the writer's failure to distinguish between fact and opinion. Did the writer of the paragraph about children ever bother to ask what factual basis he had for his opinions? He assumes as self-evident that young children lose their identity and freedom as they grow up. But is it true to say that a child of three or four has a wider range of choices or a more clearly defined individuality than a child of nine or eleven? Clearly, in handling topics of any complexity, writers need to examine their own underlying assumptions and to question the external evidence and authority for their views. If they take the time to do this, they are more likely to spot the flaws in their own generalizations and to discover how much *more* there is to be said.

Another useful device is making a list of the concrete images, details, and examples you want to include. One way is the strict outline form:

1. Drama in Robert Frost's Imagery
   A. Natural settings
      —For example, a boy climbing to top of birch tree
   B. Domestic settings
      —For example, wife crouching on stairs in "Home Burial"

If you find this method too mechanical, at least jot down the specific items which can *illustrate* and *deepen* your generalizations. In the footnotes to the following example, notice how the writer has visualized the concrete details to give the generalizations some real content:

> Working as a door-to-door magazine salesman in and around St. Louis last summer gave me more than just extra spending money. It gave me a chance to meet types of people[1] I might otherwise never have known, and some practical experience[2] I am glad I had.
> *The last two generalizations could stand expansion.*
>
> [1]Young wives of construction workers living in trailers, retired jazz musicians and newsstand operators living in boarding houses, electronic engineers in suburbs.
>
> [2]How to keep temper when insulted, how to walk through a neighborhood not showing fear, how to size up a person's tastes by the way he keeps lawn or TV show he's watching.

An excellent way to get depth is to practice building up examples which contribute to the dominant idea or impression, the topic sentence. Cutting is usually easy, and you can always thin out in revising. In the following student paragraph, notice how skillfully the writer has picked his details to show why he remembers an attic which would only seem dirty and uncomfortable to an adult, and notice how he builds up these details.

Building up Details to Support a Thesis

```
The attic was the third floor of an old
Victorian house, one of those countless
look-alike monstrosities of towers and
porches and trim. To the adult eye, the
```

<u>attic was dirty and uncomfortable, but to the boy it was a sanctuary.</u> The attic always had that sneezy smell of twenty-year-old newspapers just shuffled; and its roof arched clear down to the floor at the four corners so that the boy had to play near the middle of the room. And the floor had a thick layer of--not exactly dust, not exactly dirt--dry, yet slick gray pollen that filters out of old wooden rafters. On the floor the boy had his Lionel trains and build-it-yourself brick houses and farms--but they were merely strategic positions and crucial points of supply which he, as General, and his army defended against the Enemy. The whole floor was occupied with troops marching at the slope or resting in position. Here, all bundled up in a jacket, he used to spend his dark winter evenings directing his men. He sometimes even played up here in the summer, when it was so hot his face would turn prickly red and he had to worry about the hard, black wasps knocking at the window sills. Here he would set up Gettysburg with some paper-paste mountains he had molded or trap the Enemy on an isthmus, using the rough-finished chimney as a barrier.

Notice that this method of development by specific detail moves from the general to the particular, is deductive. (We shall look at some other methods shortly.) Many effective paragraphs have this pattern of organization:

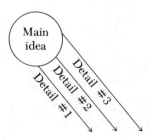

In the following paragraph, Swift attacks two hundred years of European exploration and colonizing with an extended bitter example supporting the irony of his opening and closing statements.

Illustration Supporting Ironic Comment

> But I had another reason which made me less forward to enlarge his Majesty's dominions by my discoveries. **To say the truth, I had conceived a few scruples with relation to the distributive justice of princes upon those occasions.** For instance, a crew of pirates are driven by a storm they know not whither, at length a boy discovers land from the topmast, they go on shore to rob and plunder, they see an harmless people, are entertained with kindness, they give the country a new name, they take formal possession of it for their King, they set up a rotten plank or stone for a memorial, they murder two or three dozen of the natives, bring away a couple of more by force for a sample, return home, and get their pardon. Here commences a new dominion acquired with a title by **divine right.** Ships are sent out with the first opportunity, the natives driven out or destroyed, their princes tortured to discover their gold, a free license given to all acts of inhumanity and lust, the earth reeking with the blood of its inhabitants: and this execrable crew of butchers employed in so pious an expedition is a **modern colony** sent to convert and civilize an idolatrous and barbarous people.
>
> —JONATHAN SWIFT

(2) Other Methods of Paragraph Development

There are many ways of developing paragraphs, and each has its advantages. One of them, development by *specific detail*, has already been considered. In actual practice, writers are apt to employ a combination of methods; a few of the most useful are worth illustration and analysis.

The first of these methods is development by *definition*. Here, a writer limits the range of a term's application. In this kind of development, the writer uses a number of sentences to tell the reader what the key term or terms signify. A few words about definitions are in order here.

In formal logic, a term is defined by referring it to a general class (or genus)—i.e., by classifying it—and then distinguishing it from others in the general class it belongs to. To take a simple example, one might begin by *classifying* a pen as a "writing instrument." But since the class "writing instrument" also includes pencils, one would have to *differentiate* a pen by continuing ". . . writing instrument which makes use of a hard point and a colored fluid."

term		*class*	*differentiation*
Pen	is	a writing instrument	making use of a hard point and a colored fluid.
Pencil	is	a writing instrument	with a core of solid-state material like graphite inside a wooden or plastic case.

A description of the object can include all kinds of details—the pencil has a chewed end, used to cost five cents, peels in bits of yellow paint—but these details are irrelevant to the definition of the term. Similarly, examples do not constitute a definition, although they can certainly help to clarify a definition. To say that a Dixon Ticonderoga, #2 Soft is an example of a pencil is not the same as specifying what the meaning of the term "pencil" is.

Much of the time a writer can successfully define technical terms or concrete words by using an appositive construction.

DEFINITION BY APPOSITION The X-ray showed a crack in the *tibia, or shinbone.*

Please analyze the importance of the *denouement—the final unraveling or outcome of the plot*—in *Lord Jim.*

Tonight the moon will be in *apogee, that is, at the point in its orbit farthest from the earth.*

Sometimes, however, especially when dealing with complex or highly abstract terms, a writer will need a fuller definition. He may spend several paragraphs, not just one, in defining the term if the term is crucial to a long essay or research paper. To do so, he should observe certain principles.

First, avoid circular definitions. "Democracy is the democratic process" and "An astronomer is one who studies astronomy" are circular definitions. When words are defined in terms of themselves, no one's understanding is improved.

Second, avoid long lists of synonyms if the term to be defined is an abstract one. When a paper begins, "By education, I mean to give knowledge, develop character, improve taste, draw out, train, lead," the reader knows he is in for the shotgun treatment. The writer has indiscriminately blasted a load of abstract terms at the reader, hoping one will hit.

Third, avoid loaded definitions. Loaded definitions do not restrict key terms but make an immediate appeal for emotional approval. A definition beginning "By federal aid to education I mean government meddling and thought control" is loaded with pejorative emotional connotation. Conversely, "By federal aid to education I mean one of the great blessings of democratic planning" is loaded with favorable emotional connotation. Such judgments can be vigorous conclusions to a discussion, but they invite argument, not clarification, when offered as definitions.

The following student paragraph illustrates the process of definition. The writer first classifies Sarah Woodruff and Clarissa Dalloway as belonging to the class of people having "certain heroic qualities." She then clarifies and limits the term "heroic" by rejecting one set of meanings (control and domination) and choosing another (sensitivity, endurance, independence). To further limit the concept, the writer then discusses how each character is "heroic."

Definition by Distinction

> The central characters in John Fowles's
> The French Lieutenant's Woman and Virginia
> Woolf's Mrs. Dalloway are women who embody
> certain heroic qualities that set them
> apart from what one character calls "the
> great niminypiminy flock of women in
> general." These two women, Sarah Woodruff
> and Clarissa Dalloway, are not heroic in
> the traditional masculine, aggressive
> sense of the word. They do not seek to
> control or to dominate but to cultivate a
> sensitivity, to endure, and to remain free
> of masculine narrow-mindedness. They
> possess a power that allows them to remain
> open to the compelling vitality of life.
> Their heroism is their ability to be
> responsive to reality, to feel even if it
> entails suffering and uncertainty; and
> this heroism spurs others on to live in the
> presence of life, with all its beauty and
> terror. Sarah is a free woman, and through
> her sensitivity, forbearance, and courage,
> she liberates Charles, a man caught in the
> petrifying forces of Victorian society,

> preoccupied with duty and piety. Clarissa
> Dalloway's radiant, vital presence at her
> party, a ritual of community, helps to
> liberate her guests from their shells of
> individual solitude and memory. It is in
> this sense and these ways that they
> are heroic.

The following example by a professional writer will illustrate how extended definitions are formulated, developed and put to use. Notice that Lionel Trilling begins by contrasting snobbery with class pride and then, having indicated what the term "snobbery" does not signify, goes ahead in the next paragraph to indicate what it does signify. He restricts the term's application.

Definition by Restriction

Snobbery is not the same thing as pride of class. Pride of class may not please us but we must at least grant that it reflects a social function. A man who exhibited class pride—in the day when it was possible to do so—may have been puffed up about what he was, but this ultimately depended on what he *did*. Thus, aristocratic pride was based ultimately on the ability to fight and administer. No pride is without fault, but pride of class may be thought of as today we think of pride of profession, toward which we are likely to be lenient.

Snobbery is pride in status without pride in function. And it is an uneasy pride of status. It always asks, "Do I belong—do I really belong? And does he belong? And if I am observed talking to him, will it make me seem to belong or not to belong?" It is the peculiar vice not of aristocratic societies which have their own appropriate vices, but of bourgeois democratic societies. For us the legendary strongholds of snobbery are the Hollywood studios, where two thousand dollars a week dare not talk to three hundred dollars a week for fear that he will be taken for nothing more than fifteen hundred dollars a week. The dominant emotions of snobbery are uneasiness, self-consciousness, self-defensiveness, the sense that one is not quite real but can in some way acquire reality.

—LIONEL TRILLING

A second method of development is by *subdivision* and *classification*. Here the writer enumerates and distinguishes the main aspects of a topic, either as an introduction to a further discussion or for identification. The material can vary in subject matter—the major kinds of job opportunities in a community, the legal requirements a candidate must fulfill, the types of people one meets while working. The writer's concern should be to keep the features or classifications distinct.

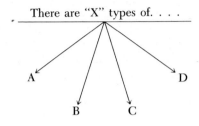

Subdivision and Classification

But the major disappointment in the book [*The Status Seekers*] is Packard's unclarified ideas about status—although the literature he himself cites could have clarified his ideas had he thought about it longer and harder. **There are at least three kinds of status, all of which the author touches upon without distinguishing. The first is** status-by-definition. If whites are defined as superior to Negroes, then any white, no matter how shiftless and ignorant, is superior to any Negro, no matter how talented and useful. **Then there is** status-by-consumption, in terms of which Bill is superior to Joe if Bill has a handsomer car, a more expensive house, or a more fashionable suit of clothes than Joe can display. **Finally there is** status-by-achievement, in which the individual is regarded as superior who, in his chosen line of endeavor, does a better job than others: the ball player who hits .375 or the scientist who solves a previously insoluble problem.

—S. I. HAYAKAWA

A third method is development by *comparison* or *contrast*. Here, a writer stresses likenesses or differences. To be effective, the paragraph should state the main point of the comparison early and should be organized so that the reader does not have to jump back and forth from one subject to another. Joseph Wood Krutch makes the point of the contrast very clear at the beginning of the following example:

Contrast

> Sociologists talk a great deal these days about "adjustment," which has always seemed to me a defeatist sort of word suggesting dismal surrender to the just tolerable. The road runner is not "adjusted" to his environment. He is triumphant in it. The desert is his home and he likes it. Other creatures, including many other birds, elude and compromise. They cling to the mountains or to the cottonwood-filled washes, especially in the hot weather, or they go away somewhere else, like the not entirely reconciled human inhabitants of this region. The road runner, on the other hand, stays here all the time and he prefers the areas where he is hottest and driest. . . .
>
> —Joseph Wood Krutch

One special type of comparison is *analogy*, discussed at length in Chapter 11. As a method of illustration, analogy can simplify and clarify complex relationships. In the following student paragraph, for example, the writer was faced with the problem of showing how the characters in William Faulkner's short story "Spotted Horses" could continue to admire and tolerate a man who continually fleeced them. To solve this problem, the student used the apt analogy of a game of pool with Willie Hoppe, for many years the world champion.

Analogy for Characterization

> "That Flem Snopes," says the narrator. "I be dog if he ain't a case now." The townspeople had respect for a good horse trader and Flem Snopes was that. Since money was of grotesque importance to these people who had to dig for every penny, they admired a man who could come by it easily and cleverly. Ironically, when Flem skinned someone of his last nickel and kept the fact to himself, the people would interpret Flem's silence as sheer modesty, while the victim laughed off as hopeless any thought of retribution. <u>Their admiration and toleration of Flem is not hard to understand. It was like a game of pool</u> in which you lose so decisively to Willie Hoppe that you feel no bitterness--merely a sense of pride and awe at having played the master at all. After Willie has beaten

you and quietly taken off the stakes, you
admit sheepishly to others you were licked
before you started and put the cue back on
the rack instead of taking it into some
dark alley to wait for Willie. Most people
didn't even try to beat the time-honored
master, Flem Snopes, at his game of
swindling.

Professional writers often try to make difficult abstract ideas concrete through analogy, and they take care, while developing their
paragraphs, to be sure the reader understands that the analogies
are illustrations, not proof. In developing the following paragraph,
for instance, Lincoln Barnett calls his analogy "this little fable."

Analogy for Description

**The distinction between Newton's and Einstein's ideas about
gravitation has sometimes been illustrated by picturing a little
boy playing marbles in a city lot.** The ground is very uneven. An
observer in an office ten stories above the street would not be
able to see these irregularities in the ground. Noticing that the
marbles appear to avoid some sections of the ground and move
toward other sections, he might assume that a [semi-magnetic]
"force" was operating which repelled the marbles from certain
spots and attracted them toward others. But another observer on
the ground would instantly perceive that the path of the marbles
was simply governed by the curvature of the field. In this little
fable Newton is the upstairs observer who imagines that a "force"
is at work, and Einstein is the observer on the ground, who has no
reason to make such an assumption. Einstein's gravitational laws,
therefore, merely describe the field properties of the space-time
continuum. . . .

—LINCOLN BARNETT

A fourth method is development by *cause* and *effect*. Here, the
writer stresses the connections between a result or results and the
preceding events. The writer may begin with the causes or with the
effects, but in either case he raises the question of connections and
makes it the basis for his paragraph development.

Causes and Effects Linked

> Here is one of the most familiar forms of the vicious circle of poverty. The poor get sick more than anyone else in the society. That is because they live in slums, jammed together under unhygienic conditions; they have inadequate diets, and cannot get decent medical care. When they become sick, they are sick longer than other groups in society. Because they are sick more often and longer than anyone else, they lose wages and work, and find it difficult to hold a steady job. And because of this, they cannot pay for good housing, for a nutritious diet, for doctors. At any given point in the circle, particularly when there is a major illness, their prospect is to move to an even lower level and to begin the cycle, round and round, toward even more suffering.
>
> —MICHAEL HARRINGTON

Often, cause-and-effect paragraphs are the basis for a whole paper. The first paragraph may raise the question of causes, the second paragraph eliminate some alternatives, the third focus on the remaining possibilities. Or the first paragraph may state the effect, the second raise the question, and the remaining ones analyze the cause or causes. Chapter 11 discusses the principles underlying cause-and-effect reasoning in some detail.

Depending on that nature of the material, a writer may use any *combination* of the methods just discussed to develop a paragraph adequately. The following paragraph has been pulled apart to show how its topic is developed by means of definition, contrast, and example.

TOPIC	London has one great advantage for Americans: since they know the language, they can easily get to know the people and their culture.
DEFINITION	By culture I do not mean the treasures of the British Museum or the Tate Gallery. I mean, rather, the underlying assumptions, attitudes, and values which give the specific flavor to British life.
CONTRAST	In other foreign countries this sense of the real life of the people is difficult to achieve. Americans in Paris may be able to ask simple questions and understand simple directions, but unless they know French very well, they remain onlookers, outsiders, and they miss the subtleties of the French outlook on life.
EXAMPLE	In London, every native is a potential acquaintance and a source of knowledge of British life.

The landlord at your bed and breakfast place will not only tell you how to get to Buckingham Palace; his incidental remarks may reveal a good deal about the English class system. A Cockney newsdealer gave me . . . .

A well-developed paragraph gives the reader as much relevant information as he needs for a full understanding of the point. To help yourself write well-developed paragraphs, try to

a. Use concrete diction which helps your reader see and feel the object or event, and select your details purposefully so that he cannot doubt what they illustrate.
b. Revise undeveloped paragraphs by identifying trite or vague generalities, distinguishing the opinions which need fuller explanation and evidence, and making a list of the details and examples to be included.
c. Determine whether a particular method of paragraph development, such as by definition or by contrast, best suits your immediate ends or whether a combination of methods will be necessary.

Exercises for Paragraph Development

Exercise 1

(Exercises 1 and 2 are for practice in working with concrete detail and diction.)

Pick one of the following topics and write two paragraphs about it. Make the diction of your first paragraph as vague, general, and trite as you can. Then, still describing the same event, make the diction of your second paragraph as concrete and clear as you can.

A man shaving sleepily with a dull razor
A student trying to stay awake in the front row
A teacher who cannot sit still or stay in one place
A man or woman shopping for clothes

Exercise 2

List six or eight details which you could use in describing one of the following subjects. Then organize the details into a well-developed paragraph.

Subway or bus passengers after midnight
Customers in a pet shop
The amusement section of a fair or carnival
A public swimming pool on a hot day
A college dining room at noon
A large crowd at a rock concert
People watching monkeys at the zoo

Exercise 3

(Exercises 3 through 8 are for practice in working with different methods of paragraph development. Your instructor may ask you to develop one or more of your choices into paragraphs.)

Pick one of the following and list several details you could use in developing a paragraph by specific detail.

A lazy roommate
A dull movie
An annoying lecturer
A successful party
An ideal campsite
A persistent salesperson
A spoiled child

Exercise 4

In a short paragraph for each, define any two of the following terms. Be sure to distinguish each term from other terms which are sometimes used as loose synonyms for it. For example, if you were to pick the term "chuckle," you would need to differentiate it from terms like "giggle" and "laugh."

a. Pond   e. Rage
b. Coupe   f. Bowl
c. Violin   g. Macadam
d. Pantomime   h. Biscuit

Exercise 5

Choose one of the following terms and define it in a paragraph or two.

a. Ecology   b. Propaganda

c. Isolationism   d. Women's Liberation
e. Lobbyist   f. Hypothesis

Exercise 6

Pick one of the following and list the main categories you would use in developing a paragraph by subdivision. Then write the paragraph.

The traits of a goof-off
The traits of a good talker
The best ways to study ineffectively
The kinds of movies students prefer

Exercise 7

Pick one of the following. List the main points you would use in developing the paragraph by comparison and contrast (or analogy). Then write the paragraph.

Dating in high school and dating in college
Arguing and discussing
Living at college and living at home
What is meant by the expression "mathematics is a language"
What is meant by saying an ethnic group "has its own culture"

Exercise 8

Pick one of the following and develop it in one or more paragraphs of cause and effect.

Why I have been uncertain about my major
Why teen-age marriages often fail
How a bull session can clarify one's thinking
How automobiles could be designed for greater safety

Exercise 9

This exercise is designed for practice in analyzing the methods of paragraph development used by professional writers. For each of the paragraphs below, identify the method or combination of methods used by the writer. Pick out the topic sentence (or make up one if there is none) and study each paragraph carefully to see what are its main points and what kind of evidence or detail is offered in support.

> The American people, more than any other people, is composed of individuals who have lost association with their old landmarks. They have crossed an ocean, they have spread themselves across a new continent. The American who still lives in his grandfather's house feels almost as if he were living in a museum. There are few Americans who have not moved at least once since their childhood, and even if they have stayed where they were born, the old landmarks themselves have been carted away to make room for progress. That, perhaps, is one reason why we have so much more Americanism than love of America. It takes time to learn to love the new gas station which stands where the wild honeysuckle grew. Moreover, the great majority of Americans have risen in the world. They have moved out of their class, lifting the old folks along with them perhaps, so that together they may sit by the steam pipes, and listen to the crooning of the radio. But more and more of them have moved not only out of their class, but out of their culture; and then they leave the old folks behind, and the continuity of life is broken. For faith grows well only as it is passed on from parents to their children amidst surroundings that bear witness, because nothing changes radically, to a deep permanence in the order of the world. It is true, no doubt, that in this great physical and psychic migration some of the old household gods are carefully packed up and put with the rest of the luggage, and then unpacked and set up on new altars in new places. But what can be taken along is at best no more than the tree which is above the ground. The roots remain in the soil where first they grew.

> —WALTER LIPPMAN

Biologists used to entertain themselves by speculating as to what would happen if, through some unthinkable catastrophe, the natural restraints were thrown off and all the progeny of a single individual survived. Thus Thomas Huxley a century ago calculated that a single female aphis (which has the curious power of reproducing without mating) could produce progeny in a single year's time whose total weight would equal that of the Chinese empire of his day.

Fortunately for us such an extreme situation is only theoretical, but the dire results of upsetting nature's own arrangements are well known to students of animal populations. The stockman's zeal for eliminating the coyote has resulted in plagues of field mice, which the coyote formerly controlled. The oft repeated story of the Kaibab deer in Arizona is another case in point. At one time the deer population was in equilibrium with its environment. A number of predators—wolves, pumas, and coyotes—prevented the deer from outrunning their food supply. Then a campaign was begun to "conserve" the deer by killing off their enemies. Once the predators were gone, the deer increased prodigiously and soon there was not enough food for them. The browse line on the trees went higher and higher as they sought food, and in time many more deer were dying of starvation than had formerly been killed by predators. The whole environment, moreover, was damaged by their desperate efforts to find food.

—RACHEL CARSON

I suppose that obvious things are the hardest to define. Everybody thinks he knows what a story is. But if you ask a beginning student to write a story, you're liable to get almost anything—a reminiscence, an episode, an opinion, an anecdote, anything under the sun but a story. A story is a complete dramatic action—and in good stories, the characters are shown through the action and the action is controlled through the characters, and the result of this is meaning that derives from the whole presented experience. I myself prefer to say that a story is a dramatic event that involves a person because he is a person, and a particular person—that is, because he shares in the general human condition and in some specific human situation. A story always involves, in a dramatic way, the mystery of personality. I lent some stories to a country lady who lives down the road from me, and when she returned them she said, "Well, them stories just gone and shown you how some folks *would* do," and I thought to myself that that was right; when you write stories, you have to be content to start exactly there—showing how some specific folks *will* do, *will* do in spite of everything.

—FLANNERY O'CONNOR

All of the disconnector virtues—courage, perseverance, rectitude, chastity, ambition, honor, dutifulness, self-discipline, temperance, purity, self-reliance, impartiality, incorruptibility, dependability, conscientiousness, sobriety, asceticism, spirituality—are ecologically unsound. All express the same arrogant assumption about the importance of the single individual in society and the importance of humanity in the universe. To imagine that it matters (except to those in immediate contact with him) whether or not a man is righteous, holy, or self-actualized is the height of pomposity.

The opposite virtues—cowardice, distractibility, sensuality, inability to complete tasks or resist temptations, partiality, dependency, inconsistency, corruptibility, and so on—are humble virtues. They express humanity's embeddedness in a larger organic system—a system that has its own laws and justice. As such they ultimately have higher survival value than the disciplines since they serve to reconnect the individual with his or her environment. This is not to say that the arrogant virtues should be extirpated from the human repertory. We need only recognize the *price* of the disconnector virtues.

—PHILIP SLATER

It is seldom that an English judge or magistrate does not at least wince or yawn when a psychiatric opinion is being read; often he speaks his mind. This is a favourite. "It is not going to hurt your victim any the less to know that you knocked her down because of some complex or other." True. Just as it is not going to hurt any the less if what knocked her down had been a falling branch or brick. We no longer think of cutting down the tree or burning down the house; we've become quite rational towards inanimate things. The tree may need a prop; those bricks may need more mortar; the hooligan may need some treatment or another kind of life. The chief difference is that we know more about roofs and trees; men and women being of course more complex, and we much less willing to learn.

—SYBILLE BEDFORD

8b   Paragraph Coherence

Within every paragraph the sentences should be arranged and linked in such a manner that readers can easily follow the thought. It isn't enough for readers to know what each sentence means; readers must also see how each sentence is related to the one which precedes it and how it leads into the one which follows it. The connections may be clear enough to the writer but not at all clear to readers: incoherence means that the relationships have not been shown, not that they don't exist. Coherence is *continuity* within and between paragraphs. The means of securing continuity are, first, the arrangement of sentences in a logical order and, second, the use of special devices such as the repetition of key words to link sentences.

(1) Logical Order of Ideas

Though a topic sentence will help give focus to a paragraph, you need a consistent pattern of organization within the paragraph to ensure continuity. The particular pattern will depend on the kind of material which is to go into the paragraph. The four patterns to be discussed include chronological order, spatial order, deductive order, and inductive order.

The pattern most often used for narrating personal experiences, summarizing steps in a process, and explaining historical events and movements is *chronological order*—the arranging of events in an orderly time sequence. If the time sequence of a narrative is unclear or disorderly, incoherence can result. Diagrammed, chronological order means

$$A \rightarrow B \rightarrow C \rightarrow D, \text{ not } C \rightarrow A \rightarrow D \rightarrow B.$$

For instance, in revising the following paragraph for greater coherence, the writer placed her motives first [1] and then arranged the rest of the paragraph in an orderly chronological sequence—routine [2], first week on the job [3], following weeks on the job [4], conclusion at the summer's end about the value of interesting work [5]. (The brackets and numbers have been added here for illustration.)

Patterned Chronologically

> Last summer I took a job as a waitress.
> [1] My motives at the time were purely
> ulterior: I had been attracted by local
> fables of the generous tips left by tour-
> ists and thought I would earn some easy
> money towards a college wardrobe. [2] My
> routine was the regular one: take orders,
> carry food, clean up the table, and
> repeat--eight hours a day, six days a
> week. During that first week [3], I could
> only stumble home after a day's work and
> fall in bed. Even when I had become
> accustomed to the routine [4], I never had
> any trouble distinguishing between the
> drudgery of that hot, noisy restaurant and
> the relaxation which came naturally but
> too briefly with the leisure of a cool

> evening. By the end of the summer [5], I had
> firmly resolved never to take another job
> unless the work itself was interesting.

An important pattern of organization is *spatial order,* useful for many kinds of description. This pattern helps provide coherence by arranging visual details in some consistent sequence—from left to right, right to left, east to west, west to east, from the distant to the near, or from the near to the distant. If the writer moves haphazardly from one place to another, this randomness produces an incoherent pattern. Diagrammed, spatial order can mean

$$A$$
$$\downarrow$$
$$B$$
$$\downarrow \quad \text{or} \quad A \rightarrow B \rightarrow C \rightarrow D, \text{ or their opposites.}$$
$$C$$
$$\downarrow$$
$$D$$

It can also mean

$$A \nearrow^{B} \searrow_{C} \quad \text{or} \quad \begin{matrix} A \rightarrow B \\ \downarrow \\ D \leftarrow C \end{matrix}$$

and variations thereof.

In the following paragraph, the writer begins with the sky, moves down to the girls, down from them to the cart and the man, and then concludes with the skeleton, a real climax.

Spatial Pattern

> The night was clear and cool. There was
> only a small crescent moon and the small
> blue stars, cold and far away. A biting
> wind from snowy Taos Mountain made the
> girls shiver as they crouched close to the
> embankment and looked down at the proces-
> sion passing beneath them. Janet heard
> loud squeaking and creaking and rose up for
> a better look. She saw the Carreta del
> Muerto, the cart of death, passing

beneath. A bent-over man was pulling the crude wooden cart on large wheels. On top of the cart sat a figure of death, an intricately carved skeleton representing expert craftsmanship and a detailed knowledge of the human body. The figure was veiled in a black cloak and held a drawn bow and an arrow nocked for flight. The skeleton's eyes were obsidian, shiny stones to catch the pale moonlight and show that death was alive, his eyes searching the darkness. He rode in the middle of the procession, instilling fear in the heart of every man, for the mystery of death is veiled, and no man can tell where he will strike next.

A paragraph laid out in *deductive order* makes a well-known logical structure. This pattern of organization is one which moves from a general statement to the particular details which support or explain it. Diagrammed, deductive order can mean

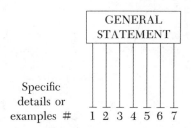

If details are scattered throughout the paragraph, the reader may be left with a blurred memory of miscellaneous information. The original of the following paragraph began with a clear general statement—"The Roman Empire expanded because the Romans were great organizers as well as fine builders and engineers"—but the paragraph jumped from bridges and roads to language and religion, from language and religion to law and citizenship, from law and citizenship to the training of soldiers, from the training of soldiers back to bridges and roads. To make the paragraph coherent, the student revised it by dividing it into two paragraphs and grouping his ideas accordingly.

Patterned Deductively

> The Roman Empire expanded because the Romans were great organizers as well as fine builders and engineers. When they conquered a territory, they systematically tried to make it a willing part of the Empire. They brought Roman law and the promise of Roman citizenship and they introduced Latin as a common language. Sometimes they recruited and trained native men to become Roman soldiers, as in the case of the members of the German tribes who became part of the Praetorian Guard, the Emperor's personal soldiers. But they did not try to change all of the religious beliefs and social customs of the conquered people. They did not, for example, try to complel the Egyptians to accept the Roman gods.
>
> Moreover, when the Romans conquered a territory, they constructed key cities and highways to consolidate their military and financial power in the colony. London, for instance, was built as a military depot and trade center. The excellent roads and bridges built by Roman engineers to the main administrative city gave the Romans good control over the surrounding countryside. A few of these bridges and roads in France and Italy are still in use today.

Another pattern for organizing paragraphs is arrangement by *inductive order*. The inductive paragraph is organized with the details at the beginning and in the middle, and with an ending which is a summary or generalization, usually the topic sentence. Diagrammed, inductive order means

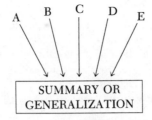

Details A B C D E → SUMMARY OR GENERALIZATION

The inductive pattern is the complementary counterpart of the deductive; some of the preceding deductively arranged material about the Romans might just as easily have been arranged and more fully developed in this pattern:

Inductive Pattern

> Roman roads were built on a solid stone base and paved with flat rocks. They were crowned on the top and ditched along the sides for drainage. They were designed to run in almost straight lines and to go over hills, not around them. Roman armies used them as military highways--ten to twenty feet wide--to move legions rapidly and to supply them adequately. These roads led to and from key administrative cities such as London, originally built as a depot and trade center, and gave the Romans good control over the surrounding countryside. In Britain alone, a great series of roads radiated from the southeast to all parts of the island. <u>Thanks to these superbly designed roads linking cities and ensuring rapid troop movement, the Romans could hold conquered territory and expand the Empire.</u>

(2) Special Devices for Coherence

The other means of achieving coherence include the use of transitional words, the use of linking pronouns, the repetition of key words, and the use of parallel structure. Usually, experienced writers employ *all* these means, and they are not much interested in the label attached to the method they use. Instead, they are concerned to achieve coherence accurately and gracefully. But here it will be helpful to discuss separately each technique available to you for improving paragraphs which lack coherence. What happens when the available means are not fully employed can be seen in the following paragraph:

Disjointed

I was a naive child. My parents sheltered me. All playmates were picked with care. I wasn't allowed to join any of the gangs that roamed the neighborhood so freely, and the TV shows I saw and books I read were carefully picked. When I went to camp, I was on my own. I expected the other campers to "play fair" and abide by the rules. At the dinner table, one camper opened my eyes, as well as making them sting, when he blew pepper in them. He had invited me to see something in his hand. I was surprised the next day when I found another camper reading a comic book called "Tales of the Horror from the Crypt." He lounged on my bunk and dripped a melting candy bar onto my blanket. This was the beginning of my real education. I had to learn how to make my own decisions about people and situations and act on these decisions for myself.

Though it has unity and development, the paragraph generally lacks coherence because the writer too often leaps and jumps erratically from one sentence to the next, as reading aloud will make especially clear. Revised by slight rephrasing and the addition of connecting words, the paragraph becomes easier to follow:

More Coherent

I was a naive child <u>because</u> my parents sheltered me. <u>They picked</u> my playmates carefully and kept me from joining any of the gangs that so freely roamed the neighborhood. They censored the TV I watched and the books I read. Thus, when they sent me away to camp, I was on my own for the first time in my life, and as a result of my training, I expected the other campers to "play fair" and abide by the rules. The first camper to open my eyes, as well as make them sting, did so at the dinner table by blowing pepper into them, after inviting me to see something in his hand. Another camper surprised me the next day when I found him reading a comic book called "Tales of the Horror from the Crypt" as he lounged on my bunk and dripped a melting candy bar onto my blanket. That summer at camp was the beginning of my real education. For the first time I had to learn how to make my own decisions about people and situations and act on these decisions myself.

In the revised passage, *the writer is no longer thinking in single sentences only.* Instead, he has looked for the continuity among his ideas and for the most accurate means of showing this continuity in each case.

Transitional words and phrases serve to indicate different relationships. Here is a chart of relationships and appropriate transitional words:

1. Result or consequence: *hence, consequently, as a result, therefore.*
2. Comparison or contrast: *similarly, likewise, however, on the other hand, yet, still, nevertheless.*
3. Example or illustration: *as an illustration, for example, specifically, for instance.*
4. Additional aspects or evidence: *moreover, furthermore, also, too, next, besides, in the first place, first.*
5. Conclusion or summary: *in conclusion, to sum up, to conclude, in short.*

Notice the careful use of transitional words in the following passage:

Relationships Indicated

Past and future are two time regions which we commonly separate by a third which we call the present. **But** strictly speaking, the present does not exist, **or** is at best no more than an infinitesimal point in time, gone before we can note it as present. **Nevertheless** we must have a present; **and so** we get one by robbing the past, by holding on to the most recent events and pretending that they all belong to our immediate perceptions. If, **for example,** I raise my arm, the total event is a series of occurrences of which the first are past before the last have taken place; **yet** I perceive it as a single movement executed in one instant of time.

—CARL BECKER

Sentences also may be connected by linking pronouns which have clear antecedents. This technique is an effective way of avoiding needless repetition. Notice in the following example how Henry James substitutes "it" for "symbolism" and later for "this suggestion" and how he uses the phrase "*this* suggestion" to point back to the entire preceding sentence.

Linking Pronouns

In **The Scarlet Letter** there is a great deal of symbolism; there is, I think, too much. **It** is overdone at times, and becomes mechanical; **it** ceases to be impressive, and grazes triviality. The idea of the mystic A which the young minister finds imprinted upon his breast and eating into his flesh, in sympathy with the embroidered badge that Hester is condemned to wear, appears to me to be a case in point. **This** suggestion should, I think, have just been made and dropped; to insist upon **it,** and return to **it,** is to exaggerate the weak side of the subject. Hawthorne returns to **it** constantly, plays with **it,** and seems charmed by **it;** until at last the reader feels tempted to declare that his enjoyment of **it** is puerile.

—HENRY JAMES

Paragraph coherence is also maintained *by the repetition of key words* which are related to a central idea. In the following passage, notice the key words *darkness, deep sea,* and *blackness* and the words related to them by contrast such as *sunlight, red rays,* and *surface:*

Key Words Repeated

Immense pressure, then, is one of the governing conditions of life in the **deep sea; darkness** is another. The unrelieved **darkness** of the **deep waters** has produced weird and incredible modifications of the **abyssal** fauna. It is a **blackness** so divorced from the world of the **sunlight** that probably only the few men who have seen it with their own **eyes** can visualize it. We know that **light fades out rapidly with descent below the surface.** The **red rays** are gone at the end of the first 200 or 300 feet, and with them all the **orange and yellow warmth of the sun.** Then the **greens** fade out, and at 1,000 feet only a **deep, dark brilliant blue** is left. In **very clear waters** the **violet rays** of the spectrum may penetrate another thousand feet. Beyond this is only the **blackness** of the **deep sea.**

—RACHEL CARSON

Continuity can also be sustained by *parallel structure,* which calls attention to similar ideas. This coordination of equally important ideas is often useful with introductory or summary paragraphs, though its use is by no means confined to such paragraphs. In the following example, the first paragraph is taken from the beginning of a chapter, the second from near its conclusion.

To "become a pueblo" **meant to adopt** many of the ways and political forms and ambitions of townspeople. **It meant to accept** the tools, leadership, and conceptions of progress which were then being offered to the villagers of Yucatan by the leaders of Mexico's social revolution. **It required** the inhabitants **to give up** some of the isolation which was theirs in the remote and sparsely inhabited lands that lay apart from the goings and comings of city men. In future they would be a part of the political and economic institutions of Yucatan, of Mexico, and—though of course they would not have put it so—of the one world that was then in the making.

. . .

Chan Kom had attained its loftiest political objective. **It had become** the head of its own municipality. **It had made** itself into a pueblo, a community of dwellers—some of them—in masonry houses. **It had** a municipal building, with a stone jail; a school building, also of masonry; a masonry church—and a masonry Protestant chapel. **It had** two gristmills and four stores. **It had** two outdoor theatres and a baseball diamond.

—ROBERT REDFIELD

Notice how the parallel structure in the first three sentences of the second paragraph restate what it meant for Chan Kom to achieve its "loftiest political objective." Notice how the parallel structure in the last three sentences of the second paragraph lists equally important features in a "community of dwellers." And notice how the parallel structure of the second paragraph harks back to the parallel structure of the first paragraph—from what Chan Kom "had attained" back to what "it required" to become a pueblo.

If the paper is to read smoothly, the reader must be able to see *the connections between the paragraphs* as well as the relationships within a paragraph. Even though a paragraph is well-constructed in itself, it may fail to be an integral part of the paper. Indeed, from the reader's viewpoint, it is more important that a paragraph should carry him along from one point to the next than that it should be a little masterpiece in itself. Aside from the short transitional paragraphs discussed in Chapter 7, the main devices for providing coherence among paragraphs are the same as those for providing coherence within a paragraph—transitional words, linking pronouns, key words repeated, and parallel structure.

Probably more important than any of these devices is the *arrangement* of the material so that a paragraph ends with some reference to the idea that is to be taken up next. In the following example, taken from Turner's "The Significance of the Frontier in American History," notice how continuity is sustained by the progression of the argument:

Continuity by Arrangement of Material and Focused Thesis

. . . Up to our own day [1893] American history has been in a large degree the history of the colonization of the Great West. The existence of an area of free land, its continuous recession, and the advance of American settlement westward, explain American development [thesis].

Behind institutions, behind constitutional forms and modifications, lie the vital forces that call these organs into life and shape them to meet changing conditions. The peculiarity of American institutions is the fact they have been compelled to adapt themselves to the changes of an expanding people—to the changes involved in crossing a continent, in winning a wilderness. . . . [omission of the rest of a long paragraph]

In this advance, the frontier is the outer edge of the wave—the meeting point between savagery and civilization. . . . [omission of the rest]

The American frontier is sharply distinguished from the European frontier—a fortified boundary line running through dense populations. The most significant thing about the American frontier is that it lies at the hither edge of free land. . . . [omission of the rest of the paragraph]

In the settlement of America we have to observe how European life entered the continent, and how America modified and developed that life. . . . The frontier is the line of the most rapid and effective Americanization. . . . [rest of paragraph suggests how, and concludes] And to study this advance, the men who grew up under these conditions, and the political, economic and social results of it, is to study the really American part of our history.

—FREDERICK JACKSON TURNER

Exercises for Paragraph Coherence

Exercise 1

Pick an aspect of a subject you know well and jot down about a dozen nouns or noun phrases connected with it—e.g., hard wax, soft wax, backache, shammy, clean rags, car washed, shady spot, lots of time, etc. Then arrange the items in a logical order, discarding any that won't fit, and write a *coherent* paragraph from your outline.

Exercise 2

Pick one of the following topics. Then write two separate paragraphs about it in which you try to develop the same idea each time but use a *different* pattern of organization for each paragraph.

The pleasure of being a good tennis player (or poker player, or dancer, or whatever).
The most effective way to put things off without feeling guilty
The most offensive commercial on TV
How to make your advisor (or teacher) remember your name
How to keep your temper in a traffic jam

Exercise 3

Analyze the paragraphs you have written for exercise 2 to determine what specific devices you have used most frequently for coherence.

Exercise 4

Compare the rough draft and the final version of one of your papers to determine how much you revised for coherence. If you made changes, were they to improve the order used (e.g., making time sequence clearer), to supply more specific links, or to sharpen up the thrust of the whole argument? Or were they a combination of these?

Exercise 5

For the following paragraphs, identify the pattern of organization and the specific transitional devices used in each.

> When we are children, though, there are categories of films we don't like—documentaries generally (they're too much like education) and, of course, movies especially designed for children. By the time we can go on our own we have learned to avoid them. Children are often put down by adults when the children say they enjoyed a particular movie; adults who are short on empathy are quick to point out aspects of the plot or theme that the child didn't understand, and it's easy to humiliate a child in this way. But it is one of the glories of eclectic arts like opera and movies that they include so many possible kinds and combinations of pleasure. One may be enthralled by Leontyne Price in "La Forza del Destino" even if one hasn't boned up on the libretto, or entranced by "The Magic Flute" even if one has boned up on the libretto, and a movie may be enjoyed for many reasons that have little to do with the story or subtleties (if any) of theme or character. Unlike "pure" arts which are often defined in terms of what only they can do, movies are open and unlimited. Probably everything that can be done in movies can be done some other way, but—and this is what's so miraculous and so expedient about them—they can do almost anything any other art can do (alone or in combination) and they can take on some of the functions of exploration, of journalism, of anthropology, of almost any branch of knowledge as well. We go to the movies for the variety of what they can provide, and for their marvelous ability to give us easily and inexpensively (and usually painlessly) what we can get from other arts also. They are a wonderfully *convenient* art.
>
> —PAULINE KAEL

> The village to which our family had come was a scattering of some twenty to thirty houses down the southeast slope of a valley. The valley was narrow, steep and almost entirely cut off; it was also a funnel for winds, a channel for the floods, and a

jungly, bird-crammed, insect-hopping sun trap whenever there happened to be any sun. It was not high and open like the Windrush country, but had secret origins, having been gouged from the escarpment by the melting ice caps some time before we got there. The old flood-terraces still showed on the slopes, along which the cows walked sideways. Like an island, it was possessed of curious survivals—rare orchids and Roman snails; and there were chemical qualities in the limestone springs which gave the women pre-Raphaelite goitres. The sides of the valley were rich in pasture and the crests heavily covered in beech woods.

Living down there was like living in a bean pod; one could see nothing but the bed one lay in. Our horizon of woods was the limit of our world. For weeks on end the trees moved in the wind with a dry roaring that seemed a natural utterance of the landscape. In winter they ringed us with frozen spikes, and in summer they oozed over the lips of the hills like layers of thick green lava. Mornings, they steamed with mist or sunshine, and almost every evening threw streamers above us, reflecting sunsets we were too hidden to see.

Water was the most active thing in the valley, arriving in the long rains from Wales. It would drip all day from clouds and trees, from roofs and eaves and noses. It broke open roads, carved its way through gardens, and filled the ditches with sucking noises. Men and horses walked about in wet sacking, birds shook rainbows from sodden branches, and streams ran from holes, and back into holes, like noisy underground trains.

—LAURIE LEE

What man most passionately wants is his living wholeness and his living unison, not his own isolate salvation of his "soul." Man wants his physical fulfillment first and foremost, since now, once and once only, he is in the flesh and potent. For man, the vast marvel is to be alive. For man, as for flower and beast and bird, the supreme triumph is to be most vividly, most perfectly alive. Whatever the unborn and the dead may know, they cannot know the beauty, the marvel of being alive in the flesh. The dead may look after the afterward. But the magnificent here and now of life in the flesh is ours, and ours alone, and ours only for a time. We ought to dance with rapture that we should be alive and in the flesh, and part of the living, incarnate cosmos. I am part of the sun as my eye is part of me. That I am part of the earth my feet know perfectly, and my blood is part of the sea. My soul knows that I am part of the human race, my soul is an organic part of the great human race, as my spirit is part of my nation. In my own very self, I am part of my family. There is nothing of me that is alone and absolute except my mind, and we shall find that the mind has no existence by itself; it is only the glitter of the sun on the surface of the waters.

So that my individualism is really an illusion. I am part of the great whole, and I can never escape. But I *can* deny my connections, break them, and become a fragment. Then I am wretched.

What we want is to destroy our false, inorganic connections, especially those related to money, and re-establish the living organic connections, with the cosmos, the sun and earth, with mankind and nation and family. Start with the sun, and the rest will slowly, slowly happen.

—D. H. LAWRENCE

Voice and Audience 9

"Why are you writing?" someone asks. "Because I have to," we answer, short of time and temper and certainly out of patience with silly questions. Besides, the answer is true enough. Most of us write not because we choose to, but because we are told to by parents, by teachers, by employers. If we want another present from Uncle Henry or an *A* in Economic Theory or the job as District Manager, we write the letter, the term paper, the report, whether we feel like writing or not.

But there are occasions now and then when we write because we have something we want to say with clarity and feeling and power. The composition of a letter to someone we love or the declaration under fire of a value we believe in can move us to choose our words carefully, to change the order of our sentences, to revise and write again until we feel certain that what we have written will move another person. In such a creative act we can almost hear our voice in the words on the page and see the look of recognition on the face of the person we are addressing. Moments like this are rare, but they produce the best writing, and the best is always rare.

While ordinary composition is not so intense, we still can bring to routine assignments a human concern. If we resolve to be personally committed to any act of writing, to care about what we say and how we say it, such an involvement will compel us to write vigorously and well. Writing becomes mechanical and inhuman only if we fail to listen to our personal voice and to the imagined voice of the listener beside us.

Writing begins as dialogue. It is one person speaking to another about something of importance to both of them. We write because we wish to extend the one-to-one relationship where all communication begins to a larger number of persons for a longer time to come. As we become literate and learn to write the language of written discourse, our audience widens, our knowledge of the world and its history deepens, and our awareness of self expands. Our writing skills must grow in complexity and scope if they are to keep pace with this mature experience.

9a The Writer's Voice

In spoken dialogue, our facial expression, gestures, and tone of voice determine to a great extent the way our audience responds to what we say. The pitch, volume, and pace of our speech tell our audience whether we are serious or mocking, authoritative or questioning—in short, how we feel about our subject matter. In writing, we must translate these physical and auditory signals into visual symbols, so that the eyes of our audience will hear the tones of our voices.

One of the pleasures of learning to write well is the discovery that we have a number of writing voices and that the more proficient we become as stylists, the more voices we have at our disposal. On one occasion we may speak from the authority of personal experience; on another as the questioning investigative reporter or the reasonable observer who gathers and evaluates evidence. Our written tone-of-voice can vary from ironic or wry to formal, elegant, funny, passionate, casual, or grim.

Before we can write consistently with any voice, we must know exactly how we feel about the topic. We must try to say what *we* think, not what we think someone else (usually the teacher) wants to hear. Instead of abandoning our personal voice, we must write with a lively sense of self. The reader must be convinced that we know exactly what we want to say and that we consider it important.

Such confident writing demands self-examination. As you collect material, go beyond what the author says. Ask yourself what you think about his statements. Do they square with your experience, or the recorded experience of other writers? As you go through a book, get involved in an active exchange of ideas with the author. Take notes on a separate sheet of paper. Summarizing comments will map areas of the material that you find important. Question marks and exclamation points help to start an argument with the author. Comments like "Right on" or "Hogwash!" may help you discover what you think and where you stand.

For flexibility, cultivate a number of personal voices, and learn to shift easily from one to another. To discover how the written voice is altered by a shift in point of view, experiment in your preliminary drafts by beginning in the first person and ending in the third, by shifting from the singular to the plural. The degree of responsibility for what we say changes considerably from "I know" to "you know," to "we know." The old parlor game of Conjugations matches degrees of frankness with the person spoken to, or of: *I* look healthy and well nourished; *you* are a trifle overweight; *she* is getting fat.

9b Audience

In spoken dialogue, we can see whether or not other people understand what we are saying, whether they approve, when they object. As writers, alone with our thoughts and our typewriters, we must imagine how the audience will react to what we write. To do this, try to visualize your intended audience. Will your readers be older, younger, or about the same age as yourself? What do they know about the subject matter—more or less than you do, or about as much? Is the audience of the same race, religion, or sex as you are? What is your own feeling toward such an audience: affection, distrust, anxiety, fellowship? You need to decide whom you want to reach before you can select the appropriate voice for making contact with them.

Some writers find it helpful to visualize a specific member of the audience they are addressing. While in the British Museum reading a book entitled *The Natural Inferiority of Women*, Virginia Woolf began to draw a picture of the kind of man she imagined the author to be. To her surprise she found that her sketch of the angry author also revealed her own anger, and she was able to trace its source: "the professor's statement about the mental, moral, and physical inferiority of women." "One does not like," she continues, "to be told that one is naturally the inferior of a little man—I looked at the student next to me—who breathes hard, wears a ready-made tie, and has not shaved this fortnight."

To her surprise, Woolf discovered that the assumption of inferiority which had blinded the professor to his anger against women revealed her own anger against men. In coming to terms with her feelings, she gained the rhetorical advantage; the book she subsequently wrote, *A Room of One's Own,* is an exemplar of modulated tone. Only when we are in control of our feelings and ourselves can we control the responses of others.

Good writers can adapt to a number of audiences. We make such adjustments of tone and style every day. If we are explaining a bridge to a small child, we don't use the vocabulary of a structural engineer. If we are speaking to strangers, we don't use slang or obscenity or the familiar dialects which we use with close friends or family. The person who is sincerely trying to communicate, rather than impress or confound, makes every effort to find the language appropriate to the audience.

In a writing course you can assume, unless otherwise instructed, that the students and the instructor constitute your audience. Most teachers, when they read student papers, try to exemplify the informed and questioning mind that should be the result of a university education. Keep such an audience in mind, but remember also that your classmates, though of your generation, may represent geographic areas and cultures different from your own. Becoming aware of these different provinces and comparing them with your own provincial outlook will help you to discover the assumptions you bring to your writing and the prejudices your audience brings to its reading.

Part of the task of writers is learning to anticipate the objections of an audience. In reading fiction or watching a play, we willingly suspend disbelief, as Coleridge says, but in reading exposition or argument, we seldom do. In fact, the tension generated by our unspoken objections contributes to the excitement we discover in expository discourse. "Prove it . . . show me . . ." we insist in conversation. As writers, we try to imagine when the audience will begin to look incredulous or skeptical, and then to do something about it.

We must also be always alert for signs of a listener's boredom. While the sound of one hand clapping may be the ultimate of Zen enlightenment, the sound of one voice droning on and on is apt to put a listener to sleep. We must keep in mind that our audience is distracted by a number of things, like the inclination to read something else, or the disinclination to read at all. If we care about our audience, we must be careful to keep them interested, and we do this best when we are ourselves interested in the subject.

Don't hesitate to bring your own biases to bear on the topic. Prod the topic with questions. How do I, as a young person, or a Black, or a Pre-law student, or a woman, or a southerner—a poet, a gambler, a Buddhist, a hopeless romantic or a confirmed skeptic—feel about the problem of ecology? How does my personal history—the fact that my grades are lousy but my lovelife good, that I like to swim and hike and want to own a car, that I like to be alone at times and crowded together with people at others—how does all this affect my attitude toward water and trees, toward babies and oil wells, solar energy, condominiums, and plastics? What sort of objections would someone have if I advocated the banning of the internal combustion engine? What sort of objection would I have if someone stole my car? What sort of evidence might convert either of us to the other's point of view? Every topic is potentially controversial, and controversy is always interesting.

To sum all this up, you should speak in one of your own natural voices, not in the inhuman abstractions of the bureaucrat. And you should keep your intended audience always in mind and try to make reading pleasant and comprehension easy for them.

Exercise 1

Observe your instructors and your classmates in the courses you are taking. How much do the instructors rely on body language or gesture to convey information as they lecture or lead discussions? How much information does the "audience" (the class) reveal through body language? How attentive is the instructor to this language? Be prepared to translate into words your interpretation of these gestures.

Exercise 2

Analyze the point of view this chapter is written from. Is it consistent, or does it change; if so, where and why? What tone does the point of view (or points of view) convey? Is the tone appropriate to the audience and the subject matter?

Exercise 3

Make a list of your own assumptions about the following topics and of the objections you would anticipate on the part of the intended audience.

TOPIC	AUDIENCE
The right of women to obtain an abortion.	The trustees of a Catholic Hospital.
The legalization of marijuana.	High school seniors.
The vitality of the institution of marriage and the family.	Your parents in a letter.
The abolition of the combustion engine.	Stockholders of General Motors.
The necessity for National Health Insurance.	American Medical Association.
Prohibiting the distribution of birth control devices.	Membership of the Planned Parenthood Association.
Public control of television programming.	President of a major T.V. network.

Try to visualize these audiences. Draw a picture of a representative member of that audience. What does the picture tell you about your feelings for the audience and for the subject matter?

Exercise 4

How would you make the following topics interesting?

The equal distribution of funding to female and male athletic programs in colleges and universities

Violence and sex in the contemporary cinema

The grading system as an obstacle to education

The selling of nuclear arms to foreign countries

Racial prejudice in high school

The patient's right to determine in terminal cases when medical assistance should be stopped

Do prisons rehabilitate criminals?

Should foreign languages be required courses in elementary schools?

The enforcement by local governments of air pollution regulations

Mandatory spaying of cats and dogs

Exercise 5

The Danish theologian, Søren Kierkegaard, made notes in his *Journal* for writing a novel about a madman which began in the third person and ended in the first. Try a similar experiment on any topic in which you begin a paragraph in the third person singular and end in the personal "I". What happens as the point of view shifts?

10 | Plan and Organization

If a topic for a paper is assigned, you must be sure you understand what you are being asked to do. This is especially important if you are asked to write an "essay" question on an examination. If you have any doubt about what the question calls for, ask for clarification. If a theme assignment requires that you comprehend certain reading materials, do the reading early enough so that you can discuss obscure points with the instructor or members of the class. Talking about a subject generates critical thinking and makes for fluent writing.

Word limits are usually assigned as an indication of approximate scale, not as absolute restrictions. Your instructor is not going to count the number of words in your paper; don't waste time doing it yourself. Ordinarily, you will find that the real problem is not filling up space but keeping within the rough limits set by a teacher or editor. If your first draft seems too short, look for more material, not more padding. It is a courtesy to your audience to present your argument as incisively as possible, but if your first draft goes far beyond the set limit, cut down the topic instead of trying to compress everything into a few pages.

10a   Limiting a Subject

The process of limiting, or cutting down, a topic to manageable size is particularly important when you are free to choose your own subject. Complete freedom of choice can be confusing, especially when preliminary reading shows you how complicated things really are. Suppose for example that you have been concerned about the importance of conserving the world's natural resources. When you begin to explore this large subject, you may be tempted to throw up your hands in despair. Such topics as natural scenery, agricultural lands to grow food for increasing millions of people, limited supplies of oil and natural gas, other possible sources of energy (solar, geothermal, nuclear) and their potential hazards and advantages, pollution of the air by exhaust gases from factories and cars, pollution of rivers and lakes by industrial wastes or sewage, inadequate water supply in urban areas, the necessity of controlling population growth—even a book would be too short to cover it all. How do you start?

The answer is "Don't start, yet." That is, don't begin to write until you have limited the topic to a size you can handle comfortably. Instead of trying to say something about all the topics included under "Conservation of Natural Resources," choose one of them, and start to explore it in detail.

Suppose you choose other sources of energy than the now prevailing oil, coal, and natural gas. Alternate sources are, mainly, solar, nuclear, and geothermal. In its direct form, solar energy is relatively simple—heating space or water by concentrating the sun's rays. But the possibilities of utilizing indirect solar energy—harnessing the wind, developing natural water power, taking advantage of temperature differences in the sea, recycling organic wastes like garbage or sewage, converting vegetable fuel to alcohol or artificial "natural" gas—are still too broad for a single paper. You might choose one of these subtopics and explore it, or you might move on to consider nuclear power. Here you would find two main subdivisions—energy from nuclear fission (splitting the atom) and energy from nuclear fusion. The latter, still in an experimental stage, would involve some highly technical special knowledge.

Unless you know a good deal about nuclear physics, you'd better try the simpler process—nuclear fission, now used widely to generate electricity. This process, you will soon discover, is highly controversial. Its advantages and disadvantages are hotly debated by physicists whose expert knowledge does not keep them from violent disagreement. Is the process economically justifiable, considering the enormous cost of building nuclear reactors? Is the process safe enough to justify tripling the number of our nuclear plants?

If you decide to limit yourself to exploring this latter question, you may have cut down your topic to a manageable size. When you begin reading on the relative safety of present nuclear power plants, you will find that critics of nuclear power point to three chief hazards: the danger of the accidental escape of radioactive material at a reactor, the danger of plutonium falling into the hands of terrorists bent on nuclear blackmail, and the problem of safely disposing of the violently poisonous nuclear "ash." These three points may still be too much to cover in a short paper. How about taking only one of them?

Suppose you choose only the first of these—the possible danger of accident at a nuclear power plant. You will still find differences of opinion, and you may gather more material than you will actually use. That is normal; don't worry about it. You will now be in a position to select items to suit your topic. You may, for example, come across an account of a near-accident at the Browns Ferry plant in Alabama and decide to use it as one example of the human error which can render the best of safety devices inoperable.

It should be clear by now that you can't limit a subject to an appropriate size by just sitting at your desk and thinking. You need to get over to the library and inform yourself a little. The more you read, the more possible lines of development will suggest themselves; and by a process of narrowing and eliminating, you can arrive at a unified topic of about the right size for the space at your disposal. As you organize and write up this material, you may want to cut a bit here, or add there, depending on your purpose, but at least you will have something to work with.

10b Defining Your Purpose

Before you do much actual writing, you should define your purpose in writing at all. What am I trying to do with this material? Do I want to present objectively both sides of some controversial question? Am I trying to convince my audience that nuclear reactors are safe, or dangerous? Unless you have clearly defined your purpose, you may wander away from the main point of the paper.

By the end of the first draft, your stand on the issue should be clear, and you should be able to express your purpose in a single, unambiguous sentence which sums up the central thesis the paper develops. In most essays, although by no means all, the thesis statement is expressed in the opening paragraph and is a useful guide for letting the reader know where the writer is going. In some essays the thesis is not finally stated until the concluding paragraph. Such holding back of the thesis statement can provide a dramatic turn to the essay and give the reader a sense of discovery. No matter where the thesis is placed, there should be no question as to what the writer's commitment to the subject matter is. A thesis is specific, not general; sharply phrased, not vague. Such a statement as "Adolescence is a difficult period in the life of an American," does not commit the writer to anything because it does not focus specifically on the subject matter. Be relentless in asking yourself why you believe what you do. Your preliminary notes might read like this: adolescence is hard because my body and my thinking seem out of gear with the rest of the world. I want everything and never have any money. I have to make decisions which will affect my whole life, and yet I don't know what I want. No one ever gave me any guidelines about sex, and I'm still muddled about it. I never had enough allowance to treat my friends, so when I'd find money I'd pocket it and feel guilty about it later. I had to take College Boards when I was seriously considering dropping out of school, and that's why I'm not in the advanced English class.

Depending upon your purpose, the topic, "Adolescence—What About It?" can be turned in a number of directions and lead to a number of thesis statements:

Some American adolescents lie, steal, and commit vandalism because they are frustrated at a critical period of their development.

Adolescent misbehavior can be cut down by a strict curfew enforced by jail sentences for those who violate it.

The creation in American families, schools, and churches of puberty rituals like those of primitive societies would help the young to bridge the gap between an immature individual and adult society.

201

10c Organization

A sharply defined thesis statement will help you to organize the material you want to cover. While good writing is always orderly, there is no set formula for organizing a paper. Often organizing the material and formulating a thesis coincide during the act of composition. Sometimes, however, sorting and arranging the subject matter will lead to a sharper understanding of what your thesis commitment is. Conversely, clearly defining the thesis may suggest a pattern of organization most suited to the purpose of the paper. Many writers do not discover the final design of their argument until the second or third draft; others make a structured plan that changes little in concept or content from the preliminary jotting down of ideas to the final typing.

We all have our own writing styles, our own methods of organization, and what works for one writer does not necessarily work for another. You should study, however, the procedures—notes, topic outline, sentence outline—which have helped other writers to shape ideas into a convincing arrangement. You should also learn to recognize bad habits you may have acquired which interfere with efficient organization.

Exposition often depends for its effectiveness not only on how clearly ideas are explained but also on how cohesively they are drawn together. A teacher of Wayne Booth's once admonished him never to write a sentence which did not have something to do with the sentence that preceded it and something to do with the sentence that followed. That, says Booth, was the soundest writing advice he ever received. The careful and craftsmanlike placing of sentence to sentence lays the foundation for solid organization. Indeed, the word *cohere* means literally to cling or stick together. The strongest arguments depend on such firm cohesion.

In order to achieve this coherence you should have an overall sense of the structure of the paper. The function of a building affects an architect's conception of the whole structure; similarly, the purpose of a paper—to persuade, to inform, to evaluate, to tell how—influences its design. A paper which describes a process is usually organized into a step-by-step explanation of the procedure; an essay which draws a moral from a personal experience might narrate that experience in chronological order and then explain the lesson it teaches. Even a rough plan—a series of notes scattered on the table—will help you figure out what are the major and minor ideas, what information can be tucked into a sentence parenthetically, what point needs supporting evidence, what assumption calls for an explanation.

A plan will also help you decide what to include or to eliminate, what evidence is pertinent, what style convincing. Knowing where you are going with your topic is like planning for a journey. You will pack cotton or wool, ski boots or sandals, insect repellent or Ben-Gay depending upon the weather, the terrain, the occasion, the company. Such foresight is important in writing. While you may feel comfortable with a casual, slangy style, the kind you speak to friends, it may be as inappropriate to your purpose as blue jeans would be at a formal wedding. You need not abandon such a style entirely, any more than you would throw away the jeans you decided not to wear. Save them for a camping weekend, when formality would be a downright hazard.

As a preliminary exercise, jot down all the ideas that come to mind as you think about the topic. Even though much of this material may be discarded in the end, random or free writing can break the block which often forms when we try to think through an issue. In such free writing, don't be concerned about ordering ideas. Let words, phrases, or, if you choose, whole sentences flow into written notes, governed by no particular logic and unstemmed by critical judgments. Sorting can come with later reflection. For the moment, surrender to the flow of associative thought. You may be delighted to discover how many opinions and ideas you have on a particular subject.

Because it is in the nature of the human animal to classify and categorize, you may, looking back on a mass of freely gathered language, begin to see a pattern. Connections between ideas seem to appear spontaneously. As you develop a preliminary outline, trust this sense of proportion. You may want to revise and rearrange after the entire design is constructed, but at this early stage of writing pay attention to your mind's natural inclination for shape and progression. You are discovering what you feel and think about a topic, and a hunch gathered during this random excursion and later analyzed and followed through, may develop into a forceful thesis statement.

10d   The Introductory Paragraph

Few rules of writing are binding, but it is usually desirable that the introductory paragraph (1) seize and hold the reader's attention, (2) indicate efficiently and gracefully the subject matter of the paper, and (3) reveal, implicitly or explicitly, the writer's attitude toward the subject matter. Most writers write the introductory paragraph a number of times. And since its success depends on your understanding of the complete essay, especially of the conclusion, you may well write its final version last of all.

Don't be timid about taking a first plunge into writing. Just begin, remembering that any beginning can be changed, or even discarded, in the final draft. Try to create in a reader the illusion that you are beginning at the beginning, even though you have written and discarded three or four versions before you were satisfied. Polishing for tone—the selection of this word rather than that—may be the last thing you do before handing in the essay.

Any number of ways of organizing a paragraph (see Chapter 8) can be used in an introduction; the reasoning may be inductive or deductive; the paragraph itself long or short; the opening sentence abrupt or meditative. One method, used by a student in the following excerpt, is to begin with a sharp contrast and an injection of controversy:

> There is no longer just a generation gap. It is often open, deep hostility now. In the 1950s, youth was condemned for its apathy and concern with personal and economic security. In the 1960s, it was attacked for its involvement in political and peace movements and its rebellion against sterile education and the war-as-usual. Knowing that earlier generations were denounced for contradictory reasons, many students can see no reason at all why they should listen to adult America.

Another method is to open with a key quotation from the work under discussion, as the student writer of the following example did:

> It is the "quick, compact imagery of a single statement that forms the basis of

Navajo poetry," says Oliver LaFarge.
This remark can well be illustrated in
LaFarge's own story of Navajo life,
Laughing Boy, a novel in which things are
perceived and identified through "quick,
compact imagery." The first image ties the
protagonist, Laughing Boy, to his environment: "His new red headband was a bright
color among the embers of the sun-struck
desert, undulating like a moving graph of
the pony's lope"--a simple statement,
surely, but nonetheless a "compact image"
of the movement of a man on his horse over
flat ground.

Still another way is to begin with a short, clear summary or characterization and lead up to a focusing statement:

The Hawaiian Islands are anchored in a
position where they receive sea swells the
year round. The contour of the ocean floor
and the structure of the reefs turn these
swells into beautiful breaking waves,
which make Hawaii a surfer's paradise. I
have been surfing in this paradise every
day for the last seven years, and I can tell
you that there probably is no more purely
natural act than surfing. You are at one
with nature's most basic element--the
living sea. But as changing times bring
"progress" to the islands, so is there a
change in surfing.

Avoid beginning essays with generalities and platitudes: "Pollution
nowadays is a very important issue" or "It is obvious to everyone
that children watch too much television." Such inept openings dis-
courage even the most determined reader. Neither is the proclama-
tion "This essay will discuss" likely to spark reader interest. Avoid
scrupulously the complaining tone, "While no one can write on
a topic as difficult and complex as this one, I will nevertheless
attempt . . ." or the apology, "I am but one small sail in the sea
of human opinion . . ." Confidence, assertiveness, authority charac-
terize the most successful opening paragraphs.

10e   The Main Body

Those paragraphs between the introduction and the conclusion of a paper constitute the body of the argument. While the middle of the paper should take into account all the points listed in an outline, each heading need not require full paragraph development. Whether to devote more than a sentence or two to a specific heading depends upon your judgment of the importance of a point, since the more space you give an idea the more significant it will appear to the reader. Commonly accepted judgments or matters of fact and history can be stated briefly or summarized, but stands on controversial issues may need the support of concrete evidence and the reasonable proof a logically developed paragraph provides.

In papers which argue a thesis through the analysis of particular examples, the evidence should be arranged in ascending order of importance. Otherwise you miss the opportunity to convince a skeptical reader through the accumulation of solid proof and run the risk of jarring your audience with anticlimax. Keep your reader alert by varying the length and structure of your sentences and paragraphs, and fasten paragraphs together with strong transitional sentences.

The most important points of transition in a paper are those leading from the introductory paragraph to the main body of the essay and from the body of the essay to the conclusion. The last sentence of the opening paragraph and the first sentence of the concluding one often determine the persuasiveness of your argument. In revision, examine these tension points for their focus, their logical coherence, their assertion, tone, and grammatical structure to make sure they support, firmly and unshakably, what you are saying.

10f   The Conclusion

While the conclusion of the paper is a vital part of the composition, if only because of its final effect upon the reader, it is the one most often neglected by student writers: either they end too abruptly or meander through a tedious summary of the major points of the argument. Unfortunately, there are too many formulas to end a paper—the grandiose "therefore"; the limp but modest "so"; the circular and soporific "in conclusion I have shown . . ." Resist these

pat transitions since they avoid the task of demonstrating the significance of the argument, which is the obligation of a well-written
conclusion.

A conclusion is not a one-sentence tag; it should not apologize for
itself or the essay, and it should never introduce a new idea. Rather
than summarize what has gone before, the best conclusions mark the
arrival of the essay at the destination announced in the introductory
paragraph. An essay should end with the ease and authority of a
musical composition which brings its themes to a unified, harmonious
resolution, giving the reader a sense of finality. One student ended a
700-word theme on Chekhov's play *The Seagull* this way:

> When the curtain falls on The Seagull, one
> has the feeling that the story is not at all
> ended, that the action continues behind
> the curtain. Reflecting on this, one may
> find that the secret of Chekhov's effect
> lies in avoiding the overly dramatic, the
> play in which everything builds to one
> climax centered in one character. Chekhov
> has allowed the themes of love and death,
> of dreams and reality, to unfold in the
> random, senseless way that they occur in
> our lives.

Often the feeling of completeness which a well-written conclusion
conveys can be created by picking up a word or phrase from the
introduction or recalling an earlier example. Such returns, of course,
should make it clear that since we have read the body of the essay,
we understand these references in a new way. An essay is not a circle.
If we only arrive where we began, we have not gotten anywhere.

The student who argued that the increasing number of surfers in
Hawaii would either have to discipline themselves to share the waves
or expect state regulation of the sport picked up from the opening
paragraph the key word, *sea,* and echoed *living* in the noun *life,*
to tie together the beginning and the end of his paper:

> Unless we treat the sea with the consider-
> ation that it deserves as a source of
> wonder, pleasure, and life, sacrificing
> our own selfish desire to catch the big
> wave regardless of who or what is in the
> way, we can look forward to the regulation

> of surfing. Police patrolling the beaches,
> floodlights stuck into the sand for day
> and night surfing, licenses, permits,
> tickets--these are not pleasant pros-
> pects. But neither are the fights, the
> racial name-calling, the indifference to
> another surfer's safety which one en-
> counters all too often in Hawaiian waters.
> To live in a world of change we must learn
> to change ourselves.

No competent writer dashes off a conclusion at the last moment. When we finish reading an essay we should feel that it could not have ended any other way. Writing which creates this sense of completion is the result of thought and revision, but the result—a satisfied and agreeable reader—will justify the effort.

10g The Formal Outline

The most obvious use of the formal outline—and the reason it is so often required by teachers—is to help the writer and the reader anticipate the main divisions of the topic and the connections between ideas and evidence. There are three types of formal outlines: the paragraph outline, the topic outline, and the sentence outline. In the paragraph outline, which is used mainly to outline reading, the topic of each paragraph is summarized in sentences which follow the order of the paragraphs. The topic outline consists of brief phrases or single words, numbered and lettered to show the order and importance of ideas. The sentence outline has a complete statement, a sentence, for every item in the outline and has a thesis at the beginning.

Whether to use an outline and what form to use depends on the writer and on the requirements of the assignment. If your writing is criticized for lack of coherence or unity or the logical relationship of ideas, you might experiment with the topic or sentence outline to sketch clearly the blueprint of your plan for composition. Both the topic and sentence outline indicate, by numbering and indentation, which are the main points and which are the subordinate points. The following system of numbering and lettering is nearly universal:

I. ....

   A. ....

   B. ....

      1. ....

      2. ....

         a. ....

         b. ....

II. ....

Coordinate points—those of equal importance—should be indented the same distance from the left margin. The main heads (I, II, III) are farthest to the left; the subheads (A, B, C) are indented several more spaces to the right. Rarely will you need to go farther than the third subhead (a, b, c).

For topic outlines capitalize the first letter of the word beginning the heading but do not punctuate the end of the entry since it is not a sentence. For sentence outlines, begin with a capital letter and end with a period or other terminal punctuation.

The headings and subordinate items in the topic and the sentence outline should correspond to the logical divisions and subdivisions of the material. The indentation and numbering of items should indicate parallelism or subordination of ideas. The pattern

I. ....

   A. ....

   B. ....

II. ....

indicates that A and B are parallel ideas under I, and that the larger division II is parallel in content with I. Each topic that is subdivided should have at least two subheads. Since a genuine division produces at least two parts, a lone subtopic is not really a subdivision, but rather a part of the preceding point.

Study the following topic outline, and sentence outline (based upon the sample research paper on pages 269–95) to determine the characteristics and utility of each type.

Topic Outline

Anne Bradstreet's Homespun Cloth:
The First American Poems

I. Biographical introduction
   A. Anne Bradstreet's voyage to
       Massachusetts Bay
   B. Her reaction to the New World
II. The Puritan Dilemma
   A. Conflict between impulse
       and dogma
       1. Love of this world
       2. Love of God and submission to
          His will
   B. Bradstreet's dilemma
       1. Rebellion against the New World
       2. Submission to God's will
III. First volume of poems
   A. Publication without author's
       permission
   B. Bradstreet's reaction
   C. Public reaction
       1. Favorable reception in her day
       2. Modern preference for her
          later poems
IV. Handicaps of a woman poet in
    colonial America
   A. Physical handicaps
       1. Harsh living conditions
       2. Endless labor raising
          eight children
   B. Psychological handicaps
       1. Woman's duty to do housework
       2. General distrust of poetry as
          "Devil's Library."
       3. Writing believed dangerous for
          tender female minds
          a. Governor's wife
          b. Sister Sarah
          c. Anne Hutchinson
V. Bradstreet's best poetry produced
   by tension
   A. Conflict between love of this
       world and of Heavenly Kingdom
   B. Increased interest in personal
       experiences

        1. Fear of death and love
          of husband
        2. Autumnal splendor declaring
          the glory of the Lord
        3. Adjusting to early death
          of grandchildren
        4. Loss of home and possessions
          in a fire
    C. Bradstreet's solution of
      this dilemma
      1. God's providence to be accepted
      2. Inevitable human rebellion
        against such dogma
  VI. Conclusion: Final success of
    Bradstreet's homespun muse

Sentence Outline

Anne Bradstreet's Homespun Cloth:
  The First American Poems

Thesis: The contradictions of "the Puritan
Dilemma" produce a tension that gives
vitality to the homespun Muse of Anne
Bradstreet's later poetry.

   I. A sheltered childhood in England was
     poor preparation for the New World.
    A. The voyage to Massachusetts Bay
      was long and difficult.
    B. At first sight of the New World
      Anne Bradstreet's heart rose
      in revulsion.
  II. Though she shared the Puritan
     dilemma, she had special problems.
    A. All Puritans felt some conflict
      between human impulse and dogma.
      1. It is human nature to love the
        things of this world.
      2. Man is required to love God and
        submit to His will.
    B. Anne Bradstreet also had a
      private dilemma.
      1. She rebelled against the harsh
        life of the New World.

    2. She felt that she must submit to God's will and live there.

III. Her first volume of poems was published in 1650.

  A. It was printed in England without her knowledge or consent.

  B. Bradstreet had hoped to clothe her "rambling brat" in better trim but had nothing on hand but "homespun cloth."

  C. Public reaction shows the difference between her time and ours.

    1. Her contemporaries loved her didactic verse.

    2. Modern readers prefer the homespun cloth of later poems.

IV. A woman poet in colonial America faced major obstacles.

  A. The physical handicaps were serious.

    1. At first living conditions were almost intolerable.

    2. Raising eight children demanded endless labor.

  B. Serious psychological handicaps were imposed by the tradition of male dominance.

    1. Women were supposed to devote themselves to housework.

    2. Poetry was generally distrusted as the "Devil's Library."

    3. Intellectual activity was believed to be dangerous for tender female minds.

      a. There were the examples of the Governor's wife, and of

      b. Sister Sarah, and of

      c. Anne Hutchinson.

V. The tension produced by these obstacles made Bradstreet's later poetry her best.

  A. Like all Puritans she felt a conflict between this world and the Kingdom of Heaven.

    B. As she became used to America, she
       showed increasing interest in her
       own personal experience.
       1. Her fear of death emphasized
          her love of her husband.
       2. The splendor of autumn color
          was good in itself, as well as
          declaring the glory of the Lord.
       3. Adjusting to sorrow at the
          early deaths of some grand-
          children was very difficult.
       4. Losing all her possessions
          when her house burned down
          showed her how much she had
          depended on small, familiar
          things.
    C. Eventually Anne Bradstreet worked
       out a solution to her dilemmas.
       1. She tried to make herself
          accept and believe in God's
          providence.
       2. But she also accepted as in-
          evitable some human rebellion
          against such dogma.
VI. Conclusion:
   The human voice of her homespun muse
   gives her a major place among
   American poets.

Exercise 1

Analyze an essay in the text used in your writing course or a chapter
in a text for another course you are taking or an article in a magazine
such as *Scientific American, Harper's, Atlantic Monthly, Natural History*
to discover what the thesis of the essay is. Does the essay have a thesis
statement, and if so, where does it appear?

Exercise 2

Decide what your position or commitment is regarding the following
topics. On the basis of that decision, formulate in one sentence the
thesis statement which would be the foundation for a 500–700 word

essay about the subject. Then analyze your statement to see whether or not it leads to a pattern of organization or development. If not, re-examine the thesis statement for vagueness and generalities.

Images of minority groups in television programs
Defense spending in the current fiscal year
The meaning of "sexual freedom"
Nonviolence as a response to violence
Science fiction as an art form
Playing a musical instrument
The place of athletics in college life
The eating habits of American children
Law enforcement in your local community

Exercise 3

Test the value of Wayne Booth's rule for good writing (page 202) by exchanging papers with a fellow student and examining in conference each of your essays to see if the sentences in every paragraph have something to do with the ones that precede and the ones that follow them. Frankly discuss the structure of your papers, the effectiveness of the opening paragraph and the conclusion, the strength of the crucial points of transition. Offer specific suggestions on how the organization of the paper might be improved.

Exercise 4

Select some controversial subject about which you have strong convictions—pollution, drugs, child care centers, education. Prepare a thesis and sentence outline of the position you oppose. Then construct a thesis and sentence outline for a 1,000 word composition which answers the most telling arguments of the opposition.

Exercise 5

Take an in-class theme, an essay test, or a short composition you had trouble organizing and make paragraph, topic, and sentence outlines of it *as it was written*. Then construct revised paragraph, topic, and sentence outlines for it. Be prepared to write a revised version from one of the new outlines if your instructor should ask you to.

Sound Logic | 11

Any expository writing which is more than just a bare summary of dates and events involves reasoning: making generalizations, drawing deductions, arriving at conclusions. You may be explaining your actions or beliefs; you may be discussing a book you find persuasive or unpersuasive; you may be arguing for or against some new policy. In each case, you are trying to convince your readers, and if you credit them with intelligence, you will want to convince them by reason.

As used in this chapter, the term "logic" applies in the broad sense of sound and adequate reasoning. The treatment is necessarily brief, ignoring many technicalities more suitably taken up in a full course in logic.[1] It also omits discussion of certain specific expository techniques which help clear reasoning but which are more properly taken up elsewhere: the definition and restriction of terms, the ways of achieving paragraph coherence, and the ways of achieving sentence coherence (see index).

This chapter cannot teach you "how to be logical." But it can supplement the comments of your teachers, who are often forced to confine themselves to such labels as "logic" or "coh" (coherence).

---

[1]For a more detailed treatment of the materials discussed throughout the chapter, see Monroe K. Beardsley's *Thinking Straight* (3rd Edition, Prentice-Hall, 1966). For a more technical treatment, see Irving M. Copi's *Introduction to Logic* (4th Edition, Macmillan, 1972).

Since these are only labels, the real challenge you face is the rethinking of your materials, and here the chapter may be helpful. It tries to indicate some of the most common errors in logic and some precautions you can take. Above all, the chapter argues that unsound reasoning is often the result of ignorance rather than intentional deception or incurable bigotry: *the writer has not known enough,* and perhaps not cared enough, about the subject and so has generalized hastily. Clear and persuasive arguments require clear and persuasive evidence.

11a The Structure of an Argument

Definitions are usually the preliminaries of an argument. Having defined capital punishment as "execution, the death penalty for a crime," you can then argue for or against it. One "argument," or "reason," you might give for capital punishment is that it deters murder. A "reason," or "argument," against it might be that it does not deter murder. Note that the words "argument" and "reason" are interchangeable and that they imply an identical process of thinking.

In most discussions of logical analysis, the word *argument* signifies any two statements connected in such a way that one is drawn from the other. The argument has two parts: a *premise* (or evidence) and an *inference* (or immediate conclusion):

premise or evidence	*inference or immediate conclusion*
Capital punishment deters murder.	It should be continued.
Because it does not deter murder,	capital punishment should be abolished.

We use arguments constantly in writing and in speaking, and we recognize them by the actual or implied presence of connectives like "because," "so," and "since," and by auxiliaries like "ought," "should," and "must." The structure of an argument, then, is an observed fact or set of facts, or else a generalization presumably based on facts (the premise), leading to a conclusion (the inference). And usually we intend, though we may not always state explicitly, a final conclusion or *point* of the argument:

premise ———————→ *inference*
I'm tired out **because** I've been studying too hard.

↓ *final conclusion*
So I'll take a break now.

final conclusion ←— *inference* —————————→ *premise*
She wasn't angry.   She didn't mean it *since* she was joking about
                     it later.

Usually, a final conclusion has several arguments, not simply one, to
support it. The inference of one argument may be the premise for
the next, and so on in a chainlike pattern to the final conclusion, the
clasp:

premise 1 and . . .   *premise 2*
Hayes has an A− average and an   Brookes a B− average and an
IQ of 130.   IQ of 125.

    (inference from premises 1 and 2 *becomes premise 3*)
Since Hayes is obviously brighter and more energetic,

        (inference from premise 3 *becomes premise 4*)
he should do better work in a restricted creative writing course.

final conclusion
Consequently he certainly should be given preference over Brookes.

Several distinct strands of argument may be knotted into the one
final conclusion, itself often the beginning of a paper or conversation:

final conclusion
There is no clear reason for preferring Hayes over Brookes.

first argument introduced   *premise 1*
In the first place, both students are in the superior IQ range. The
standard is irrelevant in this case (*inference* from premise 1).

second argument introduced   *premise 1*
In the second place, the fact that Hayes has a higher grade average is
no proof he has the special interest or talent this course requires (*negative inference* from premise 1).

third argument introduced   *premise 1 and so on to the end*
Moreover, I learned from talking with Brookes that. . . .

Just as a paragraph can develop several arguments to support one
conclusion, so several paragraphs can each develop one or more
arguments to support a thesis, itself a final conclusion. And just as an
outline can help you sort out your arguments for the paragraph, it
can also help you sort them out for the paper. But nothing has been
said yet about the kind of argument used and its content. So far, we
have considered an argument's structure, not its truthfulness. An
argument's structure may be quite consistent, yet its premises and
conclusions unsound. Two common causes for unsound arguments

are the writer's failure to examine the key assumptions and the failure to distinguish between fact and judgment. Each of these causes requires a separate discussion.

11b Key Assumptions

A key assumption is a connection between the premise and the inference, which is taken for granted *before* the argument is advanced; and it is a *presupposed* relationship between the argument and the final conclusion. Consider the argument we have looked at earlier about the two students. Unless you *took for granted* that high grades and creativity are related, you couldn't very well argue that Hayes's superior average was proof that he would do better work in the writing course than Brookes and that *therefore* Hayes ought to be given priority. The key assumptions underlying the argument or arguments must be sound before they are built upon. If they are unsound, the whole thing collapses. If the assumptions are unjustified, the writer risks overlooking troublesome details which do not support them, and he may find unreal evidence which does. For example, if he were to assume that academic success and creativity are related, he would have to overlook the students with mediocre averages who are gifted painters, dancers, or dramatists and the intelligent honor students who seem to lack imagination, or at least seldom do more than safe, thorough work. The writer might, moreover, find an unreal significance in the difference between an IQ of 130 and one of 125, and from this trivial difference make a flimsy inference. And, finally, IQ tests are in themselves open to question in some areas.

To take another example, when students write about short stories narrated by a first person "I," they sometimes assume there must be a one-to-one correspondence between the narrator and the author in real life—that what happens to the narrator of the story is exactly what happened to the author. By failing to distinguish between the "I" as a device for telling the story and the writer's personal identity, the analysis turns the story into autobiographical self-confession and distorts fact and fiction alike.

There are at least a couple of things you can do to help protect yourself against unsound assumptions and arguments built on them. First, you can get into the habit of detecting your own key assumptions by asking yourself what you have taken for granted in your argument. If the assumptions need defending, defend them; if they need explaining, explain them. Second, you can make it a practice to ask what other people are taking for granted in their arguments. If their key assumptions need challenging, challenge them.

Exercise 1

Consider the following arguments. Each (in one variation or another) is popular; each has one or more key assumptions. Analyze the argument to determine the key assumptions it makes and which of these assumptions, if any, would need to be explained or defended.

1. A great many of the movies that Hollywood makes give an unfair picture of American life because they show mainly its violence and obsession with sex.
2. Enriched courses for gifted students are a valuable addition to the high school curriculum because such courses offer these students a chance to fulfill college requirements and to begin specializing earlier.
3. Many fraternities (or sororities) are hypocritical because they choose members on the basis of family, money, and appearance.
4. Civil rights laws are often useless because you can't legislate morality.
5. A politician who takes an unpopular position during an election is foolish because it simply increases his or her chances of losing.

11c The Differences between Fact and Judgment

As the preceding exercise may have suggested, what can be proved and what one approves of do not always coincide. The differences between fact and judgment, though not always easy to determine in a given case, are important. A *fact* may be defined as any statement, any declarative sentence, which can be proved true. The definition says nothing about who does the proving, what his or her qualifications are, or how he proves it. *It merely stipulates the possibility of verifying the statement,* the central idea intended here. It rules out commands, questions, and exclamations as provable assertions—no one will try to prove or disprove utterances like "Shut the door!" "How old is she?" or "Wow!"

The definition eliminates more than these obvious examples. "Water is wet"; "A yard has three feet"; "New York has more people than Chicago"; "Shakespeare was born in 1564"—most people would agree that such statements are all "facts." But saying "Water is wet" isn't the same as saying "The paint on the door is wet." The first sentence is either a *tautology*, a needless repetition of an idea to anyone familiar with the qualities of "waterness," or else instructions to a very young child on *how to identify* the feeling of liquid on his fingers. To say "A yard has three feet" is also to state a truth-by-definition—quite different from saying "The track was only ninety-nine yards long." We can touch the paint and measure the track and thereby answer "Yes, it is" or "No, it isn't" to the assertion. But what point is there in responding "Yes, it is" or "No, it isn't" to statements like "Water is wet" or "A yard has three feet" except to agree with the definition?

Some statements are verifiable facts because they are stated in *quantifiable* terms, that is, in such a way that what is asserted can be weighed, measured, or counted: "Jean weighs eighty pounds," "The last discus throw was 147 feet long," "There are two bluebooks apiece for the thirty-five of you." Even in these cases, of course, you assume that the scale or the tape measure is accurate, that neither has been jiggled, and that your index finger has not missed a cover or pointed at the same head twice. Other facts presuppose greater faith: If you believe "New York has more people than Chicago" and "Shakespeare was born in 1564" are factual statements, you are not simply accepting the authority of an almanac and an encyclopedia. You are trusting the accuracy and conscientiousness of every census taker hired in these cities by the Bureau of the Census in 1970 and the reliability of scholars who have inspected the parish records of baptism in Stratford-on-Avon.

Admittedly, life is too short for anyone to verify personally more than a fraction of the "facts" he learns and many things have to be taken on authority. Still, you ought to cultivate the habit of skeptical analysis in reading and writing. It can help you detect those judgments which are unverifiable and which are often "proved" in writing by heavy underlining and double exclamation marks and in conversation by rising voices and tempers. How, for instance, can one prove (or disprove) such statements as "You can't change human nature" or "Materialism is the greatest threat to our way of life"?

A judgment is a conclusion expressing some form of approval or disapproval. The term should not be dismissed because it is taken to connote "mere opinion." There are, after all, reasonable grounds and confirming facts for "good judgment" as well as the arbitrary assump-

tions and disregarded facts in "poor judgment." Sometimes the judgment is a fairly simple, safe inference from the facts, as in the
judgment "Helen Wills Moody was one of the finest tennis players in
the game's history," which is based on her winning the Women's
National Singles seven times, the Women's National Doubles three
times, and the Women's Singles at Wimbledon eight times. The
phrase "one of the finest" is a judgment of her record. Sometimes, a
judgment is a complicated inference from many facts, none of which
is immediately clear. Consider three propositions, in which the
judgments are italicized:

1. In 1920, there were 6,448,343 farms in America with a total acreage
    of 955,844,000 acres; by 1973, farms were larger and fewer, totaling
    2,844,000 in number and accounting for 1,090,000,000 acres.
2. Between 1920 and 1973, the American farm *has become more ef-
    ficient through improved mechanization and specialization; it is
    now able to cultivate more land and feed a larger population with
    fewer people doing the farm work.*
3. *Profit-seeking specialization and mechanization are destroying the
    small, self-sufficient family farm in America and the deep attach-
    ment to the land and tradition that are so much a part of the
    family farm.*

The first statement contains the terms "larger" and "fewer," which
possibly connote a judgment of greater efficiency but which certainly
denote a factual inference—that fewer farms and a greater total
acreage mean larger farms. The statement is clearly factual and the
inference results from a simple computation. The second sentence,
a judgment, not only presupposes the first statement's facts ("now
able to cultivate more land . . .") but presupposes others. To prove
"improved mechanization and specialization," the writer would need
figures showing the increased use of electricity and various kinds of
power machinery and the increased percentage of farms that raise
only crops or livestock, or produce dairy goods. The evidence exists,
of course, to defend the judgment that "the American farm has become more efficient."

In the third statement, the judgment is far more conspicuous than
in the first two, and the facts are less immediately evident. To prove,
for example, the existence of "the small, self-sufficient family farm"
with its "deep attachment to the land and tradition" would require
detailed information about income, expenses, size of family, acreage
worked, period of ownership without tenancy, length of political and

religious affiliations, and a study of attitudes towards marriage, education, and the like. Such information, whether in the form of statistics or the extensive observations of qualified reporters, would have to include the New York family raising sheep and a few cows, some acres of wheat, and garden tomatoes; the North Carolina family raising a hillside of tobacco and corn, supplemented by hogs and hunting; the Illinois family running a small dairy and orchard; and the Colorado family raising grain and beef near the foothills of the Rockies. Then the information about all of these families would have to be analyzed to see whether there is such a type as "the small, self-sufficient family farm" with distinct values or whether there are sharply different regional variations.

You can no more help making judgments about human actions and goals than the writer of the third statement could help feeling strongly about the changes taking place in the American farm. In fact, the writer might say that information about income and attitudes towards marriage had little to do with his judgment, that he was talking about qualities which could only be experienced personally. The grounds for this judgment might be his or her own life on a small Iowa farm or New Mexico ranch; novels like Willa Cather's *O Pioneers!*, Steinbeck's *The Red Pony*, or Harriet Arnow's *The Dollmaker;* short stories like those in Hamlin Garland's *Main-Travelled Roads;* movies like *Hud;* or the memoirs of a country doctor. The question would then be what other qualities are slighted. Do the films, fiction, and memoirs show only loyalty, belief, the close-knit family, and hard work? What of the fatigue and boredom, the bigotry and blighted vision, the drudgery and failure they reveal? Fiction, films, and memoirs are images of possibility, not mathematical probability: they can make us see, feel, and share the intensity and variety of human life in a particular time and place rather than convince us of statistical likelihood. If the writer argues that their details and experiences are "factually typical," he then *assumes as true* what only statistics or the extensive testimony of many qualified observers could confirm.

When you make judgments, then, express your facts clearly and accurately, and show clearly the way in which the facts warrant your judgment; when you don't know the facts, or have reason to suspect their authority, suspend judgment. And don't be reluctant to ask others to do the same. Try to distinguish between those judgments which involve personal preference and are not provable and those which may be supported by evidence and arguments. For your college writing, this advice implies your willingness to do research; to distinguish among facts, statements which may be factual, and judgments; and to tolerate uncertainty. The last is especially hard to do: often the experts in specialized fields are so much at odds that either you are tempted to give the matter up entirely or else arbitrarily decide "one side *must* be right, the other wrong, so I will choose." If, for example, you were to look up the statistics and analyses on capital punishment, you would find no clear-cut agreement among the criminologists, psychologists, and various law officials as to what the figures prove—and no agreement among the statisticians, either. But lives, the victim's, the accused murderer's, and their families', are too important to be forgotten about simply because you cannot prove conclusively that capital punishment is or is not a deterrent. There are other factual grounds which may help you form a judgment: How many innocent men have been executed, or how many saved at the last minute? Do the poor and the uneducated receive the death sentence more frequently than others convicted of murder? How often are murderers declared insane, later to be released to commit another murder?

As has been pointed out, we cannot verify personally more than a fraction of the "facts" we learn, and necessarily we have to take many things on authority. Still, when experts disagree about their facts and their judgments, there are a few helpful guides.

The *first guide* is to be sure that a supposed expert is an authority on the subject at hand. If a famous physicist and chemist differ about disarmament, you may have to suspend judgment so far as their argument about the technical difficulties is concerned, but you don't have to feel that either of them is an expert on Russia and Russian foreign policy. Other writers and scholars have made the study of Russian aims and behavior their life's work, and you should turn to them.

A *second guide* is to consider the experts' probable motives in relation to their testimony. An executive for a major car manufacturer who testifies that "all reasonable efforts have been taken to make economical, unpolluting cars" may well not be as reliable an authority as an independent trade magazine or engineering firm.

A *third guide* is to see whether others in the field agree about the strengths or weaknesses in an expert's research. Suppose that you are doing a project on the attitudes of high school students towards their teachers. If book reviewers generally praise a husband and wife team for their studies of suburban students but criticize their failure to study inner-city students as thoroughly, you would want to confine yourself to the couple's discussion of suburban students only, and look elsewhere for evidence about the feelings of inner-city students.

Exercise 2

For practice, consider the following statements. Determine which parts of each are facts and which parts are judgments. For each judgment, decide what kind(s) of facts or evidence, if any, could be cited to support the judgment.

1. Smoke Cigarmellos! They last longer, burn cooler, and are easier on you than cigarettes. They are cleaner and cheaper than pipes.
2. Julius Caesar, Rome's greatest general and ruler, was assassinated in 44 B.C. by Cassius, Brutus, and other personal enemies.
3. A meter equals 39.37 inches.
4. A kilometer contains 1,000 meters.
5. Kareem Abdul-Jabbar is one of the finest offensive players of all time in professional basketball.
6. If one compares the number of talented women now entering law schools with the number fifteen years ago, one sees how wasteful of abilities those sexist admissions policies were.
7. More often than not, European journalists and writers who travelled in America during the first half of the nineteenth century were surprised by our belligerent nationalism and confident optimism, though why they should have expected a young country to be otherwise is a puzzling question.
8. Since language changes, the criteria of what is good or bad usage also change.
9. Since language changes, there can be no criteria of what is good or bad usage except what the majority is willing to accept at any given moment.
10. Real mastery of a foreign language means the ability to think in the language, not simply to translate headlines and signs, word by word.
11. A recent classification of land use in Afghanistan estimates 76% wastelands, 5% meadows and pastures, 1.5% forests and woodland, 14% arable, and 3.5% cultivable but unused.
12. The early bird catches the worm—but who wants the worm?

11d Faulty Reasoning

The failure to examine key assumptions and to distinguish between fact and judgment is by no means the only cause of faulty reasoning. Of the other causes, hasty generalizing is one of the most common.

(1) Hasty Generalizations

To generalize is to *draw conclusions* about a *whole class* or *group*, after studying some members of the group. A hasty generalization is one drawn from too few individuals or from nontypical individuals. Suppose, for example, that after meeting three bright and articulate fraternity rush chairmen, you are convinced that most outstanding male students belong to fraternities. Do you have reason to question this generalization? Yes, because your sampling may be quite unrepresentative and in any case is quite small. The chairmen were probably chosen for their jobs because they are so impressive. But even so, suppose you still have a hunch that the outstanding students are fraternity members. How would you establish such a generalization?

Establishing an effective generalization usually requires several steps. First, you would have to identify the group "outstanding student" by defining it as, say, those on the college's honor roll. Otherwise the generalization is no more than a vague judgment about a vague, unidentified group of people. You would then have to show that there was a higher percentage of fraternity men on the honor roll than of nonfraternity men. Otherwise, the outstanding student is no more likely to be a fraternity member than not.

To establish an effective generalization, you have to identify clearly the group or groups about which you are generalizing, and you must study enough individual members of the group to ensure they represent the group as a whole. Failure to observe these principles usually results in hasty generalizations.

Not all generalizations can be as easily established as the one above. In cases where all the relevant facts about a limited group are available, one may indeed generalize by simply counting or checking accurately—a parking attendant inspects each car on the lot and generalizes that all headlights are off; a dean reviews all the high school transcripts and generalizes that every freshman has had at least a year of foreign language before entering the college. But much of the time it is not possible to do a complete check. Necessarily, one also generalizes by *induction*, that is, by observing a number of specific examples of the group and then concluding that other examples will *probably* be like those observed. Young children use induction when, after grabbing at two or three cats, they conclude that all cats scratch. Later on, when they understand what grabbing is and when they have seen more cats, they learn to generalize that most cats will not scratch unless they are grabbed. Pollsters use induction when they question a representative *sample* of the voters to determine how all voters feel or will probably vote. If their cross-section is not representative, as happened in 1948, they will be embarrassed. A consumers' research organization uses induction when it purchases all different brands of a mass-produced item, tests several samples of each brand carefully, and then generalizes about which brands are likely to be the best buys and in what ways.

The stereotype is one form of hasty generalizing—the trite, unchanging picture of an ethnic group, a profession, or a social role. "He was the typical Italian father, singing with gusto and crying 'Mamma mia!'" "She was the typical college student, a dirty-looking hippie." Other stereotypes include the dumb athlete ("a real jock"), the crooked politician ("You can't trust any of them"), the absent-minded professor, etc. Stereotypes are crude caricatures which deny the variety and diversity of actual life.

Oversimplification is another form of hasty generalizing. Usually, it entails making a question seem easier than it is. Statistics, especially, can lead to oversimplifying. For example, if two groups have a markedly different class average on a reading comprehension test, you could not generalize that every member of the first class was better than every member of the second. Since a few very high scores might have pulled up some mediocre ones in the averaging, you would have to compare all the individual scores to reach such a conclusion. Still less would you be entitled to simplify the results by generalizing that one group was "innately" better than the other. You would have to know a good deal about the income and education of the parents, the reading matter (if any) in the homes, each child's previous training, and other crucial factors before drawing any conclusions.

The unqualified generalization makes a third form of hasty generalizing, the exaggerated claim made from insufficient evidence. Several years ago, on the basis of a peace petition signed by a few thousand college students, a commentator generalized that all under-graduates were becoming pacifists. His sampling was highly inade-quate. He ignored not only those who refused to sign but also those who were being drafted. The unqualified generalization is a rather frequent weakness in college writing—e.g., "All the freshmen think 'Orientation Week' is a waste of time" or "Not one woman student in the whole college trusts the Dean." To the question "How do you know? Have you talked with *every* freshman or every woman?" the writer usually answers: "Of course not, but I know several [or some] people who feel . . . ." The least the writer can do is to rephrase the generalization more accurately and responsibly by identifying the approximate numbers involved and the source of the real evidence: "Several of us who are freshmen and attended 'Orientation Week' with high hopes have decided that . . ." or "After the women on our corridor had met with the Dean, we agreed that . . . ."

In order to generalize effectively, you need to know some criteria of generalizations. Since generalizations are made about classes or groups, *the first criterion of generalizations is that the evidence be typical of the class or group.* A theme using students in remedial English as the basis for generalizing about the writing abilities of all members of the freshman class would be as unconvincing as a theme that used the Panthers to generalize about the political at-titudes of all Blacks.

Often, though, the untypicality is less crude, more a question of interpretation than of outright error. Are Hemingway's heroes and heroines in *A Farewell to Arms* and *The Sun Also Rises* "typical" of the period in their disillusionment with World War I and its after-math? Was the fear of "majority faction" by the authors of *The Federalist* "typical" of the Constitution's other proponents? If you read Hemingway's novels or *The Federalist* essays, you will agree on some conclusions: Hemingway's heroes and heroines do distrust "causes" and conventional moralities—they say so and ignore them; Hamilton and Madison often speak of "majority faction" especially in *Federalist 10.* Many of your most interesting writing assignments will be ones like these, or at least ones in which you use complex facts for complex judgments. *When you have to evaluate typicality, define what features you believe typical and show how these features are found in the evidence.* If you had read only the two Hemingway novels, but none by F. Scott Fitzgerald, John Dos Passos, or Ford Madox Ford about this period, you would want to confine your dis-cussion of typicality to Hemingway's novels.

The second criterion of generalizations is that the evidence be adequate. Americans spending a few days in London or Madrid, Europeans touring in the United States for two weeks, or students visiting Washington, D.C. for a weekend have many superficial impressions, some of them probably accurate. But if they generalize "The English are reserved" or "Americans are friendly but ignorant," they reveal more about themselves than about the English or Americans. Other examples of inadequate evidence are the essay citing those convicted during the Watergate trials to show that all of the hundreds of people appointed by Nixon were unreliable, or a term paper citing Janis Joplin's death to show that all rock stars are deeply unhappy, tormented people. Like typicality, adequacy is sometimes difficult to judge—the anthropologist with only a jaw fragment and a few bones or the archeologist with only a faded temple painting may have to infer what he can and hope for more evidence. *But you can assist yourself and your reader by saying why you think your evidence is adequate and for what, if there is likely to be doubt.* If only one half of the 250 freshmen vote for class officers, you have adequate evidence that "something" is wrong with morale, but you would have to talk with many of the nonvoters to find out what it is.

The third criterion of generalizations is that the evidence be relevant. Figures showing that all sororities on campus have a "C" average or better would not be proof that sororities produce outstanding students. The figures would be more *pertinent* to the generalization that sororities care enough about their eligibility to satisfy academic requirements. In a different fashion, the fact that an artist or musician was once a communist or a fascist is irrelevant evidence to prove his work incompetent, if you define incompetence as a lack of artistic ability or skill. The only way he can be shown to be incompetent is by musical or artistic standards of performance. You might find it personally distasteful to attend his exhibit or recital, but if you condemn his present work because of his past associations, you adopt the propaganda view of art and the illogic used by the Nazis in persecuting "non-Aryan" writers and writing, and by the Communists in their harassment of Pasternak, Solzhenitsyn, and others.

The fourth criterion of generalizations is that the evidence be accurate. This standard seems self-evident, yet if you were to read through the long, careful book reviews in such publications as *Scientific American,* the *American Historical Review,* or the *Journal of American Folklore,* you would find two common criticisms: that the writer has been careless about checking facts, and indiscriminate about sources. In cases of extreme carelessness, the reviewer legitimately questions the author's right to be trusted, regardless of how original the ideas are. In addition to the advice available in this volume (see Chapter 12), the most helpful guides you have are the ones for expert testimony: Does the information come from a recognized source? What are the person's announced motives or position in relation to the evidence? What agreement is there among others in the field about the strengths or weaknesses in the researcher's work? Like an editor or reviewer, your teacher has greater confidence and pleasure in conclusions based on accurate evidence.

(2) Mistaken Causal Relationships

Mistaken causal relationships are errors in reasoning about cause and effect. Perhaps the two most frequent kinds are the *post hoc, ergo propter hoc fallacy* and the *reductive fallacy.*

The post hoc, ergo propter hoc fallacy is the error of arguing that because *B* follows *A, A* is the cause of *B.* Sequence is not proof of a causal relationship. The fact that *B* follows *A* is *not* proof that *B* was caused by *A.* Primitive beliefs like a full moon "causing" pregnancy and their modern equivalent in the television commercial connecting marriage with a change in deodorant are easy enough to laugh at. But clear thinking on serious social problems can be obscured by this fallacy. For example, the assertion that heroin addiction is the result of smoking marijuana not only ignores the fact that most people who try or use pot never touch heroin, but it may divert attention from the real need—the understanding of the psychological and physiological factors which do contribute to addiction. And what of the unqualified generalization which makes the loss of religious belief the cause of crime? Crimes are committed by people who profess religious belief; not every person who loses his faith commits a crime.

The reductive fallacy occurs when simple or single causes are given for complex effects, creating a generalization based on insufficient evidence. In history when motives and events are enormously complicated and cannot be exactly duplicated, such generalizations as "Athens fell because of mob rule," "Luther caused the Reformation," or "The need to rebel caused the campus demonstrations of the 1960's" are *reductive.* That is, instead of specifying the mob or Luther as *one important condition,* these assertions make Luther or the mob the *single agent* of causation. Such generalizations tend to reduce history to caricature. Strictly speaking, historians rarely uncover the cause or causes of events. Rather, they try to decide which conditions were important and were more probably necessary for the event to take place. In scientific studies when a sequence cannot be directly observed and controlled and the investigator cannot know whether Y is the result of X only or W and X together, or whether X and Y are both the result of W, he speaks of a *correlation.* In 1964 when the Surgeon General announced a high correlation between cigarette smoking and lung cancer, he indicated that one was probably a *contributory cause* of the other. But since not all heavy smokers die of lung cancer and since there is evidence that industrial fumes and car exhaust are injurious in this regard, one cannot say that smoking is the *only* cause of lung cancer. Insofar as he cannot directly isolate, identify, and control each factor in a sequence, the scientist, like the historian, usually observes the test of sufficiency: *only if A alone is sufficient to produce B can it be called the cause.*

Except for laboratory reports in physics or chemistry and perhaps a research project in psychology or education, you will seldom have space or occasion in college writing to prove a strictly causal relationship. Usually, so far as causal relations are concerned, you will be judging or reporting on research done by others, or else trying to determine what the probable connections are between an effect you have observed or experienced and events preceding it.

To let your readers judge the *sufficiency* of your argument, define its conditions and limitations as clearly as you can. With complex relationships, it is often helpful to know that there is a significant difference between saying "It is due to" and "It has been helped by," just as there is between saying "Luther caused" and "Luther contributed to" or "The reason for the Revolution" and "One reason for the Revolution." The limited statement can be more exact because it is more tentative: it implies that other conditions, other contributing factors, may be as important as the one singled out for discussion. This kind of exact tentativeness requires careful, analytical thinking. When you analyze complex historical events and personalities, complex social issues and complex motives, avoid the reductive fallacy.

(3) Reasoning by Analogies

An analogy is a comparison between two different things or events showing the way or ways in which they are similar. To illustrate, for example, how the novelist works, one could draw the analogy between the writer and the potter: both begin with a rough idea or image, but discover the particular shape of the plot or vase as they work with their materials, often modifying the outlines several times before they are satisfied.

Analogies can vividly illustrate and clarify difficult ideas. They have been fruitful in science because they have suggested new lines of research and testing: Franklin saw a similarity between lightning and electric sparks; the similarity between x-rays and the rays emitted by uranium salts raised questions about the source and nature of this energy, and eventually led to Marie Curie's discovery of radium; mathematicians like John von Neumann, instrumental during the early development of computers, saw an analogy between the way the human nervous system works and the way a relay of vacuum tubes can be made to work. But in science, an analogy only sets up a hypothesis to be proved or disproved. Though it suggests a possibility, it is *not* proof by itself.

An analogy can be illustrative or suggestive, but it cannot be conclusive. You do well to suspect any conclusions which are supported only by an analogy. Sometimes, a false analogy offered as proof is relatively easy to detect. The student who argued that the new African countries should have federated into a United States of Africa to solve their political and economic problems ignored some obvious dissimilarities with the American colonies. The latter, unified by language and a common foe, had in most cases a long tradition of local self-government. African countries are separated from each other by deep linguistic and cultural differences and in several cases are inwardly divided by tribal rivalries. This analogy also ignores the difficulties we had—the failure of the Articles of Confederation and the opposition to the Constitution.

Often, however, false analogies may be more deceiving. Two principles will help you cope with them:

1. The more concrete similarities there are, and the more instances that can be cited, the higher is the possibility that the conclusion is true.
2. The greater the magnitude of the differences and the more irrelevant the similarities that do exist, the less is the chance the conclusion is true.

False analogies obscure the real issues of and prevent clear thinking about serious and difficult questions. To detect analogies used as proof, examine the argument to see if any evidence is offered other than a comparison between two different things or events. In your own writing, if you think an analogy is essential to your argument, rethink your entire case: don't allow yourself to be taken in by shallow or deceiving similarities.

(4) Avoiding the Question

When writers fail to give relevant evidence for their arguments or fail to draw relevant inferences, they are *avoiding the question.*

Begging the question is one such common failure. A question is begged when writers use as a proven argument the very point they are trying to prove. For example, columnists who argue that the poor are lazy and cite families on relief as "evidence" are assuming *without proof* that only lazy opportunists would take relief—the very point *to be demonstrated.*

The *ad hominem* argument is a second common form, the argument "to the man." Here, the tactic is to condemn the morals, the motives, the friends, or the family of one's opponent and to divert attention from the substance of the opponent's argument. The evaluation of expert testimony should not be confused with the *ad hominem* argument: in the former, you *ask* what a person's professional credentials are and the reasons for his position—that is, you attempt to distinguish between fact and judgment; in the latter, you *insinuate* by sarcasm or similar means that a person's word is untrue or his case unsound because there is something wrong with him.

The *straw man* is another device commonly used for avoiding the question. As the label implies, the technique is to stuff, set up, and knock down a position which is not being contested. If the question is whether or not Shylock deserves his punishment and the writer goes to great lengths to prove that bitterness can make a man lonely, he is erecting a straw man. The issue is whether Shylock is treated too severely, by either his own standards or Christian ones. No one argues the fact that bitterness can isolate people.

(5) False Alternatives

The false either/or deduction is a common but easily avoided error. The error lies in assuming that there are only two alternatives and that if one of them is true, the other must be false. If parents tell a child, "You must be lazy because the only reasons for poor school work are laziness or stupidity, and I know you aren't dumb," the parents commit this error. They ignore other alternatives: the child may be bored with easy work, or he may lack adequate training, or he may be unhappy for a variety of reasons. Ideological slogans often make this kind of phony simplification—"Communism versus Capitalism," "The Free World versus Tyranny," "Education versus Indoctrination," and the like. The careful writer will rethink the false alternatives in order to discover what the more complex possibilities really are.

Exercise 3

To sharpen your eye for others' fallacies, take a newspaper and turn to the editorial and opinion section. Go through it carefully, isolating and analyzing the logical errors you find. Better still, if there's an issue you feel strongly about or a column you find particularly objectionable, write a letter pointing out *how* the reasoning is unsound.

Exercise 4

To sharpen your eye for fallacies in your own writing, go over some of your back papers as if they had been written by a stranger. What kinds of logical errors do you find? Now, try revising the material logically, as if you were doing a favor for a good friend.

Exercise 5

Analyze each of the following generalizations by the four criteria suggested. Be prepared to explain which generalizations are defective and in what ways.

1. From a recent faculty committee meeting: "Students are making a farce out of the government's low interest loan program for college financing. The percentage of students who deliberately default is steadily rising, and there's no reason to think it will drop or that students will begin to feel responsible for paying the money they owe. The whole program is just a waste of the taxpayer's money."
2. From a recent "Letters to the Editor": "Christmas is more commercialized and materialistic this year than it has ever been before. Read the business page and notice the record sales reported

by every major city in the country. People are spending at an all-time high just to gratify their love for belongings."
3. From a recent college newspaper: "This school has the worst meals of all the state colleges. Any athlete or debater can tell you the meals you get at other colleges make the ones we get look awful."
4. From *Guinness Book of World Records:* "The only admissible evidence upon the true height of giants is that of recent date made under impartial medical supervision. Biblical claims, such as that for Og, King of Bashan, at 9 Assyrian cubits (16 feet 2½ inches) are probably due to a confusion of units. Extreme mediaeval data from bone measurements refer invariably to mastodons or other non-human remains. Claims of exhibitionists, normally under contract not to be measured, are usually distorted for the financial considerations of promoters. There is an example of a recent 'World's Tallest Man' of 9 feet 6 inches being in fact an acromegalic of 7 feet 3½ inches."

Exercise 6

Analyze each of the following statements of causal relationship to determine which ones are guilty of the *post hoc, ergo propter hoc fallacy* or the *reductive fallacy.*
1. There must be a conspiracy. No country as powerful and as wealthy as ours could have suffered the reverses it has for the last thirty years by accident. Things don't just happen that way; someone plans them.
2. Every child in that remedial reading class watches at least twenty hours of television a week. With all that passive sitting, no wonder they can't read!
3. More than two-thirds of the people in our school district voted against the school bond issue. The only explanation is sheer selfishness; they were afraid of higher taxes.
4. Since 1940, the government has gotten bigger and bigger and taxes have gone higher and higher. The conclusion is obvious.

Exercise 7

Analyze each of the following analogies to determine whether it is used as an illustration, a hypothesis suggesting further investigation, or proof.

1. From a student theme: "The sight of a monkey pushing through the jungle, leaping from tree to tree, seems 'natural' and, perhaps, graceful. However, when a monkey is placed in a small cage or zoo, his boundings from side to floor to side to ceiling seem antic and 'unnatural.' The satirist employs the same technique of limitation. He confines his subject, as it were, to a small cage, or at least one tree, for purposes of close observation. The setting in which he moves his object is limited and its barriers are precisely drawn. The satirist, in effect, traps the victim in his most ridiculous positions and does not allow him to wander off or in any way escape an intensely mocking portrayal."

2. From a composition handbook: "Many of the rules in this book, making no mention of exceptions or permissible alternatives, are dogmatic—purposely so. If a stranger is lost in a maze of city streets and asks for directions, one doesn't give him the several possible routes, with comments and cautions about each. He will simply become more confused and lost. One sends him arbitrarily on one route without mentioning equally good alternative ways. Likewise, the unskilled writer can best be set right by simple, concise, stringent rules."

3. From a student editorial: "The administration never gets tired of telling us that the state college is part of society as a whole. It harps on student responsibility for 'good taste' in plays and publications, student responsibility to obey state laws about drinking and driving, and student responsibility for property. By the same line of reasoning, then, how can the administration claim it has the final right to approve of campus organizations and their speakers? If the state university is part of 'society as a whole,' it ought to recognize *our* rights as well as our obligations. We aren't asking for the privilege of being subversive; we are asking for the civil rights we have in 'society as a whole'—the rights to hear whom we wish and join the groups we wish."

4. From a student theme: "The college has the same obligation to satisfy the student that a store does to satisfy a customer. Students and their parents pay the bills and they ought to have a much freer say about what courses they take. No clerk would think of telling a customer he had to buy several things he didn't want before he could buy the item he came for. And no store would keep as clerks some of the men the college keeps as professors. They can't even sell their product."

5. From a medical journal: "If you place a number of mice together in fairly close quarters and then systematically introduce an increasing variety of distractions—small noises, objects, movements—you increase the probability of neurotic behavior. Cannot something like this process help explain the growth of neurotic behavior in our ever more crowded, complex society? The possibility is worth considering."

Exercise 8

Pick one of the following analogies and write a paragraph using the analogy as proof. Then, in a second paragraph, show precisely how the analogy is false or misleading, as you have developed it.

1. The family budget and the federal budget
2. The referee in boxing and the arbiter in labor disputes
3. The captain of a ship and the president of a democracy
4. Tastes in art and tastes in food
5. Packaging the goods well and giving a lecture well

Exercise 9

The following statements contain unsound reasoning. Identify the different kinds of fallacies and specify what change, if any, would improve the argument.

1. Either you trust a person or you don't. And you don't do business with someone you don't trust. The same principle ought to be observed in foreign affairs: you don't do business with countries you can't trust.
2. Anyone with a grain of sense would have known the county didn't need to buy land for a park. But those officials don't learn easily. It wasn't proof enough for them that a majority voted against the purchase in the election. They had to go to the state legislature and get voted down, too.
3. Freshman "Hell Week" is one of the oldest and dearest traditions of the college. Many of us alumni can remember having our heads shaved and getting up at midnight for roll calls and jogs around the track. Those of us on the Alumni Board oppose the abolition of the custom. We find the arguments for doing away with "Hell Week" childish and tiresome. We were good enough sports to go along with the sophomores in our time.

4. I don't see why I received such a low grade on this term paper. I put in hours of work on it and did several rough drafts. And I followed the format you asked for. It doesn't seem fair.

5. Opposition to the new expressway comes only from a small, loud, selfish minority of home owners who are holding out for more money. State engineers say the proposed route is the cheapest and safest to build. State appraisers have made fair offers, which even the owners themselves admit are equal to average market prices. Hence the inescapable conclusion is that these few hold-outs are willing to sacrifice the public good for their own private gain.

6. To be an actor, you have to lack self-restraint. That's why people become actors. All you have to do is look at any famous star and you'll see the living proof.

7. "If you're not part of the solution, you're part of the problem."

8. "Reflection on Ice-Breaking"
   Candy
   Is dandy
   But liquor
   Is quicker
   —OGDEN NASH

Exercise 10

The following is a satire, written by a student, of the arbitrary assumptions, unexamined generalizations, and misleading analogies, which all too often are found in print. In analyzing the argument, see how many of these logical errors you can find.

"Why Have Teachers?"

In the early days of America, before the establishment of compulsory schooling, moral standards were high. People were contented with the simpler virtues. Girls learned to sew, cook, and keep house; men, to farm or work at some trade. Marriages were stable and happy; there was no such thing as divorce. Today this happy scene has changed--the morals of modern America are corrupted. Every newspaper carries stories of murder, embezzlement, adultery, and divorce. What has caused this shocking situation? Is it possible to regain the happy state of the early America?

The most influential institution during the formative years of each American is the school, governed and dominated by the teachers. From these teachers children learn the human faults of blind obedience, prejudice, and the betrayal of one's kind in the form of tattling. These early sown seeds bear the bitter fruit of low morality. Clearly, teachers do much to undermine the morality of American children, and through them, that of society.

The obvious solution is to eliminate the teacher as much as possible. The modern child is increasingly capable of educating himself. There are more college students today than ever before, a fact which proves that youth today possess superior intelligence. By educating themselves, they would not be subjugated to the influence of teachers. They would share their knowledge willingly, each gaining from the other, with no one person dominating the others.

As applied to colleges, this would mean that students would gather in pleasant informal surroundings and discuss intelligently matters with a common appeal, as was done in the medieval university. Not only would they enrich their knowledge, but they would also learn how to compromise and see each other's viewpoint. By obtaining many viewpoints instead of the one our system presents, the students would learn to know their own minds and think objectively instead of receiving opinions on a silver platter.

Cynics will sneer that this system is impractical, that students need guidance and even indoctrination in fundamentals before they can think on their own. Nothing could be further from the truth! One of the

most clear-thinking, intelligent men in
this nation's history, Abraham Lincoln,
was almost entirely self-educated. Think
of the effect on our society of an entire
generation with the training and characteristics of Lincoln. The present immo-
rality would disappear; a high moral
standard would be developed. The group
that is undermining morality would be
minimized in its influence, and the education of American youth placed where it
belongs--in the hands of these same youth.

The Long Paper

A theme in a freshman composition course is usually short, from 500 to 700 words. It fills two or three typed double-spaced pages, and a first draft of it can be written at one sitting. Most often you write a short theme out of your own head, the material coming from your own experience, knowledge, or reading. In any case, if you are writing on something you know about at first hand, collecting information on the subject is no problem.

In upper-division courses, and later in "real" life, you will probably need to write at greater length. A long paper may be required in a seminar or as a report on independent study; business and professional men and women have to write reports, digests and summaries, legal briefs, or feature articles. Such an assignment, often running to more than a thousand words, presents special problems. You will be writing, not fiction or reminiscence or personal experience, but some form of exposition—descriptive or analytic or argumentative.

An essential first step, before you begin to write, is to get together the information you need. Even if you already know something about the subject, you will want to check on recent developments, and in most cases you will have to do some digging around in the library if you are to know what you are talking about. You can't even decide on your particular topic, nor adapt it to fit the space available, until you know something about the subject. Part of this chapter, accordingly, will be about locating material in books and magazines.

You will also need to know the conventional methods of documentation—that is, indicating to the reader by footnotes or other references the sources of your material. Failure to indicate the source of a quotation or paraphrase will lead the reader to assume that it is your own writing, and if it is not, you will be guilty of plagiarism. Passing off other people's words, sentences, or ideas as your own, whether it is deliberately or ignorantly done, is a serious offense. In college it can lead to dismissal; in the business world it can lead to a damage suit. Various safeguards against this misfortune will be discussed later in this chapter.

A long paper cannot ordinarily be written at a single sitting, and you will need to plan your time accordingly. The venerable but foolish custom of neglecting an assignment till the day before and then sitting up all night to finish it simply will not work here. After three or four hours, even experienced professional writers feel fatigue and know that whatever they write thereafter will be poorer and poorer. So the first rule is to plan ahead and begin writing early enough so that you can finish in several sessions, a day apart, instead of in one desperate coffee-soaked night.

Ernest Hemingway long ago laid down two basic rules for writers. First, always stop when you are going good. Don't write yourself out at any session, for if you say everything you have in mind, you may have trouble getting started next day when you return to the job. Make yourself stop when you still know exactly what is to come next, and you will find it easy to pick up the thread of your discourse next day. Second, to insure continuity, begin each writing session by reading everything that has gone before, or at least the preceding five or ten pages. By the time you come to the place where you stopped writing, you should be back into the mood and spirit of the piece, and you may even have recovered your momentum. This is as important to a writer as to a football team.

But the first problem when you begin a long paper is to get some information together, and the first place to go is the library.

12a   The Library

The library is the heart of a college or university, and students should learn to use it effectively. Since the amount of information one can carry in his head is small compared with the vast amount stored in print, an important part of one's college education is learning how to find needed information. Every student should be able to use the card catalog, be familiar with important reference books, and know how to use bibliographies and periodical indexes.

(1) The Card Catalog

The card catalog is the index of the library. All books and bound periodicals are listed on 3 × 5 cards, which are filed in alphabetical order in labeled drawers. A book is often listed three times: by author's name, by title, and by general subject. In large university libraries, the subject cards may be filed in a separate alphabetical order and kept in a separate Subject Catalog. Author and title cards usually make up the main catalog, in one single alphabetical listing.

Subject cards are intended to help you find books on a particular subject when you don't know the authors or the titles. The chief value of subject cards is to direct you to the section of the stacks where books on your topic are kept. A little browsing around the area indicated by one call number will usually lead you to a number of relevant books. If these are serious studies of the subject, they will contain bibliographies (that is, lists of other books in the field), and soon you will have so many references that you can begin to pick and choose. The main thing is to get a start, and the subject cards can often help.

Exercise 1

a.   By consulting the author cards, see if your library has the following books. If so, list the place of publication, the publisher, and the date of publication.

1.   *The Culture of Cities,* by Lewis Mumford
2.   *Animals as Social Beings,* by Adolf Portmann
3.   *The Subversive Science: Essays toward an Ecology of Man,* by Paul Shepard.
4.   *Literature and Film,* by Robert Richardson
5.   *Structuralism,* by Jean Piaget
6.   *Blues People,* by LeRoi Jones
7.   *The Armies of the Night,* by Norman Mailer
8.   *Language,* by Edward Sapir
9.   *On the Contrary,* by Mary McCarthy
10. *Briefing for a Descent into Hell,* by Doris Lessing

SAMPLE CATALOG CARDS

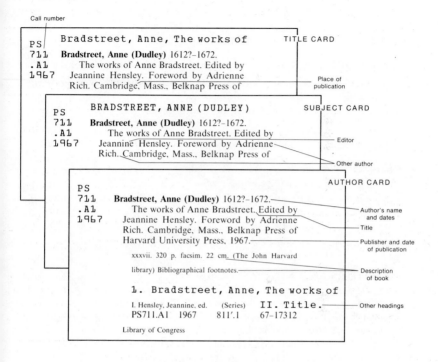

Call number

PS / 711 / .A1 / 1967

Bradstreet, Anne, The works of   TITLE CARD
Bradstreet, Anne (Dudley) 1612?-1672.
    The works of Anne Bradstreet. Edited by
Jeannine Hensley. Foreword by Adrienne
Rich. Cambridge, Mass., Belknap Press of — Place of publication

PS / 711 / .A1 / 1967

BRADSTREET, ANNE (DUDLEY)   SUBJECT CARD
Bradstreet, Anne (Dudley) 1612?-1672.
    The works of Anne Bradstreet. Edited by — Editor
Jeannine Hensley. Foreword by Adrienne
Rich. Cambridge, Mass., Belknap Press of — Other author

PS / 711 / .A1 / 1967

    AUTHOR CARD
Bradstreet, Anne (Dudley) 1612?-1672. — Author's name and dates
    The works of Anne Bradstreet. Edited by — Title
Jeannine Hensley. Foreword by Adrienne
Rich. Cambridge, Mass., Belknap Press of
Harvard University Press, 1967. — Publisher and date of publication

    xxxvii. 320 p. facsim. 22 cm. (The John Harvard
    library) Bibliographical footnotes. — Description of book

    1. Bradstreet, Anne, The works of
    I. Hensley, Jeannine, ed.   (Series)   II. Title. — Other headings
    PS711.A1   1967   811'.1   67-17312

    Library of Congress

b. Find a title card for a work of nonfiction and note any differences from the author card.

c. Select five of the books which are nonfiction and obtain the following information on each:

1. What subject headings is each book catalogued under?
2. What are at least two other books—call number, author, and title—under one of the same general subject headings?

(2) Standard Reference Books

Another way of getting a start is to use the guidebooks in the Reference Room—encyclopedias, dictionaries, indexes, bibliographies. It pays to get acquainted with such standard reference books, and their location on the shelves, early in your college career. Some of the important ones are listed below.

GUIDES TO REFERENCE BOOKS

Gates, Jean Key. *Guide to the Use of Books and Libraries.* 3rd ed. 1973.
The Reader's Adviser. 2 vols. 11th ed. 1968–69. 12th ed., Vol. I (American and British Literature), 1974.
Winchell, Constance M. *Guide to Reference Books.* 8th ed. 1967.

GENERAL ENCYCLOPEDIAS

Chambers' Encyclopedia. 15 vols. 1964.
Collier's Encyclopedia. 24 vols. 1965.
Encyclopedia Americana. 30 vols. 1971.
Encyclopedia Britannica. 24 vols. 1968.
Encyclopedia International. 20 vols. 1964.
New Columbia Encyclopedia. 1 vol. 1975.

GAZETTEERS AND ATLASES

National Geographic Society, *Atlas of the World.* 1963.
Palmer, R. R., ed. *Rand McNally Atlas of World History.* 1970.
Pergamon World Atlas. 1968.
Seltzer, L. E., ed. *Columbia-Lippincott Gazetteer of the World.* 1962.
Shepherd, William R. *Historical Atlas,* 9th ed. 1973.
Times (London) *Atlas of the World.* 5 vols. 1958–1960.

REFERENCE BOOKS FOR SPECIAL SUBJECTS

Art and Architecture

Bryan, Michael. *Bryan's Dictionary of Painters and Engravers.* 5 vols. Rev. ed. by George C. Williamson, 1964.
Encyclopedia of World Art, 15 vols. 1959–68.
Haggar, Reginald C. *Dictionary of Art Terms.* 1962.
Hamlin, T. F. *Architecture through the Ages.* Rev. ed. 1953.
Myers, Bernard S., ed. *Encyclopedia of Painting.* 3rd ed. 1970.
Zboinski, A., and L. Tyszynski. *Dictionary of Architecture and Building Trades.* 1963.

Biography

American Men and Women of Science. 12th ed. 1971–1974. This set
   includes scholars in the physical, biological, and social sciences.
Current Biography. Monthly since 1940, with an annual cumulative
   index.
Dictionary of American Biography. 22 vols. and index. 1928–58.
Dictionary of National Biography. (British). 22 vols. and supplements.
Directory of American Scholars. 4 vols. 6th ed. 1974. This set includes
   scholars in the humanities.
National Cyclopaedia of American Biography. 1898–1906.
Webster's Biographical Dictionary. 1972.
Who's Who (British), *Who's Who in America*, *International Who's
   Who*. Brief accounts of living men and women, frequently revised.
Who's Who of American Women. 1958–.

Classics

Avery, C. B., ed. *New Century Classical Handbook*. 1962.
Hammond, N. G. L. & H. H. Scullard, eds. *Oxford Classical Dictionary*.
   2nd ed. 1970.
Harvey, Paul, ed. *Oxford Companion to Classical Literature*. 1937.

Current Events

Americana Annual. 1923–. An annual supplement to the *Encyclopedia
   Americana*.
Britannica Book of the Year. 1938–. An annual supplement to the
   Encyclopaedia Britannica.
New York Times Index. 1913–.
Statesman's Year Book. 1864–. A statistical and historical annual giving
   current information about countries of the world.
World Almanac. 1868–.

Economics and Commerce

Coman, E. T. *Sources of Business Information*. 2nd ed. 1964.
Greenwald, Douglas, and others. *McGraw-Hill Dictionary of Modern
   Economics*. 2nd ed. 1973.

Historical Statistics of the United States: Colonial Times to 1957. 1960. Continuation to 1962 and revisions, 1965.

International Bibliography of Economics. 1952–.

Munn, Glenn G. *Encyclopedia of Banking and Finance.* 7th ed. 1973.

Statistical Abstract of the United States. 1879–.

Education

Burke, Arvid J. and Mary A. Burke. *Documentation in Education.* (The 5th ed., renamed, of Alexander's *How to Locate Educational Information and Data.*) 1967.

Deighton, Lee C., ed. *The Encyclopedia of Education.* 10 vols. 1971.

Ebel, Robert L., and others. *Encyclopedia of Educational* Research. 4th ed. 1969.

World Survey of Education. 5 vols. 1955–72.

History

Adams, James T., ed. *Dictionary of American History.* 2nd ed. 6 vols. 1942–61.

Cambridge Ancient History. 12 vols. 1923–39. 3rd ed. 2 vols. 1970–75.

Cambridge Mediaeval History. 8 vols. 1911–36.

Langer, William L., ed. *Encyclopedia of World History.* 5th ed. 1972.

Morris, Richard B., and Graham W. Irwin, eds. *Harper Encyclopedia of the Modern World.* 1970.

New Cambridge Modern History. 14 vols. 1975.

Sarton, George. *Horus: a Guide to the History of Science.* 1952.

Literature and Drama
A. American

Cunliffe, Marcus. *The Literature of the United States.* Rev. ed. 1967.

Hart, J. D. *Oxford Companion to American Literature.* 4th ed. 1965.

Kunitz, S. J., and H. Haycraft. *Twentieth Century Authors.* 1942. First supplement, 1955.

Leary, Lewis. *Articles on American Literature 1900–1950.* 1954; *1950–1967.* 1970.

Parrington, V. L. *Main Currents in American Thought.* 3 vols. 1927–30.

Spiller, Robert E., and others. *Literary History of the United States.* 4th ed. 2 vols. 1974.

B. British

Baugh, A. C., and others. *A Literary History of England.* 2nd ed. 1967.
Craig, Hardin, and others. *A History of English Literature.* 4 vols. 1950.
Harvey, Paul, ed. *Oxford Companion to English Literature.* 4th ed. 1967.
Sampson, George. *Concise Cambridge History of English Literature.* 3rd rev. ed. by R. C. Churchill, 1970.
Watson, George, ed. *The New Cambridge Bibliography of English Literature.* 4 vols. 1972.
Wilson, F. P., and Bonamy Dobrée, eds. *Oxford History of English Literature.* Begun in 1945, this major series of reference works will soon include all fourteen projected volumes.

C. Continental and General

Fleischmann, Wolfgang Bernard, ed. *Encyclopedia of World Literature in the 20th Century.* 3 vols. 1971.
Grigson, Geoffrey, ed. *The Concise Encyclopedia of Modern World Literature.* 1971.
Leach, Maria, and Jerome Fried, eds. *Funk & Wagnalls Standard Dictionary of Folklore, Mythology, and Legend.* 1949–50.
MacCulloch, John A., and others. *Mythology of All Races.* 13 vols. 1964.
Preminger, Alex, F. J. Warnke, and O. B. Hardison, eds. *Encyclopedia of Poetry and Poetics.* 1965.
Steinberg, Sigfrid Henry. *Cassell's Encyclopedia of World Literature.* 2 vols. 1954.

D. Drama

Gassner, John, and Edward Quin, eds. *Reader's Encyclopedia of World Drama.* 1969.
Hartnell, Phyllis, ed. *Oxford Companion to the Theatre.* 3rd ed. 1967.

Music and Dance

Apel, Willi. *Harvard Dictionary of Music.* 2nd ed. 1969.
Beaumont, Cyril W. *A Bibliography of Dancing.* 1963.
De Mille, Agnes. *The Book of the Dance.* 1963.
Ewen, David. *The World of Twentieth Century Music.* 1968.

Grove, George. *Dictionary of Music and Musicians.* 9 vols. 5th ed. 1954. Supplement. 1961.

Sachs, Curt. *World History of the Dance.* 1937.

Scholes, P. A. *Oxford Companion to Music.* 10th ed. 1970.

Thompson, Oscar. *International Cyclopedia of Music and Musicians.* 10th ed. 1974.

Westrup, J. A., ed. *The New Oxford History of Music.* 10 vols. 1957–74.

Philosophy

Copleston, Frederick. *A History of Philosophy.* 8 vols. Rev. ed. 1950.

Edwards, Paul, ed. *Encyclopedia of Philosophy.* 8 vols. 1967.

Urmson, J. O., ed. *The Concise Encyclopedia of Western Philosophy and Philosophers.* 1960.

Political Science

Burchfield, Laverne. *Student's Guide to Materials in Political Science.* 1935. Useful for earlier periods.

Frankel, Joseph. *The Making of Foreign Policy: An Analysis of Decision-Making.* Rev. ed. 1967.

Huntington, Samuel P. *Political Order in Changing Societies.* 1968.

Morgenthau, Hans. *Politics among Nations.* 4th ed. 1967.

Political Handbook of the World. 1927–.

Smith, Edward C., and A. J. Zurcher, eds. *Dictionary of American Politics.* 2nd ed. 1968.

White, Carl M. and others. *Sources of Information in the Social Sciences.* 1964.

Psychology

Drever, James. *Dictionary of Psychology.* Rev. ed. by H. Wallerstein, 1964.

The Harvard List of Books in Psychology. 4th ed. 1971. Annotated.

Psychological Abstracts. 1927–.

Religion

Buttrick, G. A., and others. *Interpreter's Dictionary of the Bible: An Illustrated Encyclopedia.* 4 vols. 1962.

Cross, F. L., ed. *Oxford Dictionary of the Christian Church.* 1961.
Ferm, Vergilius. *Encyclopedia of Religion.* 1945.
Hastings, James, ed. *Encyclopaedia of Religion and Ethics.* 12 vols. and index. 1908–27.
Jackson, S. M., and others. *New Schaff-Herzog Encyclopedia of Religious Knowledge.* 12 vols. and index. 1949–51.
McDonald, William J., and others, eds. *New Catholic Encyclopedia.* 15 vols. 1967.
Werblowsky, R. J. Z. and Geoffrey Wigoder, eds. *The Encyclopedia of the Jewish Religion.* 1965.

Science—General

Deason, Hilary. *A Guide to Science Reading.* 1963.
McGraw-Hill Encyclopedia of Science and Technology. 15 vols. 3rd ed. 1970.
Newman, James R., and others. *Harper Encyclopedia of Science.* 4 vols. Rev. ed. 1967.

Life Sciences

Benthall, Jonathan. *Ecology in Theory and Practice.* 1973.
De Bell, Garrett, ed. *The Environmental Handbook.* 1970.
Gray, Peter, ed. *Encyclopedia of the Biological Sciences.* 2nd ed. 1970.
Kerker, Ann E., and Esther M. Schlundt. *Literature Sources in the Biological Sciences.* 1961.
Smith, Roger C., and W. Malcolm Reid, eds. *Guide to the Literature of the Life Sciences.* 8th ed. 1972.

Physical Sciences

Larousse Encyclopedia of the Earth: Geology, Paleontology, and Prehistory. 1961.
Le Galley, Donald P., and A. Rosen, eds. *Space Physics.* 1964.
Parke, Nathan G. *Guide to the Literature of Mathematics and Physics.* 2nd ed. 1958.
Universal Encyclopedia of Mathematics. 1964.
Van Nostrand's International Encyclopedia of Chemical Science. 1964.

Sociology and Anthropology

Hauser, Philip M., ed. *Handbook for Social Research in Urban Areas.* 1965.

International Bibliography of Sociology. 1951–. Annual.

International Encyclopedia of the Social Sciences. 17 vols. 1968.

Kroeber, A. L., ed. *Anthropology Today: An Encyclopedic Inventory.* 1953.

Siegel, Bernard J. *Biennial Review of Anthropology.* 1959–. Contains a subject index.

Social Work Year Book.

Exercise 2

To familiarize yourself with Constance M. Winchell's *Guide to Reference Books,* pick one of the following questions and run down the answer. Consult the *Guide* for likely sources; then check the sources themselves; finally, record on a 3 × 5 card the question, the answer(s), and the sources which were most helpful. Use complete bibliographic form for sources.

1. If, in the eighteenth century, you had been convicted of "pradprigging," what would have been your crime and, in all probability, your punishment?

2. What Mexican hero-god carried a cross and what did it symbolize?

3. In what decade did the population of the United States shift from a predominantly rural to a predominantly urban one?

4. Why might a librarian view with alarm a type of book introduced in 1769 by James Granger?

5. Why are brushes made of camel hair and when did the practice begin?

6. What biographer of Johann Sebastian Bach has also written books on Jesus and Paul?

Exercise 3

Each of the following topics is too broad for a research paper of 1,500 to 2,000 words, but each has several possible, more restricted subjects within it. By using the card catalog and appropriate reference works, locate at least three books and three articles on a specialized aspect of one general topic. Then compose a thesis, a short outline, and a working bibliography for a research paper of 1,500 to 2,000 words.

1. African influences on jazz   2. American cartoon strips

3.	Atomic power plants	12.	Organic foods
4.	Book censorship	13.	Pesticides
5.	Chemical basis of heredity	14.	Pop art
6.	Ecology of oceans	15.	Prison riots
7.	Electronic computers	16.	Public television
8.	European films of the 1970's	17.	Sensitivity groups
9.	Existentialism in literature	18.	Urban planning
10.	Ghetto schools	19.	Utopian novels
11.	Gun control laws	20.	Women's Liberation

(3) Finding Information in Periodicals and Newspapers

Magazines and newspapers like the *New York Times* are the principal sources of information for topics of current interest and recent events. To find this information, you will need to consult periodical indexes like the following:

Readers' Guide to Periodical Literature. 1900—. Alphabetical list under author, title, and subject.

International Index to Periodicals. 1907—. Devoted chiefly to the humanities and the social sciences.

Poole's Index to Periodical Literature. 1802-1881; 1882-1906. Useful for earlier periodicals.

Book Review Digest. 1905—.

New York Times Index. 1913—.

These indexes list alphabetically, by author and by subject, important articles in magazines of general circulation. If you are investigating a more specialized subject, you may need to get information from the various scientific and learned journals. To find relevant articles in these, use specialized indexes like the following.

Applied Science and Technology Index. 1957—.

Art Index. 1929—.

Biography Index. 1946—.

Biological Abstracts. 1926—. Includes ecological materials.

Business Periodicals Index. 1958—.

Current Anthropology. 1960—.

Economic Abstracts. 1953—.

Education Index. 1929—.

Engineering Index. 1884—.

Historical Abstracts. 1955—.

Music Index. 1949—.

PMLA, "Annual Bibliography." 1921–68. Since 1969 this is entitled
MLA International Bibliography. It is published separately from
PMLA in four volumes: I, English and American literature; II, foreign
literature; III, linguistics; IV, the teaching of foreign languages.

Psychological Abstracts. 1927–.

Public Affairs Information Service. 1915–. Political affairs, economics,
and government.

Sociological Abstracts. 1953–.

Zoological Record. 1864–.

Here are two sample entries from the *Readers' Guide.* They refer
to the same article, but the first is a subject entry, the second an
author entry.

> MASSACHUSETTS BAY colony
> Anne Hutchinson versus Massachusetts. W.
> Newcomb. il pors Am Heritage 25:12–15+
> Je '74
>
> NEWCOMB, Wellington
> Anne Hutchinson versus Massachusetts. il
> pors Am Heritage 25:12–15+ Je '74

Notice that these entries are not in the form you will use in your own
bibliography. The abbreviations are explained on the first pages of
each volume of the *Guide.* The article referred to, "Anne Hutchinson
versus Massachusetts," was written by Wellington Newcomb. It
appeared in June, 1974, in Volume 25 of *American Heritage* on pp.
12–15 and later pages. The article is illustrated with portraits.

12b The Long Paper

(1) Preliminary Bibliography

A list of books and articles related to a particular topic is called a
bibliography, and you will need to make one of your own for a long
paper. The bibliography you compile when you begin a paper is
"preliminary" because you will alter it as you discover new references and discard references that turn out, as some will, to be useless.
To make such changes easy, and to facilitate alphabetizing, you
should put each reference on a separate card or slip of paper. A good
size is 3 × 5 inches, easily distinguished from the larger slips on
which you will put your actual notes.

Include on each bibliography slip all the information that will be
needed for the final bibliography at the end of your paper. For a

book you will need the name of the author or editor, the exact title
of the book including any subtitle, the place and date of publication,
and the name of the publisher. For an article in a periodical, you
will need the author's name if the article is signed, the title of the
article (in quotation marks), the name of the periodical (italicized),
and an indication of the exact volume and pages. Ordinarily, volume
number, date, and page numbers will serve, but in newspapers and in
magazines like *Newsweek* which begin each issue with page 1, you
will need to give the date of the particular issue in which the article
appears. The standard form for bibliographic entries, which differs
slightly from that of a footnote reference, is illustrated on page 266.

Use common sense in choosing the items for your preliminary
bibliography. Don't waste time, for example, in collecting references to obscure publications not in your library. Inter-library loans
are possible but time-consuming, and you will find it much more
rewarding to explore the resources of your own library. If your topic
is new—a relatively recent event or discovery or notable person—look
for information in newspapers and periodicals, rather than in books.
The writing and publishing of a serious book takes, usually, from
two to five years; but magazines try to keep up with the times, and
indexes to periodicals appear in monthly installments.

Remember, too, to check for original dates of publication whenever you are dealing with a paperback book or with a collection of
essays. Some paperbacks will represent the original edition of a work,
and some collections will be composed of material never printed
before. But others will be reprints, or made up of reprints; and then
you must be careful to get the original date of publication (which
should be on the copyright page) or the source of the article (which
should be either at the bottom of the first page of the article or in a
list of sources at the beginning or end of the book). You need to do
this for two reasons: first, because you will need this information for
your footnotes and bibliography; and second, because you will feel
like a fool if you refer to a 1975 paperback as "one of the latest works
on this subject," only to discover too late that it's a reprint of something written in 1920.

(2) Evaluating Material

When you look into the actual books and articles referred to in your
bibliography, you will find some of them unsatisfactory—too skimpy,
too prejudiced, irrelevant, or just plain ignorant. Pick out the good

ones and discard the rest, but be sure you are taking account of both sides of controversial issues. If your topic is, for example, "How Safe Is Nuclear Power?" you will run across pamphlets published by utility companies. These may not be actually biased, but they are almost certain to be extremely optimistic about the desirability of nuclear power plants. They should be checked with articles on the other side, which may in their turn be biased or exaggerated.

As authorities, scientists are generally preferable to public relations men, but scientists also disagree with each other. Read both sides—the scientists who signed Dr. Hans Bethe's statement in favor of nuclear energy and those members of the Union of Concerned Scientists who have come out against expanding nuclear power plants. If you feel incompetent to judge between them, present both sides. Whether your paper is meant to prove a point or just to lay out the facts, you will need to know both sides of controversial questions.

(3) Limiting the Topic

As you revise your own bibliography—discarding useless references and adding new and better ones—you should be looking ahead to the next two steps: collecting information and limiting the topic to a suitable size.

Suppose you are looking into alternate sources of energy—that is, substitutes for our rapidly disappearing stocks of oil, coal, and natural gas. The more you read about solar energy—its direct application to heating water or houses and its various secondary forms, based on winds and waves and temperature gradients, not to mention planned biological transformation and concentration of sunlight—the more surprised you may be by the breadth of the subject. If you try to include all alternative sources of energy, you won't have time or space to do a thorough account of any one of them. The solution is obvious: limit your topic by choosing three or four alternate sources, or even just one, that can be treated in detail.

How do you choose? On what principle do you select parts of a topic and discard the rest? There are many answers. You might choose those that interest you most. Or, being severely down-to-earth, you might work only on those sources that have already been tested in the laboratory.

Or you could take up those that seem most practicable, technically or economically or even politically. You may find that you will need to limit your paper still further—perhaps to the technical and economic aspects of one alternative source, like geothermal power.

Notice how these three processes—revising your bibliography, reading and evaluating material, and limiting your topic—go hand in hand. You have to find out something about the subject before you can know how to limit it, or how much limitation is needed. Limiting the subject will require changes in your bibliography, too. Not only will you discard references to articles no longer relevant, but you will be turning up new references in every book or article you read.

A useful guide in all three processes is a tentative plan. This can be a fairly detailed outline or a few notes to remind yourself what points you want to cover. The essential thing is to use the plan as a guide, but to keep it tentative and not be bound by it. The more you read, the more you may find it desirable to change this, or modify that, or emphasize some new points. No one can tell in advance what kind of material he will find, nor what will interest him most. The tentative plan should develop as your reading fills out and changes your original ideas on the subject.

(4) Taking Notes

The most important advice here is to put each note on a separate card or sheet. To organize your material, you must break it down into small units, and unless each unit is on a separate card, you will find it difficult to bring together from different sources all the notes on a single topic. Write your notes on cards (at least 4×6 inches) or on half sheets of theme paper. If more than one card is needed for one point, use the back or clip on another card with the subject and source as a heading.

1. State the topic of the note in the upper left-hand corner. (Other corners may be used for the library call number and other information.) The exact source, including the author, the title, and the page, can go along the bottom edge of the card. (See page 256.) It is not necessary to include the place of publication, the publisher, and the date on each card since your bibliography cards will contain full information.
2. Always put quotation marks around quoted material, and quote exactly, even to the punctuation marks and the spelling. Do not use quotation marks for paraphrases or summaries.

3. If parts of a quotation are omitted, ellipsis marks should be used to show where the omission occurs—three spaced periods (. . .) to indicate an omission within a sentence, four spaced periods (or three added to end-punctuation) to indicate an omission at the end of, or beyond the end of, a sentence. Brackets—[ ]— should enclose words which are not part of the quotation but which you have inserted for clarity. If, for example, there is an obvious error in the text, you may insert after it the word *sic* (Latin for "thus") in brackets, to show that the quotation is exact even though it contains an error: [*sic*].

A note is usually a direct quotation, a paraphrase in your own words, or a summary of main points. The disadvantage of quoting directly is that it may waste space, and hence time; a paraphrase is usually shorter. But the great advantage of direct quotation in your notes is that you can check the precise wording without going back to the book. When you actually write the paper you will use direct quotation sparingly: ordinarily a paraphrase or a summary, sometimes including a brief excerpted phrase from the original, will be more effective. But in your notes, copy out as many direct quotations as time permits, indicating them of course by quotation marks.

Direct Quotation

> Control of smoke
> "Smoke is... more easy to control than liquid effluents, because it proclaims itself to all the world. A stream of water running from a factory into a river or a sewer is not conspicuous, and the connivance of an official inspector may be arranged. But black smoke belching from a high stack stands out against the sky for every voter to see. The housewife in particular bristles up in wrath, and a politician recognizes a good vote-getting issue."
>
> George R. Stewart, <u>Not So Rich as You Think</u>, p. 125.

Paraphrase and Direct Quotation

> Control of smoke
> Smoke is easier to control than liquid effluents.
> Since dirty water draining from a factory is
> usually invisible to the public, "the connivance
> of an official inspector" can be arranged more
> easily than when "black smoke [is] belching
> from a high stack ... for every voter to see."
>
> George R. Stewart, *Not So Rich as You Think*, p. 125.

Summary

> Control of smoke
> Smoke can be more easily controlled than liquid
> effluents because it is more conspicuous. Liquid
> factory wastes are usually invisible to the public,
> but smoke from a high stack attracts the
> attention of voter and politician alike.
>
> George R. Stewart, *Not So Rich as You Think*, p. 125.

(5) Proper and Improper Use of Source Material

The basic principle of scholarship is to make use of the discoveries and conclusions of previous investigators. Life is too short to permit repeating all the investigations of the past. What a professor tells you in class is in part a summary of the work of others, supplemented by what he has found out by his own research.

In writing a long paper, you will want to use ideas and material from a number of sources, and that is permissible so long as you name the sources. Unless you do, a reader is entitled to assume that what he is reading is your own idea, expressed in your own words. If he discovers later that it is actually the idea or the language of someone else, he will conclude that you are trying to pass this material off as your own. This is dishonesty, a moral fault. In the classroom it is called cheating, and among writers it is called plagiarism. In either case it can have serious consequences.

Avoiding plagiarism is not always as clear-cut and simple as it may sound. In practice, it is often impossible to give the sources for everything one writes. Where, for example, did I get (since I certainly was not born with) the definition of plagiarism just given? I really don't know. For years I've heard plagiarism talked about, and I have read about it and even studied examples of it in student papers. In short, my knowledge of what the term means is common knowledge, part of the vocabulary of the language I use. Generally known facts, like the discovery of America by Columbus, are also considered common knowledge. One is not required to indicate the sources of the fact that a mile is 5,280 feet and that a red light, in this country at least, means Stop.

If, however, I write that "a study of 125 randomly selected freshmen showed that only 29% considered snitching more reprehensible than cheating," my failure to indicate who made the study implies that I did it myself. And since I didn't, I could be accused of plagiarizing the work of someone else. If I write "a study by A. G. White[1] showed that 29% . . ." etc., and if I indicate in a footnote[*] that the source is an article entitled "Moral Judgments in the Classroom," which appeared in 1972 on page 223 of Volume 6 of the *Review of Education,* I am using White's material properly.

---

[*]For the proper form of such a footnote, see pp. 264–66.

12b

Even if I indicate the source of my information, I may be plagiarizing if my paraphrase is too close to the language of the original. Suppose a paragraph in White's article reads

> The students used in the study were chosen from a middle-western university thought to be generally representative of middle-class views on ethical questions. Standard statistical techniques were employed to insure an adequate sample of the freshman class.

If in my paper this turns up as "The students were selected from a mid-western university in which middle-class views on ethical matters prevail. To insure a representative sampling of freshmen, standard statistical techniques were used," I am guilty of plagiarizing.

It is true that, in a paraphrase, I will need to use some of the words that occur in the original; it is both difficult and unnecessary to find accurate synonyms for "middle-western," "university," "freshman," and the like. But it is not enough to merely invert the order of the clauses in the second sentence of the original and to change "chosen" to "selected," and "adequate sample" to "representative sampling." To use material legitimately, you must say it in your own language, fit it into your own context, and connect it with what goes before and after in your paper. A patchwork of paraphrases and quotations, loosely connected, is not a paper you can call your own—nor, in all probability, would you want to. If it is to be your paper, you must use the source material to support, or test, or illustrate your own ideas, and in most instances, you will paraphrase rather than quote directly. When you do quote you must do so exactly.

(6) Writing the Paper

When you have collected as much information as you need, or have time for, convert your tentative plan into a final outline. Expand, cut, and reorganize so that the outline represents what you finally want to say. The new outline should be as detailed as possible, since you will actually write your paper from it.

Next, sort out your notes, putting together those that relate to the various subpoints in your outline. This will bring together the notes which explain or justify or give evidence for the points you want to make. If you find you have no notes at all for a subpoint in the outline, ask yourself some questions. Is the point really important?

Should you look for more material, should you try to write it up out of your own head, or should you simply omit the point altogether? You're in charge here. Use your judgment.

From this point on, beyond reminding you of the principles of order, coherence, emphatic statement, and careful choice of words—matters already discussed in this handbook—a teacher can only give you advice based on experience. I find, for example, Hemingway's advice very useful: write the first draft by hand, not on the type-writer. A soft pencil or a smooth-flowing ballpoint pen helps your writing to flow naturally, instead of jerking along in a staccato mechanical rhythm. It also helps to keep the first draft fluid and easy to revise. There is something final-looking about typewritten copy that discourages the impulse to make changes. Moreover, deleting a typed sentence is awkward and time-consuming, but with one satisfying swoop of the pen you can wipe out a whole sentence, or even a paragraph, and start over again. Allow plenty of space so that words or phrases can be inserted between the lines, in place of those you cross out. If the order of sentences in a paragraph needs to be changed, you can indicate this quickly and clearly with freehand lines as visual guides.

In writing the first draft, try any device that enables you to keep going rapidly so that you don't lose your train of thought. If you can't think of the right word, leave a generous blank and go on. The main idea at this stage is to get your ideas down on paper while they are hot. The time to agonize in cold blood over the exact word or the most concisely emphatic sentence pattern is in revision. Hemingway's other bit of advice is also worth remembering: Don't write yourself out. Stop while you're going good and know just what's coming next, so that you can get started readily at your next writing session.

Don't neglect transitional words, phrases, and sentences. Give the reader lots of signposts so he will know at all times where he is. *However* signals a concession to the opposite point of view; *in the second place* locates a stage in a progressive pattern. A sentence like "Two types of evidence support this theory" alerts the reader to the structure of the paragraphs that follow. If in doubt, use more transitional phrases rather than fewer. They can always be crossed out in revision, but if they seem appropriate to you, they will proba-bly be helpful to a reader and should be retained.

If you have time, put the first draft of the whole paper in a drawer for a day or two (at least overnight) before beginning to revise it. Revision is the hardest part of a writer's task, and it is helpful to come at it refreshed and with a clear mind. This is the time for simple mechanical repairs: looking up the spelling of difficult or troublesome words, checking rules of punctuation and mechanics, looking for your likely faults in sentence structure. Decide how much direct quotation you will use, how much summary. If you see lots of long quotes on a page, look again to see if they can't be shortened. Check your paraphrases to make sure they're not uncomfortably close to plagiarism. Put footnotes into their full form now, while there's still time for a last mad dash to the library; check spellings of names and titles, correctness of page numbers. Most importantly, this is the time to test each sentence to see if it really says what you intend. Set a high standard here. Don't be satisfied with the mere hope that a reader will be able to understand your meaning. Try to write so that your reader cannot misunderstand.

The final version of your paper—the one you will hand in—should be typed, double spaced, or written neatly in ink. Follow the suggestions in section 17a (mechanics) for manuscript style. If your instructor requires it, prepare and submit a detailed outline, which will serve as a table of contents. Doublecheck footnotes for correct form, and prepare a final bibliography. When you submit the paper, put it in a folder or secure it by paper clips, but do not staple the pages together. Most instructors will want to separate the pages to facilitate checking and making corrections.

(7) Footnotes

The number of footnotes in a long paper cannot be prescribed in hard and fast rules. All quotations should be documented, of course, and all titles of books. Beyond this, use your judgment. Give references to the most important sources of your information, especially on controversial issues. If you have only four footnotes in a thousand-word paper, you probably aren't doing justice to your sources. If you have five footnotes on every page, you probably are documenting needlessly.

When a paper is to be submitted for publication, most editors prefer to have the footnotes on separate sheets at the end of the paper. Some instructors also prefer this method for term papers. Ask about it. If footnotes are placed at the bottom of each page, the first footnote should be separated from the last line of the text by triple spacing. Footnotes and bibliography entries are double spaced for college papers. Use arabic numerals rather than asterisks or other symbols to indicate the reference of the footnote in the text. Number the footnotes consecutively throughout the paper. In the text the reference numerals should be placed slightly above the line and immediately after the name, quotation, sentence, or paragraph to which the footnote refers. In the footnote itself, the reference number should also be placed slightly above the line. Information given in the text of the paper need not be repeated in the footnote. For example, if you say "Angus Wilson maintains that . . . ," the footnote would begin with the title of the book, instead of the author's name.

A footnote can be thought of as an abbreviated sentence. Its first line is indented five spaces from the left-hand margin, and the first word is capitalized. The footnote ends with a period. Only the first footnote reference to a book or periodical article needs to be written out in full. For later references, use the brief form illustrated on page 263.

The footnote form prescribed and used in this section follows that of *The MLA Style Sheet*, Second Edition. A footnote should contain the following items in the sequence here given:

1. The author's name, first name first. Since footnotes are not in alphabetical order, there is no need to put the last name first.
2. The title of the book, underlined to indicate italic type. If the reference is to an article in a periodical or in a book, the author's name is followed by the title of the article, in quotation marks, and this is followed by the name of the periodical (or book) underlined. Use commas to separate these elements.
3. Information regarding the place and date of publication. For books, this consists of the city in which the book was published, a colon, an abbreviated name of the publisher, and the date, all enclosed in parentheses. For articles, the title of the periodical underlined, followed by the volume number in arabic numerals, the date in parentheses, and the page number.
4. Page number. The abbreviation of *page* is *p.;* the plural is *pp.* If a book is printed in more than one volume, use Roman numerals to indicate numbers between one and ten. In such a case, the abbreviation *p.* is not used: e.g., II, 46.

The following six footnotes illustrate first and second footnote references.

[1]Perry Miller and T. H. Johnson, *The Puritans* (New York: Harper, 1963), p. 18.

[2]Rosemary M. Laughlin, "Anne Bradstreet: Poet in Search of Form," *American Literature*, 42 (1970), 16.

[3]Miller and Johnson, p. 65.

[4]Ann Stanford, "Anne Bradstreet," in *Major Writers of Early American Literature*, ed. Everett Emerson (Madison: Univ. of Wisconsin Press, 1972), p. 37.

[5]Ibid.

[6]Laughlin, p. 19.

The following additional words and abbreviations are sometimes used in footnotes, bibliographies, and references:

anon.	anonymous
b.	born
c. or ***ca.*** *(circa)*	about (used with dates)
cf. *(confer)*	compare or consult
d.	died
diss.	dissertation
ed.	edition, editor, or edited by
et al.	and others (used of people only)
f., plural ***ff.***	and following page(s)
ibid.	the same
id. or ***idem***	the same; usually the same author
l., plural ***ll.***	line(s)
loc. cit. *(loco citato)*	in the place already cited
ms., plural ***mss.***	manuscript(s)
n., plural ***nn.***	note(s)
N.B. *(nota bene)*	take notice, mark well
n.d.	no date (of publication) given
n.p.	no place (of publication) given
n. pag.	no pagination used in book

(The three preceding abbreviations tell your reader that the publisher of your reference work has omitted information you would normally include in your footnote.)

op. cit. *(opere citato)*	in the work cited

(This abbreviation must be used with the author's name, to identify the work being cited. If two works by the same author have been referred to, this abbreviation cannot be used. The general tendency today is to avoid such abbreviations altogether, and to use the author's name, plus a short title if one is needed.)

passim	here and there, throughout

rev.	revised, revision; review, reviewed by (Write out word if necessary to prevent ambiguity.)
sc.	scene
sic	so, thus
st., plural *sts.*	stanza(s)
trans.	translator, translation, translated by
v., plural *vv.*	verse(s)
vol., plural *vols.*	volume(s)

The following list illustrates the chief footnote forms used in the first reference.

Book by One Author

[1]Elizabeth Wade White, *Anne Bradstreet: "The Tenth Muse"* (New York: Oxford Univ. Press, 1971), p. 52.

Book by One Author, Revised or Later Edition

[2]Roy Harvey Pearce, ed., *Colonial American Writing,* 2nd ed. (New York: Holt, 1969), p. 34.

Book by One Author, Reprint of an Older Edition

[3]Sumner Chilton Powell, *Puritan Village* (1963; rpt. New York: Anchor, 1965), p. 61.

Book by One Author, Translated

[4]Ursula Brumm, *American Thought and Religious Typology,* trans. John Hoaglund (New Brunswick, N.J.: Rutgers Univ. Press, 1970), pp. 49–50.

Book by One Author, Part of a Series

[5]George M. Waller, ed., *Puritanism in Early America,* 2nd ed., Problems in American Civilization (Lexington, Mass: Heath, 1973), p. 67.
[6]Josephine K. Piercy, *Anne Bradstreet,* Twayne's United States Authors Series, No. 72 (1965; rpt., New Haven, Conn: College and University Press, 1965), p. 14.

Book by Two Authors

[7]Perry Miller and T. H. Johnson, *The Puritans* (New York: Harper, 1963), II, 47.

A work with three authors would use this same style, with the authors being listed as A, B and C. If a work has more than three authors, the custom is to cite only the name of the first author mentioned on the title page and to complete it with et al. or with the English equivalent, "and others."

An Edited Text

[8]Robert Hutchinson, ed., *Poems of Anne Bradstreet* (New York: Dover, 1969), p. 48.

[9]William Bradford, *Of Plymouth Plantation: 1620–1647*, ed. Samuel Eliot Morrison (New York: Knopf, 1952), pp. 101–02.

Signed Essay in a Book by Several Contributors

[10]Ann Stanford, "Anne Bradstreet," in *Major Writers of Early American Literature*, ed. Everett Emerson (Madison: Univ. of Wisconsin Press, 1972), p. 38.

[11]Robert D. Richardson Jr., "The Puritan Poetry of Anne Bradstreet," *Texas Studies in Lit. and Lang.*, 9 (1967), rpt. in Sacvan Bercovitch, ed., *The American Puritan Imagination: Essays in Revaluation* (London and New York: Cambridge Univ. Press, 1974), pp. 112–13.

Article in a Journal

[12]Rosemary M. Laughlin, "Anne Bradstreet: Poet in Search of Form," *American Literature*, 42 (March, 1970), p. 5.

Article in a Weekly Magazine

[13]D. Davis, "American Hurrah: European Vision of America," *Newsweek*, 5 Jan. 1976. p. 36.

Anonymous Magazine Article

[14]"ALA Pictorial Scrapbook," *American Libraries* 7 (Jan. 1976), pp. 42–43.

Anonymous Encyclopedia Article

[15]Bradstreet, Anne Dudley," *Encyclopedia Britannica,* 1974, Micropaedia II, 221.

Anonymous Newspaper Article

[16]"Women's Roles to be Featured," *Boston Sunday Globe,* 4 April 1976, p. 93, col. 5.

A Book Review

[17]John Harris, "A Free Press Underground," rev. of *The Books of the Pilgrims,* by Lawrence D. Geller and Peter J. Gomes, *Boston Sunday Globe,* 11 April 1976, p. A15, col. 1.

(8) The Final Bibliography

At the end of the paper (after the footnotes, if they are on separate sheets), add your final, alphabetized, bibliography. This may be a list of all those works mentioned in either your text or your footnotes (often called a "List of Works Cited"), or it may include all books and articles you have consulted at length, whether they were actually used in writing the paper or not. This would be a "List of Works Consulted." If your instructor does not specify one form of bibliography or the other, the choice is up to you.

The form of a bibliographic entry differs slightly from that of a footnote reference. Authors are listed with surname first, to make alphabetizing easy. The items within each reference are generally separated by periods instead of commas, but colons and semicolons remain as they were.

Sample Bibliography

"ALA Pictorial Scrapbook." *American Libraries,* 7 (Jan. 1976), 42–43.
"Bradstreet, Anne Dudley." *Encyclopedia Britannica.* 1974. Micropaedia II, 221.
Brumm, Ursula. *American Thought and Religious Typology.* Trans. John Hoaglund. New Brunswick, N.J.: Rutgers Univ. Press, 1970.
Laughlin, Rosemary. "Anne Bradstreet: Poet in Search of Form." *American Literature,* 12 (1970), 1–17.
Miller, Perry, and others, eds. *Major Writers of America.* 2 vols. New York: Harcourt, 1962.

——————, and T. H. Johnson. *The Puritans.* New York: Harper, 1963.
Vol. 2.

*The long dash indicates that Miller is the first-named author for this as
well as for the preceding book. Books by the same author, or having the
same senior author, are listed in alphabetical order.*

Powell, Sumner Chilton. *Puritan Village.* 1963; rpt. New York: Anchor,
1965.

Richardson, Robert D., Jr. "The Puritan Poetry of Anne Bradstreet." *Texas
Studies in Lit. and Lang.,* 9 (1967); rpt. in *The American Puritan Imag-
ination: Essays in Revaluation.* Ed. Sacvan Bercovitch. London and
New York: Cambridge Univ. Press, 1974, pp. 105–122.

Stanford, Ann. "Anne Bradstreet." *Major Writers of Early American Literature.* Ed. Everett Emerson. Madison: Univ. of Wisconsin Press,
1972, pp. 33–58.

Waller, George M., ed. *Puritanism in Early America,* 2nd ed. Problems in
American Civilization. Lexington, Mass: Heath, 1973.

Comments

Spacing between the lines of footnotes: in a manuscript which is going to be set in type by a printer, the footnotes are always double spaced, and for the convenience of editor and printer they are typed all together on pages at the end of the article.

If a typed manuscript is in its final form, as in a thesis or dissertation, or if it is to be duplicated by photographing or xeroxing, the footnotes are placed at the bottom of each page and made to stand out by single spacing, with double spacing between footnotes. (This is the form recommended for term papers by some handbooks.) *The MLA Style Sheet*, however, recommends double spacing the footnotes at the bottom of each page of a term paper for greater ease in reading and in making corrections. This is the form used here.

Footnote 1. Notice that an explanatory sentence may be included in a footnote.

Footnote 2. The passage in the text, quoted rather than paraphrased to preserve its vivid phrasing, could be located by the page number of Hensley's edition of the *Works*. But the author's name, Adrienne Rich, is essential to a reference, and the explanatory "foreword to" is useful, though not essential.

SAMPLE PAPER

Anne Bradstreet's Homespun Cloth:
The First American Poems

by Suzanne E. Conlon

In 1630 a young Englishwoman sailed for the New World with her husband and parents aboard the <u>Arbella</u>, the flagship of the Winthrop fleet carrying Puritan settlers from Southampton to the Massachusetts Bay Colony.[1] As usual, the voyage was rough and uncomfortable, "with its alternations of danger and boredom, three months of close quarters and raw nerves, sickness and hysteria and salt meats."[2] Nor was the

---

[1]Elizabeth Wade White, <u>Anne Bradstreet: "The Tenth Muse"</u> (New York: Oxford Univ. Press, 1971), p. 103. Biographical information is drawn from this book and from the <u>Dictionary of American Biography</u>, ed. Dumas Malone, I, 577–78.

[2]Adrienne Rich, "Anne Bradstreet and Her Poetry," foreword to <u>The Works of Anne Bradstreet</u>, ed. Jeannine Hensley (Cambridge: Harvard Univ. Press, 1967), ix.

Comments

Footnote 3. Since this second quotation is from the same page of the same article in the same book as #2, the standard abbreviation *ibid.*, "in the same place," is adequate. *The MLA Style Sheet* recommends that the abbreviation be written without underlining, since usage differs and it is easier for an editor to add underlining than to erase it.

Footnote 4. Though most of the bibliographical information repeats that of the preceding footnote, the form of reference used here is necessary to make clear that the quotation is from Anne Bradstreet herself, not from Adrienne Rich or Jeannine Hensley.

Footnote 5. The phrase "the Puritan dilemma" is widely used by American historians. The reference given here is to one of numerous discussions of the term.

landing quite what the eighteen-year-old bride
had expected -- "the wild coast of Massachusetts Bay, the blazing heat of an American
June, the half-dying, famine-ridden frontier
village of Salem, clinging to the edge of an
incalculable wilderness."[3]

Forty years later Anne Bradstreet was to
report her feelings in a letter "To My Dear
Children": "I found a new world and new manners, at which my heart rose [in revolt]. But
after I was convinced it was the way of God, I
submitted to it. . . ."[4]

This combination of revulsion and submission
pervades Anne Bradstreet's poetry. It represents an interesting variation on "the Puritan
dilemma"[5] as it was experienced by a sensitive,
cultivated, and pious woman of early New
England. "The Puritan was always trying to

---

[3]Ibid.

[4]The Works of Anne Bradstreet, ed. Jeannine
Hensley (Cambridge Univ. Press, 1967), p. 241.
All quotations from Bradstreet will be taken
from this volume.

[5]See Perry Miller and T. H. Johnson, The
Puritans (New York: Harper, 1963), II, 287.

Comments

The long quotation has been cut down by the two omissions indicated by the ellipsis marks (. . .). The words omitted are irrelevant to the point being made here. Since the second omission occurs within a sentence, three spaced periods are sufficient.

achieve a balance between this world and the next. . . . One could not safely turn one's back on this world, for the simple reason that God had made it and found it good; yet one could not rely upon . . . an earthly life which was, at last, insubstantial."[6]

Anne Bradstreet's dilemma was a little different but produced the same conflict between opposite impulses. Instead of loving the New World, she at first hated the harsh life it imposed on colonists, but this feeling went against her conviction that God's will demanded her to stay there and submit. Eventually she managed to strike a kind of balance: despite periods of doubt and depression, she bore and raised eight children in the wilderness near Andover and in intervals stolen from her scanty leisure time, she wrote five long didactic poems. With their publication in 1650, she became America's first poet.

The poems had been collected in manuscript as a present for her father, Thomas Dudley, an educated gentleman and future governor of the colony; they were not meant to be published.

---

[6]Robert D. Richardson, Jr., "The Puritan Poetry of Anne Bradstreet," <u>Texas Studies in Literature and Language</u>, 9 (1967), 317–318.

Comments

The spelling used in quotations is that of the original. Because seventeenth-century spelling is not expected to meet twentieth-century rules, there is no need to use [sic] or otherwise comment upon it.

Footnote 7. Note that the form of Footnote 4 has made it unnecessary to cite the edition again here.

But her brother-in-law took the manuscript
with him on a journey to England and had it
printed, as a family surprise for Anne, under
the pompous title The Tenth Muse, Lately Sprung
Up in America. His introduction is equally
pompous and painfully condescending: "I doubt
not but the reader will . . . question whether
it be a woman's work, and ask, is it possible?
If any do, take this as an answer from him that
dares avow it: it is the work of a woman,
honoured, and esteemed where she lives, for
her . . . exact diligence in her place, and
discrete managing of her family occasions, and
more than so, these poems are the fruit but of
some few hours, curtailed from her sleep and
other refreshments."[7]

Anne Bradstreet's reaction to the success of
The Tenth Muse was a witty reproach to those
"friends, less wise than true," who had exposed
to the public that "ill-formed offspring of my
feeble brain."[8] She goes on to say that she had
hoped to trim her "rambling brat" in better
dress, "but nought save homespun cloth i' th'

---

[7]John Woodbridge, "Epistle to the Reader," in
Bradstreet, Works, p. 3.

[8]"The Author to Her Book," p. 221.

Comments

Anne Bradstreet's poem, "The Author to her Book," is reprinted below. Note that the writer has selected from it just those phrases she needs and has fitted them smoothly into her own sentence structure. This technique creates a concise and effective summary.

THE AUTHOR TO HER BOOK

Thou ill-formed offspring of my feeble brain,
Who after birth didst by my side remain,
Till snatched from thence by friends, less wise than true,
Who thee abroad, exposed to public view,
Made thee in rags, halting to th' press to trudge,
Where errors were not lessened (all may judge).
At thy return my blushing was not small,
My rambling brat (in print) should mother call,
I cast thee by as one unfit for light,
Thy visage was so irksome in my sight;
Yet being mine own, at length affection would
Thy blemishes amend, if so I could:
I washed thy face, but more defects I saw,
And rubbing off a spot still made a flaw.
I stretched thy joints to make thee even feet,
Yet still thou run'st more hobbling than is meet;
In better dress to trim thee was my mind,
But nought save homespun cloth i' th' house I find.
In this array 'mongst vulgars may'st thou roam.
In critic's hands beware thou dost not come,
And take thy way where yet thou art not known;
If for thy father asked, say thou hadst none;
And for thy mother, she alas is poor,
Which caused her thus to send thee out of door.

Footnote 9. See comment on p. 280.

house I find." It is an odd phrase to describe
the mixture of pedantic learning, dull mor-
alizing, and poetic cliché that made the book
popular in its own time. Modern readers are apt
to pass over these once-fashionable quater-
nions -- rambling four-part exercises in
poetic diction -- in favor of the genuine
homespun of her later verses, written when her
European heritage had faded from memory and she
turned for material to the timeless events of a
woman's personal life. These poems still
stand, three hundred years later, as honest
testaments of the human condition as seen from
one woman's point of view.

Anne Bradstreet's poetic output is the more
surprising when one considers the handicaps
that a woman poet on the frontier had to over-
come. At the very beginning of their new life,
the Dudleys and Bradstreets, though among the
richer founders of the Bay Colony, probably
lived in wigwams or caves dug into the hillside. Anne Bradstreet's father reported that
they had "no table, nor other room to write in
than by the fireside upon my knee," and that
they often lived upon "clams and museles and
ground nuts and acorns."[9] Even when living

---

[9]Quoted in Poems of Anne Bradstreet, ed.
Robert Hutchinson (New York: Dover, 1969), p. 4.

Comments

Note that the reference to *Paradise Lost* is not footnoted, since both the poem and its characterization of Eve would be familiar to anyone who is sufficiently interested in Puritan poetry to be reading an essay on Anne Bradstreet. As it is a book-length poem, its title is underlined.

conditions improved, the unending labor of feeding, clothing, and caring for eight children must have left little time for poetry or other diversions.

In addition, a good Puritan woman was supposed, like Eve in <u>Paradise Lost</u>, to base her life on submission to God and husband. It was her duty to love God and to subordinate her own interests to the welfare of her father, husband, and family. Anne Bradstreet was fully aware of "each carping tongue / Who says my hand a needle better fits."[10] Such critics held that it was an aberration for a woman to write at all, and that it was certainly unseemly, if not actually sinful, for a Puritan woman to write poetry.

To the Puritan mind, poetry represented attachment to the things of this world: to words rather than to the dogma words were meant to communicate, to the natural world rather than the Heavenly Kingdom, to loved ones rather than to God. Cotton Mather, the great Puritan preacher, announced magisterially that the poets were "the most numerous as well as the most venomous authors" in the Devil's Library

---

[10]"The Prologue," p. 16.

Comments

Footnotes 9 and 11. The phrase "quoted in" shows that the writer is borrowing a passage which was already a quotation when she found it in her source. Since both speakers, "Anne Bradstreet's father" and "Cotton Mather, the great Puritan preacher" are identified in the text, there is no need to put their names in the footnotes. For the correct form when it is necessary to identify the speaker, see Footnote 12.

on earth.[11] Any woman who attempted to join this company was apt to come to a bad end, like the wife of the governor of Hartford, Connecticut, who had lost her wits through devoting herself entirely to reading and writing: "If she had attended her household affairs, and such things as belong to women, and not gone out of her way . . . to meddle in such things as are proper for men, whose minds are stronger, etc., she had kept her wits, and might have improved them usefully and honourably in the place God had set her."[12]

There was also the example of her husband's sister Sarah, disgraced in her family for "Irregular prophecying"[13] and preaching in England, as well as her friend Anne Hutchinson, expelled by the Massachusetts Bay Colony for

---

[11]Quoted in American Poetry and Poetics, ed. Daniel G. Hoffman (Garden City: Anchor, 1962), p. 253.

[12]John Winthrop, The History of New England from 1630 to 1649 (Boston, 1826), quoted in Ann Stanford, "Anne Bradstreet: Dogmatist and Rebel," New England Quarterly, 39 (1966), 374-375.

[13]White, Anne Bradstreet, p. 176.

Comments

Here the writer is moving from the first main section of her paper, which dealt with Anne Bradstreet's earlier poems and with the background against which she wrote them, to the second main section, which will be concerned with a closer look at Bradstreet's later poetry. She makes her transition effectively, using one further quotation from Bradstreet's early work to support her point that "there is another voice in this first volume" which foreshadows the "more original, confident, personal voice" of the later poems. (Note that she concentrates her own and the reader's attention on the voice of the poem, which is relevant to the point she is making; she does not speak of the subject of the poem, which is less relevant.)

listening to the inner voice of God rather than
to the elders of the Church. Such consequences
of speaking out -- madness, heresy, banishment
-- should have warned Bradstreet not to risk
poetic fame and may have prompted her humble
request to be rewarded, if at all, with a wreath
of "thyme or parsley," rather than laurel.[14]
And most of Anne Bradstreet's early poems are,
indeed, too imitative and lifeless to merit a
genuine poet's wreath.

Yet there is another voice in this first
volume, a forceful, ironic, intelligent voice
that has its wits about it, as in these lines
from "In Honour of Queen Elizabeth":

> Now say, have women worth? or have they
>   none?
> Or had they some, but with our Queen is't
>   gone?
> Nay masculines, you have thus taxed us
>   long,
> But she, though dead, will vindicate our
>   wrong.
> Let such as say our sex is void of reason,
> Know 'tis a slander now but once was
>   treason.

> (pp. 197-98)

As she set about revising her poems and
adding to them in the second edition, Anne
Bradstreet drew upon this more original,
confident, personal voice. Instead of writing

---

[14]"The Prologue," p. 17.

Comments

The Sidney quotation is well enough known that it does not need to be documented. Note that this quotation, being run into the text, is put inside quotation marks and that therefore the words of the poet's muse, which would normally appear inside regular quotation marks, have been placed inside single quotation marks. Whenever possible, repeated citations from the same author should have their references incorporated into the text, as has been done here. A parenthetic (p. 224) is no more distracting to the reader than a super-script number[14]; and it is certainly easier on the typist. In general, you would not use this form if you needed to include a long title in it; but a short title could be given (e.g., "Contemplations," p. 205).

If a long poem were being quoted, a line reference (ll. 62-65) would probably substitute for the page reference. In a formal foot-note, you might use both, with the line numbers preceding the page number. Some very long poems, such as *Paradise Lost*, are divided into books; then you would give book and line numbers (I. 49-50). For a play, you would give act, scene, and line numbers, with Act I, scene 3, lines 47-50 appearing as (I.iii.47-50).

what she thought was expected of a Puritan
poet, she began to imitate the practice of her
distant relative, Sir Philip Sidney: "'Fool,'
said my muse to me, 'look in thy heart and
write.'" The tension generated by the persistent conflict between the duty owed to God and
the loyalty and love given to her husband and
children gives strength and vitality to her
later poems -- elegies on the deaths of grandchildren, verse letters to her absent husband,
a meditation on the fire that destroyed her
house and personal possessions.

"Before the Birth of One of Her Children"
expresses her fears, well founded in the Seven-
teenth Century, of dying in childbirth. Her
sadness arises not so much from terror of the
after life, for she had the Puritan's confidence in salvation, but from imagined grief
at leaving the husband in whose arms she had
lain for so many years. The salt tears that
dropped on her manuscript fell also for her
"little babes" who might be left motherless or,
worse, in the power of a "step-dame" (p. 224).

"Contemplations," by common consent the most
successful of her poems, has as its underlying
theme the truth that earth as well as heaven
declares the glory of the Lord. Looking at the
autumnal splendor of the New England landscape, Bradstreet asks

If so much excellence abide below,
How excellent is He that dwells on high,
Whose power and beauty by his works we
    know?

(p. 205)

Though the poem unflinchingly faces the passing
of fragile beauty and human life into the ever-
lastingness of God, the poet nevertheless
lingers for a long, loving look by the river's
bank, admiring the autumn color which "seemed
painted, but was true" until her senses were
rapt and she knew not what to wish. "Contemplations" has been called the first American
nature poem, foreshadowing Bryant and the
Romantics.[15]

Another theme that calls out the best in
Bradstreet is the terrible mystery of the early
death of children. Three of her grandchildren,
including her namesake Anne, died within a
period of five years, and Bradstreet's protest
at this eradication of "plants new set . . . and
buds new blown"[16] is at first bitter, revealing

---

[15]Hyatt H. Waggoner, American Poets from the
Puritans to The Present (Boston: Houghton
Mifflin, 1968), p. 8.

[16]"In Memory of My Dear Grandchild Elizabeth
Bradstreet," p. 235.

Comments

On this page and the next, quotations from several poems are used to support single points. Since this part of the paper deals primarily with Anne Bradstreet's own attitudes, as revealed in her poetry, numerous quotations from her works are used, and fewer references are made to the works and opinions of scholars. The quotations remain brief and to the point.

a dark root of anger and grief that had grown
during years of hardship, sickness, and the
loss of loved ones. In the end, as always, she
submits:

> Three flowers, two scarcely blown, the
>   last i' th' bud,
> Cropt by th' Almighty's hand; yet is He
>   good. . . .
> Such was His will, but why, let's not
>   dispute,
> With humble hearts and mouths put in the
>   dust,
> Let's say He's merciful as well as just.[17]

But one can still hear in the later poems, as on
the <u>Arbella</u>, the rising protest of her heart
against the desolation of life in this new
world.

One of the senseless accidents of life that
the Puritan was bound to accept as part of God's
merciful Providence was the loss of worldly
goods. When the Bradstreet house burned down,
through the carelessness of a servant, Anne
lost not only her shelter from New England
weather but all the little personal possessions that had helped make life in the raw new
world more tolerable. Her reaction was

---

[17]"On My Dear Grandchild Simon Bradstreet,"
p. 237.

typical: sorrow at the sight of her treasures now in ashes, but

> . . . when I could no longer look,
> I blest His name that gave and took,
> That laid my goods now in the dust.[18]

Compared to the modest wealth she had known in England, her American treasures must have been paltry, but losing them was still painful, and her grief was real as she looked at the places

> Where oft I sat and long did lie:
> Here stood that trunk, and there that
>   chest,
> There lay that store I counted best. . . .

The Puritan's answer to all this was well known to Anne Bradstreet. She had written some lines of stern comfort to her son Samuel when his wife died:

> Cheer up, dear son, thy fainting bleeding
>   heart,
> In Him alone that caused all this smart;
> What though thy strokes full sad and
>   grievous be,
> He knows it is the best for thee and me.[19]

---

[18]"Upon the Burning of Our House," p. 292.

[19]"To the Memory of My Dear Daughter-in-Law, Mrs. Mercy Bradstreet," p. 239.

Comments

The writer returns to a more general topic for her conclusion, summing up the points she has made in her paper. The early and late books are again compared, the experts once more cited. Now the writer returns to the questions of the reception accorded Bradstreet's poetry. She mentions again the "recognition that came with the 1650 publication," then brings the topic up to date by mentioning nineteenth- and twentieth-century critical responses. The choice of John Berryman, in particular, as a figure to end with—a contemporary poet now first brought in to join contemporary critics in speaking of a seventeenth-century poet—helps create a strong ending for the paper. Language as vivid and original as this is always a good note to end on.

The new poems published in <u>Severall Poems</u> were not intended for publication any more than those in <u>The Tenth Muse</u> had been,[20] but it is these letters, elegies, and prayers, in which the Old World and its old history are forgotten and the New World and its trees and small graves remembered, which assure her a prominent place in the American tradition. The recognition that came with the 1650 publication seems to have freed her from writing the poetry she felt a good poet ought to write and enabled her to write poems about what she saw and touched and held and lost.

Still it was not until the Nineteenth Century that literary historians began to give her the critical appraisal she deserved.[21] And perhaps not until 1956, with the publication of John Berryman's <u>Homage to Mistress Bradstreet</u>, did she become completely accessible to her literary descendants. Berryman confessed: "I did not choose her--somehow she chose me--one point of connection being the almost insuper- able difficulty of writing high verse at all in

---

[20]White, p. 361.

[21]Josephine K. Piercy, <u>Anne Bradstreet</u> (New York: Twayne, 1965), pp. 116-17.

a land that cared and cares so little for it."[22]
But whether we care for her or high verse or
not, she is there, as Berryman writes, "a
sourcing whom my lost candle like the firefly
loves."

---

[22]Quoted by Adrienne Rich in her foreword
to The Works of Anne Bradstreet, from an interview with John Berryman in Shenandoah, Autumn,
1965.

List of Works Cited

American Poetry and Poetics. Ed. Daniel G.
    Hoffman. Garden City: Anchor, 1962.

Bradstreet, Anne. The Works of Anne
    Bradstreet. Ed. Jeannine Hensley. Cam-
    bridge: Harvard Univ. Press, 1967.

Dictionary of American Biography. Ed. Dumas
    Malone. New York: Scribner's, 1928-37.

Hutchinson, Robert, ed. Poems of Anne
    Bradstreet. New York: Dover, 1969.

Miller, Perry, and T. H. Johnson. The Puritans.
    New York: Harper, 1963. Vol. 2.

Piercy, Josephine K. Anne Bradstreet. New
    York: Twayne, 1965.

Rich, Adrienne. "Anne Bradstreet and Her
    Poetry." Foreword to The Works of Anne
    Bradstreet. Ed. Jeannine Hensley. Cam-
    bridge: Harvard Univ. Press, 1967. pp.
    ix-xx.

Richardson, Robert D. Jr. "The Puritan Poetry
    of Anne Bradstreet." Texas Studies in
    Literature and Language, 9 (1967), 317-31.

Stanford, Ann. "Anne Bradstreet: Dogmatic
    Rebel." New England Quarterly, 39 (1966),
    373-89.

----. "Anne Bradstreet." <u>Major Writers of
Early American Literature</u>. Ed. Everett
Emerson. Madison: Univ. of Wisconsin
Press, 1972. pp. 33-58.

Waggoner, Hyatt H. <u>American Poets from the
Puritans to the Present</u>. New York: Dell,
1968.

White, Elizabeth Wade. <u>Anne Bradstreet: "The
Tenth Muse."</u> New York: Oxford Univ. Press,
1971.

Sentence Fragments and Comma Splices

13

To correct fragments and comma splices, you must be able to recognize them, either by their sound, or "feel", when the sentence is read aloud, or by analysis of sentence structure. For the latter method, study Chapter 4 carefully. To get the feel for complete sentences, read your sentences aloud, listening to their accents, pitch, and rhythm. For example, say this sentence aloud. Notice that you pause after *example* and that you end the sentence by lowering the pitch of the last syllable of *aloud*. Try it on other sentences in this paragraph, making yourself notice how you say them.

13a Types of Sentence Fragments

A careless writer, putting the period in too soon, may seriously mislead the reader by cutting off a piece of the full sentence. If the piece does not contain an independent clause, a clause which can stand by itself as a complete sentence, the result is a *sentence fragment*. For example:

The purpose of reciting five minutes in French was to encourage imitation of the recording. **Thus putting emphasis on intonation, rhythm, and pronunciation.**

This was meant to be one complete sentence. As it is written, how-ever, the last part is a fragment, a participial phrase without subject or verb. This phrase should be attached to the previous sentence:

> The purpose of reciting five minutes in French was to encourage imi-tation of the recording, thus putting emphasis on intonation, rhythm, and pronunciation.

Learn to recognize the common types of sentence fragments and how to correct them.

(1) Appositive Phrase

FRAGMENT   The crowd which attended the local track meet was the usual one. **Parents, friends of the athletes, and people looking for a good tan.**

The three nouns "parents," "friends," and "people" are in apposition to "one," and the appositive phrase should be attached to the rest of the sentence.

CORRECTED   The crowd which attended the local track meet was the usual one—parents, friends of the athletes, and people looking for a good tan.

(2) Prepositional Phrase

FRAGMENT   The receptionist was expected to appear efficient and serene, but it was impossible. **With the telephone ringing constantly and clients arriving every half hour for appointments.**

CORRECTED   The receptionist was expected to appear efficient and serene, but it was impossible with the telephone ringing constantly and clients arriving every half hour for appointments.

The prepositional phrase beginning with "With" modifies "impossible" and should be attached to it. Or the phrase might be made into an in-dependent clause and written as a separate sentence.

CORRECTED   The receptionist was expected to appear efficient and serene, but it was impossible. The telephone rang constantly and clients ar-rived every half hour for appointments.

(3) Participial Phrase

FRAGMENT   I was surprised at the commotion in the magazine's office. Reporters, copywriters, and secretaries were rushing all over the place.

Running up and down the aisles, conferring with the editors, and talking in little groups.

Running, conferring, and talking are participles parallel in structure with rushing; that is, they are part of the first sentence and should be attached to it.

CORRECTED   I was surprised at the commotion in the magazine's office. Reporters, copywriters, and secretaries were rushing all over the place, running up and down the aisles, conferring with the editors, and talking in little groups.

FRAGMENT   She had good reason for coming to college and choosing the one she did, unlike some of her classmates. **Having planned for several years to become a doctor.**

CORRECTED   Unlike some of her classmates, she had good reason for coming to college and choosing the one she did, having planned for several years to become a doctor.

(4) Infinitive Phrase

FRAGMENT   After a good deal of arguing, I finally received permission from my parents. **To work for Project Head Start that summer and perhaps even during the fall semester.**

CORRECTED   After a good deal of arguing, I finally received permission from my parents to work for Project Head Start that summer and perhaps even during the fall semester.

(5) Dependent Clause

FRAGMENT   The first car was trying to get far enough ahead to pull off safely. **While the second car kept close in an effort to pass.**

CORRECTED   The first car was trying to get far enough ahead to pull off safely, while the second car kept close in an effort to pass.

Note that the fragment could have been corrected by omitting the conjunction "while" and making two complete sentences.

FRAGMENT   After so many weeks of worrying, I was grateful to learn of the college's loan funds. **Because I didn't know where I could turn for help or see how I could take a part-time job.**

CORRECTED   After so many weeks of worrying, I was grateful to learn of the college's loan funds because I didn't know where I could turn for help or see how I could take a part-time job.

Usually the best way to correct a sentence fragment is to join it to the sentence of which it is logically a part. Sometimes, however, it is better to change the fragment into a full sentence, by adding a verb, a subject, or whatever else is lacking.

13b Permissible Incomplete Sentences

Certain elliptical expressions are equivalent to sentences because the missing words are clearly understood. Such permissible incomplete sentences include the following:

(1) Questions and Answers in Conversation

Why not?   Because it's late.
How much?   Two dollars.

(2) Exclamations and Requests

At last!
This way, please.

(3) Transitions

So much for the first point.
Now to consider the next question.

In addition, fragments are sometimes deliberately used for particular effects, especially in narrative or descriptive writing. In most expository writing, however, there is seldom occasion or excuse for writing fragmentary sentences.

ACCEPTABLE   He watched the needle swing rhythmically from one side of the dial to the other. Back and forth. Over and over. Beginning to get sleepy.

Exercise 1

For each of the following sentences, identify the cause of the fragment and correct it in whatever way seems most effective.

1. When you really get down to it, homework is more likely to be assigned in the academic subjects. Whether they are English, math, science, or some language.
2. One thing which I dislike very much is a person with a mean streak. A person who will go out of his way to do harm to others.
3. During the day the eel lies buried in the mud or concealed under rocks or in seaweed. But at night begins its prowling for food.
4. As this summary indicates, the first part of the story is deceiving. So far, just another tale about a college boy—maybe the all-American ideal—who gets his girl and job and is living on easy street.
5. For some people, life is only boring or painful. Especially if the person has no purpose, no goal in life.
6. The number of the very rich and the very poor having been reduced, leaving most Americans in one large middle class.
7. I now think that my high school was too progressive in some ways. Meaning that it didn't teach how to read and write correctly.
8. The head librarian threatened to close the stacks to all students. Because the cost of replacing stolen books was mounting each year.
9. Tyrone Guthrie's movie production of *Oedipus Rex* was very impressive. Although it took me a while to get used to the masked actors.
10. The City Council's decision to limit speed on a road in the campus but not on a street near an elementary school seemed ridiculous. Since small children are less able to cross streets responsibly.
11. Long hours of practice after classes, the weekends usually taken up with games, and most evenings spent in study. Athletes have little time for working their way through college.
12. Historians are interested only in the more civilized societies that have existed in the past. The ones that have produced great works of art, science, or technology.
13. Every month, the entire research staff spends a full day together in informal conference. To discuss at length current problems and propose and criticize new ideas.
14. A description of being lost in the Grand Canyon when Schuyler's life was saved by a discarded semi-rotten orange.
15. The distance between the stars is immense. So immense that it is difficult to find a unit of measurement which will help one grasp it imaginatively.

13c   Correcting Comma Splices

Do not join two main clauses with only a comma between them (comma splice).

COMMA SPLICE   I'm sure that the teen-agers of today didn't invent cheating, it must have been going on for quite a long time.

A comma splice (sometimes called a "comma fault") is two or more independent clauses separated *only* by a comma. The result can be either a misreading, as in

I wonder if he is thinking, he probably won't tell.

or a failure to show clear sequence and relationship, as in

There was an extremely heavy rain on Monday night, after the storm was over, the streams were overflowing.

You can catch many comma splices in revision by reading your paper aloud: if you drop your voice or pause conspicuously at a comma, check the sentence to see if it is two separate statements.

To correct a comma splice, you have several alternatives. Some illustrations follow.

(1) Subordination of One Main Clause

Correct the comma splice by subordinating one of the main clauses. The commonest subordinating conjunctions include *because, which, since.*

COMMA SPLICE   The banks were closed, John couldn't get the necessary money.

SUBORDINATION   *Since* the banks were closed, John couldn't get the necessary money.

COMMA SPLICE   There are many good reasons for working in the summer, only a few of them can be discussed.

SUBORDINATION   There are many good reasons for working in the summer, only a few *of which* can be discussed.

or

SUBORDINATION   *Of* the many good reasons for working in the summer, only a few can be discussed.

(2) Coordination of Clauses by Conjunction

Correct the comma splice by using a coordinating conjunction to join the two main clauses if you want to give them equal emphasis.

COMMA SPLICE   We will add another room to the house this summer, painting will have to wait until next year.

COORDINATION   We will add another room to the house this summer, *but* painting will have to wait until next year.

COMMA SPLICE   Reading is partly a matter of personal taste, every reviewer ought to keep this fact in mind.

COORDINATION   Reading is partly a matter of personal taste, *and* every reviewer ought to keep this fact in mind.

The most usual pattern is the coordinating conjunction (*and, but, for, nor, or*) preceded by a comma. When long, complex clauses punctuated internally by commas are joined, a semicolon along with a coordinating conjunction may be needed to show the main division of the sentence.

COMMA SPLICE   As the development of the atomic bomb, the computer systems, and guided missiles shows, technology, indeed basic scientific research itself, is often determined by political and military considerations, many people do not recognize this interdependence and instead regard changes in technology as changes which simply "happen."

COORDINATION   As the development of the atomic bomb, the computer systems, and guided missiles shows, technology, indeed basic scientific research itself, is often determined by political and military considerations; *but* many people do not recognize this interdependence and instead regard changes in technology as changes which simply "happen."

(3) Coordination of Clauses by Semicolon

Correct the comma splice by using a semicolon to join the two main clauses. This method is appropriate when the relationship between the two statements is to be implied, rather than stated explicitly.

COMMA SPLICE   Gambling is like a drug, after a while the gambler finds it impossible to stop.

CORRECTED BY SEMICOLON   Gambling is like a drug; after a while the gambler finds it impossible to stop.

(4) Separation of Clauses into Sentences

Correct the comma splice by making each main clause into a sentence. Use this method if you want to emphasize the separation between the two statements.

COMMA SPLICE There was an extremely heavy rain on Monday night, after the storm had passed, the streams were overflowing.

TWO SENTENCES There was an extremely heavy rain on Monday night. After the storm had passed, the streams were overflowing.

(5) Commas with Short Independent Clauses

Commas without conjunctions may be used between short independent clauses for special effects or emphasis. Short, closely related independent clauses in a series are occasionally joined only by commas. Such punctuation is often used in narratives, more sparingly in expository writing.

ACCEPTABLE The wind blew, the shutters banged, the children trembled.

(6) Semicolon with Conjunctive Adverbs

Two main clauses linked by a conjunctive adverb require a semicolon or a period between them. One of the commonest forms of the comma splice is the use of the comma between two main clauses linked by a conjunctive adverb. Such conjunctive adverbs as *also, besides, hence, however, instead, moreover, then,* and *therefore* should be preceded by a semicolon or period when they introduce a second independent clause.

COMMA SPLICE I hadn't read the test very carefully, therefore I was surprised that I had done so well on it.

CORRECTED I hadn't read the test very carefully; therefore I was surprised that I had done so well on it.

COMMA SPLICE To a majority of the economists a gloomy forecast seemed inevitable, however three of the experts were unfashionably cheerful.

CORRECTED To a majority of the economists a gloomy forecast seemed inevitable; however, three of the experts were unfashionably cheerful.

Omitting the semicolon or period before the conjunctive adverb can result in grotesque misreading.

The sergeant had command of his temper and his men, also the general who was reviewing that day was in a good mood.

One way to tell a conjunctive adverb from a pure conjunction is to try to change its position in the sentence. A conjunctive adverb need not stand first in its clause:

We had been told to stay at home; **moreover,** we knew that we were not allowed to play outside after dark.

We had been told to stay at home; we knew, **moreover,** that we were not . . .

A pure conjunction will fit into the sentence only at the beginning of its clause:

We had been told to stay at home, **and** we knew . . .

13d   Fused Sentences

Do not fuse two main clauses by omitting all punctuation between them.

FUSED SENTENCE   He took the job he was offered otherwise he would have had to borrow more money.

The fused sentence is a more blatant error than the comma splice since it often results in serious misreadings. To correct a fused sentence, use any of the means for correcting the comma splice.

REWRITTEN   To avoid borrowing money, he took the job he was offered.

CORRECTED   He took the job he was offered; otherwise he would have had to borrow more money.

FUSED SENTENCE   Congress passed the bill only after long hours of debate there was strong feeling on both sides.

CORRECTED   Congress passed the bill only after long hours of debate. There was strong feeling on both sides.

Exercise 2

In the following sentences, revise the comma splices or fused sentences by whatever means seems most effective. Be prepared to explain the reasons for the means you choose.

1. On most report cards there is a special place for marking effort this is put there so that the teacher can show how hard a student has tried.

2. I obeyed my elders, but I always weighed the facts and formed my own judgments, apparently this independence of mine made some adults angry.

3. But why shouldn't carols be played in shops and stores it's all in the spirit of Christmas.

4. But Huck doesn't pray, instead he thinks of all the times that Jim has been good to him.

5. Once in her room she did a few dance steps, looked at her un-made bed, and shrugged unconcernedly, then she glanced out the window in hopes of catching sight of her little brother.

6. But with the first of September the warm days were over, cold winds began to blow, stirring up freshly turned dirt in the grave-yard and causing old Charles to cast apprehensive glances at the sky.

7. Ironically, the population migration has been especially great to places like Arizona, New Mexico, and Southern California, these are places with a limited water supply.

8. There was a long string of gas stations outside the city, any driver could fill up easily.

9. We found the sea too choppy for sailing or swimming, we stayed on shore.

10. Permission was not granted for the interview, however the re-porters never gave up hope.

11. The new dictionary was more than a revision of the old one, the compilers had redefined each entry and included many more examples of usage.

12. The critic wrote that as the commercials became longer and more offensive, the shows became shorter and more innocuous, also she felt advertisers ought to be forced to watch the commericals.

13. In speech class he announced he would give a demonstration-lecture on how not to pack a suitcase, after he was finished, the other students clapped reluctantly.

14. The counselor gathered the paddles, came down to the pier, and untied the canoe then he waited while the campers climbed in.

15. The medical insurance was cheap and comprehensive, according to its advertisers, the people who bought it soon claimed other-wise.

Grammatical Usage

14

14a Agreement

In standard English a verb agrees with its subject in person and number. That is, if the subject is first person (*I*), the verb is first person (*am*); if the subject is plural, (*they*), the verb is plural (*are*). The rule is simple enough in theory, but in practice we occasionally make agreement errors for a number of reasons.

In the first place, the third person singular of many verbs is formed by the addition of *s* (he/she/it walk*s*), while *s* added to a noun forms the plural (noun*s*). We have to live with this inconsistency in the language, but we should be aware that it can be a source of confusion. Another difficulty is that some writers speak a dialect which does not observe the agreement convention. Furthermore, all of us from time to time violate the principle in conversation, either in haste or carelessness or in sheer forgetfulness of how we began the sentence. It is easy to understand why agreement is a troublesome rule for some writers. Perhaps the pronoun is so far away from its antecedent (the word it refers to) that the writer forgets what the antecedent is. Or a writer may be uncertain whether a compound subject, like "Either Angela or Carol," should be considered singular or plural. Such questions will be discussed in following sections.

Another problem, sociological rather than grammatical, arises from the lack in English of a singular pronoun which refers to either sex.

For centuries it has been a convention to use the masculine third-person singular pronoun to refer to a noun of which the gender is either unknown or irrelevant.

A *child* should be taught to take care of *his* teeth.

This convention, however, has led to some bizarre constructions:

> At her strongest and most characteristic, she [Edith Wharton] is a brilliant example of the writer who relieves an emotional strain by denouncing his generation.
>
> —EDMUND WILSON

To avoid such a logical inconsistency, don't hesitate to use the feminine pronoun where its antecedent is clearly female, as in the example above. You can avoid the problem entirely by casting general statements about human beings in the plural: "*Children* should be taught to take care of *their* teeth."

Avoid the "everyone . . . his" construction when possible, in consideration of those women in your audience who might feel uncomfortable with a pronoun which sometimes refers to them, sometimes not. Some writers in published books use first "he," then "she" to refer to the sexually neutral *person, artist, student;* others frown on this practice as confusing and inconsistent. A number of new pronouns have been suggested to replace "his or her": *tes, shis, vis.* Experimenting with these forms will teach you, if nothing else, how difficult it is to break ourselves of old language patterns and introduce new words into our grammar.

(1) Agreement of Subject and Verb

Everyone knows that a pet *requires* care, whereas pets *require* care. Violations of this principle usually occur when (1) it is not clear which word is the simple subject or (2) when there is doubt whether the subject is singular or plural.

1. Which word is the subject?

Modifying phrases do not change the number of the subject.

NONSTANDARD   A program of two Bergman films were shown last night.

> *It is easy to become confused here, since the pattern "films were shown" is a familiar one. But the simple subject in this sentence is "program," and the verb must agree with it.*

STANDARD   A *program* of two Bergman films *was* shown last night.

Although phrases like "accompanied by," "as well as," and "together with" suggest a plural idea, they do not change the number of the subject.

STANDARD   The *prisoner,* accompanied by guards and her lawyer, *was* in the courtroom.

STANDARD   The *property,* as well as the guest house and the extra garage, *is* up for rent.

When two nouns are connected by some form of the verb *to be,* the first noun is the grammatical subject, and the verb agrees with it.

STANDARD   The first *thing* we noticed *was* the tuna boats.

STANDARD   The tuna *boats were* the first thing we noticed.

When the subject follows the verb, a common error is to make the verb agree with the word which precedes it.

NONSTANDARD   Beyond the old mud fort was the endless sands of the desert.
What was beyond the fort? The "sands," and they "were."

In sentences beginning with *there is* or *there are,* you will always find the subject following the verb.

There *are* a million *laughs* in this bouncy little comedy.
There *is* only one correct *solution* to the problem.
There *is* a long *list* of jobs to be done before we leave.
There *are* many *jobs* to be done before we leave.

2.   Is the subject singular or plural?

When compound subjects are joined by *and* they are usually considered to be plural.

STANDARD   *Mathematics* and *science are* my best subjects.

STANDARD   The *evaluating, hiring,* and *training* of the applicant *are* left to the Personnel Department.

There are, however, some exceptions to this principle. If the two nouns of a compound subject refer to the same person, the verb should be singular.

STANDARD   This young bachelor and man-about-town *was* finally discovered to be an imposter.

Sometimes two compound nouns are needed to indicate one thing.

STANDARD   Bacon and eggs *is* the typical American breakfast.

In informal English, a singular verb is occasionally used when a compound subject follows the verb.

FORMAL   In the office there *are* a *desk,* a *chair,* and a filing *cabinet.*

INFORMAL   In the office there *is* a desk, a chair, and a filing cabinet.

When *each* or *every* is used to modify the compound subject, a singular form of the verb is used.

STANDARD   Each soldier and sailor *was* given a complete examination.

STANDARD   Every camera and light meter *has* been reduced in price.

Two or more subjects joined by *or* or *nor* usually take a singular verb form.

STANDARD   Local information or a good road map *is* needed to get you
to the camp.

STANDARD   Neither the producer nor the consumer *was* treated fairly.

When one subject is singular and one is plural, the verb agrees with the subject nearer it.

STANDARD   Neither my brother nor my sisters *have* ever been there.

In informal English, a plural verb is occasionally used when a *neither . . . nor . . .* construction expresses a plural idea.

STANDARD   Neither the union nor the company *seem* to like the plan.

Collective Nouns

Collective nouns, like *class, committee, team, family, number,* are considered singular when they refer to the group as a unit. If you want to emphasize the individual members of the group, you may use the plural form of the verb.

STANDARD   The *committee was* unanimous in its recommendations.

STANDARD   The *class were* unable to agree on a day for the party.
   Many writers would feel this sentence to be awkward, even though correct, and would rephrase it: "The members of the class were unable. . . ."

STANDARD A large *number* of votes *is* required.

STANDARD A large *number* of notes in his journal *are* inaccurate.

STANDARD The *number* of correct answers *was* small.

Indefinite Pronouns

Indefinite pronouns, like *each, every, either, neither, any, some,* and their compounds with *–one* or *–body,* are singular in number and should be followed by singular verb forms.

STANDARD *Each* of the boys *was* tested.

STANDARD *Either* of them *is* qualified for the job.

STANDARD *Neither* of the speakers *was* willing to answer questions.

In speech and in informal writing, especially in questions, a plural verb is common.

INFORMAL *Are either* of the boys qualified for the job?

COLLOQUIAL *Each* of the children *have* their own room.

None, some, more, most, and *all* may be either singular or plural, depending on the context and the intended meaning.

STANDARD *None* of the money *was* wasted.

STANDARD *None* of the dresses *are* paid for.

STANDARD *Most* of the pie *has been* eaten.

STANDARD *Most* of the students *have read* that play.

Relative Pronouns

The relative pronouns *who, which,* and *that* take a singular verb form when the antecedent is singular, a plural verb form when the antecedent is plural.

STANDARD Betsy is the kind of *woman who prefers* to earn her living.
 The antecedent of who *is* woman.

STANDARD This is one of those *motors that were* imported from Japan.
 The antecedent of "that" is "motors." The sentence is about one of a group of motors—those that were imported from Japan.

Nouns Ending in s

Some abstract nouns which are plural in form are grammatically singular—e.g., *aesthetics, economics, linguistics, mathematics, news, physics, semantics.*

STANDARD   Physics *was* the hardest course I had in high school.

Note that certain nouns ending in s have no singular form and are always plural: *trousers, scissors, measles, forceps.* Some nouns ending in *ics* (*athletics, politics, statistics*) may be either singular or plural, often with a distinction in meaning.

STANDARD   Athletics [the collective activity] *builds* the physique.

STANDARD   Athletics [particular sports and teams] *are* his favorite
pastime.

STANDARD   Statistics *is* my most difficult course.

STANDARD   Statistics *show* that . . . .

Latin Plurals

Words like *data* and *strata* are Latin plurals, but there is a strong tendency in current English to treat them as collective nouns, which may be either singular or plural.

FORMAL   We must classify all the data that *have* been collected.

ACCEPTABLE   This data *was* collected in a survey.

STANDARD   These *strata go* back to the Miocene period.

Exercise 1

Give reasons for using the singular or the plural verb form in the following sentences.

1. Every one of the nine men on the team (is, are) important.
2. The close relationship with professors and fellow students (makes, make) the small college the choice of many entering freshmen.
3. Doug sprawled in the chair and knocked over one of the lamps which (was, were) on display.
4. There (has, have) never been hard feelings between the families on this street.

5. The symptoms of lead poisoning (varies, vary) with each individual case.
6. Next in the waiting line (was, were) an elderly lady and her grandson.
7. He believes that athletics (improves, improve) school morale.
8. Up goes the starter's gun, and each of the runners (becomes, become) tense.
9. The doctor said that there is always a possibility the infection will return but that so far there (has, have) been no signs of its recurrence.
10. The family (takes, take) its annual vacation during August.
11. A majority of the hospital's patients (has, have) some kind of medical insurance.
12. Either the *Times* or the *Tribune* (is, are) a reliable source of news.
13. The catcher, as well as the pitcher and the coach, (was, were) arguing furiously with the umpire.
14. Her chief interest in life (was, were) horses.
15. Slater is one of those legislators who (has, have) always opposed spending.

Exercise 2

In the following sentences, determine the cause of the faulty agreement and supply the correct form of the verb.

1. In addition, there is the students who cheat because they have never been taught differently.
2. The author's portrayal of the guests and the games add up to an extremely vivid picture of that particular society, with its petty concerns and rituals.
3. Another of the unpopular activities that take place during freshman week are the roll calls.
4. The theme of suffering, its causes and its consequences, are treated by Shakespeare, Tolstoy, and Conrad.
5. The first thing which catches your eye are the headlines.
6. The fact that the children are so beautiful and so intelligent add to their goodness and make ghosts appear even more evil.
7. Everyone else in the story have readjusted to their roles, and Pam is the only one who is injured by the experience.
8. But their way of expressing themselves are totally different.

9. These products of automation may have made life more pleasant but has reduced the population from hardworking pioneers to button-pushing time-servers.
10. She is one of the women who has made this country what it is.

(2) Agreement of Pronoun and Antecedent

Pronouns should agree in number with the words they refer to—their antecedents.

STANDARD   Many *people* pay a genealogist to look up *their* ancestry.
"People," the antecedent, is plural, and so the correct pronoun is "their."

STANDARD   My *uncle* paid a genealogist to look up *his* ancestry.
"His" agrees with "uncle."

Such indefinite antecedents as *each, either, neither, everyone, everybody, someone, somebody, anyone, anybody* are followed in Edited English by a singular pronoun.

STANDARD   *Everyone* at times finds *himself* facing failure.

STANDARD   *Anybody* can eat *his* meals at the Club.

The terms *everyone* and *anybody* include my sister, and she never finds "himself facing failure" nor eating "his meals at the Club." Many women object to this illogical construction, but to fill it out—"eats his or her meals"—is awkward and wordy. Such a sentence, however, can often be improved by rewriting.

REVISED   Everyone at times faces failure.

REVISED   Anybody can eat meals at the Club.

Compound antecedents are usually considered plural when joined by *and*, singular when joined by *or* or *nor*.

STANDARD   My father encouraged *Henry* and *me* not to postpone *our* trip.

STANDARD   Neither the senator nor his press secretary would admit that *he* was responsible.

If a singular pronoun, even though correct, produces an awkward or clumsy sentence, the plural pronoun is often acceptable in informal writing.

ACCEPTABLE   Almost everybody eats some fruit as a part of *their* basic diet.

When the antecedent is a collective noun, the singular pronoun is used to emphasize the cohesiveness of the group, the plural to emphasize the separate individuals.

STANDARD   The *audience* showed *its* approval by applause.

STANDARD   The *audience* were cheering, booing, whistling and stamping *their* feet.

Note in the sentence above that the verb "were" also is in the plural form. Be consistent. If the verb form shows the antecedent to be singular, the pronoun should be singular. If the verb is plural, the pronoun should be plural.

INCONSISTENT   The *jury is* about to return and give *their* verdict.

CONSISTENT   The *jury is* about to return and give *its* verdict.

Demonstrative pronouns (*this, these; that, those*) are sometimes used as adjectives and should then agree in number with the words they modify.

NONSTANDARD   *These kind* of vegetables are grown in the Valley.

STANDARD   *This kind* of vegetable is grown in the Valley.

STANDARD   *These kinds* of vegetables are grown in the Valley.

Exercise 3

Give reasons for using the singular or plural form of the pronoun in the following sentences. Be prepared to say which pronoun forms would be acceptable in speech and informal writing but would be discouraged in college writing.

1. Maybe some day each person will have (his, their) own helicopter for commuting to the city.
2. Nobody needs servants because nobody has more housework than (he, they) can manage.
3. The school was preparing to put on (its, their) annual May Day Dance.
4. Any parent hopes to get the best education for (his, their) children.
5. The congregation were divided in (its, their) feelings about the new minister.

6. Neither Faulkner nor T. S. Eliot won the Nobel Prize in literature until well after (he, they) had written (his, their) most important works.
7. Each man and woman must make (his, their) own decision.
8. The United States has to look out for the rights of (its, their) citizens.
9. Neither Macbeth nor the Emperor Jones cared how (he, they) got what (he, they) wanted.
10. I believe that a person should never ask someone else for advice on (his, their) problems.

Exercise 4

In the following sentences, determine the cause of the faulty agreement and supply the correct form of the pronoun.

1. Either the members or the secretary may submit their objections.
2. The family was quite frank in stating their opinions.
3. These kind of scrimmages can be very bruising.
4. Each camper was supposed to bring their own bedding.
5. Now that everything was perfect, he was going to make sure they stayed that way.
6. Dorm meetings are always a spectacle because someone always loses their temper.
7. The prisoner's attitude toward society is largely determined by the treatment they receive in prison.
8. Every new proposal was vetoed by the chairman because he thought they weren't practical.

14b Case of Pronouns and Nouns

Case means the changes in the form of a noun or pronoun that show how it is used in a sentence: *man, man's, he, his, her, them,* etc. English nouns used to have many case forms, but over the centuries the forms have been reduced to those which indicate possession. Most pronouns, however, have three case forms: NOMINATIVE (or subjective) when the pronoun is the subject of a verb, the POSSESSIVE (or genitive) case to show possession, and the OBJECTIVE case when the pronoun functions as a complement—the object of a verb or preposition.

NOMINATIVE	I	we	he	she	it	they	who
POSSESSIVE	my	our	his	her	its	their	whose
OBJECTIVE	me	us	him	her	it	them	whom

As with agreement, people usually get case right without consciously thinking about it. But a few constructions can cause writers trouble.

(1) Compound Constructions

A noun and a pronoun used in a compound construction should be in the same case; the same principle applies to constructions like *we boys* and to appositives.

My father and *I* often hunt together.
"I" is a subject of the verb "hunt."

The professor invited my father and *me* to his house.
Because a construction like "my father and I" is so familiar, it is easy to slip into using it even when, as here, the objective case is needed. He invited my father and he invited "me," not "I."

Between you and *me*, Porter doesn't have a chance to win.
The compound construction "you and me" is the object of the preposition "between."

My father always spanked *us boys* for staying out late.

We boys always tried to avoid being seen coming in.
In the first sentence, "us boys" is the object of "spanked." In the second, "we boys" is the subject of "tried."

Most of the float was designed by two members of the class, Howard and *me.*
Since "two members" is the object of the preposition "by," the appositive should also be in the objective case. However, in speech, "Howard and I" would be fairly common. After all, Howard and I did it.

(2) *Who* in Dependent Clauses

When in doubt about the case of the relative pronoun *who*, try a personal pronoun in its place. If *he* or *they* sounds right, use *who*; if *him* or *them* fits the grammatical context, use *whom*.

Here is a man *who* can explain eclipses.
Would you say of this man that "him can explain eclipses"?

Prentice is the man *whom* I told you about.
The preposition "about" needs an object, like "him" or "whom."

Note that a parenthetical expression like *I think* or *he says* does not change the case of the pronoun.

The woman *who* I thought would accept the nomination changed her mind.
I thought "she" would accept the nomination, and so the relative pronoun should be the nominative "who."

Here are extra bluebooks for *whoever* needs them.
The relative pronoun is the subject of "needs." "Whomever" would be correct in a sentence like "Give the tickets to whomever you choose." But most speakers and many writers would find the construction too formal and would rephrase the sentence: "Give the tickets to anyone you choose."

In formal writing, the interrogative pronouns *who* and *whom* are used exactly like the relative pronouns.

Who is coming to the party?

Whom are you expecting at the party?
"Whom" is the object of "are expecting."

In speech and in much informal writing, there is a decided tendency to use *who* as the interrogative form whenever it begins a sentence, no matter what its construction in the sentence. *Whom* is usually avoided unless it directly follows a preposition. Since the use of *who* and *whom* is often picked on as a crucial test of literacy, it is safer to use the formal case form in Edited English.

INFORMAL   **Who** are you expecting for dessert?

FORMAL   **Whom** are you expecting for dessert?

INFORMAL   **Who** are you driving with?

FORMAL   With *whom* are you driving?

(3) Complement of *to be*

In formal writing, the complement of the linking verb *to be* is in the nominative case.

The members of the delegation are *you*, your *sister*, and *I*.

We hoped the speaker would be President Markson, but it was not *she*.

A voice on the telephone asked for Professor Poynter, and I said, "This is *he*."

In speech and informal writing, the form "It is me" and analogous forms like "I thought it was her" and "It wasn't us" are commonly used. In college writing, such forms usually occur in dialogue, where informality is appropriate.

When the infinitive form of *to be* is used, its complement is always in the objective case.

I wouldn't want to be *him*.

(4) Pronoun after *than, as,* or *but*

After *than* or *as*, the case of a pronoun is determined by its use in the shortened clause of which it is a part.

My cousin is taller than *I* [am].

They take more photographs than *we* [do].

I can type as well as *he* [can].

He chooses you more often than [he chooses] *me*.

I thought her as guilty as [I thought] *him*.

But is sometimes used as a preposition meaning "except." In such constructions, the object of *but* should be in the objective case.

By morning everyone had left but *them*.

At Judy's party all the children had a good time but Judy and *me*.

(5) Possessives with Gerund

A noun or pronoun modifying a gerund should be in the possessive case.

Julie's giggling disturbed those around her.

Alan's father and mother approved of *his* joining the Navy.

The subject of a gerund, however, should be in the objective case.

We could hear *John* snoring.

We saw *them* washing the dishes.

Exercise 5

In each sentence, choose the proper case form and be prepared to explain your choice.

1. My brother is a better skier than (I, me).
2. If Harvey hadn't finished college, my parents would never have permitted Betty and (he, him) to get married.
3. There was no comment from the two members (who, whom) I thought were sure to protest.
4. All the students (who, whom) I talked to seemed to like the new coach.
5. My father used to nag us—my sister and (I, me)—about using his pipe cleaners to make bracelets.
6. All the family went to the funeral but (I, me).
7. The new dictator won't be sure of (who, whom) he can trust.
8. His father objects to (him, his) watching sports every spare minute he can.
9. The reward was divided between my older brother and (I, me).
10. The Holes have not lived here as long as (we, us).
11. That year we finally had a teacher (who, whom) won the respect of all of (we, us) students (whom, whom) she had in class.
12. Only two members of the family are double-jointed in the thumb, my mother and (I, me).
13. Another good reason for (him, his) joining the Coast Guard is the chance for special training.
14. The ten remaining tickets will be given to (whoever, whomever) applies first.
15. I would hate to be (he, him).

14c Correct Use of Adjectives, Adverbs, and Verbs

Most adverbs are formed by adding *ly* to the adjective: *clear, clearly; immediate, immediately,* etc. But note that some adjectives also end in *ly:* a *friendly* gesture, a *manly* appearance, *monthly* payments. A few adverbs have the same form as the adjective: *far* out, *much* pleased, I *little* thought, do it *right,* run *fast,* go *slow.* The dictionary will tell you whether a word functions as an adjective or an adverb, or both.

The car stopped **suddenly.**
The adverb modifies the verb "stopped."

The car came to a **sudden** stop.
The adjective modifies the noun "stop."

(1) Adjectives with Linking Verbs

Verbs like *be, become, seem, appear,* as well as verbs indicating the use of the five senses (*look, feel, taste, sound, smell*) are often used to link an adjective to the subject of a sentence. Do not use the adverbial form as the complement of a linking verb.

The swimmer
- looked
- seemed
- felt
- sounded
- became
- was

cold.

I felt **terrible** about my mistake.

I knew I had played **terribly.**

The melon tasted **sweet,** and my aunt smiled **happily.**

Though the surgeon looked **tired,** he felt my ankle **carefully.**

I smelled the fish **cautiously,** but it smelled **fresh.**

Watching him, Betty felt **uneasy.** (*tells something about Betty*)

Betty watched him **uneasily.** (*tells how she watched him*)

I felt **bad** about her illness. (*adjective complement of* "felt")

I felt **badly** bruised. (*adverb modifying* "bruised")

In speech, the following adjectives are often used to modify a verb or an adjective:

COLLOQUIAL He looks **real** good in blue.

COLLOQUIAL I slept **good** last night.

COLLOQUIAL Today I feel **some** better.

COLLOQUIAL We were **sure** glad to see them again.

14c

In writing, use the corresponding adverbs: *really* good, slept *well,* *somewhat* better, *surely* (or *certainly*) glad.

(2) Comparatives and Superlatives

Formal writing distinguishes between the comparative and superlative in making comparisons. The comparative is used in speaking of two persons: "He was the *taller* of the two." The superlative is used when three or more are being compared: "He was the *tallest* man on the team." In speech and informal writing this distinction is not always observed, and the superlative is often used in comparing two persons or things.

FORMAL He was the **more** influential of the two vice-presidents and the **most** powerful of all the stockholders.

INFORMAL Of the two styles offered, the first was the **most** popular.

According to logic, adjectives like *perfect* or *unique* should not have comparative or superlative forms; a thing is either perfect or not perfect, and since *unique* means "the only one of its kind", no object can be more unique than another. Consequently, formal writing tends to avoid expressions like *most perfect* or *more unique,* even though it regularly uses modifiers indicating an approach to the absolute, like *nearly perfect* playing, or an *almost unique* diamond. Informal writing often uses the superlative form, *most perfect,* but *rather unique* and *the most unique* were considered unacceptable by 94% of the Usage Panel of *The American Heritage Dictionary.*

FORMAL Holmes is the **most nearly perfect** actor we have seen this season.

INFORMAL Holmes is the **most perfect** actor we have. . . .

ACCEPTABLE We, the people of the United States, in order to form a **more perfect** union. . . .

Exercise 6

Correct the use of adjectives and adverbs as may be necessary to bring the following sentences up to the level of standard *written* English.

1. If you listen close, you should be able to hear it quite distinct.
2. The colors in the living room contrasted harshly and looked shockingly.

3. People today live more secure because of new drugs and anti-biotics.
4. I am sure I didn't do too good on the objective part of the final.
5. The sky was clear and the air smelled freshly.
6. In the laboratory we were shown a seemingly impossibility.
7. An exciting documentary affects me quite different from a dramatized story about the same thing.
8. We were real pleased that so many people were willing to help.
9. That disastrous Thursday started out quite normal.
10. The sunset was beautiful that evening, but the sky looked threateningly the next morning.
11. During the whole time that Blaisdel was chairman, business went along very smooth.
12. The trick worked as perfect as we had hoped.
13. By looking real close at the ballot, I could see somebody had changed it.
14. A small minority of students have given this university a real bad image.
15. At the end of the play, he finds that defeat tastes bitterly.

14d Tense and Mood of Verbs

Tense means variations in the form of a verb to indicate time differences. There are six principal tenses in English.

PRESENT
I **believe** this is the right thing to do.

PAST
I **mowed** the lawn, and my sister **pruned** the bushes.

FUTURE
I **will fly** to Denver next month.

PRESENT PERFECT
I **have tried** to encourage him, but he **has** never **dared** to dive.

PAST PERFECT
She **had finished** the assignment by the time I arrived.

FUTURE PERFECT
He **will have arrived** before we get to the station.

(1) Sequence of Tenses

Every native speaker of English knows the following tense patterns:

When I **press** this button, the motor **begins** to run.

The instant he **pressed** the button, the motor **began** to run.

If you **press** (or **will press**) the button, the motor **will start.**

Now that he **has pressed** the button, he **expects** the motor to start.

Since he **had pressed** the button, he **expected** the motor to start.

Ignoring these patterns occasionally produces a monstrosity like "When he died, his fellow citizens realized how much he contributed to the community, and since then they collected funds for a memorial."

CORRECT SEQUENCE OF TENSES   When he **died** [a particular time in the past], his fellow citizens **realized** [from that time on] how much he **had contributed** [up to the time of his death] to the community, and since then they **have been collecting** [from that time to the present] funds for a memorial.

An infinitive should be in the present tense unless it represents an action earlier than that of the main verb.

July 14, 1789, must have been a great day **to be alive** [not **to have been alive**].

I realized later that it was a mistake **to have chosen** [not **to choose**] the life of an artist two years earlier.

Statements that are permanently true should be put in the present tense (sometimes called the "timeless present") even though the main verb is in the past.

Copernicus **found** that the Sun **is** the center of our planetary system. [Not **was;** it still **is.**]

I **insisted** that the Amazon River **is** longer than the Nile.

The present tense is often used in book reviews and criticism for describing a novel, play, or movie. But statements about the facts of a dead author's life are normally in the past tense.

Oliver La Farge's novel **is** the story of a young Navajo whose wife **seeks** revenge for her mistreatment by a white man.

The setting of Hawthorne's short stories **is** the New England village that Hawthorne **knew** so well. [The setting of the stories is still the same; Hawthorne knew them in the past.]

(2) Principal Parts of Irregular Verbs

Irregular verbs are a small group which, instead of forming their past tenses by adding *ed* (*start, started*), change the vowel to indicate the past tense and the past participle (*begin, began, begun*). The principal parts consist of (1) the present infinitive (*begin*); (2) the past tense (*began*); (3) the past participle (*begun*). All tense forms can be derived from the three principal parts. The first principal part is the basis for all present and future tenses, including the present participle; the second principal part is used for the simple past tense— "I began the job yesterday." The third principal part is used in all the compound tenses: "I have begun," "he had begun," "the job was begun," etc.

In the speech of children, errors in the use of principal parts of the irregular verbs are common: "I throwed the ball," "We brung it home," "He has went home." The following list gives the principal parts of some irregular verbs which are apt to be confused.

present	simple past	past participle
begin	began	begun
bid **(offer)**	bid	bid
bid **(command)**	bade	bidden
bite	bit	bitten
blow	blew	blown
break	broke	broken
bring	brought	brought
burst	burst	burst
choose	chose	chosen
come	came	come
dive	dived (dove)	dived
do	did	done
draw	drew	drawn
drink	drank	drunk
eat	ate	eaten
fall	fell	fallen
fly	flew	flown
forget	forgot	forgotten (forgot)
freeze	froze	frozen

get	got	got (gotten)
go	went	gone
grow	grew	grown
know	knew	known
lie	lay	lain
ride	rode	ridden
ring	rang	rung
rise	rose	risen
run	ran	run
see	saw	seen
shrink	shrank (shrunk)	shrunk
sing	sang	sung
speak	spoke	spoken
spring	sprang (sprung)	sprung
steal	stole	stolen
swim	swam	swum
swing	swung	swung
take	took	taken
throw	threw	thrown
wear	wore	worn
write	wrote	written

(3) *Shall* and *will*

More space may be spent on the distinctions between the verbs *shall* and *will* than the topic warrants. But since very formal writing preserves the traditional distinction, it deserves an explanation. To express the simple future (the tense which indicates an event yet to occur), Formal English demands *shall* in the first person and *will* in the second and third persons. To express determination, promise, or prophecy, *will* is used in the first person and *shall* is used in the second and third person.

Simple Future
{
If you don't mind, I *shall join* you and we *shall go* together.
If you don't hurry, you *will be* late.
When he arrives, he *will* probably *be* tired.
}

Determination etc.
{
Despite the inconvenience, we *will pay* the bill.
He *shall do* as I tell him.
Thou *shalt* not *kill.*
You *shall* not *escape* the consequences of your crime.
}

In most speech and writing these distinctions are ignored. To express the simple future, *will* is used for all three persons. *Shall* is rarely used at all in informal speech and writing, except in questions, as a polite substitute for *let's,* or to find out what the person addressed wants.

> Shall we go now? (Meaning "Let's go.")

> Shall I leave the window open? (Meaning "What would you like?")

(4) Subjunctive Mood

Subjunctive forms of the verb are used much less than formerly. In speech, the subjunctive is retained only in formulas like "If I were you. . . ." Informal writing, however, often uses, and formal writing demands, the subjunctive on a few occasions:

Condition
Contrary to Fact

{ I wish I *were* younger.
If this *were* Saturday, we would be at the lake.
Though the dog has just had his supper, he acts as if he *were* still hungry.

Indirect
Imperative

{ The terms of the will require that the funds *be spent* on education.
Her lawyer insists that she *open* a savings account.

Motions
and Resolutions

{ I move that the minutes *be approved.*
Resolved, that this question **be submitted** to arbitration.

Exercise 7

Correct any errors in the use of verbs in the following sentences.

1. She wore a faded blue dress, and her dusty gray shoes were once white.
2. The astronomer said that the moon was approximately 239,000 miles from the earth.
3. For a reader who had never run across advertising of this kind, a further explanation may be necessary.
4. Zephyr, our cat, would lay on the floor for hours and played with a ball of string.
5. He would have liked to have told her what he thought of her.
6. If I had chose physics as my major, I wouldn't have to write all these papers.

7. It was a serious mistake to have been so candid.
8. The book had laid right where I had put it.
9. The water level began to raise, and by noon it had rose ten feet.
10. She recognized the boy who had spoke to her at the dance.

Exercise 8

For each of the following sentences choose the proper verb form and be prepared to justify your choice.

1. I wouldn't tolerate such noise if I (*were, was*) you.
2. He moved that the motion (*is, be*) approved.
3. His mother insists that he (*come, comes*) in right now.
4. If Alaska (*was, were*) a warmer state, its population would be larger.
5. He acts as if he (*was, were*) drunk, and he probably is.
6. (*Shall, Will*) the play begin promptly at eight?
7. I am determined that he (*shall, will*) not escape punishment.
8. That bell sounds as though it (*was, were*) cracked.

Exercise 9

Correct all grammatical errors in the following sentences.

1. Most ski accidents are the results of someone being careless or thinking they are more skillful than they really are.
2. But along with increased speed comes many new problems in jet design.
3. Their bird was setting right on the perch, right where they left him three hours earlier.
4. The adolescent feels that if they do not conform, they will be unpopular.
5. Intercollegiate sports, even though the whole student body does not participate in it, provides amusement for most of the students.
6. Certain basic traits in humans, such as love of power, is a real obstacle to a peaceful world.
7. I know several people in my class whom I'm convinced scarcely opened a book in four years.
8. Criminals receive very fair trials in our country in that he is considered innocent until proved guilty.
9. Her favorite reading matter are novels, preferably science fiction.

10. According to the report, the company will give a bonus to whomever discovers the source of leakage.
11. Extra work was assigned to we students who came in late.
12. Every time any of us open a newspaper, we read of new trouble abroad.
13. The foreman of the lumber gang told Stan and I to report early the next morning.
14. Anyone with a little practice can learn to drive, can't they?
15. Within the broad limits of the assignment there are a great variety of topics for students to choose from.
16. He says he always feels bad after he had worked hard.

Punctuation   15

Punctuation is, at best, a minor aid to clarity of communication. A sentence which is badly constructed or poorly phrased cannot be saved by punctuation alone; it must be revised or phrased more accurately.

Some rules for the use of punctuation are intended to make communication easier, but many rules can be justified only on the grounds of accepted editorial practice. Moreover a good deal of punctuation is optional. A writer may use commas or not, depending on his taste or his intention, in such a sentence as the following:

Eleven All-Americans would not in fact guarantee a good team.

Eleven All-Americans would not, in fact, guarantee a good team.

Most readers would probably feel that setting off the *in fact* gives it a little more emphasis, but either sentence is correct.

The rules in the following sections specify where punctuation marks are needed and, occasionally, where they are acceptable. Beyond this, you must use your judgment. If you are in doubt and no positive rule covers the point, you will probably be safer to omit the punctuation mark.

15a   **End Punctuation**

(1) The Period

Use a period to mark the end of a declarative or imperative sentence.

CORRECT   This is an example of a declarative sentence.

CORRECT   Use a period at the end of a sentence like this.

A period is also used after abbreviations, like *Dr., Mr., Ph.D., etc.,* A.D., *Calif., Inc.* For the proper use of abbreviations see Chapter 17.

Three spaced periods (. . .), called ellipsis marks, are used to indicate the omission of a word or words from a quoted passage. If the omitted words come at the end of a sentence, a fourth period is needed.

CORRECT   We hold these truths to be self-evident: that all men . . . are endowed by their Creator with certain unalienable rights. . . .

Similarly, three (or four) periods are sometimes used in dialogue and interrupted narrative to indicate hesitation and pauses. Beginning writers should use these with caution.

CORRECT   He inspired uneasiness. That was it! Uneasiness. Not a definite mistrust—just uneasiness—nothing more. You can have no idea how effective such a . . . a . . . faculty can be.

—JOSEPH CONRAD

(2) The Question Mark

Use a question mark after a direct question.

CORRECT   Where did you find such information?

CORRECT   How much of the White Sands is gypsum?

CORRECT   Looking at me, the officer said, "Where do you live?"

An indirect question should be followed by a period, not a question mark.

CORRECT   He asked what had caused the delay.

CORRECT   I wonder how many Americans walk to work these days.

A request which is phrased as a question for politeness' sake is followed by a period.

CORRECT   Will you please send me your latest catalog.

(3) The Exclamation Mark

Exclamation marks are appropriate only after statements which would be given unusual emphasis if spoken. This mark is seldom appropriate to expository writing. Do not use it to lend force to flat statements or ironic remarks.

INAPPROPRIATE   The professor suggested that we take out our notebooks since he was going to give us a little (!) test.

15b   The Comma

The comma is perhaps the most used and, consequently, the most abused punctuation mark. It separates coordinate elements within a sentence, and sets off certain subordinate constructions from the rest of the sentence. Since it represents the shortest breath pause and the least emphatic break, it cannot separate two complete sentences.

A primary function of the comma is to make a sentence clear. Always use commas to prevent misreading: to separate words which might be erroneously grouped together by the reader.

(1) To Separate Independent Clauses

Two independent clauses joined by a coordinating conjunction (*and, or, nor, but, for*) should be separated by a comma. Note that the comma is always placed before the conjunction.

CORRECT   I failed German in my senior year of high school, *and* it took me a long time to regain any interest in foreign languages.

CORRECT   She went through the motions of studying, *but* her mind was elsewhere.

Very short independent clauses need not be separated by a comma if they are closely connected in meaning.

CORRECT   The bell rang and everyone left.

Coordinating conjunctions are often used to join the parts of a compound predicate: that is, two or more verbs with the same subject. In such a sentence a comma is not required to separate the predicates. However, if the two parts are long or imply a strong contrast, a comma may be used to separate them.

CORRECT   We *measured* the potassium and *weighed* it on the scale.

CORRECT   Mr. Fossum *demonstrated* the differences between preserving wood with oil and with shellac, **and** advised the use of oil for durable table tops.

CORRECT   To our dismay, the suede could not be *washed* at home nor *dry cleaned* at an ordinary place, **but** *had to be sent* to a specialist.

When the clauses of a compound sentence are long and are also subdivided by commas, a stronger mark of punctuation than a comma may be needed to separate the clauses from each other. For this purpose a semicolon is regularly used.

CORRECT   For purposes of discussion, we shall recognize two main varieties of English, Standard and Nonstandard; and we shall divide the first type into Formal, Informal, and Colloquial English.

(2) To Separate Elements in Series

Separate words, phrases, or clauses in a series by commas. The typical form of a series is *a, b,* and *c.* A series may contain more than three parallel elements, and any of the coordinating conjunctions may be used to connect the last two. If *all* the elements of a series are joined by coordinating conjunctions (*a and b and c*), no commas are necessary to separate them.

SERIES OF ADJECTIVES   The shy devil-fish blushes in blue, red, green, or brown.

SERIES OF PHRASES   Water flooded *over the riverbed, over the culverts, and over the asphalt road.*

SERIES OF PREDICATES   The bear *jumped away from the garbage can, snarled at the camper, and raced up the tree.*

SERIES OF NOUNS   *Resistors, transistors, capacitors, and connectors* are small electronic parts.

SERIES OF INDEPENDENT CLAUSES   Stone was hauled twelve miles, casing was built as the hole deepened, and a well 109 feet deep was completed in Greensburg, Kansas.

The comma before the last item in a series is omitted by some writers, but its use is generally preferred since it can prevent misreading.

MISLEADING   The three congressional priorities are nuclear disarmament, the curtailment of agricultural trade and aid to underdeveloped countries.

Without the comma before "and," "agricultural trade" and "aid to underdeveloped countries" can be read as compound objects of "curtailment of," and the reader reaches the end of the sentence still waiting for the third priority. No such misreading occurs if the comma is included.

(3) Uses with Coordinate Elements

Adjectives modifying the same noun should be separated by commas if they are coordinate in meaning. Coordinate adjectives are those which could be joined by *and* without distorting the meaning of a sentence.

CORRECT   Bus lines provide inexpensive, efficient transportation.

The adjectives are coordinate: transportation which is "inexpensive" and "efficient."

Sometimes, however, an adjective is so closely linked with the noun that it is thought of as part of the noun. Such an adjective is not coordinate with a preceding adjective.

CORRECT   Paynes bought a spacious summer cabin.

This does not mean "a cabin which is spacious and summer." "Summer" indicates the kind of cabin; "spacious" describes the summer cabin.

Note that numbers are not coordinate with other adjectives and are not separated by commas.

CORRECT   They screened in two large, airy outdoor porches.

"Two" and "large" should not be separated by a comma. But since the two outdoor porches were "large" and "airy," a comma is used to separate these two coordinate adjectives.

Coordinate words or phrases which are sharply contrasted are separated by commas.

CORRECT   He is ignorant, not stupid.

CORRECT   Our aim is to encourage question and debate, not criticism and argument.

An idiomatic way of asking a question is to make a direct statement and add to it a coordinate elliptical question. Such a construction should be separated by a comma from the direct statement.

CORRECT   You will come with us, won't you?

CORRECT   He won't test on last semester's units, will he?

Another idiomatic construction which requires a comma is the coordinate use of adjectives, as in *the more . . . , the more . . . .*

CORRECT   The faster the bird, the higher the metabolism.

CORRECT   The more a candidate meets voters, the more he may learn about their concerns.

Exercise 1

Insert the proper punctuation marks where they are required in the following sentences, and give a reason for your choice.

1. Seven legislators from the southern part of the state changed their votes and with their aid the bill was passed.
2. During many periods of history men's clothing has been no less extravagant in cut color and richness of fabric than women's and there have been times when men's clothes have been the gaudier.
3. By the end of the twenty-mile hike we were all fairly tired and some of us were suffering from sore feet as well.
4. Three of the editors argued that the article was biased and malicious and voted to reject it in spite of the distinguished name of the author.
5. The teller at the bank looked dubiously at the check I offered him and even though I knew the check was good I could feel a guilty look freezing on my face as his doubts increased.
6. Painted surfaces should be washed with a detergent sanded lightly and covered with a thin coat of plastic varnish.
7. I painted the house a warm deep pearl gray.
8. His latest novel was marred by pretentious writing the absence of solid characterization and a hackneyed plot.
9. I believe that a state lottery can be useful because it can provide revenue for education increase employment and relieve the tax burden.
10. I judge people of any race by what they say and how they act not by the color of their skin.

(4) To Set Off Nonrestrictive Modifiers

A dependent clause, participial phrase, or appositive is nonrestrictive when it can be omitted without changing the main idea of the sentence. A nonrestrictive modifier gives additional information about the noun to which it refers. A restrictive modifier, on the other hand, restricts the meaning of the word to which it refers to one particular group or thing. If it is omitted, the main idea of the sentence is changed. One check is to read the sentence aloud: if the voice pauses and drops slightly before and after the modifier, the modifier is probably nonrestrictive; if the voice is sustained and unhesitant before and after the modifier, the modifier is probably restrictive and is *not* set off by commas.

Nonrestrictive Clauses and Phrases

Note that *two commas* are required to set off a nonrestrictive modifier in the middle of a sentence; one comma is sufficient if the modifier is at the beginning or end of the sentence.

NONRESTRICTIVE CLAUSE   My faculty advisor, **who had to sign the program card,** was very hard to find.

If the clause were omitted, some information would be lost, but the sentence would still make the same point: that my advisor was hard to find.

RESTRICTIVE CLAUSE   A faculty advisor **who is never in his office** makes registration difficult.

Omitting the clause here changes the sense completely. The purpose of the clause is to limit the statement to a certain kind of faculty advisor— those who are never in their offices.

nonrestrictive clause
CORRECT   I found the letter under the door, **where the postman had put it.**

restrictive clause
CORRECT   The letter was still **where the postman had put it.**

nonrestrictive phrase
CORRECT   Uncle Jasper's letter, **lying unclaimed in the dead letter office,** contained the missing document.

restrictive phrase
CORRECT   We have had many complaints about letters **undelivered because of careless addressing.**

Notice how the meaning of a sentence may be altered by the addition or the omission of commas:

CORRECT   The board sent questionnaires to all members, who are on Social Security.

Nonrestrictive clause. The sentence implies that all members are on Social Security.

CORRECT   The board sent questionnaires to all members who are on Social Security.

Restrictive clause. The questionnaire is sent only to some members, those on Social Security.

Nonrestrictive Appositives

Appositives are usually nonrestrictive and hence are set off by commas. If, however, an appositive puts a necessary limitation upon its noun, it is restrictive and no punctuation is necessary.

NONRESTRICTIVE APPOSITIVE   Scientists working with cryogenics have produced temperatures within a thousandth of a degree of absolute zero, *approximately 459.7 below zero Fahrenheit.*

RESTRICTIVE APPOSITIVE   The noun cryogenics comes from a Greek word meaning "icy cold."

Note that an appositive used to define a word is often introduced by the conjunction *or.* Such appositives are always set off by commas to distinguish them from the common construction in which *or* joins two coordinate nouns.

CORRECT   The class found a fine specimen of pyrite, *or fool's gold.*

CORRECT   We couldn't decide whether to plant phlox or coral bells.

Note that an abbreviated title or degree (K.C.B., USMC, M.D., Ph.D.) is treated as an appositive when it follows a proper name.

CORRECT   He was introduced as Robert Harrison, *L.L.D.,* and he added that he also held a Ph.D. from Cornell.

Exercise 2

Insert commas in the following sentences to set off nonrestrictive clauses and participial phrases. In doubtful cases, explain the difference in meaning produced by the insertion of commas.

1. King Leopold of Belgium who was Queen Victoria's uncle also gave her a great deal of advice.
2. Many people who have never been to the United States think of it as a country of wealth and luxury where everyone lives on the fat of the land.
3. Some years ago I lived in a section of town where almost everyone was a Republican.
4. With the advent of the jet engine which is more efficient at high than at low altitudes aircraft could attain greater heights.
5. The astronauts who had been trained for any circumstance were calm when launching was called off at the last minute.
6. The student hoping to get a C without too much work should stay out of Economics 152.
7. We shall have to hire a caretaker if you can't find time to keep the place neat and orderly.
8. The packing plant where I worked all summer is on the Aleutian Islands.
9. She has made a special study of the native women who are monogamous.
10. The average American tired of last year's models and seeking something new is an easy prey for the designers who capitalize on herd psychology and the craving for novelty.

(5) To Set Off Parenthetic Elements

Parenthetic is a general term describing explanatory words or phrases which are felt to be intrusive and subordinate. That is, they interrupt the normal sentence pattern to supply additional, supplementary information, and they are accordingly set off by commas or other punctuation marks. In the widest sense of the term, nonrestrictive modifiers are a kind of parenthetic element. Many other sentence elements may become parenthetic if they are removed from their regular place and inserted so that they interrupt the normal order of a sentence.

For example, adjectives normally are placed before the words they modify: *Two tired, hungry boys came into camp.* If the adjectives are inserted elsewhere in the sentence, they become parenthetic and should be set off: *Two boys, tired and hungry, came into camp.* Similarly, it is possible to rewrite a sentence like *I am certain that space science will bring some unexpected discoveries* so that one clause becomes parenthetic: *Space science, I am certain, will bring some unexpected discoveries.*

CORRECT   The minutes, I regret to say, need several additions.

CORRECT   The discovery that mammals can learn to breathe under water may, in the opinion of some experts, lead to a technique which will prevent drowning.

Transitional Words

Transitional words and phrases, like *however, moreover, indeed, consequently, of course, for example, on the other hand,* are usually set off by commas, especially when they serve to mark a contrast or the introduction of a new point. In short sentences where stress on the transitional word is not needed or desired, the commas are often omitted.

CORRECT   The beginning violinist needs patience. For example, six lines of music can have 214 bowing variations.

CORRECT   The best beef should be bright red and be marbled with pure white fat. However, a customer may be fooled by tinted lighting which, in fact, cheats the buyer.

CORRECT   The court ruled, consequently, that no damages could be collected.

Notice that *however* is sometimes used as a regular adverb, to modify a particular word rather than as a sentence modifier, and that when so used it is not set off by a comma.

CORRECT   However much he diets, he does not lose enough weight.
Since "however" modifies "much," it is not set off.

Dates and Addresses

Multiple elements of dates, addresses, and references are set off by commas. If only one element (day of month, year, city, etc.) appears, no punctuation is needed.

CORRECT   April 4 is her birthday.

CORRECT   New York is her native state.

CORRECT   Act IV moves toward the climax.

But if other elements are added, they are set off by commas.

CORRECT   April 4, 1953, is the date of her birth.

CORRECT   The return address was 15 South Main Street, Oxford, Ohio.

CORRECT   The quotation is from *King Lear*, II, ii, 2.

Direct Address, Interjections, yes and no

Nouns used as terms of direct address, interjections, and the words *yes* and *no* should be set off by commas.

CORRECT   Miss Kuhn, would you like to be a teaching assistant?

CORRECT   This preposterous charge, ladies and gentlemen, reveals my opponent's ignorance.

CORRECT   Oh, yes, we have a more expensive rental.

Quotation Expressions

Quotation expressions such as *he said* are set off by commas when used with a direct quotation.

CORRECT   "When I was young," he said, "seeing a monoplane was exciting."

Do not use a comma to set off an indirect quotation.

CORRECT   The jeweler said that he could reset the sapphire.

CORRECT   They told us that they had sent a wire.

When the quotation contains two independent clauses and the quotation expression comes between them, a semicolon may be required to prevent a comma fault (see section 13c).

CORRECT   "Please try," he said; "you could win."

CORRECT   "Please try," he said. "You could win."

CORRECT   "I'd like you to try," he said, "but I won't insist."

For other rules regarding the punctuation of direct quotations, see section 15d.

Absolute Phrases

An absolute phrase should be set off by commas. An absolute phrase consists of a participle with a subject (and sometimes a complement) not part of the basic structure of the sentence but serving as a kind of sentence modifier. It usually tells when, why, or how something happened.

CORRECT   The gale having quieted, highway workers began to clear fallen trees and signs from the roads.

CORRECT   The marks on her transcript didn't annoy her, grades representing only part of her education.

Exercise 3

Insert commas where they are required to set off parenthetic elements or to follow conventional usage.

1. Money is not to be sure the only problem that people worry about.
2. Yes I have lived in Minnesota most of my life but I was born in Seattle Washington.
3. My uncle formerly one of the richest men in Woodstock promised to put me through college.
4. In the first place there is no evidence Mr. Jones that my client was driving a car on July 14 1965.
5. Teaching of course has certain disadvantages class size being what it is.
6. "From here" said Mr. Newman "you can see the car double-parked in the alley."
7. The study of Latin or of any other foreign language for that matter helps to clarify English grammar.
8. My cousins tired and wet returned from their fishing trip at sunset.
9. Stricter laws it is argued would be of no use without more machinery for their enforcement.
10. Portland Maine was not as I remember an unpleasant place for a boy to grow up in.

(6) To Set Off Introductory Elements

A dependent clause coming first in the sentence is usually set off by a comma. If a dependent clause follows the main clause, however, a comma is used only when the dependent clause is nonrestrictive.

CORRECT   If you see him, tell him to write me soon.

Introductory adverbial clause, set off by a comma.

CORRECT   Since the melting point of tallow is 127° Fahrenheit, slow-burning candles are made with beeswax.

CORRECT   Tell him to write me as soon as he can.
Restrictive adverbial clause following main clause.

CORRECT   Take a trip abroad now, even if you have to borrow some money.
Nonrestrictive adverbial clause following main clause.

An introductory verbal phrase (participial, gerund, or infinitive) is usually followed by a comma. A prepositional phrase of considerable length at the beginning of a sentence may be followed by a comma.

participial phrase
CORRECT   **Suffering from disease, overcrowding, and poverty,** the people of Manchester were prime victims of the early Industrial Revolution in England.

gerund phrase
CORRECT   **After seeing the poverty and unfair treatment of the working class people,** Mrs. Gaskell wrote several protest novels.

infinitive phrase
CORRECT   **To understand Hemingway's uneasy friendship with F. Scott Fitzgerald,** one must know something of Hemingway's attitude toward Fitzgerald's wife, Zelda.

long prepositional phrase
CORRECT   **Soon after his first acquaintance with Fitzgerald,** Hemingway took an intense dislike to Zelda.

(7) To Prevent Misreading

Use a comma to separate any sentence elements that might be incorrectly joined in reading and thus misunderstood. *This rule supersedes all others.*

MISLEADING   Ever since he has devoted himself to athletics.

CLEAR   Ever since, he has devoted himself to athletics.

MISLEADING   Inside the house was brightly lighted.

CLEAR   Inside, the house was brightly lighted.

CORRECT   Soon after, the minister entered the chapel.

CORRECT   To elaborate, the art of Japanese flower arranging begins with simplicity.

(8) Misuse of the Comma

Modern practice is to use less, rather than more, punctuation in narrative and expository prose. A good working rule for the beginner is to use no commas except those required by the preceding conventions. Here are some examples of serious errors caused by excessive punctuation. In all the following sentences, the commas should be omitted.

INCORRECT   His ability to solve the most complicated problems on the spur of the moment, never failed to impress the class.
The comma erroneously separates subject and predicate.

INCORRECT   The men who lived in the old wing of the dormitory, unanimously voted to approve the new rules.
If the clause is restrictive, no commas should be used; if the clause is nonrestrictive, two commas are required.

INCORRECT   During chapel the minister announced, that the choir would sing Handel's *Messiah* for Easter.
The comma erroneously separates an indirect quotation from the rest of the sentence.

INCORRECT   Gigi is so tall, that she may break the record for rebounds.
The comma erroneously splits an idiomatic construction, "so tall that."

Do not put a comma before the first member or after the last member of a series, unless the comma is required by some other rule.

INCORRECT   For lunch I usually have, a sandwich, some fruit, and milk.
The comma after "have" separates the whole series from the rest of the sentence. It should be omitted.

INCORRECT   Rhode Island, New Jersey, and Massachusetts, were the most densely populated states in 1960.
The comma after "Massachusetts" erroneously separates the whole series from the rest of the sentence.

CORRECT   Rhode Island, New Jersey, and Massachusetts, in that order, were the most densely populated states in 1960.
The comma after "Massachusetts" is required to set off the parenthetic phrase "in that order."

Exercise 4

Some of the following sentences omit necessary commas, while others contain unnecessary and misleading ones. Punctuate the sentences correctly and be prepared to justify each comma you use and the eliminations you make.

1. The person who used to speak precisely and clearly, may now mumble and run words together the way a favorite television star does.
2. Some parents feel there should be a limit to the amount of home-work which students are assigned but I feel most teachers are quite reasonable about the amount given.
3. When one cheats, he cheats no one, but himself.
4. This purity of spirit combined with the courage to stand up for what he believes, makes Huck the great character that he is.
5. Finally when Ike is fully initiated the chase begins.
6. A certain coffee commercial is amusing because it uses puppets, and is different from other advertisements.
7. The skeptical writer proposes questions hoping for answers.
8. I could readily understand for instance, that primitive man who was ignorant and easily terrified, might develop a caste of medi-cine men.
9. The band, bunting and fireworks were planned but these were not enough to assure the parade's success.
10. It is soon evident, in the story, *Lucky Jim,* by Kingsley Amis, that Margaret is unstable, and that Dixon feels insecure and inferior.
11. He is apparently disgusted with his job, and the rest of his environment.
12. Their faces, like the faces of the rest of the villagers are grotesque and primitive.

15c The Semicolon

The semicolon indicates a greater break in the sentence than the comma does, but it does not have the finality of a period. Its most important use is to separate two independent clauses not joined by a conjunction. As a device for creating compound sentences from shorter sentences, the semicolon may easily be overworked. If a conjunction expresses the relationship between the two parts of your sentence, use the conjunction. The semicolon should be reserved for use when the relationship between two statements is so clear that it is unnecessary to state it explicitly.

(1) To Separate Principal Clauses

When the independent clauses of a compound sentence are not joined by a conjunction, a semicolon is required.

CORRECT I do not say that these stories are untrue; I only say that I do not believe them.

CORRECT In India fourteen main languages are written; several hundred dialectical variations are spoken.

The conjunctive adverbs (*so, therefore, however, hence, nevertheless, moreover, accordingly, besides, also, thus, still, otherwise,* etc.) are inadequate to join two independent clauses. A semicolon is required to separate two independent clauses not connected by a pure conjunction. Using a comma instead produces a comma splice (see section 13c).

COMMA SPLICE Our plan was to sail from Naples to New York, however, an emergency at home forced us to fly instead.

CORRECT Our plan was to sail from Naples to New York; however, an emergency at home forced us to fly instead.

CORRECT From the high board, the water looked amazingly far away; besides, I was getting cold and tired of swimming.

CORRECT The loan account book must be sent with each monthly payment; otherwise, there may be disputes as to the amount still owing.

If the clauses are short and closely parallel in form, commas are frequently used between them even if conjunctions are omitted.

CORRECT The picture dimmed, the sound faded, the TV failed.

CORRECT The curtains fluttered, the windows rattled, the doors slammed.

(2) To Separate Clauses When Commas Are Inadequate

Even when two independent clauses are joined by a coordinating conjunction, a semicolon may be used to separate the clauses if the clauses are long or are subdivided by commas.

CORRECT   The Northwest Ordinance of 1787, drafted by Jefferson, is generally noted because it established government of territory north of Ohio and west of New York; *yet* one of its most important statutes was the allocation of land and support for public schools.

CORRECT   In recognition of her services, the principal was given a farewell dinner, a record, and a scroll; *and* a new elementary school was named after her.

A semicolon is used to separate elements in a series when the elements contain internal commas. That is, when a comma is not a strong enough mark of separation to indicate the elements of a series unmistakably, a semicolon is used instead.

AMBIGUOUS   One day of orientation was led by Mr. Joseph, the chaplain, Mrs. Smith, a French teacher, and the Dean.
How many led orientation?

CORRECT   One day of orientation was led by Mr. Joseph, the chaplain; Mrs. Smith, a French teacher; and the Dean.

CORRECT   Bibliography may include Randall Jarrell, *Poetry and the Age*; Northrup Frye, *Anatomy of Criticism*; and Edmund Wilson, *The Shock of Recognition*.

Be sure that semicolons separate coordinate elements. Using a semicolon to separate an independent clause and a subordinate clause is an error similar to writing a sentence fragment, and just as serious.

INCORRECT   Young people tend to reject parental authority; although they are searching for other adults as models.

CORRECT   Young people tend to reject parental authority, although they are searching for other adults as models.

Exercise 5

Some of the following sentences contain semicolons which are unnecessary or incorrect, while other sentences lack needed semicolons. Correct the punctuation and be able to justify each semicolon you use or omit.

1. Joseph is reluctantly picked up by a passing stagecoach; and then only after one of the passengers notes that they could be held legally responsible if a naked stranger should die for lack of aid.

2. More understandable than any of her other criticisms are her remarks about the educational system, however, even these are not very specific.
3. Our technology has developed the telephone for the talebearer; the car for the speedster; and the elevator for children.
4. A novel dealing with the affectations of a past society may become dated, and one must consider this possibility when judging it, otherwise, the book will suffer undue criticism.
5. He was not admitted to the honor society; although he was a good athlete and a top student.
6. The second edition of the book, published in 1922, is relatively scarce and hard to find; but the third edition, published four years later, can be seen in almost any store selling old books.
7. Sometimes I get so interested in a book that I stay up until I finish it; regardless of whether I have classes the next morning or not.
8. Since air is dissolved by water at the surface only, the shape of an aquarium is important, too small an opening may cause an oxygen deficiency.
9. I might ask here; "What is the most important thing in life?"
10. The sculptor can work for more than a week on the same clay model; because clay can be kept soft and pliable for a long time.

Exercise 6

Explain the punctuation in the following sentences. In order to do so, you will need to distinguish between principal clauses, subordinate clauses, and phrases.

1. There are no set rules which actors must follow to become proficient in their art; however, there are certain principles regarding the use of mind, voice, and body which may help them.
2. The book covered the life of Lotta Crabtree from birth to death; it painted her as one of the most colorful figures of early California.
3. Her forehead was wrinkled, her mouth was firm and tense, but her eyes had a dreamy, reminiscent look.
4. The unconscious sailor would then be taken to an outbound ship to be sold to the captain at a price ranging from $100 to $300, depending on how pressed the captain was for men; and he would regain consciousness somewhere in the Pacific Ocean, without the slightest idea of where he was or where he was going.

5. Among the colorful figures in the book are Johnny Highpockets, a simple-minded settler; Charley Tufts, formerly a professor at Yale; and the author of the book himself.
6. A grove of cypress trees, wind-blown and shaggy with Spanish moss, still grows on the headland, as it did when Stevenson first explored the area.
7. Somervell, the only son of a hard-working country doctor and a mother who had been trained as a school teacher, was born in a quiet, secluded farming town in Arkansas on August 21, 1892.
8. In most respects the hotel is admirably located; it is near the corner of Fifth Avenue and 52nd Street, within walking distance of convention headquarters.
9. On the postcard was a reproduction of a watercolor by John Piper; it showed the interior of Ingelsham Church.
10. Since air is dissolved by water at the surface only, the shape of an aquarium is important; too small an opening may cause an oxygen deficiency.

15d Quotation Marks

(1) To Enclose Direct Quotation

Use quotation marks to enclose a direct quotation, but not an indirect quotation. A direct quotation gives the exact words of a speaker. An indirect quotation is the writer's paraphrase of what someone said.

INDIRECT QUOTATION He said that he would call.

DIRECT QUOTATION He said, "I will call."

> *The indirect quotation does not give the speaker's exact words; the direct quotation does and is enclosed with quotation marks.*

The expression *he said* is never included within the quotation marks. If the actual quotation is interrupted by such an expression, both halves must be enclosed by quotation marks.

CORRECT "I am interested," he said, "so let's talk it over."

CORRECT "It all began accidentally," Jackson said. "My remark was misunderstood."

(2) To Quote Several Sentences

If a quotation consists of several sentences, uninterrupted by a *he* or *she said* expression, use one set of marks to enclose the entire quotation. Do not enclose each separate sentence. If a quotation consists of several paragraphs, put quotation marks at the beginning of each paragraph and at the end of the last paragraph.

CORRECT Barbara replied, "Right now? But I haven't finished my paper for Economics. Call me in a couple of hours."

CORRECT Poor Richard has a number of things to say about diet:
"They that study much, ought not to eat so much as those that work hard, their digestion being not so good.
"If thou art dull and heavy after meat, it's a sign thou hast exceeded the due measure; for meat and drink ought to refresh the body and make it chearful, and not to dull and oppress it.
"A sober diet makes a man die without pain; it maintains the senses in vigour; it mitigates the violence of the passions and affections."

A quotation within a quotation is enclosed with single quotation marks. Be sure to conclude the original quotation with double marks.

CORRECT The lecture began, "As Proust said, 'Any mental activity is easy if it need not take reality into account.'"

(3) To Indicate Implied Speech

Quotation marks are frequently used for implied speech, but are not customarily used for unspoken thoughts.

CORRECT He tried to cry, "She is there, she is there," but he couldn't utter the words, only the sounds.

—JAN DE HARTOG

CORRECT It was a momentary liberation from the pent-up anxious state I usually endured to be able to think: At least I'm not them! At least I'm not those heavy, serious, righteous people upstairs.

—ROBERT LOWRY

(4) Misuse in Paraphrase

Use quotation marks around material directly quoted from another writer, but not around a paraphrase of an author's ideas.

CORRECT John Selden pinpoints our attitude toward virtues when he defines humility: "Humility is a virtue all preach, none practise, and yet everybody is content to hear. The master thinks it good doctrine for his servant, the laity for the clergy, and the clergy for the laity."

CORRECT   John Selden describes humility as a virtue we all praise, but few practice. We expect to observe it in those who deal with us, while overlooking our own chances to be humble.

If you quote only a few words from a well-known writer and work them into your own sentence, quotation marks may be omitted.

CORRECT   During childhood it was easy to see that others should share toys, but during adulthood it is not easy to do unto others as you would have them do unto you.

(5) Longer Quotations

When a borrowed quotation runs to several lines of print, it should be set off by indenting and single-spacing. Quotation marks should not be used to set off such material, though they may be required within the quotation.

CORRECT   T. S. Eliot begins the essay "Tradition and the Individual Talent":

> In English writing we seldom speak of tradition, though we occasionally apply its name in deploring its absence. We cannot refer to "the tradition" or to "a tradition"; at most, we employ the adjective in saying that the poetry of So-and-so is "traditional" or even "too traditional." Seldom, perhaps, does the world appear except in a phrase of censure. If otherwise, it is vaguely approbative, with the implication, as to the work approved, of some pleasing archaeological reconstruction.

(6) Verse Quotations

A quotation of more than one line of poetry should be set off by indenting and single-spacing, without quotation marks. Be sure to keep the line lengths exactly as they are in the original.

CORRECT   Boileau has captured a quality inseparable from fine satire:

> But satire, ever moral, ever new.
> Delights the reader and instructs him too.
> She, if good sense refine her sterling page,
> Oft shakes some rooted folly of the age.

A quotation of one line of verse, or part of a line, should be enclosed in quotation marks and run in as part of your text.

CORRECT   Lytton disliked the false heroics of Henley's **"**My head is bloody but unbowed.**"**

If parts of two lines of verse are run in to the text, indicate the line break by a slash (/):

CORRECT   Stark Young and Rex Stout both found book titles in Fitzgerald's "never grows so red / The rose as where some buried Caesar bled."

(7) Punctuation with Quotation Marks

At the end of a quotation, a period or comma is placed inside the quotation mark; a semicolon or colon is placed outside the quotation mark.

CORRECT   "Quick," said my cousin, "hand me the flashlight."

CORRECT   The bride and groom said, "I do"; the ladies in the audience wept.

CORRECT   I have only one comment when you say, "All people are equal": I wish it were true.

A question mark or exclamation mark goes inside the quotation mark if it applies to the quotation only, and outside the quotation mark if it applies to the whole sentence.

CORRECT   My mother asked, "Did you arrive on time?"

CORRECT   Did the invitation say "R.S.V.P."?

CORRECT   He called irritably, "Move over!"

CORRECT   Above all, don't let anyone hear you say, "I give up"!

(8) To Indicate Titles

Titles of books, poems, plays, musical compositions, etc., may be enclosed in quotation marks, but the preferred practice is to italicize titles of books, journals, plays, and major poetic or musical works, and to use quotation marks for the titles of chapters, articles, short poems, and songs. Titles of paintings and other objects of art are regularly enclosed in quotation marks.

CORRECT   The fourth section of Isak Dinesen's *Out of Africa* is entitled "From an Immigrant's Notebook."

CORRECT   Carl Orff's cantata ***Carmina Burana*** opens and closes with "Fortune, Empress of the World."

(9) Misuse for Humorous Emphasis or with Slang

If occasionally you want to indicate that a word or phrase should be heavily stressed or deserves special attention, use italics, not quotation marks. Humor or irony should be indicated by the context. Using quotation marks to call attention to an ironic or humorous passage is like poking your listener in the ribs when you have reached the point of a joke. If you use slang at all, take full responsibility for it. Do not apologize for a phrase by putting it in quotation marks.

Exercise 7

Insert quotation marks where they are necessary in the following sentences.

1. The Dean replied that he knew very well freshmen had trouble getting adjusted. But, he added, it doesn't usually take them eight months to find themselves.
2. I hope said Professor Painter that someone can identify a quotation for me. It's from the end of a sonnet, and all I can remember is Like a lean knife between the ribs of Time.
3. President Turini, according to the *Alumni Magazine,* believed that the chief values of a liberal education were nonmaterial; but on another page she was quoted, in the course of a speech delivered in Seattle, as saying that a college education is essential for any person who does not plan to marry money.
4. I asked whether Professor Lawrence still began his first lecture by saying My name is Lawrence and I wish I were not here, as he always did when I was in college.
5. The program said that the musical Hello, Dolly is based on Thornton Wilder's play The Matchmaker.
6. Take a chair, said my tutor, and smoke if you like. He picked up my paper. Tell me honestly, he said; is this the best you can do?
7. Madame Lenoir said, As my first number I will sing the song Der Leiermann, from Schubert's *Winterreise.*
8. When asked To what do you attribute your success? Henderson always answered Sleeping late in the morning.

15e　Other Punctuation Marks: Apostrophe, Colon, Dash, Parentheses, Brackets

(1) The Apostrophe

The chief uses of the apostrophe are to indicate the possessive case of nouns and indefinite pronouns, to mark the omission of letters in a contracted word or date, and to indicate the plural of letters or numerals.

Possessive Case

Nouns and indefinite pronouns which do not already end in *s* form the possessive by adding an apostrophe and an *s*.

CORRECT　a child's toy　　children's toys
　　　　　one's dignity　　Cole Porter's songs

Plural nouns which end in *s* (*boys, girls*) form the possessive by adding an apostrophe only.

CORRECT　girls' hockey　　the Ellises' orchard
　　　　　boys' jackets　　the Neilsons' garage

Singular nouns which end in *s* (*Thomas, kiss*) form the possessive by adding an apostrophe and an *s* if the *s* is to be pronounced as an extra syllable.

CORRECT　Thomas's poems　King James's reign　the kiss's effect

But if an extra syllable would be awkward to pronounce, the possessive is formed by adding the apostrophe only, omitting the second *s*.

CORRECT　Socrates' questions　Moses' life　Euripides' plays

The personal pronouns *never require an apostrophe*, even though the possessive case ends in *s: his, hers, its, ours, yours, theirs*.

In joint possession the last noun takes the possessive form. In individual possession each name should take the possessive form.

JOINT POSSESSION　Marshall and Ward's St. Paul branch

INDIVIDUAL POSSESSION　John's, George's, and Harold's separate claims.

Note also these preferred forms: *someone else's book; my sister-in-law's visit; nobody else's opinion.*

Contractions

Use an apostrophe to indicate omissions in contracted words and dates.

| CORRECT | haven't | doesn't | isn't | it's | o'clock |
| | have not | does not | is not | it is | of the clock |

| CORRECT | the class of '38 |

Plural of Letters and Numerals

The plural of letters and of numerals is formed by adding an apostrophe and an *s*. The plural of a word considered as a word may be formed in the same way.

CORRECT   Her *w*'s were like *m*'s, and her *6*'s like *G*'s.

CORRECT   His conversation is too full of *you know*'s punctuated by *well*'s.

(2) The Colon

The colon is a formal mark of punctuation, used primarily to introduce a formal enumeration or list, a long quotation, or an explanatory statement.

CORRECT   Consider these three viewpoints: political, economic, and social.

CORRECT   Tocqueville expresses one view: "In the United States we easily perceive how the legal profession is qualified by its attributes . . . to neutralize the vices inherent in popular government. . . ."

CORRECT   I remember which way to move the clock when changing from Daylight Saving Time to Standard Time by applying a simple rule: spring ahead, fall backwards.

Note that a list introduced by a colon should be in apposition to a preceding word; that is, the sentence preceding the colon should be grammatically complete without the list.

UNDESIRABLE   We provide: fishing permit, rod, hooks, bait, lunch, boat, oars.

CORRECT We provide the following items: fishing permit, rod, boat, oars, etc.

CORRECT We provide the following: fishing permit, rod, lunch, boat, etc.

CORRECT The following items are provided: fishing permit, rod, lunch, boat, etc.

The colon may be used between two principal clauses when the second clause explains or develops the first.

CORRECT Intercollegiate athletics continues to be big business, but Robert Hutchins long ago pointed out a simple remedy: colleges should stop charging admission to football games.

A colon is used after a formal salutation in a business letter.

CORRECT Dear Sir: Dear Mr. Harris: Gentlemen:

A colon is used to separate hour and minutes in numerals indicating time.

CORRECT The train leaves at 9:27 A.M., and arrives at Joplin at 8:15 P.M.

In bibliographical references, a colon is used between the place of publication and the name of the publisher.

CORRECT New York: Oxford University Press

Between the parts of a Biblical reference a colon may be used.

CORRECT *Proverbs* 28:20

(3) The Dash

The dash, as its name suggests, is a dramatic mark. Like the comma and the parentheses, it separates elements within the sentence, but what the parentheses says quietly the dash exclaims. To signal a summary statement, the dash is more informal than the dignified colon—and more emphatic. Use the dash cautiously. Its flashy interruption can create suspense and energy in a sentence, but its frequent use often indicates a writer who has not learned how to punctuate with discrimination.

A dash is used, as a separator, to indicate that a sentence is broken off or to indicate a sharp turn of thought.

CORRECT The application requested a transcript and had space to enter extracurricular activities, interests, hobbies—need I say more?

CORRECT From noon until three o'clock, we had an excellent view of all that can be seen of a battle—i.e., nothing at all.

—STENDHAL

Dashes may be used to set off appositives or parenthetic elements when commas are insufficient.

CORRECT Three pictures—a watercolor, an oil, and a silk screen—hung on the west wall.

If the commas were used to set off "a watercolor, an oil, and a silk screen" the sentence might be misunderstood to refer to six pictures. The dashes make it clear that only three pictures are meant.

CORRECT By the time the speech was over—it lasted almost two hours—I was dozing in my chair.

Since the parenthetic element is an independent clause, commas would be insufficient to set it off clearly.

When a sentence begins with a list of substantives, a dash is commonly used to separate the list from the summarizing statement which follows.

CORRECT Relaxation, repose, growth within—these are necessities of life, not privileges.

CORRECT The chance to sit on a committee with no big issues to debate, the prospect of introducing bills which will never be reported, the opportunity to write speeches that will rarely be delivered—these are not horizons toward which an able man will strain.

—HAROLD LASKI

(4) Parentheses

Parentheses, like dashes and commas, are used to enclose or set off parenthetic, explanatory, or supplementary material. Arbitrary rules indicating which marks to use cannot be laid down. Commas are most frequently used, and are usually sufficient, when the parenthetic material is very closely related in thought or structure to the rest of the sentence. If the parenthetic material is long or if it contains commas, dashes would customarily be used to set it off. Parentheses are most often used for explanatory or supplementary material of the sort which might be put in a footnote—useful information which is not essential. Parentheses are also used to enclose numbers which mark an enumeration within a sentence.

CORRECT It was, perhaps, this very sensibility to the surrounding atmosphere of feeling and speculation which made Rousseau more directly influential on contemporary thought (or perhaps we should say sentiment) than any writer of his time.

—James Russel Lowell

CORRECT His last story ("Success à la Steinberg") lacked imagination and any relevance to the cartoonist named in the title.

CORRECT In general, the war powers of the President cannot be precisely defined, but must remain somewhat vague and uncertain. (See Wilson's *Constitutional Government in the United States*.)

CORRECT The types of noncreative thinking listed by Robinson are (1) reverie, or daydreaming, (2) making minor decisions, (3) rationalizing, or justifying our prejudices.

(5) Brackets

Brackets are used to enclose a word or words inserted in a quotation by the person quoting.

CORRECT "For the First Amendment does not speak equivocally. It prohibits any law 'abridging the freedom of speech, or of the press.' *It must be taken as a command of the broadest scope that explicit language, read in the context of a liberty-loving society, will allow.*" [Italics added.]

CORRECT "It is clear [the message read] that the Muscle Shoals development is but a small part of the potential public usefulness of the entire Tennessee River."

CORRECT "We know more about its state [the state of the language] in the later Middle Ages; and from the time of Shakespeare on, our information is quite complete."

The word *sic* (meaning *thus*) enclosed in brackets is sometimes inserted in a quotation after a misspelling or other error to indicate that the error occurs in the original.

CORRECT He sent this written confession: "She followed us into the kitchen, snatched a craving [*sic*] knife from the table, and came toward me with it."

If one parenthetical expression falls inside another, then brackets replace the inner parentheses. (Avoid this situation whenever possible; usually [as here] it is distracting.)

Exercise 8

Insert colons, dashes, parentheses, and brackets as they are needed in the following sentences.

1. Each of its large rooms there were no separate cells in this prison housed some twenty prisoners.
2. I took part in a number of activities in high school the rally committee, dramatics, *Ayer* staff the *Ayer* is our annual, and glee club.
3. He joined the Quakers and became an occasional speaker the Quakers have no ordained ministers at their meetings in Philadelphia.
4. According to an inscription on the flyleaf, the book had been owned by Alburt *sic* Taylor.
5. The sect permits dancing but forbids some other seemingly innocent recreations card playing, for example, is banned as being the next thing to gambling.
6. According to the *Mason Report* Stearns testified as follows "I made his John Brown's acquaintance early in January 1857, in Boston."
7. The midnight programs at the Varsity Theater feature horror films, science-fiction thrillers, movies of strange monsters from the sea you know the kind of thing.

Exercise 9

Some of the following student sentences contain incorrect or misleading punctuation, while others lack needed punctuation. Correct each sentence and be prepared to justify your changes.

1. The author mentions spontaneous and joyous effort, but what is a spontaneous and joyous effort.
2. Lincoln born in 1809 in Kentucky, was brought up in a poor family in the woods.
3. What would imply greater silence and quiet meditation than the numerous s's in the sentence.
4. You have a carwash for your car; a combination washer and dryer for your laundry; and a portable dishwasher for your dishes.
5. His goal had been to set up camp at this particular place along the river—No other place would do even though other places would have been faster to get to, and now he had done it.

6. It is the setting that is significant, without the setting there would be no story.

7. Now we reach the inevitable question, how does our liberally educated man make use of his knowledge when he enters the business world?

8. However, Bernard Shaw's main purpose is not to show the tragedy of St. Joan (that is already quite evident)—but to explain the character of St. Joan.

9. In our new house, the kitchen the bathroom and the utility rooms, will have plain wood floors

10. Under the system just established a student from a family which cannot afford to send a child away to college, will have a chance for a scholarship, especially if he or she is interested in science or engineering.

Exercise 10

Punctuate the following paragraphs and be ready to give a reason for each mark used.

1. I could tell without turning who was coming. There wasnt a big flat-footed clop-clop like horses make on hard-pack but a kind of edgy clip-clip-clip. There was only one man around here would ride a mule at least on this kind of business. That was Bill Winder who drove the stage between Reno and Bridgers Wells. A mule is tough all right a good mule can work two horses into the ground and not know it. But theres something about a mule a man cant get fond of. Maybe its just the way a mule is just as you feel its the end with a man whos that way. But you cant make a mule part of the way you live like your horse is its like he had no insides no soul. Instead of a partner youve just got something else to work on along with the steers. Winder didnt like mules either but thats why he rode them. It was against his religion to get on a horse horses were for driving

    Its Winder Gil said and looked at Davies and grinned. The news gets around dont it

    I looked at Davies too in the glass but he wasnt showing anything just staring at his drink and minding his own thoughts.
    —WALTER VAN TILBURG CLARK

2. A few teachers and college administrators have begun to discover that student-made films say as much . . . about students, their present frustrations and aspirations, as about film-making itself. Some contend that these movies are the best guides to the

intellectual and emotional world of students and that even a cursory glance will provide penetrating insights into what is really behind the recent upheavals at Berkeley and other institutions. On a kind of hunch the American Council on Education a relatively conservative organization in higher education has screened dozens of student-made films to learn more about what undergraduates are thinking. No one has clarified the reasons why these films are so revealing but most people believe that it has a great deal to do with the fact that students are expressing themselves in a medium which they feel is their own and which therefore they can trust.

Not unexpectedly student films are characterized by a spirit of revolt they are anti-establishment anti-system anti-conformity. In some pictures this takes the form of a relatively clear statement. Take The Bulb Changer a whimsical comedy produced by a Northwestern student in which the title character completely fouls up an entire community's traffic-light system after he suffers an injustice at the hands of his superior at the local bureaucracy.

More often however the "message" in a student film is stated obliquely. A film entitled Another Yesterday made by two undergraduates at the University of Pennsylvania's Annenberg School of Communication is ostensibly a documentary account of the humdrum life of a young Negro prizefighter. We follow him from the time he awakes at 600 A.M. and starts his roadwork until he returns from the gym to his dingy one-room apartment following a 900 P.M. workout. Boxing is his profession but most of the time he devotes to it is actually moonlighting before and after his regular job as a stevedore. Part of the sound track gives us the highlights of a boxer's day a straightforward professionally composed narrative. The startling element however is an interwoven narration spoken flatly and without emotion from Camus' novel The Stranger for example Mother died today or was it yesterday it doesn't really matter.

In this second narrative thread the film-makers felt they had captured the essence of what was really going on. Predictably they waited until the last minute to add the sound assuming that their teacher wouldn't understand and would veto the whole project.

—DAVID C. STEWART

Spelling

Misspelling of common words is regarded by the general public as a sure sign of lack of education. College graduates cannot afford to be poor spellers. They need not be, since most misspelling is a habit and habits can be changed with a little effort.

The first step is to make a list of words which you misspell. Have someone give you a series of spelling tests on the words listed in section 16e. These are all common words frequently misspelled. Difficult words like *asphyxiate* or *symbiosis,* which occur infrequently in ordinary writing, need not be learned, since you can consult a dictionary for the spelling of any word which is obviously difficult.

Add to the list all words which are misspelled on your themes, and study the list. Look carefully at the letters of each word, pronounce the word a syllable at a time, write the word repeatedly to fix the pattern in your mind. Invent mnemonic devices—pictures, jingles, associations—to help you remember particular spellings. For example, a student might remember the distinction between *capital* and *capitol* by associating capitAl with WAshington and capitOl with dOme. Learn the common prefixes and suffixes, and analyze words to see how they are formed. For example:

disappoint = dis + appoint
dissatisfied = dis + satisfied
misspelling = mis + spell + ing
really = real + ly

```
unnecessary  = un + necessary
undoubtedly  = un + doubt + ed + ly
government   = govern + ment
carefully    = care + ful + ly
incidentally = incident + al + ly
```

See how many words in the list of *Words Commonly Misspelled* can be analyzed into a root word with prefixes or suffixes. If you find exceptions, look for an explanation in the Spelling Rules.

When you have finished the final draft of a paper, proofread it carefully before you hand it in. (Proofread for spelling errors separately if you have trouble with spelling.) It is no excuse to say that you knew the correct spelling of a word but that your pen slipped. Misspellings due to typographical errors or general carelessness are still misspellings.

16a   Trouble Spots in Words

Learn to look for the trouble spots in words and concentrate on them. Common words are almost always misspelled in the same way. That is, a particular letter or combination of letters is the trouble spot, and if you can remember the correct spelling of the trouble spot, the rest of the word will take care of itself. *Receive,* like *deceive, perceive,* and *conceive,* is troublesome only because of the *ei* combination; if you can remember that it is *ei* after *c,* you will have mastered these words. To spell *beginning* correctly, all you need to remember is the double *n.*

Careful pronunciation may help you to avoid errors at trouble spots. In the following words, the letters in italics are often omitted. Pronounce the words aloud, exaggerating the sound of the italicized letters:

accident*all*y	Feb*r*uary	liable
can*d*idate	gener*all*y	library
everybody	lab*o*ratory	lite*r*ature
occasion*all*y	reco*gn*ize	su*r*prise
proba*b*ly	soph*o*more	temper*a*ment
quan*t*ity	stric*t*ly	us*u*ally

Many people add letters incorrectly to the following words. Pronounce the words, making sure no extra syllable creeps in at spots indicated by italics.

a**th**letics	en**tr**ance	mischie**v**ous
disas**tr**ous	heigh**t**	remem**b**rance
drown**ed**	hind**r**ance	simila**r**
e**lm**	ligh**tn**ing	um**br**ella

Trouble spots in the following words are caused by a tendency to transpose the letters italicized. Careful pronunciation may help you to remember the proper order.

child**re**n	pe**r**form	pre**jud**ice
hund**re**d	pe**r**spiration	pre**s**cription
irre**le**vant	p**r**efer	trag**ed**y

16b Similar Words Frequently Confused

Learn the meaning and spelling of similar words. Many errors are caused by confusion of such words as *effect* and *affect*. It is useless to spell *principal* correctly if the word that belongs in your sentence is *principle*. The following list distinguishes briefly between words which are frequently confused.

accept	*receive*	altar	*shrine*
except	*aside from*	alter	*change*
access	*admittance*	alumna	a woman
excess	*greater amount*	alumnae	women
advice	noun	alumnus	a man
advise	verb	alumni	men
affect	*to influence* (verb)	angel	*celestial being*
		angle	*corner*
effect	*result* (noun)	ascent	*climbing*
effect	*to bring about* (verb)	assent	*agreement*
aisle	in church	berth	*bed*
isle	*island*	birth	*being born*
all ready	*prepared*	boarder	*one who boards*
already	*previously*	border	*edge*
allusion	*reference*	breath	noun
illusion	*misconception*	breathe	verb

capital	*city*	forth	*forward*
capitol	*building*	fourth	*4th*
choose	present	ingenious	*clever*
chose	past	ingenuous	*frank*
clothes	*garments*	its	*of it*
cloths	*kinds of cloth*	it's	*it is*
coarse	*not fine*	later	*subsequently*
course	*path, series*	latter	*second of two*
complement	*to complete*	lead	*metal*
compliment	*to praise*	led	past tense of
			verb *lead*
conscience	*sense of right*		
	and wrong	loose	adjective
conscious	*aware*	lose	verb
corps	*group*	peace	*not war*
corpse	*dead body*	piece	*a portion*
costume	*dress*	personal	adjective
custom	*manner*	personnel	noun
council	*governmental*	principal	*most important*
	group	principle	*basic doctrine*
counsel	*advice*	quiet	*still*
decent	*proper*	quite	*entirely*
descent	*slope*	respectfully	*with respect*
desert	*wasteland*	respectively	*in the order*
dessert	*food*		*named*
device	noun	shone	from *shine*
devise	verb	shown	from *show*
dairy	*milk supply*	stationary	adjective
diary	*daily record*	stationery	noun
dual	*twofold*	their	possessive
duel	*fight*	there	*in that place*
		they're	*they are*
formally	*in a formal*		
	manner	than	comparison
formerly	*previously*	then	*at that time*

365

to	go *to* bed	who's	*who is*
too	*too* bad,	whose	possessive
	me *too*		
two	*2*	you're	*you are*
		your	possessive
weather	*rain* or *shine*		
whether	*which of two*		

16c Spelling Rules

Learn the available spelling rules. Spelling rules apply to a relatively small number of words, and unfortunately almost all rules have exceptions. Nevertheless, some of the rules may help you to spell common words which cause you trouble, especially those words formed with suffixes.

It is as important to learn when a rule may be used as it is to understand the rule itself. Applied in the wrong places, rules will make your spelling worse, instead of better.

(1) Final Silent e

Drop a final silent *e* before suffixes beginning with a vowel (*-ing, -age, -able,*). Keep a final silent *e* before suffixes beginning with a consonant (*-ful, -ly, -ness*).

hope + ing = hoping	hope + ful = hopeful
love + able = lovable	nine + teen = nineteen
stone + y = stony	arrange + ment = arrangement
guide + ance = guidance	late + ly = lately
plume + age = plumage	pale + ness = paleness
white + ish = whitish	white + wash = whitewash
write + ing = writing	sincere + ly = sincerely
dote + age = dotage	bale + ful = baleful

Learn the following exceptions:

dyeing	hoeing	judgment	awful
ninth	truly	duly	wholly

The *e* is retained in such words as the following in order to keep the soft sound of *c* and *g*:

noticeable	courageous
peaceable	outrageous

Exercise 1

Following the rule just given, write the correct spelling of each word indicated below.

use + ing   pale + ing
use + ful   manage + ment
argue + ment   write + ing
guide + ance   advantage + ous
nine + ty   refuse + al
pale + ness   waste + ful
immediate + ly   hope + less
please + ure   absolute + ly
manage + able   sure + ly

(2) Doubling Final Consonant

When adding a suffix beginning with a vowel to words ending in one consonant preceded by one vowel (*red, redder*), notice where the word is accented. If it is accented on the last syllable or if it is a monosyllable, *double* the final consonant.

preférr + ed = preferred   bénefit + ed = benefited
omít + ing = omitting   prófit + ing = profiting
occúr + ence = occurrence   díffer + ence = difference
réd + er = redder   trável + er = traveler

Note that in some words the accent shifts when the suffix is added.

reférred   réference
preférring   préference

There are a few exceptions to this rule, like *transferable* and *excellent;* and a good many words that should follow the rule have alternative spellings: either *worshiped* or *worshipped; traveling, traveler,* or *travelling, traveller.*

Exercise 2

Make as many combinations as you can of the following words and suffixes. Give your reason for doubling or not doubling the final consonant. Suffixes: -able, -ible, -ary, -ery, -er, -est, -ance, -ence, -ess, -ed, -ish, -ing, -ly, -ful, -ment, -ness, -hood.

occur	scrap	ravel	man	libel	glad
happen	red	kidnap	defer	will	profit
begin	equip	hazard	sum	skill	avoid
god	commit	read	stop	expel	level
shrub	equal	rid	clan	rival	jewel

(3) Words Ending in *y*

If the *y* is preceded by a consonant, change the *y* to *i* before any suffix except -*ing*.

lady + es = ladies   lonely + ness = loneliness
try + ed = tried   accompany + es = accompanies
study + ing = studying

The *y* is usually retained if it is preceded by a vowel:

valleys   monkeys   displayed

SOME EXCEPTIONS   laid, paid, said, ladylike

Exercise 3

Add suffixes to the following words. State your reason for spelling the word as you do.

mercy	relay	hardy	bounty	medley
duty	study	wordy	jockey	galley
pulley	essay	fancy	modify	body

(4) *ie* or *ei*

When *ie* or *ei* is used to spell the sound *ee*,
Put *i* before *e*
Except after *c*.

achieve	grieve	retrieve	ceiling
belief	niece	shield	conceit
believe	piece	shriek	conceive
brief	pierce	siege	deceit
chief	relief	thief	deceive
field	relieve	wield	perceive
grief	reprieve	yield	receive

SOME EXCEPTIONS   either, leisure, neither, seize, weird.

16d

Hyphenation

A hyphen is used, under certain circumstances, to join the parts of compound words. Compounds are written as two separate words (*city hall*), as two words joined by a hyphen (*city-state*), or solid as one word (*townspeople*). In general, the hyphen is used in recently made compounds and compounds still in the process of becoming one word. Because usage varies considerably, no arbitrary rules can be laid down. When in doubt consult the latest edition of an unabridged dictionary. The following "rules" represent the usual current practice.

(1) Compound Adjectives

Words used as a single adjective *before* a noun are usually hyphenated.

fine-grained wood	three-quarter binding
strong-minded woman	matter-of-fact statement
far-sighted proposal	so-called savings
well-informed leader	old-fashioned attitude

When these compound adjectives *follow* the noun, they usually do not require the hyphen.

CORRECT   The snow-covered mountains lay ahead.

CORRECT   The mountains are snow covered.

When the adverb ending in *-ly* is used with an adjective or a participle, the compound is not usually hyphenated.

CORRECT   highly praised organization, widely advertised campaign.

(2) Prefixes

When a prefix still retains its original strength in the compound, use a hyphen. In most instances, however, the prefix has been absorbed into the word and should not be separated by a hyphen. Contrast the following pairs of words:

ex-president, excommunicate	pre-Christian, preconception
vice-president, viceroy	pro-British, procreation

Note that in some words a difference of meaning is indicated by the hyphen:

She recovered her strength.

She re-covered her quilt.

(3) Compound Numbers

A hyphen is used in compound numbers from twenty-one to ninety-nine.

CORRECT   twenty-six, sixty-three, *but* one hundred thirty.

(4) Hyphen to Prevent Misreading

Use a hyphen if necessary to avoid ambiguity.

AMBIGUOUS   A detail of six foot soldiers was on duty.

CLEAR   A detail of six foot-soldiers was on duty.

OR

CLEAR   A detail of six-foot soldiers was on duty.

Exercise 4

Should the compounds in the following sentences be written solid, with a hyphen, or as two words? Consult a recent edition of a good dictionary, if necessary.

1. We need an eight foot rod.
2. All the creeks are bone dry.
3. She gave away one fourth of her income.
4. The United States is a world power.
5. Who was your go between?
6. He is very good looking.
7. The younger son was a ne'er do well.
8. Let us sing the chorus all together.
9. They are building on a T shaped wing.
10. She is getting a badly needed rest.
11. Are you all ready?
12. The leak was in the sub basement.
13. He was anti British.
14. She does her work in a half hearted manner.
15. I don't like your chip on the shoulder manner.

16. They always were old fashioned.
17. A high school course is required for admission.
18. I do not trust second hand information.
19. He is as pig headed a man as I ever knew.
20. She will not accept any thing second rate.

16e Words Commonly Misspelled

The following list is composed of some ordinary words that are often misspelled. If you learn to spell correctly those which you usually misspell, and if you will look up in a dictionary words which are obviously difficult or unfamiliar, your spelling will improve remarkably.

Have a friend test you on these words—fifty at a time. Then concentrate on the ones you miss. To help you remember correct spellings, trouble spots are indicated by boldface italic type in most of the words.

ab*s*ence	*all* right	as*c*end
absor*p*tion	al*r*eady	as*so*ciation
ab*s*urd	al*to*gether	ath*l*etic
abund*a*nt	al*w*ays	attack*ed*
ac*a*demic	am*a*teur	attend*a*nce
accident*all*y	am*o*ng	audience
ac*comm*odate	anal*y*sis	av*ai*lable
ac*c*umulate	a*nn*ua*ll*y	awkward
ac*c*urate	apo*lo*gy	barg*ai*n
ach*ie*vement	a*pp*ar*a*tus	basic*all*y
ac*q*uainted	a*pp*arent	becom*i*ng
ac*q*uire	appear*a*nce	begin*n*ing
a*c*ross	appe*t*ite	bel*ie*ve
a*dd*ition*all*y	appreciate	bene*f*ited
a*dd*ress	a*pp*ro*p*ri*a*te	bound*a*ry
adequa*t*ely	ar*c*tic	brilli*a*nt
a*gg*ravate	arg*u*ment	Brit*ai*n
airplane	arith*m*etic	busi*n*ess
a*ll*otment	a*rr*angement	calend*a*r
a*ll*o*tt*ed	arti*cle*	can*d*idate

371

16e

career
category
cemetery
certain
challenge

changeable
changing
Christian
column
coming

commission
committee
comparatively
competent
competition

conceit
concentrate
condemn
confidence
conqueror

conscientious
conscious
consider
consistent
contemporary

continuous
controlled
convenience
coolly
copies

courteous
criticism
dealt
deceive
decision

definitely
descendant
describe

description
desirable

despair
desperate
dictionary
different
difficult

dining room
disappear
disappoint
disastrous
discipline

disease
dissatisfied
dissipate
divide
doctor

dying
effect
eighth
eliminate
embarrass

emphasize
entirely
entrance
environment
equipped

especially
etc. (et cetera)
exaggerate
exceed
excellent

exceptionally
exercise
existence
exorbitant
expense

experience
explanation
familiar
fascinate
feasible

February
fictitious
finally
foreign
forty

friend
gauge
government
grammar
guard

harass
hardening
height
hindrance
humorous

hurriedly
hypocrisy
illiterate
imagination
imitation

immediately
incidentally
incredibly
independent
indispensable

infinite
initiative
intelligence
interest
involve

irrelevant
irresistible
itself

16e

jealousy
knowledge

laboratory
laid
led
leisure
library

license
literature
loneliness
lose
luxury

magazine
maintenance
manufacturer
marriage
mathematics

mattress
meant
medieval
merely
miniature

municipal
murmur
mysterious
necessary
neither

nineteen
noticeable
nowadays
nucleus
obstacle

occasionally
occurred
occurrence
omission
omitted

opinion
opportunity
optimism
origin
paid

pamphlet
parallel
paralyzed
parliament
particularly

partner
pastime
perform
perhaps
permanent

permissible
persistent
personnel
persuade
physical

pleasant
politician
possess
possible
practically

preceding
predominant
prejudice
preparation
prevalent

primitive
privilege
probably
procedure
proceed

profession
professor
prominent

pronunciation
prove

psychology
pursue
quizzes
really
receive

recognize
recommend
reference
referred
religious

reminisce
repetition
representative
rhythm
ridiculous

sacrifice
safety
scene
schedule
secretary

seize
sense
separate
sergeant
severely

shining
siege
similar
sincerely
soliloquy

sophomore
specimen
speech
stopping
strenuous

stretch	thorough	using
studying	together	usually
succeed	tragedy	vengeance
suppress	transferred	village
surprise	truly	villain
susceptible	typical	weird
syllable	tyranny	writing
sympathize	undoubtedly	
temperament	unnecessary	
tendency	until	

Exercise 5

Write the infinitive, the present participle, and the past participle of each of the following verbs (e.g., ***stop, stopping, stopped***):

prefer	slam	hop	acquit
profit	begin	differ	commit
drag	equip	recur	confer

Exercise 6

Write the following words together with the adjectives ending in ***-able*** derived from them (e.g., ***love, lovable***):

dispose	compare	imagine
move	console	cure
prove	blame	measure

Exercise 7

Write the following words together with their derivatives ending in ***-able*** (e.g., ***notice, noticeable***):

trace	marriage	damage
service	charge	peace
change	place	manage

Exercise 8

Write the singular and the plural of the following nouns (e.g., ***lady, ladies***):

baby	remedy	treaty	turkey
hobby	enemy	delay	decoy
democracy	poppy	alley	alloy
policy	diary	attorney	corduroy
tragedy	laundry	journey	convoy

Exercise 9

Write the first and third persons present indicative, and the first person past, of the following verbs (e.g., **I cry, he cries, I cried**):

fancy	spy	vary	worry
qualify	reply	dry	pity
accompany	occupy	ferry	envy

Exercise 10

Study the following words, observing that in all of them the prefix is not **diss-** but **dis-:**

dis + advantage	dis + obedient
dis + agree	dis + orderly
dis + approve	dis + organize
dis + interested	dis + own

Exercise 11

Study the following words, observing that in all of them the prefix is not **u-** but **un-:**

un + natural	un + numbered
un + necessary	un + named
un + noticed	un + neighborly

Exercise 12

Study the following words, distinguishing between the prefixes **per-** and **pre-.** Keep in mind that **per** means **through, throughout, by, for;** and that **pre-** means **before.**

perform	perhaps	precept
perception	perspective	precipitate
peremptory	perspiration	precise
perforce	precarious	precocious
perfunctory	precaution	prescription

Exercise 13

Study the following adjectives, observing that in all of them the suffix is not *-full*, but *-ful:*

peaceful	forceful	healthful
dreadful	shameful	pitiful
handful	grateful	thankful
graceful	faithful	plentiful

Exercise 14

Study the following words, observing that in all of them the ending is not *-us,* but *-ous:*

advantageous	specious	fastidious
gorgeous	precious	studious
courteous	vicious	religious
dubious	conscious	perilous

Exercise 15

Study the following words, observing that in all of them the suffix *-al* precedes *-ly:*

accidentally	terrifically	exceptionally
apologetically	specifically	elementally
pathetically	emphatically	professionally
typically	finally	critically

Exercise 16

Study the following words, observing that the suffix is not *-ess,* but *-ness:*

clean + ness	plain + ness	stern + ness
drunken + ness	stubborn + ness	keen + ness
mean + ness	sudden + ness	green + ness

Exercise 17

Study the following words, observing that the suffix is not *-able,* but *-ible:*

accessible	discernible	imperceptible
admissible	eligible	impossible
audible	feasible	incompatible
compatible	flexible	incredible
contemptible	forcible	indefensible
convertible	horrible	indelible
intelligible	perceptible	responsible
invincible	permissible	sensible
invisible	plausible	susceptible
irresistible	possible	tangible
legible	reprehensible	terrible

Exercise 18

Study the following groups of words:

-ain	*-ain*	*-ian*	*-ian*
Britain	curtain	barbarian	guardian
captain	fountain	Christian	musician
certain	mountain	civilian	physician
chieftain	villain	collegian	politician

Exercise 19

Study the following groups of words:

-ede	*-ede*	*-eed*
accede	precede	exceed
antecede	recede	proceed
concede	secede	succeed

Exercise 20

Fill the blanks with *principal* or *principle*. *Principle* is always a noun; *principal* is usually an adjective. *Principal* is also occasionally a noun: the *principal* of the school, both *principal* and *interest.*

1. The _____ will be due on the tenth of the month.
2. Her refusal was based on _____.
3. This is my _____ reason for going.
4. The _____ has asked that we hold our meeting tomorrow.

5. He did not even know the first _____ of the game.
6. Can you give the _____ parts of the verb?

Exercise 21

Fill the blanks with **affect** or **effect:**

1. I do not like his _____ed manner.
2. An entrance was _____ed by force.
3. The _____ upon her is noticeable.
4. The law will take _____ in July.
5. It will be an _____ive remedy.
6. The hot weather will _____ the crops.
7. There was no serious after_____.
8. She _____ed ignorance of the whole matter.

Exercise 22

Fill the blanks with **passed** or **past. Passed** is the past tense or past participle of the verb **pass; past** can be an adjective, noun, adverb, or preposition.

1. We _____ your house.
2. She went _____ me.
3. They whistled as they _____ by.
4. He is a man with a _____.
5. My cousin is a _____ master at the art of lying.
6. That vocalist is _____ her prime.
7. Many years _____ before he returned.
8. It is long _____ bedtime.

Exercise 23

Fill the blanks with:
(a) **Its** (pronoun in the possessive case) or **it's** (contraction of **it is**).

1. _____ raining.
2. The cat has had _____ supper.
3. The clock is in _____ old place again.
4. _____ now six years since the accident.
5. I think that _____ too late to go.

(b) **Your** (pronoun in the possessive case) or **you're** (contraction of **you are**).

1. _____ mistaken; it is _____ fault.
2. _____ position is assured.
3. _____ to go tomorrow.
4. I hope that _____ taking _____ vacation in July.

(c) **There** (adverb or interjection), or **their** (pronoun in the possessive case), or **they're** (contraction of **they are**).

1. It is _____ turn.
2. _____ ready to go.
3. _____, that is over with.
4. _____ car was stolen.
5. _____ back from _____ trip.

(d) **Whose** (pronoun in the possessive case) or **who's** (contraction of **who is**).

1. _____ turn is it?
2. There is the woman _____ running for mayor.
3. _____ responsible for this?
4. _____ book is this?
5. He is one _____ word can be trusted.
6. Bring me a copy of _____ Who.
7. _____ ready to go?

Exercise 24

Circle the italicized word which is spelled correctly in each of the following sentences. Consult section 16b if necessary.

1. Everyone is going **accept, except** me.
2. People came to her every day for **advice, advise,** and she was always ready to **advice, advise** them.
3. At so high an altitude it was hard to **breath, breathe.**
4. His **breath, breathe** came in short gasps.
5. One of the sights of Washington, D.C. is the **Capital, Capitol.**
6. Albany is the **capital, capitol** of New York.
7. Before dinner I had time to change my **clothes, cloths.**
8. The tickets were sent with the **complements, compliments** of the manager.

9. The country was as dry and dreary as a ***desert, dessert.***
10. The shack in which we ***formally, formerly*** lived is still standing.
11. It's ***later, latter*** than you think.
12. The winners were ***lead, led*** up onto the stage.
13. Button the money in your pocket so you won't ***lose, loose*** it.

Mechanics | **17**

Before a paper is handed in, it should be carefully edited and corrected. An instructor has no way of knowing whether an error—in spelling, for example—is a result of ignorance or of hasty typing and careless editing. Do not expect to receive the benefit of the doubt. The following rules are designed to make your paper easier to read.

17a Manuscript

Paper should be 8½ × 11 inches in size, unless your instructor specifies some other kind. It should be unruled if you type your themes. If you use ruled paper for handwritten themes, the lines should be widely spaced to prevent crowding. Themes should be either typed or written in ink—black or blue-black; pencil is difficult to read. Write legibly. An instructor or an editor cannot do full justice to a manuscript which has to be puzzled out, one word at a time. Do not crowd your writing. Leave enough space between consecutive lines to permit editing. Write each word as an entity without gaps between the letters. Do not decorate letters with unnecessary flourishes; use plain forms. Simple, clear handwriting which can be easily read predisposes the reader in your favor. Conversely, handwriting which must be deciphered word by word makes it almost impossible for a reader to appreciate what you have written.

Observe the following conventions for arrangement of material on the page:

1. Write on one side of the sheet only.
2. Leave a generous margin—at least an inch and a half—at the left side of each page and at the top. Leave about an inch of margin at the right side and at the bottom.
3. In typewritten manuscript, double-space the lines throughout, including footnotes or endnotes. In handwritten manuscript, leave an equivalent space between lines. Use alternate lines on narrow lined paper.
4. Number all pages except the first in the upper right-hand corner. Use arabic numerals, not roman.
5. Indent uniformly for paragraphs. The usual indentation for type-written manuscript is five spaces. Indent about an inch in hand-written manuscript.
6. Center the title at least two inches from the top of the page, or on the first line if you use ruled paper. Leave extra space between the title and the first line of the composition.

Do not underline your title or put quotation marks around it (unless it is a quotation or the title of a book). Capitalize all words in the title except articles, short conjunctions, and short prepositions.

(1) Arrangement of Quotations

Observe the following conventions in reproducing quotations:

1. A quotation of only a few words may be incorporated into the text.

CORRECT

Irma Rombauer describes the Dobos Torte as a cake that "looks rich, is rich, and enriches all who eat it."

CORRECT

In <u>Childhood and Society</u>, Erik Erikson says that the young adult, "emerging from

```
        the search for and insistence on identity,"

        is now "ready for intimacy."
```

2. A quotation of more than two lines of verse or more than 100 words of prose should be set off from the main text, without quotation marks. It should be introduced by a colon if the preceding sentence has referred to the quotation, and it should begin on a new line. It should be indented from the left-hand margin. (Poetry should be centered on the page.) It should be single-spaced.

CORRECT

```
        Ruth Benedict's strong belief that

        individual rituals reflect a larger

        cultural whole is apparent in her descrip-

        tion of the dance of the Zuni Indians in

        New Mexico:

            The dance, like their ritual poetry, is a
            monotonous compulsion of natural forces
            by reiteration. The tireless pounding of
            their feet draws together the mist in the
            sky and heaps it into the piled rain
            clouds. It forces out the rain upon the
            earth. They are bent not at all upon an
            ecstatic experience, but upon so
            thorough-going an identification with
            nature that the forces of nature will
            swing to their purposes. This intent
            dictates the form and spirit of Pueblo
            dances. There is nothing wild about
            them. It is the cumulative force of the
            rhythm, the perfection of forty men
            moving as one, that makes them effective.

        As an anthropologist, Benedict is par-

        ticularly drawn to rituals because. . . .
```

3.   A quotation of poetry should be divided into lines exactly as the original is divided. If an entire line of verse cannot be written on one line of the page, the part left over should be indented.

CORRECT

```
Allons! the inducements shall be greater,
We will sail pathless and wild seas,
We will go where winds blow, waves dash, and the
     Yankee clipper speeds by under full sail.

                              --Walt Whitman
```

4.   When quoting a conversation from a story, novel, or play, be sure the quotation is exactly as it appears in the original, including the paragraphing and punctuation. (British writers commonly use a single quotation mark where we would use two.)

CORRECT

```
"Would you like some whisky?" Honora
asked.
"Yes, please," Leander said.
"There isn't any," Honora said. "Have a
cookie."
Leander glanced down at the plate of
cookies and saw they were covered with
ants. "I'm afraid ants have gotten into
your cookies, Honora," he said.
"That's ridiculous," Honora said. "I
know you have ants at the farm, but I've
never had ants in this house." She picked
up a cookie and ate it, ants and all.
                       --John Cheever
```

(2) Correcting the Manuscript

If a reading of your final draft shows the need of further alterations or revisions, make them unmistakably clear. It is not necessary to recopy an entire page for the sake of one or two insertions or corrections. Copying is necessary only when there are so many corrections as to make the page difficult to read or messy in appearance.

Words to be inserted should be written above the line, and their proper position should be indicated by a caret ($\wedge$) placed below the line. Words so inserted should not be enclosed in parentheses or brackets unless these marks would be required if the words were written on the line. Cancel words by drawing a neat line through them. Parentheses or brackets should never be used for this purpose.

17b Capital Letters

The general principle is that proper nouns are capitalized; common nouns are not capitalized. A proper noun is the name of a particular person, place, or thing: *Richard Wright, Virginia Woolf, Alaska, New Orleans, the Capitol, the United States Senate, Colorado River.* A common noun is a more general term which can be used as a name for a number of persons, places, or things: *engineer, doctor, county, town, court house, legislative body, harbor.*

Note that the same word may be used as both a proper and a common noun.

CORRECT Of all the peaks in the Rocky Mountains, Pike's Peak is the mountain I would most like to climb.

CORRECT Our beginning history class studied legislative procedure and the part our representatives play in it. When I took History 27 our class visited the Legislative Committee hearing in which the Representative from Ohio expressed his views on the Alliance for Progress.

Abbreviations are capitalized when the words they stand for would be capitalized: USN, ROTC, NBC.

(1) Proper Nouns

Capitalize proper nouns and adjectives derived from them. Proper nouns include the following:

1. Days of the week, and months
2. Organizations such as political parties, governmental bodies and departments, societies, institutions, clubs, churches, and corporations

   CORRECT the Socialist Party, the Senate, the Department of the Interior, the American Cancer Society, the Boy's Republic, the Optimists' Club, the J. E. Caldwell Company

3. Members of such organizations: Republicans, Lions, Presbyterians, Catholics
4. Historical events and periods: the Battle of Hastings, the Medieval Age, the Baroque Era
5. Geographic areas: the East, the Midwest, the Northwest
6. Race and language names: Japanese, English, Indian, Caucasian
7. Many words of religious significance: the Lord, the Son of God, the Trinity
8. Names of members of the family when used in place of proper names: a call from Mother telling about my father's trip.
9. In biological nomenclature, the names of genera but not of species: *Homo sapiens, Salmo irideus, Equus caballus*
10. Stars, constellations, and planets, but not the earth, sun, or moon unless used as astronomical names

(2) Titles

1. Capitalize titles of persons when they precede proper names. When used without proper names, titles of officers of high rank should be capitalized; other titles should not.

CORRECT   Senator Marsh, Professor Stein, Admiral Byrd, Aunt Elsa. Both the Governor and the Attorney General endorsed the candidacy of our representative. The postmaster of our town appealed to the Postmaster General.

2. Capitalize the first word and the important words of the titles of books, plays, articles, musical compositions, pictures, and other literary or artistic works. The unimportant words are the articles *a, an* and *the;* short conjunctions and short prepositions.

CORRECT   *I, Claudius; Summer in Williamsburg; Friar Felix at Large; Childhood and Society; Measure for Measure;* Beethoven's *Third Symphony;* Brancusi's "Bird in Flight"; Joni Mitchell's *For the Roses.*

3. Capitalize the first word and any titles of the person addressed in the salutation of a letter.

CORRECT   Dear Sir, Dear President Stark, My dear Sir.

In the complimentary close, capitalize the first word only.

CORRECT   Very truly yours, Yours sincerely, Yours very truly,

(3) Sentences and Quotations

1. Capitalize the first word of every sentence and of every direct quotation. Note that a capital is not used for the part of a quotation that follows an interpolated expression like "he said" unless that part is a new sentence.

CORRECT   "Mow the lawn diagonally," said Mrs. Grant, "and go over it twice."

CORRECT   "Mow the lawn twice diagonally," said Mrs. Grant. "It will be even smoother if the second mowing crosses over the first one."

CORRECT   Mrs. Grant said, "Mow the lawn twice."

Following a colon, the first word of a series of short questions or sentences may be capitalized.

CORRECT   The first aid questions were dull but important: What are the first signs of shock in an accident victim? should he be kept warm? should he eat? should he drink?

2. Capitalize the first word of every line of poetry except when the poem itself does not use a capital.

CORRECT   I am a part of all that I have met;
Yet all experience is an arch wherethrough
Gleams that untraveled world whose margin fades
Forever and forever when I move.
How dull it is to pause, to make an end,
To rust unburnished, not to shine in use!
—TENNYSON

CORRECT   last night i heard
a pseudobird;
or possibly
the usual bird
heard pseudome.
—EBENEZER PEABODY

Exercise 1

What words in the following sentences should be capitalized? Why?

1. A canary-colored buick convertible was driving north on fountain avenue.

17c

2. Although many of the natives can speak spanish, they prefer their own indian dialect.

3. A novel experiment in american education was announced on monday by the yale school of law and the harvard school of business administration.

4. "I'm going out to the country club," said chris; "want to come along?"

5. Although technically a veteran, he had served in the coast guard for only two weeks toward the end of the second world war.

6. the douglas fir, often sold under the name oregon pine, is neither a fir nor a pine.

7. He makes these regional divisions: the east, the old south, the middle west, and the far west.

8. When I left high school I intended to major in economics, but in college I became interested in science and graduated as a biology major.

9. Buddhists, christians, jews, and moslems attended the conference, which was held at ankara, the capital of turkey.

10. Both the rotarians and the lions meet in the private dining room of the piedmont inn.

17c Writing Numbers

Usage varies somewhat, but the following practices are widely accepted. One general principle is that all related figures in a particular context should be treated similarly: for consistency, do not use figures for some and words for others.

1. Numbers from one to ten and round numbers which can be expressed in one or two words are usually written out: *three people in line,* *seven hundred* reserved seats, *five thousand* tickets. All numbers that begin a sentence are spelled out, even though they would ordinarily be represented by figures: *Four hundred sixty dollars was too high a price.*

2. For ordinary usage, figures are appropriate for the day of the month (*June 23*), the year (*1929*), and street numbers (*400 University Circle*).

3. Figures are used for long numbers (*a capacity of 1,275 gallons*), page and chapter numbers (*chapter 14, page 372*), time expressed

by A.M. and P.M. (*from 11* A.M. *to 2* P.M.), and exact percentages, decimals and technical numbers (*7.31 inches, 8.5 percent interest, 38th parallel*).

4.   After a dollar sign ($) figures are always used: *My share of the job paid $177.90, but I had $27.50 in expenses.* If a number is short and followed by dollars or cents, it may be spelled out: *I paid twelve dollars for the reservation.*

17d   Abbreviations

Minimize the use of abbreviations in ordinary expository prose. Spell out Christian names, the words in addresses (*Street, Avenue, New Jersey*), the days and months of the year, units of measurement (*ounces, pounds, feet, hour, gallon*). Volume, chapter, and page should be spelled out in references in the text, but abbreviated in footnotes, parenthetical citations, and bibliographies.

CORRECT   Eliott Brodie of 372 West 27th *Avenue,* Kenosha, moved on *December* 16, 1970.

CORRECT   The quotation is on *page* 267 of the *third edition.*

CORRECT   For further information on proper terms for addressing dignitaries, consult the appropriate section in the latest Webster unabridged dictionary ("Forms of Address," *pp.* 51a–54a).

The following conventions are generally observed:

1.   A few standard abbreviations are in general use in all kinds of writing: *i.e.* (that is), *e.g.* (for example), *etc.* (and so forth), *vs.* (versus), A.D., B.C., A.M., P.M., (or *a.m., p.m.*), Washington, *D.C.* Names of some organizations and of many government agencies are commonly represented by their initials: *CIA, GOP, NATO, CAA, TVA,* etc. Dictionaries vary in their preferences for using periods with these abbreviations.

Some abbreviations require periods (*Ph.D., N.Y., Col., oz.*), but others are regularly written without periods (*FBI, Na, ROTC*). The correct form of standard abbreviations can be found in your dictionary, usually in regular alphabetical order, sometimes in a separate appendix.

2. Civil, religious, and military titles are spelled out except the following ones:

a. Preceding names: *Mr., Messrs., Ms., Mrs., Dr., St.* (for *Saint*). *(The) Rev.* and *(The) Hon.* are used only when the surname is preceded by a Christian name: *Rev. Henry Mitchell,* (or *Mr. Mitchell* or *Father Mitchell*), not *Rev. Mitchell.*
b. Following names: *Esq., M.D., Sr., Jr., Ph.D., M.A., LL.D.,* etc. Do not duplicate a title before and after a name.

WRONG   *Dr.* Rinard Z. Hart, *M.D.;*

CORRECT   *Dr.* Rinard Z. Hart, or Rinard Z. Hart, *M.D.*

For the correct forms of titles used in addressing officials of church and state, consult an unabridged dictionary.

3. In technical writing, directions, recipes, and the like, terms of measurement are often abbreviated when used with figures.

CORRECT   32°**F.**; 1,500 **rpm**; 25 **mph**; ½ **tsp.** salt and 2 **tbs.** sugar; 12 **ft.** 9 **in.**; 5**cc.**; 2 **lb.** 4 **oz.**

Abbreviations like *Co., Inc., Bros.,* should be used only when business organizations use them in their official titles. The ampersand (&) is used only when the company uses the symbol in its letterhead and signature.

WRONG   D. C. Heath & Co., D. C. Heath and **Co.,**

CORRECT   D. C. Heath and Company

Exercise 2

Correct any errors in abbreviations in the following sentences.

1. Dr. Geo. C. Fryer lives on Sandy Blvd. near Walnut St.
2. I have worked for the Shell Oil Co. since Oct., '57.
3. We expected to go to N.Y. for Xmas.
4. The Acme Corp. ships mail-order goods C.O.D.
5. I was in Wash., D.C., on Aug. 10, 1975.
6. Mt. Whitney, which is 14,495 ft. high, is located in SE California.
7. The drive to Lexington, Ky., took us 3 hrs., 17 min.
8. A temperature of 32°F. is equivalent to zero on the cent. scale.
9. He bought three fl. oz. of aromatic spirits of amm.
10. Turn back to the 1st page of Ch. 3 and read pp. 18–22.

17e Use of Italics

Italics are used for certain titles, unnaturalized foreign words, scientific names, names of ships and aircraft, and words considered *as* words. To italicize a word in a manuscript, draw one straight line below it, or use the special underlining key on the typewriter, thus: `King Lear`.

1. In the titles of books, monographs, musical works, and such separate publications, italicize all words. (Do not italicize the author's name.) In the titles of newspapers, magazines, and periodicals, only the distinctive words are italicized. The article *The* in newspaper titles is usually not italicized, but printed in regular (roman) type. (Note that *The* is italicized in the preceding sentence since it refers to the word itself, used as the subject of is.)

CORRECT *The Blithedale Romance.* Edmund Wilson's *The Shock of Recognition. Of Stars and Men. Dictionary of Foreign Terms.* The *Atlantic Monthly. Christian Science Monitor.* The *Southern Review.* The *New York Times.*

Titles of parts of published works and articles in magazines are enclosed in quotation marks.

CORRECT The assignment is "Despondency" from William Wordsworth's long narrative poem, *The Excursion.*

CORRECT I always read filler material in the *New Yorker* entitled "Letters We Never Finished Reading."

CORRECT She hoped to publish her story entitled "Nobody Lives Here" in a magazine like *Harper's.*

2. Italicize foreign words which have not yet become accepted in the English language. If you are not certain whether a foreign word has become naturalized, consult a dictionary. Be sure to consult the Explanatory Notes to see how foreign words are indicated. Scientific names for plants and animals are italicized.

CORRECT The dancer unties a knot with her feet in the Mexican *reboza.*

CORRECT The technical name of Steller's jay is *Cyanocitta stelleri.*

3. Italicize the names of ships and aircraft, but *not* the names of the companies that own them.

CORRECT   The liner **S. S. *Constitution*** sails for Africa tomorrow.

CORRECT   He went to Hawaii on a Matson liner and returned on one of United's ***Royal Hawaiian*** flights.

4.   When words, letters, or figures are spoken of as such, they are usually italicized.

CORRECT   The misuse of ***cool*** and ***real*** is a common fault.

CORRECT   The letter *e* and the figure *2* on my typewriter are worn.

17f   Syllabication

Dividing a word at the end of a line is mainly a printer's problem. In manuscripts it is not necessary to keep the right-hand margin absolutely even, and so it is seldom necessary to divide a word at the end of a line. If such a division is essential, observe the following principles, and mark the division with a hyphen (-) at the end of the line.

1.   Divide words only *between* syllables—that is, *between* the normal sound-divisions of a word. When in doubt as to where the division between syllables comes, consult a dictionary. One-syllable words, like *through* or *strength,* cannot be divided. Syllables of one letter should not be divided from the rest of the word. A division should never be made between two letters that indicate a single sound. For example, never divide *th* as in *brother, sh* as in *fashion, ck* as in *Kentucky, oa* as in *reproaching, ai* as in *maintain.* Such combinations of letters may be divided if they indicate two distinct sounds: *post-haste, dis-hon-or, co-au-thor,* etc.

WRONG   li-mit, sinec-ure, burg-lar-ize, ver-y, a-dult

CORRECT   lim-it, sine-cure, bur-glar-ize, very, adult, co-or-di-na-tion

2.   The division comes at the point where a prefix or suffix joins the root word, if pronunciation permits.

CORRECT   be-half, sub-way, anti-dote, con-vene, de-tract

CORRECT   lik-able (or like-able), like-ly, place-ment, Flem-ish, en-force-ment, tall-er, tall-est, fall-en

EXCEPTIONS BECAUSE OF PRONUNCIATION   prel-ate,   pred-e-cessor, res-ti-tu-tion, bus-tling, prej-u-dice, twink-ling, jog-gled

3. When two consonants come between vowels (me*mb*er), the division is between the consonants if pronunciation permits (*member*). If the consonant is doubled before a suffix, the second consonant goes with the suffix (*plan-ning*).

CORRECT   remem-ber, pas-sage, fas-ten, disman-tle, symmet-rical (*but* symme-try), prompt-er (*but* promp-ti-tude), impor-tant, clas-sic, rum-mage, as-surance, oc-cident, at-tend, nar-ration, of-fi-cial-ly, com-pen-di-um, fit-ting, tel-ling.

BUT NOTE   knowl-edge

4. The division comes after a vowel if pronunciation permits.

CORRECT   modi-fier, oscilla-tor, ora-torical, devi-ate.

Exercise 3

Correct in the following sentences any errors in abbreviations, numbers, capitals, and italics.

1. He made a survey of Athletics in the Universities and Colleges in the U.S.
2. When grandmother was a girl, she lived in Lincoln, Nebr.
3. She always adds a P.S. to her letters.
4. He was traveling in the East last Winter.
5. I spent fifty cents for a pattern, $6.80 for my material, and a dollar and ten cents for trimming; so you see that my dress will cost only $8.40.
6. 1975 brought us good fortune.
7. "You will surely decide to go," he said, "For you will never have such a chance as this again."
8. After each war we resolve "That these dead shall not have died in vain."
9. Our country entered the second world war in nineteen hundred and forty-one.
10. The use of the word like as a conjunction is a very common error.
11. My Chemistry and Math. grades were high, and my grade point average was 3.2.
12. Roosevelt was elected president for a 2nd term by an Overwhelming Majority.

13. They discussed the eighteenth amendment and the methods of repealing an amendment to the constitution.
14. The president of the United States rose to greet the president of our university.
15. Queen Elizabeth 1 tried to preserve the status quo.

Definitions of Grammatical Terms

18

absolute construction, absolute phrase An absolute phrase consists of a participle with a subject (and sometimes a complement) grammatically unconnected with the rest of the sentence but usually telling when, why, or how something happened.

> *The floodwater having receded,* people began returning to their homes.
> I hated to leave home, *circumstances being as they were.*

active voice See **Voice.**

adjective A part of speech used to describe or limit the meaning of a substantive. There are the following kinds:

> DESCRIPTIVE   a *true* friend, a *poor* man.
> LIMITING   *an* apple, *the* man, *two* boys.

Notice that many kinds of pronouns regularly perform the function of an adjective.

> POSSESSIVE   *my* book, *his* sister, *your* house.
> DEMONSTRATIVE   *this* chair, *these* papers.
> INTERROGATIVE   *whose* hat? *which* one?
> INDEFINITE   *any* card, *each* boy, *some* candy.

adverb A part of speech used to modify a verb, an adjective, or another adverb. An adverb answers the questions: *Where? When? How? Why?* or *To what extent?*

> He bowed *politely.*
> *"Politely" modifies the verb "bowed."*

A *very* old woman came in.
"Very" modifies the adjective "old."

He was *too* much absorbed to listen.
"Too" modifies the adverb "much."

Substantives may be used adverbially:

He walked *two miles.*
"Two miles" modifies the verb "walked."

He walked *two miles* farther.
"Two miles" modifies the adverb "farther."

antecedent   A word, phrase, or clause to which a pronoun refers.

I saw the *house* long before I reached it.
"House" is the antecedent of "it."

This is a *problem which* cannot be solved without calculus.
"Problem" is the antecedent of "which."

appositive   A substantive attached to another substantive and denoting the same person or thing. A substantive is said to be **in apposition** with the substantive to which it is attached.

Alice, my *cousin,* was enjoying her favorite sport—*sailing.*
"Cousin" is in apposition with "Alice"; "sailing" is in apposition with "sport."

article   The word *the* is called the **definite article;** the word *a* or *an* is called the **indefinite article.** In function, articles can be classed with adjectives.

auxiliary   When the verbs *be, have, do, shall, will, may, can, must,* and *ought* assist in forming the voices, modes, and tenses of other verbs, they are **auxiliaries.**

A message *was* given to me.
He *should have* known better.
He *has been* gone a week.

cardinal number   Any of the numbers *one, two, three, four,* etc., denoting quantity, in distinction from *first, second, third,* etc., which are **ordinal numbers** and which show sequence. Cardinal and ordinal numbers can function as adjectives or as nouns.

case   The inflection of a noun (girls', friend's) or pronoun (she, her, hers) to show its relationship to other words. In English, pronouns are classified into three cases (see Chapter 14).

NOMINATIVE (OR SUBJECTIVE)   *I* spoke; *they* listened; *she* dozed.
The inflected pronouns function as subject.

OBJECTIVE   John tossed *me* the ball. I collided with two other players
and knocked *them* down.
The inflected pronouns function as indirect object, and object of the verb.

POSSESSIVE (OR GENITIVE)   *His* score and *mine* were identical. *Our*
scores were higher than *theirs.* They wondered *whose* grade was the
highest.
The inflected pronoun shows possession or a similar relationship.

In modern times, English nouns are inflected only to indicate the genitive
case: *"Jerry's* money and *Sarah's* money was invested at their *parents'*
advice; this allayed the *relatives'* fear about the *boy's* future and the *girl's*
education."

clause   A group of words containing a subject and predicate (see Chapter
4). Clauses that can stand alone as complete sentences are **independent**
(**principal** or **main**) clauses. Clauses that are not by themselves complete
in meaning are **dependent** (**subordinate**) clauses. Subordinate clauses are
used as nouns, adjectives, or adverbs. They are usually introduced by subordinating conjunctions or relative pronouns.

We heard him *when he came in.*
*"We heard him" is the main clause; "when he came in" is the sub-
ordinate clause.*

That she will be late is certain.
Subordinate clause used as a noun.

The woman **who spoke to us** is our sheriff.
Subordinate clause used as an adjective.

He will come in *when he is ready.*
Subordinate clause used as an adverb.

Clauses that play the same part in a sentence, whether they are main
or subordinate, are called **coordinate clauses.**

The bell rang and *everyone stood up.*
Coordinate main clauses.

He left *because he did not like the work* and *because the pay was low.*
Coordinate subordinate clauses.

comparison   Inflection of an adjective or adverb to indicate an increasing
degree of quality, quantity, or manner.

POSITIVE DEGREE   Our house is *cold.*
COMPARATIVE DEGREE   Their house is *colder.*
SUPERLATIVE DEGREE   Their house is the *coldest* in town.

When adjectives have one or two syllables, the comparative degree is usually formed by adding *er* to the positive; and the superlative degree is usually formed by adding *est* to the positive. To form the comparative degree of adverbs and of adjectives with more than two syllables, place *more* before the positive form; the superlative degree is usually formed by placing *most* before the positive. Some adjectives have irregular comparison: e.g., *good, better, best; bad, worse, worst* (see section 14c).

complement   Traditionally, a word or phrase added to a verb to complete the sense of the statement. It may be the direct object of a transitive verb, an indirect object, or a predicate noun or adjective (see sections 4a, 14b, and 14c).

DIRECT OBJECT   A big wave swamped our *boat.*
INDIRECT OBJECT   I paid *him* the money.
PREDICATE NOUN   Our destination was *Corsica.*
                 The referee called Sanchez the *winner.*
PREDICATE ADJECTIVE   The waves were *enormous.*
                 A limber branch made the tree-house *shaky.*

"Corsica" and "enormous" are called subjective complements (see section 4a). "Shaky" and "winner" are sometimes called objective complements (see **Objective complement***).*

complex sentence   See section 4b.

compound sentence   See section 4b.

conjugation   The inflected forms of a verb which show person, number, tense, voice, and mood. The following is a simplified conjugation of the indicative mood of the verb *see:*

		Active Voice	*Passive Voice*
		PRESENT TENSE	
sing.	1.	I see	I am seen
	2.	you see	you are seen
	3.	he (she, it) sees	he is seen
pl.	1.	we see	we are seen·
	2.	you see	you are seen
	3.	they see	they are seen
		PAST TENSE	
sing.	1.	I saw	I was seen
	2.	you saw	you were seen
	3.	he saw	he was seen

pl.	1. we saw	we were seen	
	2. you saw	you were seen	
	3. they saw	they were seen	

FUTURE TENSE

sing.	1. I shall see	I shall be seen	
	2. you will see	you will be seen	
	3. he will see	he will be seen	
pl.	1. we shall see	we shall be seen	
	2. you will see	you will be seen	
	3. they will see	they will be seen	

PERFECT TENSE

sing.	1. I have seen	I have been seen, etc.
	2. you have seen	
	3. he has seen	
pl.	1. we have seen	
	2. you have seen	
	3. they have seen	

PAST PERFECT TENSE

sing.	1. I had seen	I had been seen, etc.
	2. you had seen	
	3. he had seen	
pl.	1. we had seen	
	2. you had seen	
	3. they had seen	

FUTURE PERFECT TENSE

1. I shall have seen, etc.	I shall have been seen, etc.

See section 14d on *Shall-Will*. See also **Principal parts.**

conjunction   A part of speech used to connect words, phrases, and clauses. There are the following kinds:

COORDINATING   Pure, or simple, conjunctions: ***and, or, nor, but, for, yet.***

COORDINATING   Correlatives: ***either . . . or, neither . . . nor, both . . . and, not only . . . but*** [*also*].

SUBORDINATING   Conjunctions introducing noun clauses, adjective clauses, or adverbial clauses: ***that, when, where, while, whence, because, so that, although, since, as, after, if, until,*** etc.

Coordinating conjunctions (see section 13c) connect sentence elements that are logically and grammatically equal; i.e., they may connect two subjects or two verbs or two clauses, etc. Subordinating conjunctions (see section 13c) connect subordinate (or dependent) clauses with their principal (or independent) clauses.

conjunctive adverb   An introductory adverb, or sentence modifier, which indicates the relationship between principal clauses: *however, moreover, therefore, nevertheless, also, hence, consequently, then, furthermore,* etc. Between independent clauses a conjunctive adverb must be reinforced by a semicolon or by a coordinating conjunction (see section 13c).

coordinate   Sentence elements that are parallel in grammatical construction are coordinate. In the sentence *He and she talked lengthily and earnestly, and at last agreed, he* and *she* are coordinate; *talked* and *agreed* are coordinate: *lengthily* and *earnestly* are coordinate.

copula, or linking verb   A verb, like *to be, to seem, to appear, to become, to feel, to look,* which acts mainly as a connecting link between the subject and the predicate noun or predicate adjective.

correlative conjunctions   Coordinating conjunctions used in pairs:

> *both* my father *and* my mother
> *neither* my father *nor* my mother
> *not only* deceived us *but also* accused us of deception.

declension   See **Inflection.**

demonstrative   See **Adjective** and **Pronoun.**

direct address   A grammatical construction in which the speaker or writer addresses a second person directly.

> *Mary,* wait for me.
> *Friends, Romans, countrymen,* lend me your ears.

direct object   See **Object** and section 4a.

elliptical expression   An expression which is grammatically incomplete, but the meaning of which is clear because the omitted words are implied.

> ELLIPTICAL   *If possible,* bring your drawings along.
> COMPLETE   *If it is possible,* bring your drawings along.

finite verb   A verb which makes an assertion and can serve as a predicate, as distinguished from infinitives, participles, and gerunds.

> FINITE VERB   The alarm *rang* and I *got* up.
> VERBAL   The *ringing* alarm awoke me and I hurried *to get* up.

genitive   See **Case** and section 14b.

gerund   A verb form ending in *ing* and used as a noun. It should be distinguished from the present participle, which also ends in *ing* but is used as an adjective. (See **Participle.**)

SUBJECT OF VERB   *Fishing* is tiresome.
OBJECT OF VERB   I hate *fishing.*
OBJECT OF PREPOSITION   I have a dislike of *fishing.*
PREDICATE NOUN   The sport I like least is *fishing.*

Like a noun, the gerund may be modified by an adjective. In the sentence *They were tired of his long-winded preaching, his* and *long-winded* modify the gerund *preaching.* A noun or pronoun preceding a gerund is normally in the possessive case—e.g., *his* preaching. Since a gerund is a verb form, it may take an object and be modified by an adverb.

He disapproved of our *taking luggage* with us.
"Luggage" is the object of the gerund "taking."

Our success depends upon his *acting promptly.*
"Promptly" is an adverb modifying the gerund "acting."

idioms   An expression whose meaning cannot be determined from the literal meaning of the individual words, but which as a whole is understood and used by speakers of a particular language or region.

She *was taken in* by the practical jokes.
Every now and then, I *have a mind to tell her off.*
He is, *after all,* my brother, and I have to *stick up for him.*
He was *out of his head* for a while, but he finally **pulled himself together.**

imperative   See **Mood.**

indicative   See **Mood.**

indirect object   See **Object** and section 4a.

infinitive   That form of the verb usually preceded by *to. To* is called **the sign of the infinitive.** Since it is a verb form, the infinitive can have a subject, can take an object or a predicate complement, and can be modified by an adverb.

They wanted *me* to go.
"Me" is the subject of "to go."

They asked to meet *him.*
"Him" is the object of "to meet."

We hope to hear *soon.*
"Soon" is the adverbial modifier of "to hear."

The infinitive may be used as a noun (*To meet her* is a pleasure. He wanted *to buy my car*), or as an adjective or adverb (He gave me a book *to read.* He waited *to see you.* We are happy *to help*).

inflection   A change in the form of a word to show a change in meaning or use. Nouns may be inflected to show number (*man, men*) and the genitive case (*dog, dog's*). Pronouns may be inflected to show case (*he, him*), person (*I, you*), number (*I, we*), and gender (*his, hers*). Verbs are inflected to show person (I *go*, he *goes*), number (she *is*, they *are*), tense (he *is*, he *was*), voice (I *received* your letter, your letter *was received*), and mood (if this *be* treason). Adjectives and adverbs are inflected to show relative degree (*strong, stronger, strongest*). The inflection of substantives is called **declension;** that of verbs, **conjugation;** that of adjectives and adverbs, **comparison.**

intensive pronoun   When the pronouns *myself, himself, yourself,* etc., are used in apposition, they are called intensives because they serve to emphasize the substantives that they are used with; e.g., *I myself will do it. I saw the bishop himself.* When one of these words is used as the object of a verb and designates the same person or thing as the subject of that verb, it is called a **reflexive pronoun;** e.g., *I hurt myself. They benefit themselves.*

interjection   An exclamation that has no grammatical relation with the rest of the sentence; e.g., *oh, alas, please.*

interrogative pronoun   See **Pronoun.**

intransitive   See **Verb.**

irregular verb   A verb which forms its past tenses by a change of the root vowel: *sing, sang, sung; drink, drank, drunk.* Such a verb is sometimes called a **strong verb.** See section *14d* for a table of irregular verbs.

linking verb   See **Copula.**

mood   Inflection of a verb to indicate whether it is intended to make a statement or command or to express a condition contrary to fact.

The **indicative mood** is used to state a fact or to ask a question.

The wind is blowing.
Is it raining?

The **imperative mood** is used to express a command or a request.

Do it immediately.
Please answer the telephone.
Come up for a drink when you are in our neighborhood.

The **subjunctive mood** is used to express a wish, a doubt, a concession, a condition contrary to fact (see section 14d). In speech and in all but "edited" writing, the subjunctive mood has largely been replaced by the indicative.

WISH   I wish that I *were* able to help you.
CONDITION CONTRARY TO FACT   If she *were* older, she would understand.

modify   To describe, or limit the meaning of, a word or group of words. In the sentence "I dislike these sour oranges," *sour* describes *oranges* and *these* limits them to a nearby group. In the sentence "Sing louder," *louder* describes (modifies) *sing*. Words that modify substantives are called **adjectives;** words that modify verbs, adjectives, or other adverbs are called **adverbs.** See **Adjective** and **Adverb.** See also section 4a.

nominative   See **Case** and section 14b.

nonrestrictive modifier   A dependent clause or phrase which adds information without limiting the meaning of the word it modifies. See section 15b.

noun   A part of speech: a noun names a person, place, thing, or abstraction. There are the following kinds:

A **common noun** refers to any member of a group or class of things, or to abstract qualities; e.g., *man, village, book, courage.* Common nouns are not usually capitalized.

A **proper noun** or **proper name** is the name of a particular person, place, or thing, or event; e.g., *Jane Austen, Chicago, Domesday Book, Revolutionary War.* Proper nouns are capitalized.

A **collective noun** is the name of a group or class considered as a unit; e.g., *flock, class, group, crowd, gang, team.*

Nouns may also function as modifiers; e.g., *town hall.*

number   Inflection of verbs, nouns, and pronouns to indicate singular or plural.

object   The **direct object** (see section 4a) of a verb names the person or thing that completes the assertion made by a transitive verb. It answers the question *what* or *whom.*

Father dried the *dishes* and broke a *plate.*
I trusted *him* and followed his *advice.*

The **indirect object** (see section 4a) of a verb is the person or thing to which something is given or for which something is done. The indirect object can usually be made the object of the preposition *for* or *to.*

I built my *wife* a shelf. = I built a shelf *for my wife.*
I wrote *him* a letter. = I wrote a letter *to him.*

objective (accusative)   See **Case** and Chapter 14.

objective complement   Either a noun or an adjective that completes the predicate by telling something about the direct object.

noun
They called him a *fool.*

adj.
I like my coffee *hot.*

ordinal number   See **Cardinal number.**

participle   A verb form used as an adjective. The present participle ends in *ing;* e.g., *eating, running.* The past participle ends in *ed, d, t, en, n* or is formed by vowel change; e.g., *stopped, told, slept, fallen, known, sung.*

Since a participle is a verbal adjective, it has the characteristics of both a verb and an adjective. Like an adjective, it modifies a substantive:

The *inquiring* reporter stopped him.
Encouraged by his help, she continued her work.
Having just *returned* from my vacation, I had not heard the news.

Like a verb the participle may take a direct or an indirect object and may be modified by an adverb:

Wishing us success, he drove away.
"Us" is an indirect object, "success" a direct object,
of the participle "wishing."

Stumbling awkwardly, he came into the room.
"Awkwardly" is an adverb modifying the participle "stumbling."

parts of speech   The classification of words according to the special function that they perform in a sentence: nouns, pronouns, verbs, adjectives, adverbs, prepositions, and conjunctions.

passive voice   See **Voice** and section 5c.

person   Inflection of verbs and personal pronouns to indicate the speaker (**first person**), the person spoken to (**second person**), and the person spoken of (**third person**).

FIRST PERSON   I am, we are; I go, we go.
SECOND PERSON   you are; you go.
THIRD PERSON   she is, they are; he goes, they go.

phrase   A phrase is a group of words without a subject and predicate, and used as a single part of speech—as a substantive, verb, adjective, or adverb. See Chapter 4.

predicate   A group of words that makes a statement about, or asks a question about, the subject of the sentence (see section 4a). Thus in the sentence *Jim drove the car, drove the car* is the predicate, for it tells what the subject *Jim* did. The predicate always contains a finite verb, or verb phrase; e.g., *drove, was driving.*

The **simple predicate** is the verb alone. The **complete predicate** is the verb and its modifiers and complements.

Jim drove the car into the garage.
"Drove" is the simple predicate. "Drove the car into the garage" is the complete predicate.

predicate adjective, predicate noun   See **Complement.**

preposition   A part of speech that shows the relationship between a substantive and another word in the sentence; e.g., *in, on, into, to, toward, from, for, against, of, between, with, without, before, behind, under, over above, among, at, by, around, about, through.* The word that completes the meaning of the preposition is called the object of the preposition. In English many words may be used as either prepositions or adverbs, their classification depending on their function in the sentence. If they are followed by a substantive which, with them, forms a phrase, they are prepositions (see section 4a); if by themselves they modify a verb, they are adverbs.

He stood *behind* the chair. (*Preposition*)
The money is *in* the bank. (*Preposition*)
He came *in* while we were there. (*Adverb*)

principal clause   See **Clause** and Chapter 4.

principal parts   In English, the three forms of a verb from which all other forms are derived. They are (1) the present infinitive, (2) the past tense, and (3) the past participle: *send, sent, sent; choose, chose, chosen; swim, swam, swum.* All present and future tense forms, including the present participle, are derived from the first principal part: I *send,* he *sends,* we *will send.* The second principal part is used for the simple past tense: he *sent,* I *chose,* you *swam.* Compound past tenses and the forms of the passive voice employ the third principal part: he *has chosen,* they *had swum,* the package *was sent,* or *may be sent, is being sent, will be sent,* etc.

In learning a foreign language or in correcting unconventional English, one must know the principal parts of the irregular verbs (see section 14d). The verb *to be* is too irregular to be reduced to three principal parts.

pronoun   A part of speech, a word used to refer to a noun already used (or implied). Pronouns may be classified as follows:

PERSONAL   *I, you, he, she, it,* and their inflectional forms.
I listened to *her.*

DEMONSTRATIVE   *this, that, these, those* (see section 6b.)
This is my favorite book.

INTERROGATIVE *who, which, what.*

Who can answer this question?

RELATIVE *who, which, that,* and compounds like *whoever* (see section 4a).

This is the house **that** Jack built.

INDEFINITE *any, anyone, some, someone, no one, nobody, each, everybody, either,* etc. See section 14a.

REFLEXIVE *myself, yourself,* etc.

I hurt **myself.**

INTENSIVE *myself, yourself,* etc.

He **himself** is to blame.

RECIPROCAL *each other, one another.*

John and Mary looked at **each other.**

regular verb A verb which forms its past tenses by adding *ed* or *t: start, started; dream, dreamed* or *dreamt; buy, bought.* Also called a **weak verb.**

relative pronoun A pronoun (*who, which,* or *that*) used with a double function; to take the place of a noun and to connect clauses as does a subordinating conjunction (see section 4a).

restrictive modifier A dependent clause or phrase intended to define or limit the word it modifies (see section 15b).

sentence An independent utterance, usually including a subject and predicate, which can stand by itself and is set off by capitalization of its beginning and a period or other terminal punctuation at the end. A sentence may range in length from one word (Why?) or short phrases (What an absurd idea!) to a main clause (I saw him sitting on the fence). See Chapter 4.

From the point of view of structure, sentences are classified as *simple, compound, complex,* or *compound-complex.* See section 4b.

From the point of view of meaning or function, sentences may be classified as follows:

1. A **declarative sentence** asserts something about a subject.

   The man felt ill and called the doctor.

2. An **interrogative sentence** asks a question.

   When is she coming?

3. An **imperative sentence** expresses a command.

   Call him again.

4. An **exclamatory sentence** expresses strong feeling.

What a fool he was!

For further discussion, see Chapters 5 and 6; see also Chapter 13, especially for the discussion of so-called "incomplete" forms.

strong verb   See **Irregular verb.**

subject   The part of the sentence or clause naming the person or thing about which something is said. The subject of a sentence is usually a noun or pronoun, but it may be a verbal, a phrase, or a noun clause. See sections 4a and 14a.

NOUN   Beyond the ridge lay a high *plateau.*
VERBAL   Nowadays *flying* is both safe and cheap.
PHRASE   *To err* is human.
CLAUSE   *That she will be promoted* is certain.

The **simple subject** is a substantive, usually a noun or pronoun. The **complete subject** is the simple subject and its modifiers.

The young trees that we planted last year have grown tall.
"Trees" is the simple subject. "The young trees that we planted last year" is the complete subject.

subjective complement   See **Complement** and section 4a.

subjunctive   See **Mood** and section 14d.

subordinate clause   A dependent clause. See section 4a.

substantive   Any word or group of words used as a noun. It may be a noun, a pronoun, a clause, an infinitive, or a gerund.

superlative   See **Comparison.**

tense   Different forms of a verb that indicate distinctions in time. In English there are six tenses: the present tense, the past tense, the future tense, the perfect (present perfect) tense, the past perfect tense, and the future perfect tense. See **Conjugation** for examples. See Chapter 14 for discussion.

transitive verb   See **Verb.**

verb   A part of speech whose function is to assert that the subject exists, acts, or has certain characteristics. (The man who *is* on my left *wrote* the book; he *is* very difficult to talk to.) The verb may be a word or a group of words, but in either case its form changes to indicate time, person, mood. (He *was saying* that I *am* too young but *should have* a chance next year).

A **transitive verb** is a verb which requires a direct object (noun or other substantive) to complete its meaning.

He *shut* the *door.*
"Door" completes the statement by telling what was shut.

They *greeted her.*

An **intransitive verb** is a verb which does not require a direct object.

After a heated argument, he *left.*
The child *sat* near the fire.

A **copula,** or **linking verb,** acts mainly as a connecting link between the subject and the predicate noun or predicate adjective.

That *is* correct.
He *seems* sleepy.
She *felt* warm.

verbals   Forms of a verb (*stealing, stolen, to steal*) used as nouns, adjectives, or adverbs. See **Gerund, Participle, Infinitive,** and section 4a.

voice   Inflection of a verb to indicate the relation of the subject to the action expressed by the verb. A verb is in the **active voice** when its subject is the doer of the action. A verb is in the **passive voice** when its subject is acted upon.

ACTIVE VOICE   I rang the bell.
The subject "I" did the act of "ringing."

PASSIVE VOICE   The bell was rung by me.
The subject "bell" was acted upon by "me."

weak verb   See **Regular verb.**

Index

A, *an*, 51
Abbreviations, **17d:** 389–90
  to be avoided in nontechnical
    writing, 389
  in bibliographies, 263–64
  capitalization of, 385
  in footnotes, 263–64
Above, 51
Absolute construction, 395
Absolute phrases
  commas used with, 341–42
  defined, 75
Abstract diction, **3b:** 37–39
Abstract nouns, 313
Abstract words, to be replaced by
  concrete words, **3b:** 37–39
Accent, shown in dictionaries, 23–24
Accept, except, 51
Accuracy of meaning, 35–37. *See
  also* Diction, Effective diction.
Ad hominem argument, 232
Adapt, adopt, 51
Address, direct, 341
Addresses, use of commas in, 340
Adjective clauses, 78. *See also*
  Clauses, Dependent clauses.
Adjective phrases, 73–74
Adjectives
  clauses used as, 78
  comparative and superlative de-
    gree, formation of, 69, 397–98
  comparison of, 397–98
  as complements, 73
  compound, 369
  coordinate, 335
  correct use of, **14c:** 321–23
  defined by function, 65–67
  demonstrative pronoun as, 316,
    395
  derived from proper nouns, capi-
    talization of, 385–86
  descriptive, 395
  ending in *ly,* 321
  function in sentence, 68–69
  hyphenated, 369
  indefinite pronoun as, 395
  interrogative pronoun as, 395
  limiting, 395
  used with linking verbs, 322
  as modifiers, 68–69

  modifying same noun, use of
    comma with, 335
  as objective complements, 403–
    404
  phrases used as, 73–74
  possessive pronoun as, 395
  as predicate adjectives, 73
  in series, 334
  types of, defined, 395
  with same form as adverb, 321
Adverbial clauses, 78
  wrongly used as nouns, 127
Adverbial phrases, 73–74
Adverbs
  clauses used as, 78
  comparative and superlative de-
    grees of, 323
  comparison of, 397–98
  conjunctive, 305–306
  defined by function in sentence,
    65–67
  distinction in use between adjec-
    tive and, 322
  distinguished from adjectives, **14c:**
    321–23
  distinguished from prepositions,
    405
  formation of, 321
  function in sentence, 67
  ly form preferred in formal writ-
    ing, 323
  misplaced, 119–20
  misused with linking verbs, 322
  phrases used as, 73–74
  with same form as adjective, 321
Adverse, averse, 52
Affect, effect, 52
Aggravate, 52
Agreement, **14a:** 308–16
  avoiding awkward use of singular
    pronoun, 309, 315
Agreement, of pronoun and anteced-
    ent, 315–16
  avoiding awkward use of singular
    pronoun, 315
  with collective nouns, 316
  of demonstrative pronouns, 316
  plural antecedents with *and,* 315
  singular antecedents with *or* or
    nor, 315

409